LEARNING FROM THE PAST

WHAT HISTORY

TEACHES

US ABOUT

SCHOOL REFORM

Learning

FROM

THE

Past

EDITED BY DIANE RAVITCH

AND MARIS A. VINOVSKIS

THE JOHNS HOPKINS UNIVERSITY PRESS

BALTIMORE AND LONDON

© 1995 The Johns Hopkins University Press
All rights reserved. Published 1995
Printed in the United States of America on acid-free paper
04 03 02 01 00 99 98 97 96 95   5 4 3 2 1

The Johns Hopkins University Press
2715 North Charles Street
Baltimore, Maryland 21218-4319
The Johns Hopkins Press Ltd., London

Library of Congress Cataloging-in-Publication Data will be found at the
end of this book.

A catalog record for this book is available from the British Library.

ISBN 0-8018-4920-9
ISBN 0-8018-4921-7 (pbk.)

CONTENTS

ACKNOWLEDGMENTS

This project began in the summer of 1992 when Diane Ravitch was the assistant secretary of the Office of Educational Research and Improvement (OERI) in the U.S. Department of Education, and Maris Vinovskis was the research advisor there. Twelve of the present essays were commissioned in September 1992, and one year later a complete set of the original essays was placed in the ERIC system.

The Office of Research in OERI provided invaluable guidance and support. We are especially indebted to Joseph Conaty, the director of the Office of Research, for his expert advice, and to Jackie Jenkins for her help in drafting the purchase orders. Many other individuals within OERI helped us with thoughtful and useful comments and assistance throughout this project. As this project was completed after the change in administrations, we appreciate the continued support and encouragement we received from OERI and its new assistant secretary, Sharon Robinson.

To disseminate the materials more broadly, we sought an outside publisher. Several publishers expressed strong interest. The Publications Committee within the Office of Research decided that the Johns Hopkins University Press provided the best opportunities for broadly disseminating these essays. Most of the original essays were commissioned by the Fund for the Improvement of Education (FIE), and none of the authors or editors will receive any monetary compensation from the publication of this volume.

At the Johns Hopkins University Press, Jacqueline Wehmueller, our editor, provided enthusiastic and thoughtful assistance throughout the project. Linda Forlifer did an excellent job of copyediting—often gently persuading all of us to clarify our own thinking and writing. Jennifer Mittelstadt, at the University of Michigan, provided valuable assistance to us in proofreading.

Finally, we would like to thank all of the contributors to this volume for their willingness to set aside their existing research and writing projects in order to undertake this activity on short notice. It has been a stimulating and satisfying intellectual experience to work with such a talented and diverse set of colleagues.

INTRODUCTION

DIANE RAVITCH AND MARIS A. VINOVSKIS

American education is once again enveloped in uncertainty. And once again it is undergoing intense scrutiny, from within and from without. Propositions that at one time seemed implausible are now being seriously debated and considered. Criticisms that were previously dismissed as marginal have become part of the central discussion. No aspect of education—its governance, its quality, its cost, its effectiveness, its mission—has escaped intense review in recent years.

To historians, it may seem that there has never been a decade free of complaint about the schools and about society's other educational institutions. But policy makers, parents, employers, and other worried citizens are not content to be told that *plus ça change, plus c'est la même chose.* They see problems and they want answers or, if not answers, then at least some effort to find constructive solutions. They are right to seek change and to demand improvement, and they are right to ignore the voices of reaction who counsel complacency, inaction, and ultimately inertia. We Americans have a venerable tradition of reform; we believe that a combination of intelligence, goodwill, and energy can solve even the knottiest problems, and nothing in this collection of essays should discourage that spirit of pragmatism and optimism.

As policy makers and the public venture forth once again into the troubled waters of educational reform, they need the knowledge, experience, and wisdom that history provides. Why reinvent the wheel? Why pursue a path without knowing what happened the last time around? Just as it would be foolish and self-defeating to enter military combat without a plan and without knowledge of the terrain and of one's allies and adversaries, so reformers dare not venture forth without considering the sources of their ideas and the experiences of the past.

At a time when social, political, and economic change seems to have become a constant in human affairs, it seems safe to predict that the improvement of education will be a high priority in our society, as well as in other modern societies. The imperative of developing human capital has surged to the forefront as an issue of signal importance. Modern societies now recognize what Horace Mann claimed more than 150 years ago, that "intelligence is a primary ingredient in the Wealth of Nations." But even though the cultivation of human capital has become a high priority, educational systems continue to be riddled with inefficiencies, low standards, and poor performance. And the continued evolution of society has produced a growing underclass whose young all too often view schooling with skepticism and even disdain, as well as a middle class whose young view schooling as the route to a useful credential rather than as a means to an education.

These and other problems in American society today have historical antecedents. Unfortunately, many policy makers and analysts believe that current problems are new and unprecedented. Implicit in many current writings and actions is the unexamined belief that knowledge of history is not necessary or particularly helpful. This is regrettable because so often in retrospect a broader historical appreciation of the earlier efforts to promote educational change might have provided some useful guidance for those previous school reformers.

To develop historical perspectives on current education reforms, the Office of Educational Research and Improvement (OERI) in the U.S. Department of Education commissioned fourteen individual papers by prominent scholars (mostly historians) to analyze recent educational developments. The authors reflect a wide range of views and experiences in the field of education analysis, and all of them combine a strong understanding of the past with a keen appreciation of the policy implications of recent education reforms.

The three essays in part one examine some of the major changes in educational development and reform. Patricia Graham provides an overview of educational changes in the twentieth century. Graham discusses how existing schools reflect in part the past agendas of previous school reforms and observes how difficult it is to initiate and implement major educational reforms. She documents these points by looking at the issues of the assimilation of immigrants, the adjustment of children to modern life, and the provision of access to high-quality schooling for everyone. Although policy makers and the public continue to look to the schools to initiate rapid changes in the education of children, Graham suggests that these institutions respond rather slowly to shifts in policy directions from above.

Michael Kirst analyzes changes in educational governance reform. The years 1900–1920 and 1965–85 encompass the major shifts in governance, but the results were often unexpected and fragmentary. He finds a long-term trend away from local control of schools and toward the increasing importance of state governments and regulations—though there are still considerable variations in the role of the states today. The federal influence upon public school education has also been increasing since the 1950s. At the same time, the growing presence and power of teachers' unions at the local level has placed some additional limitations on policy options. One consequence of these shifts in power has been the diminished discretionary power of local superintendents and school boards.

Although many policy makers and analysts focus on changes in the curriculum of schools, they often ignore important changes in the health and social services provided through these institutions. Michael Sedlak examines the growth in the provision of nonacademic services in the schools since the late nineteenth century. Most of the early health and social programs were concentrated in the larger urban areas and were designed to help the children of immigrants and the poor. Using this historical perspective, Sedlak analyzes the surge of interest since the mid-1980s in expanding health and social services in the schools for certain groups of students, such as pregnant teenagers and young mothers.

The three essays in part two examine the controversies surrounding questions of equity and multiculturalism in American education. David Kirp investigates changing concerns about equity. Before 1950, Kirp argues, equity considerations were not a major factor in educational policy. He documents the growing interest in different types of equity during the past four decades and details the swings in reforms designed to eradicate inequities. Kirp illustrates how equity issues have become much more complex and controversial as the more obvious and unacceptable inequities of the past have been partially addressed.

Reed Ueda traces the construction of ethnic diversity and national identity in American education in the twentieth century. He examines earlier public school efforts to forge a national identity as a means of assimilating immigrants. Ueda goes on to analyze the growing celebrations of ethnic differences at the expense of fostering any national identity in the public schools. The shifts in attitudes toward the concept of a melting pot are used to illustrate the changing views of ethnic differences. Ueda concludes by discussing the current tensions and problems within the schools in regard to the teaching of ethnic and national identities.

The issue of multiculturalism is explored further in Gary Nash's chapter. He analyzes how the study of history in the schools and multiculturalism have been related. Nash details how historians in the past often depicted unfairly and unfavorably some ethnic groups and cultures. He also analyzes the recent trend in history books away from a narrow male-oriented and Eurocentric perspective toward a more balanced portrayal of American society. Nash is particularly concerned about some of the more recent, extreme Afrocentric formulations of the past which involve ques-

tionable historical analyses and implicitly minimize any national common-
alities.

The essays in part three address some of the major reform efforts of
today. Diane Ravitch analyzes the history of efforts to develop coherent
and consistent curriculum standards—particularly through the effects of
college admission requirements and then through the use of various national achievement tests. She concludes by tracing the more recent efforts
to establish national content standards in certain subjects. As a school
reformer she is optimistic about the ability of standards to improve the
education of children, but her training as a historian makes her cautious
about the obstacles and pitfalls that might prevent change.

Groups such as the New American Schools Development Corporation
and Whittle Communications are calling for the creation of entirely new
schools to transform American education. David Tyack shows how these
calls for the reinvention of public schools were present earlier but failed to
have much of a lasting impact. He chronicles the rise and demise of such
once-popular educational practices as flexible scheduling, performance
contracting, and machine teaching. Tyack admonishes reform advocates
today not to overpromise their school innovations, not to try to change
everything at once, and to enlist teachers as a key element of any school
reform effort.

One of the more controversial issues in school reform is the idea of
giving parents a choice of what public or private school their children
should attend. Paul Peterson analyzes the changing attitudes toward the
role of the public schools in the nineteenth and twentieth centuries. He
then goes on to discuss the emergence of the school choice movement in
the 1950s and its more recent developments in communities such as Milwaukee. As he demonstrates, the debate over choice is no longer focused
on the efficacy of public schools but is shifting toward the question of
whether poor families in the inner cities should be given the same options
as middle-class families to send their children to private schools.

In September 1989 President Bush met with the nation's governors in
an unprecedented educational summit meeting at Charlottesville, Virginia. A year later the Bush administration and the state governors announced
six national educational goals for the year 2000. These goals have been
reaffirmed by the Clinton administration, and they provide much of the
framework for current education reforms. The five essays in part four
examine these six national education goals from a historical perspective.

The first goal is concerned with the readiness of all children to attend
school, and Maris Vinovskis examines it historically. In the early nineteenth century, American parents were eager to educate their young children, and approximately 40 percent of all three-year-olds in Massachusetts
were in school in 1840. But early childhood education fell out of favor by

the eve of the Civil War, and it became necessary to reinvent early education in the Head Start Program in 1965. Vinovskis details how the goal of school readiness evolved as both the National Governors Association and President Bush placed a high premium on early childhood education in their plans. Despite increasing scholarly concern about the long-term efficacy of Head Start, that program is growing rapidly as most policy makers are committed to providing quality early childhood education to all disadvantaged students.

Goal 2 states that, by the year 2000, 90 percent of all children will graduate from high school. Joseph Kett reviews the different ways to measure dropout rates and analyzes the changes in societal attitudes toward early school leaving. As he points out, before the 1960s the emphasis among policy makers was on increasing the average amount of education received rather than focusing on dropping out—two related but not identical goals. Reducing the dropout rate became almost an obsession among many educators in the 1960s. Kett also discusses the different perspectives on school leaving today, with particular attention to the differences between educators and economists over the nature and value of a high school education.

Improvements in the competency of students in subject matter such as English, mathematics, science, history, and geography are the focus of goals 3 and 4. David Angus and Jeffrey Mirel provide a historical perspective on these two goals by analyzing changes in high school curriculum over time. The Committee of Ten in 1893 recommended that all students have a rigorous and prescribed course of study, but Angus and Mirel found that the idea that all students should decide for themselves their own course of study triumphed. One consequence of this ideology has been that the academic share of course taking has declined over time. However, Angus and Mirel detect some signs that the focus on non-academic subjects may have lessened by the mid-1980s—a shift in educational ideology that is reinforced by the emphasis in goals 3 and 4 on specific academic subjects and the call for increased student competency.

Carl Kaestle provides a historical interpretation of goal 5, which states that all adults will be literate and possess the necessary skills for good citizenship and economic success. Kaestle examines the complexity of literacy as an issue and charts an evolving, escalating definition of functional literacy in our society. He argues that we can and should interpret goal 5 to imply that all adults should achieve critical reading skills. This goal is historically unprecedented but has been slowly developing since the 1950s. To achieve it would require schools and adult literacy programs to overcome the barriers to high-level adult literacy that have long been associated with low income, minority status, lack of education, lack of meaningful adult literacy programs, and other factors.

Goal 6 calls for safe, disciplined, and drug-free schools by the year 2000. William Reese examines the changes in societal attitudes toward youth since the 1940s and the behavior of students. He found that the definition of what constitutes a safe school has shifted dramatically over time as students, parents, and educators have become increasingly concerned about the nature and extent of violence in our schools. Moreover, Reese found shifts in worries about illicit drugs in schools from considerable anxiety in the 1930s to less concern in the 1950s. Today, fear of illicit drugs in schools has resurfaced as a major issue—though there are indications that drug use among students may have leveled off. Despite the real and serious problems facing us in regard to safe, disciplined, and drug-free schools today, Reese also reminds us that most students continue to be decent and well-behaved individuals.

The authors of these essays, reflecting quite different intellectual and disciplinary orientations, provide a useful historical context for the current education reforms. They caution us about the tendency of education advocates to exaggerate the benefits of school reforms and to minimize the difficulty of implementing them. Yet, despite the problems inherent in reforming schools, they also demonstrate that major changes have taken place in these institutions over time. Although studies of past educational reforms do not necessarily provide immediate and specific suggestions for improving our present system of schooling, they do contribute to a better understanding and appreciation of the complex and diverse nature of educational development and change today.

PART ONE

Changes in Education over Time

1 ASSIMILATION, ADJUSTMENT, AND ACCESS: AN ANTIQUARIAN VIEW OF AMERICAN EDUCATION

PATRICIA ALBJERG GRAHAM

Americans have traditionally considered their schools mechanisms for social improvement. What the society has felt either unable or unwilling to undertake with its adults, it has expected the schools to accomplish with its children. The needs of this nation have shifted during this century, and with these shifts have come changing and often conflicting priorities for the schools. Citizens viewing the schools at a discrete moment in time often fail to recognize the profound external forces that have buffeted the schools in earlier decades. Thus, they often find it difficult to understand why remnants of previous social agendas for the schools persist in the face of new, contradictory demands upon the schools.[1]

American schools in the twentieth century resemble the battleships of World War II. Large, powerful, cumbersome, with enormous crews, these giants of the ocean go where they are told to go by some distant authority, which presumably understands better than anyone on the ship, including the captain, where and why they should go. Maneuverability is not their strength. When ordered to change course, they do so, but there are significant delays between the time of course direction orders and the ship going in a different direction. The bigger the change in the direction, the longer it takes for the ship to achieve the new course.

In this century American schools have been given several powerful orders to change their courses. In the early years of this century, schools were principally expected to expand and to assimilate the rapidly rising population of children, many of them either immigrants or sons and daughters of immigrants. By the middle of the century, schools were not simply to accommodate the children but also to help them to adjust to modern life, increasingly urban, suburban, and industrial and thus distinct from the rural and small town settings in which their parents had been reared. By the beginning of the last third of the century, the schools were handed the towering moral challenge of providing access to institutions that would effectively serve children of the poor and that would also enroll both black and white children. Finally, at the end of the century, directions from society have again changed, and now schools are expected to achieve high standards of academic learning with all of their students.

The teachers and administrators of American schools, like the crews of battleships, respond valiantly and often courageously to the challenges they are given. Like battleships, the schools are large, powerful, cumbersome institutions and, like battleships, they are difficult to maneuver. Profound changes in course, which have been asked of American schools in this century, do not come easily or quickly. Americans who suddenly decided in the 1980s that they wanted their children to lead internationally in mathematics and science achievement were disconcerted to realize that the schools could not accomplish this goal immediately.

The battleship metaphor has some utility in understanding schools because, like most metaphors, it suggests some helpful and provocative similarities, but the circumstances of schools and battleships are not identical. Most important, battleships have not been built since World War II, and their use in military operations has declined precipitously. In the last half of the century we have believed that other forms of military equipment served us better than battleships. All kinds of new, specialized ships have been added to the navy's arsenal: nuclear-powered submarines, guided missile destroyers, redesigned aircraft carriers, sophisticated amphibious landing craft. The navy recognized that the all-purpose battleship needed to be supplemented by other kinds of equipment to serve national needs.

Schools, however, continue to be built and to form the mainstay of our publicly determined means of rearing our children. They are our all-purpose institution for children. They have not been augmented by the educational equivalent of guided missile destroyers or sophisticated amphibious landing craft. Although families and communities are much more powerful influences upon children than are their schools, it is the schools that remain the institutions that the public attempts to manipulate to form the children. Undoubtedly, society and children would be better served if public policy directed to the young would focus more on family and community support, television restriction, and health and child care provision, but the focus has remained on the school. Such emphasis on the school is understandable because defining the problem in that way makes it containable and assignable to a certain segment of society, the educators. The broader focus, on the other hand, would necessitate changes from all of us and would be not school reform but social reform, which is even more difficult.

During this century Americans have continued to place extraordinary responsibilities upon the schools for a host of matters concerning children.

Schools, the all-purpose battleships, have attempted to respond to these multitudinous demands upon them to aid the young. Their efforts have often been heroic, but their casualties have sometimes been high. The schools are not equipped or adapted to serve all the many needs of American children. Our children require and deserve support from a fleet, not just from battleships.

AN ANTIQUARIAN VIEW OF AMERICAN EDUCATION

The legitimate concern of Americans about the educational achievement of their children today often leads them to false assumptions about the academic learning of youth in the past. The current public interest in American achievement is driven in large part by concerns about the United States' economic decline in comparison with other nations. Just as the United States once was the unquestioned leader in industrial power and now is not, sloppy thinkers in the United States have popularized the notion that the relative decline in the economic power of the United States reflects a similar decline in American academic achievement. The analogy does not hold.

Although the United States was once an unchallenged power economically and now it is not, the same circumstance is not true in education. The comparable leadership in education was in providing the *opportunity* for all children to attend school and for many to attend college. Indeed, the United States did lead the world in expanding educational opportunity to a large, heterogenous population. Simply increasing options for formal education is not the same as assuring that all children excel as a result of these opportunities.

In America we have often been satisfied with the democratic principle that all children could attend. We have not been insistent that all children would not only attend but also learn. Although attendance is important, learning is vital, and in this century we have concentrated on the former, not the latter. We have believed that, if we created institutional structures that would permit free elementary / secondary education for all and that would provide low-cost college education for many with multiple options for leaving and reentering the system, then we would have done all that was necessary. Certainly, this was much more than any other country had done for its people, and in this sense we were international leaders in education in the twentieth century.

Our focus has been upon issues of broad educational policy, not upon the exquisitely specific contexts in which adults were supposed to help children learn. By turning our attention to the large issues of building an enduring and comprehensive public educational system, we overlooked the internal realities of what actually was expected of the participants within the system and what they were really doing. We were more interested in creating a system than we were in examining what and how children were taught and what and how much they learned. The former was the purview of policy makers, always more highly regarded than the latter world of teachers and children.

For the first two-thirds of this century, it has been easy for us to assume that our children were moving smoothly through the grades, mastering the fundamentals and the complexities of English, mathematics, history, and science while learning to work cooperatively, attending school regularly and on time, and becoming ethical and participative citizens. If we judged the schools' adequacy by the performance of American adults in the work force and in the society, then it seemed that the schools were doing a reasonably good job. Between 1920 and 1940 the percentage of youth who graduated from high school grew from 17 to 50 percent. From 1940 to 1970 the growth in high school graduates continued, and then it stalled at approximately 75 percent of the age group. The current rate has increased to 86 percent when recipients of the general educational development (GED) or high school equivalency certificate are included.[2]

The rate of high school graduates going on to college remained relatively stable at just under 40 percent for the first half of this century, rising to more than 50 percent by 1965 and to about 60 percent currently. Until relatively recently white male graduates would then enter the professions, all of which required baccalaureate degrees, and the white collar work force. Female graduates predominantly entered the few careers open to them: school teaching, retail sales, secretarial work, and nursing. Only school teaching required a college degree.[3]

The remainder of the age cohort would get jobs, which was not difficult because the economy was frequently flourishing. The pay for the men's jobs would usually be adequate to support a family. Wives could stay home, care for the children, and participate in volunteer, charitable activities in the community, and husbands could hold the jobs that provided both personal identity and a salary that would assure self-respect and family authority.

A strong economy that provided a variety of well-paid jobs for persons of varying accomplishments and skills provided the foundation for these patterns of adult life. Extensive formal education and significant academic achievement were not necessary for the vast majority. Since they were neither necessary nor highly valued by the society, they were not acquired.

Thus were the schools judged. They were providing what the society needed: a few, mostly white, men with highly developed academic skills demanded by their work; some, mostly white, women and a few minority men and women with highly developed academic skills but without jobs that utilized or required their levels of education; and many white and minority men and women with quite limited formal educations that were entirely commensurate with their employment options.

The third category, limited formal education with a job that did not require anything more than that, was by far the largest in midcentury America. These were the individuals who moved into the middle class in the post–World War II years on the basis of well-paying jobs, often in settings in which unions bargained for them. Gradually, as higher education grew after World War II with the introduction of the G.I. Bill and the expansion of public colleges and universities, new graduates moved into the middle management equivalent of experienced union workers. Their salaries were also substantial, permitting a comfortable, suburban lifestyle, and their jobs demanded little formal knowledge acquired in school or college. They did not need to know foreign languages, nor was it expected that they either have or be able to communicate deep insights into history or contemporary society.

Many were expected to be good salesmen or, as it became known, "to develop skills in marketing." Others were supposed to be knowledgeable about finance, "to develop a bottom line mentality." These subjects and skills were not taught in most schools and colleges, and most of the evolving schools of business administration, where such matters were discussed, frankly did not seek entering students with high academic marks. Learning, at least as measured by grades or test scores, was not highly valued or seemingly related to success in many American careers.

While the American economy seemed strong, the union and management employees who were emerging from the American educational system convinced the nation that its schools and colleges were similarly strong. Such union jobs as these, however, are in short supply today, and many middle managers are finding that their jobs are not secure. Further, competition for good jobs, either union or management ones, is no longer limited mostly to white men. The additional consideration of white women and minorities for good jobs has further unsettled the status quo.

As the American economy undergoes tremendous realignment, business leaders are calling for employees with very different sets of skills. The schools, they believe, are not producing what American industry needs. Some would even try to place the blame for the failure of American business leadership upon the American schools for not providing the kinds of workers needed in the new world of business. Suddenly, acquisition of high levels of academic skills by high proportions of the American population has become an immediate necessity.

Business calls for improved schools while federal, state, and local governments proclaim school reform. Many educators, frequently too anxious to please those in power in the society and frequently too insecure to explain and to justify their educational judgments, have adopted with alacrity this new demand that all students must achieve "world class" standards by the year 2000.

Sensible educators know that this is utter foolishness. They recognize that profound changes must occur in American society if such appropriate and legitimate goals are to be achieved. When so many children live in families and communities that are in utter disarray, when so many live in abject poverty without sufficient food, health care, or adequate housing, then meeting academic goals is inevitably secondary to achieving decent conditions of life. When so many children live in families and communities where learning has never been taken seriously, where books are never read, where television is watched extensively on a daily basis, where immediate consumption is accepted and deferred gratification unknown, and where the sports page of the newspaper is the only section regularly studied, then such academic goals are remote from the experience, expectations, and imagination of many Americans. Accomplishing these goals, therefore, will require profound changes in the self-definition of these adults and in their attitudes toward their children, their country, and the needs of both.

The argument thus far has been that American schools have responded adroitly and efficiently to the nation's requests. What the nation has needed from its schools has varied over the century, and thus the schools' emphases have varied as well. What has been universally true, however, is that the schools have never educated all of their students well, as they are now being asked to do. They have always educated some very well. Although many who have received excellent educations have been children of the affluent, in the United States there has always been opportunity for the child of the poor and for the child of color to succeed as well. Many have succeeded, but the system has been organized to benefit occasional children of poverty or color, not all such youngsters. Similarly, it has been organized to benefit a higher proportion of the children of the affluent, but it has not been made clear to those children that achieving academically was necessary for their subsequent success in life. In fact, good jobs and the good life did not require significant academic achievement, and until quite recently most Americans have not sought such learning for themselves, their children, or their employees.

Probably the best single indicators of the organization of American schooling that benefits children of the affluent over children of the poor have been the per pupil expenditures in different school districts and average teachers' salaries. Currently, the highest per pupil expenditures generally are in suburbs where housing is expensive and consequently family incomes are likely to be high. Local funds for schools come largely from property taxes, so communities with expensive properties have more money available to pay for their schools. Such families and communities are also likely to have money available to support other activities that help their children: supervised recreational programs with good equipment, access to museums and often travel programs for high school students, or additional wholesome instructional programs, such as gymnastics or ice skating. Most important, these communities provide models in their adult populations of individuals who are successful, who have had extensive schooling, and who believe that schooling accounts in part for their success. Deerfield, Illinois, is one such community. Its annual per high school pupil expenditure is $10,510, and its average salary for high school teachers is now over $52,000. Less than 40 miles away in another suburban district, Aurora East, is a very different community with a much lower tax base. Its per high school pupil expenditure is $4,322, and its average high school teacher salary is just over $30,000. Not surprisingly, test scores are very different as well: an average of 305 and 325 for the Illinois reading and mathematics test for high school juniors in Deerfield and of 152 and 120 in Aurora East.[4]

This pattern is typical of many states. In Massachusetts, for example, affluent Wellesley, with a median home price in 1992 of nearly $299,000, spends $7,310 per pupil and has average annual teachers' salaries of $42,000; rural Winchendon, with a median home price of $86,500, spends an average of $3,794 on its pupils and pays its teachers an average of $27,900. Not surprisingly, 42 percent of Wellesley's students demonstrated "solid understanding of subject matter on Massachusetts educational assessment tests" while only 14 percent of Winchendon's pupils did.[5]

Direct comparisons of investment (per pupil expenditure and teachers' salaries) with outcomes (average test scores) mask many differences among children, their communities, and their schools. Nonetheless, what they reveal here is that Deerfield and Wellesley spend roughly twice what Aurora East and Winchendon spend on their students and teachers, and the students in Deerfield and Wellesley score more than twice as highly on standardized tests.

These kinds of results are not new. Discrepancies of these kinds have long characterized American education. What is new is that the public is now concerned about the performers at the low end. Previous attention focused upon the upper end of the distribution. Now, as we are told to be aware of the new needs for mental agility for the American work force, we are attentive to academic performances of historically low-achieving neighborhoods. The schools find their courses again being altered with new orders from on high to change direction. This demand for universal academic achievement is the fourth major course change for the schools in this century, following earlier demands for assimilation, adjustment, and access.

ASSIMILATION

For the first quarter of this century, the schools performed the aston-
ishingly successful transformation of taking many children whose family
culture and often whose family language was foreign and converting them
into adults who were Americans. The schools accomplished this extraordinary feat in large part because many of the parents were eager for their
children to become acclimated in the new land that they had chosen and in
which many of the adults would never feel at ease. They hoped, though,
that their children would achieve the dream for which they had emigrated,
whether that be economic success, social opportunity, or religious and
political freedom. Since many families lived with others of similar heritage
and since many families attended religious institutions with their former
countrymen, the school was the primary means through which the children of immigrants encountered American institutions.

Concern for converting youngsters into loyal Americans was not
unique to the early twentieth century. From the nation's beginnings in the
late eighteenth century, one of its leading educational architects, Benjamin
Rush, had urged, "Let our pupil be taught that he does not belong to
himself, but that he is public property. Let him be taught to love his family
but let him be taught at the same time that he must forsake and even forget
them when the welfare of his country requires it."[6] Although the issue for
Rush was building allegiance to a nation that was new, the manifestation of
that sentiment more than a century later was building allegiance to a
nation that was no longer new but was new to these pupils and their
families. The idea that one of the schools' chief obligations was to develop
commitment to the American nation persisted.

One of the reasons that the United States led in developing a comprehensive school system was that this country faced a special challenge. Most
of the new Americans came from countries with well-established governments and national cultures and without significant numbers of immigrants. The task in the United States, however, was to establish both the
government and the culture and to imbue the immigrants with a commitment to them. Furthermore, the success of the novel republican form of
government resting on the consent of the governed depended upon the
governed being informed. Shrewdly, American leaders from Benjamin
Rush, Thomas Jefferson, and Horace Mann on recognized that the group of
the population with whom it would be easiest to accomplish this feat were
the children, and the institutional entity with the leading responsibility
was the school. Hence, the push to comprehensive schooling in the United
States was driven by the need both to inform the citizenry so they could
govern and to assimilate the immigrants so they could be constructive
citizens.

Thus, in the early twentieth century the United States faced two challenges that it sought to meet through its school systems: informing the citizens and Americanizing the immigrants. These dual needs pushed this country to develop comprehensive schools through high school before they were common elsewhere.

Many of these schools were rigid in their procedures, forcing youngsters to adapt their youthful exuberance to the regulation of the emerging school bureaucracies. Many found this difficult and thus were "retained" in grade until they had proved themselves either flexible enough to adjust to the school rules or bright enough to master the material on their own. Figures from New York City schools in 1904 reflect the difficulty these children had in progressing smoothly through the New York City public schools. Although grade 1 had only 23 percent overage children, the percentage who were overage rose to 38 percent in grade 2, 45 percent in grade 3, and 49 percent in both grades 4 and 5. As children dropped out of school, it began to fall to 42 percent in grade 6, 32 percent in grade 7, and 25 percent in grade 8. A few years later Leonard P. Ayres reported that, of 1,000 children entering city schools in 1908 (then probably the best in the country), only 263 would reach the eighth grade and a bare 56 the fourth year of high school.[7]

The growth of school populations coincided with massive immigration in the early years of this century, creating in cities, where many immigrants chose to live, large, graded schools with newly defined procedures that teachers and administrators were expected to follow. Rural and small town schools with low enrollments and children of different ages all taught together in one or two rooms with a single teacher or a small corps of teachers disappeared rapidly in the twentieth century. What evolved were school systems led by a new breed of educators, not teachers but administrators, who saw their mission not to inspire a love of learning in the younger generation but rather to become what David Tyack and Elisabeth Hansot felicitously termed them, "managers of virtue." Their primary obligation was to assure that these diverse youngsters would grow up to become good citizens, which meant that their skills would be adequate to hold jobs, become homemakers, and avoid the perils of alcoholism or poverty.[8]

In short, the schools' principal mission was moral, to create citizens who possessed the habits of heart and will to function well in this new land and who were sufficiently if minimally literate. The schools understood that their task was given to them by the larger society, endorsed by it, and generally supported by the families and communities in which the children lived.

Some youngsters, like Leonard Covello and Mary Antin, thrived in this setting and subsequently wrote enthusiastic autobiographical pieces about it.[9] Their works are well known, and many of us have inaccurately assumed that the experiences they described were nearly universal. Others, undoubtedly the more typical, endured this regimen for as long as they could and quit, acquiring minimal literacy and a profound disinclination toward academic matters. Others also quit early, often because family demands upon them necessitated that they either help at home or work for pay. Some were thankful to leave, others regretful, but none of these latter groups was likely to eventually publish a paean to the schools.

Since the principal effort of the schools was to move the children into a smooth adulthood, capable of independence and citizenship, any of these alternatives was satisfactory from the school's point of view. It was always important that some unlikely children did well in the school, and some always did. The proportion who needed to succeed academically was small, while the proportion who needed to move smoothly into the work force was great. The schools understood this and added vocational education courses to their curriculums with broad support from business and labor and, after passage of the Smith-Hughes Act in 1917, with support from the federal government as well.

The phrase widely used to describe this phenomenon of assimilating the immigrants and their children into American society was *melting pot*. The ethnic traditions of the immigrants, over 90 percent of whom were European in the early years of the twentieth century, were to be brought together in a large cauldron, heated well, and stirred vigorously, and the viscous liquid that would emerge, the essence of Americanness, would be uniform in its consistency but different from any of its component parts, which would no longer be identifiable.[10] The melting pot image dominated discussions of Americanization throughout the first half of the twentieth century, when the focus was upon white immigrants from Europe coalescing with other white immigrants from Europe who had come to the United States as earlier generations.

Little effort was made to assimilate the 10 percent of the population who were of African ancestry. They had not come here of their own free will but rather as slaves; further, their skin was black and hence their differences from the majority population were not simply cultural but also racial. Much was made of this distinction. For African Americans, for the Native Americans, whose indigenous economies and cultures had been displaced by the Europeans, and for the Hispanics, who had settled in the Southwest before the westward migration, as well as for some Asian immigrants, melting pot rules applied differently. Schooling existed for all of these groups, and often particular efforts were made in the school to rid them of their own cultural traditions and to get them to accept uncritically the dominant culture of early twentieth-century America.

Pronouncements about the education of Native Americans capture the flavor of much public sentiment about the educational needs of all non-Europeans in the United States, who were largely assumed to be bereft of civilization. The Lake Mohonk Conference in 1884 resolved that "education is essential to civilization. The Indian must have a knowledge of the English language, that he may associate with his white neighbors and transact business as they do. He must have practical industrial training to fit him to compete with others in the struggle for life. He must have a Christian education to enable him to perform the duties of the family, the State, and the Church." Richard Pratt, the founder of the Carlisle school for Indians, allegedly put it more pithily: "Kill the Indian and save the man."[11]

Thus, assimilation into American society or, as some would argue, annihilation of family culture characterized the principal mission of schooling in America during the early decades of this century. Most educators believed that their undertaking was beneficial both to the nation and to the individual, and few argued with them. The challenge of forging a nation from these diverse ethnic and racial groups was immense, but by the outbreak of World War II patriotism was rampant in America. The children of the hyphenated Americans were simply Americans, in large part because their schools had taught them so.

ADJUSTMENT

The *Report of the Commission on the Reorganization of Secondary Education of the National Educational Association*, published by the U.S. Bureau of Education, appeared in 1918 and soon dominated professional discussions of high school education. For the next several decades, aspiring teachers fulfilling licensing requirements memorized what the document asserted were "the principal aims in education," which came to be known as the Seven Cardinal Principles:

1. health
2. command of fundamental processes
3. worthy home membership
4. vocation
5. civic education
6. worthy use of leisure time
7. ethical character

The rationale for the need for these new principles appeared in the opening sentence of the report: "Secondary education should be determined by the needs of the society to be served, the character of the individuals to be educated, and the knowledge of educational theory and practice available." The report observed that many changes were indeed taking place in society and that these necessitated changes in secondary schooling. It continued, "As a citizen, he must to a greater extent and in a more direct way cope with problems of community life, State and National Governments, and international relationships. As a worker, he must adjust to a more complex economic order."[12]

Reading these sentiments seventy-five years later, one notes that the requirements of both citizenship and employment have continued to dominate discussions of education, and appropriately so. The "international relationships" have also been an enduring issue. Yet the solution of 1918 of "adjusting" to these changes was very different from the present imperative of refocusing schooling upon academic achievement.

Of the Seven Cardinal Principles, only one, command of fundamental processes, even hinted at academic activities, and it conveyed a sense of primitive academic mastery. The remaining six all were nonacademic in their content. High school educators took this emphasis to heart and developed programs that matched the goals. The consequence of these efforts was to minimize the significance of academic learning in many high schools for many students. If the National Education Association and the U.S. Bureau of Education, the forerunner of the U.S. Department of Education, believed that these should be the goals of education, then surely this was so. Aside from some isolated academic critics, there was little dissension about these goals. Although written largely by educators, these views fit neatly with the economic needs of the nation as they changed from those of agricultural and small businesses to predominantly urban and increasingly large businesses in the years after World War I. This document was as important in its time in setting the tone for discussions of what should be done in the schools as *A Nation at Risk* was sixty-five years later.[13]

If the Seven Cardinal Principles provided the goals for American schools, then the deeper explication of them could be found in John Dewey's magisterial *Democracy and Education*, published in 1916.[14] This became the Bible of the educational reform movement then emerging; like the Bible, it was rarely read in full and was suitable for constant reinterpretation. The newly self-conscious professional educators, however, were little given to exegesis. Instead, they turned their profound energies into forming an organization, the Progressive Education Association, devoted to battling the traditional academic lockstep and replacing it with a commitment to "teaching the whole child."

Since the "whole child" was preponderantly a psychological construct, successful teaching of the whole child meant for many that the child preeminently would adjust and would have good mental health. Such a definition minimized academic learning, as did the Seven Cardinal Principles.

Yet inevitably the child was implicitly—but not explicitly—defined by his or her social contexts. School staff often tacitly recognized the limits that children's social, economic, gender, or racial characteristics placed upon them, and this recognition helped define appropriate "adjustment" for these children. In an era when testing of personality, attitude, and vocational interest was growing rapidly, these different expectations were codified most clearly in the Strong Vocational Inventory which, throughout this period, maintained different tests and different scales for boys and girls and men and women. A young woman seeking to establish how her interests fit with those of working professionals had to take the male version of the Strong to learn where her interests might lead her because there was no comparable scale for employed women, allegedly because there were too few to justify creating such a scale. Except for the nation's needs during World War II, the message was clear to young women of the mid-century: be a homemaker.

The Progressive Education Association reached its zenith of public acceptance and recognition in the 1930s, exemplified by its executive director appearing on the cover of *Time* magazine in 1938. At that time it was in the midst of sponsoring its best-known project, the Eight Year Study, also known as the Thirty Schools Study. The study eventually revealed in the midst of World War II (when most Americans were not much interested in schooling questions) that graduates of the thirty "progressive" schools participating in the study did as well in college as graduates of schools with traditional, college-preparatory academic curriculums. The unwarranted assumption accepted by many educators from these data was that curriculum and pedagogy did not make a difference in the children's subsequent educational performance. Acceptance of this assumption led many to believe that mastery of the curriculum, whatever it was, was less significant than simply participating in school life. Coming as they did at a time when attention focused on adjustment, these conclusions found a congenial reception among many educators. The Eight Year Study was not responsible by itself for reducing the emphasis upon academic achievement, but it provided the research justification that reinforced the prevalent anti-intellectual sentiment in America that academic learning was useful for some but not necessary for all.[15]

Today we would probably observe that many of the children in the progressive schools came from homes and communities in which many powerful and effective educational activities engaged them: parents who regularly read to them and discussed ideas with them, books in their homes, museums available for visits, travel with guidance and supervision, and, most of all, communities that modeled success based on education and expected the same for their children. The formal program presented by their schools, therefore, was less influential in their lives than were the broader educational experiences they were receiving outside of school. Most important, the goals of the schools and the other educational agencies with which the children were involved were either the same or, at a minimum, harmonious.

The assumption that the content of the school curriculum did not matter may have been true for those youngsters with a rich educational environment outside the schools and for whom the other potentially educational agencies had goals that were harmonious with the schools'. For those children for whom the school provided the principal route to formal learning, however, the curriculum and pedagogy were extremely important because those youngsters had few opportunities to learn elsewhere what society believed was important to know and to be able to do. The former group, with the rich nonschool educational experiences, were a small minority of American youth, and the latter, without rich educational experiences outside school, were the vast majority. But the distinction between the role of schooling and the role of other educational activities in a child's life has not attracted wide attention in America until recently.

We have tended to accept that schooling provided the same experience for everybody, not recognizing that for some schooling was a mere addition of spice to an already wholesome educational recipe. For others, though, it was the entire educational recipe. Spice alone will not suffice as a diet.[16]

Although the Progressive Education Association may have provided the research underpinnings for diminishing the significance of academic learning for most children, the operational and bureaucratic justification came with sponsorship by the U.S. Office of Education (USOE) in 1947 of the Commission on Life Adjustment Education for Youth, chaired by Benjamin Willis, then superintendent of schools in Yonkers, New York. (He eventually became the superintendent in Chicago.) The commission's reports stressed many of the same themes as the Seven Cardinal Principles. Although it alluded to academic matters, it gave its primary attention to children's nonacademic educational needs: "physical, mental, and emotional health . . . the present problems of youth as well as their preparation for future living . . . the importance of personal satisfactions and achievements for each individual within the limits of his abilities."[17]

The stimulus for the commission had come from Charles Prosser, an indefatigable leader of vocational education, who in 1945 had introduced the notion of life adjustment education at a conference and had called for the USOE to establish the commission. At that time Prosser had argued that 20 percent of American youth could benefit from an academic curriculum in high school, 20 percent from a vocational curriculum, and the remaining 60 percent from "life adjustment training." Acceptance of this formula, while never overt, has dominated high school education ever since.[18]

ACCESS

John Studebaker was commissioner of the United States Office of Education from 1934 to 1948, and it was under his leadership that the federal government gave its blessing to life adjustment education. Generally, the USOE, as it was known, was not a place of power, and Studebaker's dubious achievement in promoting life adjustment education was based partly on his longevity in the office and partly on his catching the final gasp of progressive education before its demise as a national educational ideology in the 1950s.

The next commissioner to capture and shape America's educational destiny was Francis Keppel, who served from 1962 to 1966. Keppel himself was no exponent of progressive education. Born in 1916, he grew up in a household deeply committed to education, but few would describe it as *progressive* as the term was used in his childhood. His father, Frederick Keppel, was dean of Columbia College in New York City when John Dewey was on its philosophy faculty. The campus's northern border, 120th Street, was often described as the widest in the world because it separated Columbia College from Teachers College, the leading institutional champion of progressive education. Frederick Keppel became head of the Carnegie Corporation in 1923, the foundation in the United States which probably gave more support to education than any other during the middle of the twentieth century.

At the height of progressive education's prominence in America and in the depths of the United States' Depression, young Frank was sent off to preparatory school at Groton and subsequently to Harvard College. While an undergraduate Frank actively engaged in campus life, becoming acquainted with the new president of Harvard, James B. Conant, and after graduation he received a fellowship to study sculpture in Rome immediately before World War II. That year of study in Italy remained Francis Keppel's sole formal postgraduate education. By some standards he had no qualifications as an educator, but his abilities, nurtured by his home, community, and schools, far outshone his formal qualifications.

During World War II Keppel helped design the college correspondence courses for servicemen, now known as the United States Armed Forces Institute (USAFI), and the G.I. Bill. After the war, he returned to Harvard to serve as an assistant to President Conant. When Conant exhausted his list of possible deans for the struggling School of Education at Harvard, he turned to Keppel, who in 1948 at the age of thirty-one undertook to rebuild the school.

What Keppel lacked in formal instruction in education itself he more than compensated for in intelligence applied to educational issues. He was a smart and well-read man who was deeply concerned about improving the education of all Americans. Moreover, he had insight into how to organize others to achieve these ends. Such insight is the highest art of politics. Further, he was not identified either personally or professionally with any of the extant ideological strands of the education establishment. More than any other figure in America, he eased the transition from pre-war progressive education, with its individualistic emphasis on the child and his or her adjustment, to the American educational agenda of the last half of the twentieth century, with its emphasis upon the needs of groups of children who were not well served by the existing educational structures.

In 1965, eleven years after the critical Supreme Court decision in *Brown v. Board of Education*, which prohibited segregation on the basis of race in the public schools, Keppel successfully orchestrated passage of the Elementary and Secondary Education Act, which established the principle that children from low-income homes required more educational services than children from affluent homes did. Many believed Keppel was simply interested in access, but a close look at Keppel's agenda reveals that the essence of Title I of the Elementary and Secondary Education Act, which was the most expensive element of the bill, was mandating additional *educational* activities that would enhance the academic achievement of children of the poor. Such concern for children's learning, particularly impoverished children's learning, was in dramatic contrast to the educational priorities of his predecessors.

Not all children enter school on a level playing field, Keppel argued. Children from wealthier families have more informed resources devoted to their educations than do children from poor families. Thus, if it is in the national interest for all of our children to learn, the federal government must supply additional funds to public schools to help them educate the children of the poor. Those youngsters require compensatory educational services. Typically this meant more formal instruction in reading and arithmetic. Keppel was not arguing that children of the poor should simply adjust to their circumstances of life; he believed that they must learn. That was a radical departure from the educational wisdom of his predecessor, Studebaker.

Too many poor children in America (and in most other countries as well) fell behind their classmates in academic achievement. This was true in progressive schools as well as traditional ones, largely because educators as a group had not recognized the supplementary educational services poor children required for comparable academic achievement. Few educators had the social vision that made academic achievement for all children a priority. When adjustment had been seen as the goal, it typically meant living easily within the constraints of society, a laudable goal for children of the affluent, who could be expected to replicate their parents' circumstances, but a much less laudable goal for the children of the poor, who might not choose their parents' status quo for themselves and for whom education was the primary means of securing a destiny different from that of their friends and neighbors. Thus, for children of the poor the adjustment that progressive educators sought for their students through school interventions consigned these youngsters to inferior educations. Since minimal literacy was seen as necessary for all, children in primary or elementary schools generally fared better than did older youngsters, for whom adjustment was more likely to be tied to curriculums that determined career choices: college preparatory, home economics or domestic science, industrial arts or shop, agricultural courses, secretarial programs. In high school, then, the effects of progressive education—or life adjustment—on children of the poor were often devastating.

Keppel sought to change this professional wisdom by calling for "equal educational opportunity." No one, including Keppel, knew exactly what that meant; hence, it was salable politically. No one had any idea at all how to implement it, which was also beneficial politically. Finally, the idea was much more popular with the politicians than with the educators, for the latter recognized that implementing this new notion would cause them to change their practices profoundly.

Two politicians, Wayne Morse and Robert F. Kennedy, both then members of the Senate, pushed Keppel to explain how the nation would know if Title I was having an effect. Keppel, recalling the rationale for the creation of the federal education office in 1867 (to provide information on the condition of education in the United States), proposed a national testing program. This would be the first of its kind and would assess what American children knew in a variety of subject areas. Educators were aghast at such a notion, and Keppel trod very carefully among the potent antagonists to such a proposal. He believed that it would be both faster and more politically expedient for the initial work on the tests to be done with private funds, rather than with public money. He turned to the Carnegie Corporation, of which his father, Frederick, had been president and of which he eventually became a trustee. Carnegie funded the planning of what became the National Assessment of Educational Progress (NAEP), but its operation, beginning in 1970, has been funded by the federal government, the National Center for Educational Statistics, and the National Institute of Education.[19]

In the beginning, results of the NAEP were released only by region, not by state or locality, because of political opposition from educators who did not want their states or localities identified by specific scores of their students. Such was the level of concern about academic achievement of the educators in the late sixties and early seventies. By the time of Keppel's death in 1990, the political climate had so changed that more than half of the states were now reporting their NAEP scores.

The effort to change both the ideology of adjustment and the practice of progressive education is the dominant theme of educational reform in the last third of the twentieth century. Keppel had the idea and the phrase, "equal educational opportunity." In short, he had the vision, but the American people have not yet had the will to transform that vision to a reality.

After a skirmish over desegregation of the public schools in Chicago with Superintendent Benjamin Willis and Mayor Richard Daley, Keppel left the commissionership in early 1966. Keppel's successor as commissioner, Harold Howe II, had the principal responsibility both for implementing the new Elementary and Secondary Education Act, whose passage Keppel had orchestrated, and for desegregating the schools. The *Brown* decision in 1954 had found separating the races in public schools by law inherently a violation of their constitutional rights, and Title VI of the Civil Rights Act of 1964 had provided the federal government with the leverage to do something about it. With the passage of the Elementary and Secondary Education Act, the federal government for the first time could spend money in nearly every school district in the country. To be eligible for the money, however, the district must not have segregated schools or it would be in violation of Title VI of the Civil Rights Act. Howe's dilemma was figuring out how to assure that the funds could be spent and the schools desegregated. The well-established separate housing pattern for blacks and whites in the North and the extensive formal legal and informal social structure in the South requiring segregation made school desegregation extremely complicated. Howe, appointed by President Lyndon Johnson, undertook these formidable tasks with zest. Grandson of the founder of the Hampton Institute and son of a Presbyterian minister, who was also head of Hampton Institute in the 1930s, Howe (like Keppel) did not come from the ranks of the education establishment. A graduate of the Taft School and Yale College, with a master's degree in history from Columbia, Howe, however, had substantial experience as a schoolteacher and school administrator before his federal appointment. Like Keppel he was playful with ideas. He wrote extensively, always dissociating himself from the world of educational researchers, but he wrote and spoke with clarity and charm that eluded most of the professional educators.

Howe needed all of the charm he could muster to get the southern schools to begin desegregation. He never promised that test scores would rise for either blacks or whites as a result of desegregation. His argument was simply that federal money could not go to the districts until they could prove that they had desegregated and were not in violation of Title VI of the Civil Rights Act. How to achieve that necessary desegregation was a political question that he addressed with some of his able junior colleagues at the USOE, particularly Gregory Anrig, now head of the Educational

Testing Service, which administers NAEP, and Stephen Joel Trachtenberg, now president of George Washington University.

Today the southern public schools are mostly desegregated, and today the scores on the NAEP of southern black students have risen significantly. Whether those scores have risen as a result of the Elementary and Secondary Education Act or of the desegregation of the schools or for a myriad of other reasons is unknown. The argument, however, of the post-Brown era, beginning in 1954, was that access to institutions was important.

Keppel and Howe attempted to translate a judicial ruling and Congressional law into routines that would affect the lives of many, many American school children. Initially, the South proved more amenable to those changes than did the North, where housing, not laws, were the determining consideration. Gradually, however, housing in the South, as exemplified by Gary Orfield's recent work on Atlanta, is proving as cumbersome as housing in the North. In the end, the changing residential and economic patterns in which poor, often minority, groups are concentrated in sections of cities has proved devastating for the children living there. They grow up, as William Julius Wilson documented, in circumstances in which the safest and most compassionate institution they encounter is the urban school. Most people would not give urban schools high marks for either safety or compassion, but it is those children's tragedy that for many the urban school is the bulwark of their lives. That such a bulwark exists at all is an incredible testament to the dedication and devotion of the adults who both care and work there.[20]

CONCLUSION

The prior principal goals for the schools in this century—assimilation, adjustment, and access—all have elements of merit. The nation sought assimilation as a means of dealing with its large European immigrant population, and the schools provided it. Indeed, most newly American families did wish their children to learn the language and the ways of their new country, although many did not wish their own language and culture to be denigrated in the process, as frequently occurred.

The emerging configuration of the increasingly industrial, urban, and well-paid work force in the 1940s and 1950s encouraged adjustment as a goal so that men would learn good work habits and women would learn to be happy as housewives. Parents also sought healthy psychological, mental, social, and economic adjustment for their children, although not at the expense of other qualities, such as creativity, independence, or curiosity, that might not be fostered by schools' commitments to traditional forms of adjustment.

Finally, access to educational institutions without regard to race and access to needed compensatory educational services are goals no one in the society can seriously fault, particularly after the civil rights revolution of the 1960s. These aspirations, however, have proved extraordinarily difficult to translate from theory to practice, frustrating and angering both government and families. Thus, each of these societally dictated goals for our schools in the twentieth century has merit. Complete fulfillment of each, however, has proved elusive.

The school continues to remind one of a battleship, changing course as society demands but never quite completing its journey before another new set of orders arrives to send it in another direction. "Hard right rudder," the captain shouts upon receipt of the newest coded message from Washington. With great creaking and dislocation of the movable items on board, the great ship shudders slowly into a new direction. So it is with the schools. Having tried to assimilate European immigrant children, having attempted to help youngsters adjust to life, and having sought to provide access by complying with desegregation orders and programs of compensatory education, school leaders now find themselves ordered to have all their children attain world class academic standards by the year 2000. They must try and they will, but they also need help. The battleship, the school, cannot do this alone. The rest of the educational flotilla must assist: families, communities, government, higher education, and the business community. Only then will all of our children be able to achieve that which by birthright should be theirs: enthusiasm for and accomplishment in learning.

NOTES

1. A fuller discussion of these issues can be found in Patricia Albjerg Graham, *S.O.S.: Sustain Our Schools* (New York: Hill & Wang, 1992), chap. 1.

2. Educational Policies Commission, National Education Association, and American Association of School Administrators, *Education for All American Youth: A Further Look* (Washington, D.C.: Educational Policies Commission, 1952), 3; U.S. National Center for Education Statistics, *Digest of Education Statistics, 1992* (Washington, D.C.: Government Printing Office, 1992), 109; Robert Kominski and Andrea Adams, "Educational Attainment in the United States: March 1991 and 1990," *Current Population Reports*, Population Characteristics, ser. P-20, no. 462 (May 1992): 7.

3. U.S. Bureau of the Census, *Historical Statistics of the United States: Colonial Times to 1970* (White Plains: Kraus International Publications, 1989), 379; U.S. National Center for Education Statistics, *Digest of Education Statistics,* 184.

4. "High Schools, by the Numbers," *Chicago Tribune*, 15 November 1991, sec. 2, 4.

5. Diego Ribadeneira, "Disparities between Rich, Poor Systems Often Glaring," *Boston Globe*, 25 January 1993, 16.

6. Benjamin Rush, "Thoughts upon the Mode of Education Proper in a Repub-

lic" (Philadelphia, 1786) in *Essays on Education in the Early Republic*, ed. Frederick Rudolph (Cambridge: Belknap Press of Harvard University Press, 1965), 14.

7. City of New York Department of Education, *Sixth Annual Report of the City Superintendent of Schools* (New York: City of New York Department of Education, 1904), 47; Leonard P. Ayres, *Laggards in Our Schools: A Study of Retardation and Elimination in City School Systems* (New York: Russell Sage, 1909), 14.

8. David B. Tyack and Elisabeth Hansot, *Managers of Virtue: Public School Leadership in America, 1920–1980* (New York: Basic Books, 1982).

9. Leonard Covello with Guido D'Agostino, *The Heart Is the Teacher* (New York: McGraw-Hill, 1958); Mary Antin, *The Promised Land* (Boston: Houghton Mifflin, 1912).

10. U.S. Bureau of the Census, *Historical Statistics of the United States*, 105.

11. *Proceedings of the Lake Mohonk Conference* (1884), 14, in Francis Paul Prucha, *The Great Father: The United States Government and the American Indians* (Lincoln: University of Nebraska Press, 1984), 2:687; the Pratt quote is from *Great Documents in American Indian History*, eds. Wayne Moquin and Charles Van Doren (New York: Praeger, 1973), 110, cited in Jeffrey Louis Hamley, "Federal Off-Reservation Boarding Schools for Indians, 1879–1900" (qualifying paper, Harvard Graduate School of Education, 1986), 32.

12. National Education Association, *Report of the Commission on the Reorganization of Secondary Education*, U.S. Bureau of Education Bulletin no. 35 (Washington, D.C.: Government Printing Office, 1918), in *American Education in the Twentieth Century: A Documentary History*, Classics in Education no. 52, ed. Marvin Lazerson (New York: Teachers College Press, 1987), 79–87. Quotes are from p. 80.

13. National Commission on Excellence in Education, *A Nation at Risk: The Imperative for Educational Reform* (Washington, D.C.: Government Printing Office, 1983).

14. John Dewey, *Democracy and Education: An Introduction to the Philosophy of Education* (New York: Macmillan Co., 1916).

15. Frederick Lovett Redefer, Executive Secretary of the Progressive Education Association, appeared on the cover of the 31 October 1938, issue of *Time*. The cover story, "Progressives' Progress," is on pages 31–35. Wilford M. Aiken, *Thirty Schools Tell Their Story* (New York: Harper & Brothers, 1943).

16. The preceding three paragraphs draw heavily upon Patricia Albjerg Graham, "What America Has Expected of its Schools over the Past Century," *American Journal of Education* 101 (1993): 83–98.

17. Commission on Life Adjustment Education for Youth, *Vitalizing Secondary Education: Report of the First Commission on Life Adjustment Education for Youth*, in U.S. Office of Education, *Bulletin* 3 (Washington, D.C.: U.S. Office of Education, 1951): 32.

18. U.S. Office of Education, *Life Adjustment Education for Every Youth* (1947), in U.S. Office of Education, *Bulletin* 22 (Washington, D.C.: U.S. Office of Education, 1951): 16.

19. Francis Keppel and Harold Howe II discuss their efforts to enact and implement the Elementary and Secondary Education Act in a lecture given to A-450, Historical Perspectives on the Federal Role in Education, Harvard Graduate School of Education, Cambridge, Mass. See "The Federal Government's Direct Education Efforts: The Elementary and Secondary Education Act of 1965" (4 December 1989),

tape 931, VHS Master, Gutman Library, Harvard Graduate School of Education. Other lectures by the two on this topic occurred on 5 December 1988, 30 November 1987, 1 December 1986, and 9 December 1985.

20. Gary Orfield and Carole Ashkinaze, *The Closing Door: Conservative Policy and Black Opportunity* (Chicago: University of Chicago Press, 1991); William Julius Wilson, *The Truly Disadvantaged: The Inner City, the Underclass, and Public Policy* (Chicago: University of Chicago Press, 1987).

2 WHO'S IN CHARGE? FEDERAL, STATE, AND LOCAL CONTROL

MICHAEL W. KIRST

This chapter provides an overview of the reform of U.S. education governance, highlighting the major changes since the turn of the century. The most significant changes occurred during two twenty-year periods: 1900–1920 and 1965–85. Perhaps the 1990s will prove to be yet another notable era in this regard, as curriculum, exams, and teacher certification come under increasing scrutiny nationwide.

Over time, education governance has been fundamentally transformed, but not always in the ways intended by the proponents of change. When it comes to governance reform, theory and practice have not always coincided. The history of governance changes is filled with unexpected developments, though overall there has been a gradual increase in fragmentation and complexity.

Some of these historical shifts in governance were caused by such structural changes as redistricting for the election of school boards. But others were caused by the waxing and waning of the influence of particular policy actors and by their changing level of involvement in governance issues. States have always had a role in U.S. education governance, but aggressive governors, legislators, and courts transformed the states' role between 1950 and 1992.

Governance changes also reflect major alterations in the socioeconomic environment. Sputnik, the civil rights movement, and international economic competition are three recent galvanizing influences. The crucial structural reforms of 1900–1920, for example, in large part reflected increased immigration.

Large-scale changes in education governance have been made at the expense of local discretion. School boards, local superintendents of schools, and local central administrations have all lost influence. Those whose influence has increased over time include the federal government and the states, the courts, interstate networks and organizations (e.g., teacher standards boards), private business, teacher and administrator collective bargaining groups, and community-based interest groups composed of others than education professionals.

THE ANALYTIC APPROACH OF THIS CHAPTER

"Institutional choice" provides a partial framework for this chapter.[1] Often educational policy debates focus more on what should be done than on which institutions should be authorized to make and implement policy. One crucial policy decision is the choice of a decision maker; this determines to a large extent the balance of education governance. (For example, courts have been reluctant to delegate civil rights protection to local school districts in Mississippi.) Another type of institutional choice is whether to place various functions in the hands of markets (e.g., vouchers) or politics (e.g., school board elections). The 1983–89 state reform movement, for example, included an institutional choice to enhance the curricular and testing role of state government at the expense of local control.

Clune stressed that two general characteristics of available institutions are important: agreement on substantive goals and capacity to achieve those goals. Substantive goals are crucial because of the need to ensure support for a policy. Courts may be more enthusiastic about civil rights goals than school boards are. But support must be buttressed by institutional capacity. For example, courts cannot run school districts on a weekly basis. One method of choosing institutions can be called *comparative institutional advantage*, which begins with distrust or criticism of a particular institution.

> Since no decision maker is perfect, the distrust directed at one decision maker must be carefully weighted against the advantages of that decision maker and both the advantages and disadvantages of alternative decision makers. In other words, although the logic of institutional choice typically begins with distrust, distrust itself proves nothing in the absence of a superior alternative . . . The logic of comparative institutional advantage also implies the futility of seeking perfect or ideal implementation of a policy . . . The real world offers a "least worst choice" of imperfect institutions.[2]

A problem with institutional choice analyses is the tendency to confuse predictive with normative applications. In education, policy connections between new institutional choices and education are often unclear. For instance, how much state control of curriculum will lead to how much decline in teacher autonomy? How does parent control of school choice through vouchers lead to increased learning? The *rate* of substitution is equally unclear, for example, the point at which increased federal influence in education leads to a decline in the state role. It is possible to avoid zero-sum properties through various win-win scenarios such as state curriculum content guidelines that help teachers communicate higher order thinking and do not interfere with local teacher professionalism or autonomy. In sum, institutional choice is complex, uncertain, and subject to continual political change. The accumulation of policies over many years embodies a set of preferences about which institutions should govern what components of a policy area. For example, from 1960 to 1990 states increased drastically their control of school finance.

Although most nations have established school systems based on national or state control, the United States has always emphasized local control based predominantly on small districts. In 1948 the United States had 89,000 school districts, and now it has 15,020. Moreover, unlike most countries, U.S. school governance is detached from general government that provides other services for children. Governance changes over the years have challenged these original institutional choices concerning who should govern U.S. schools.

As this history will demonstrate, reform of educational governance that results in different educational choices is often motivated by desires to change school priorities and policies.[3] Replacing those in power with those who are out of power is one way to attempt policy changes. Moreover, directly changing the objectives of schools may be more difficult politically than indirectly changing local school policies by "reforming" governance. Institutional choice becomes another policy instrument to settle temporarily the debates among the numerous and conflicting goals that the public has for education. For example, reformers at the turn of the twentieth century wanted a unitary curriculum across cities and an end to bilingual education in German, Polish, and other languages. The 1983 report, *A Nation At Risk,* implied that local control of curriculum standards was not optimal and that therefore state government should assume more control of local curricular policies.[4]

Institutional choice can also be designed to further the interests of either majorities or minorities. During the 1955–75 era the U.S. Supreme Court became more influential and created local court monitors with powers to override local school boards. These monitors were supposed to protect the rights of minorities such as blacks and handicapped children.[5]

Recent critics of educational governance have alleged that democratic government is inappropriate and dysfunctional for schools. These critics want to change institutional choice to the market through vouchers and choice.[6] Typically, changes in institutional choice result both from disagreement about goals and from widespread dissatisfaction and loss of confidence in the quality of educational outcomes. For example, New Jersey declared some of its school districts educationally bankrupt in the

TABLE 2.1 Illustrative Influences on Curriculum Policy Making

Type	National	State	Local
General legislative	Congress	State legislature	(City councils have no influence)
Educational legislature	House Committee on Education and Labor	State school board	Local school board
Executive	President	Governor	(Mayor has no influence)
Administrative	U.S. Dept. of Education	State department	School superintendent
Bureaucratic	OERI, National Science Foundation (Division of Curriculum Improvement)	State department (division of instruction)	Department chair, teacher
Professional association	National testing agencies, subject matter organization, NCTM, NSTA	Accrediting associations, NEA, state subject matter affiliates	County association of superintendents
Other private interests	Foundation and business corporations, College Board	NSF systemic state initiatives	NAACP, National Organization for Women

Abbreviations: NAACP, National Association for the Advancement of Colored People; NCTM, National Council of Teachers of Mathematics; NEA, National Education Association; NSF, National Science Foundation; NSTA, National Science Teachers Association; OERI, Office of Educational Research and Improvement.

1980s and seized control from the local school boards. The shifting patterns of influence discussed in this chapter are caused in part by different preferences for institutional choice. But increases and decreases in influence are also unintended products of other policies. For example, California's proposition 13 cut local property taxes and unintentionally, according to voter surveys, shifted control of educational policy to Sacramento.

Because of the nature of U.S. federalism, there are many contenders for new institutional choices that will shift the balance of governance influence. Table 2.1 is one way to portray the overall governance matrix. Note the important influence of private organizations such as textbook publishers, foundations, and testing agencies.[7]

As this historical review demonstrates, trends since 1960 have shifted governance upward toward nonlocal levels. The biggest political losers have been local school boards and superintendents. The biggest winners have been states and unions. The consolidation of school districts from over 130,000 to about 15,000 resulted in fewer options for consumers and enhanced demands for more choice. Is this the right balance for governing education? These are value judgments that U.S. systems must make. It is easier for many political organizations with special causes to utilize higher levels of government than to tell the local level what to do. Unions prefer school system contracts rather than negotiating at every building. But the thirty-year trend toward centralization and bureaucracy is leading to radical demands for decentralizing changes in governance, including vouchers and charter schools.

THE HISTORIC DOMINANCE OF LOCAL CONTROL

Local control is the hallmark of American education, so this history begins there and moves from the local level to the states and finally to the federal level. Indeed, the federal level was the least important actor in the history of school governance and did not play a major reform role until 1957 with the National Defense Education Act (NDEA). Local taxes provided the bulk of finance support, over 83 percent in 1930. Consequently, state government focused on minimum standards for rural schools, and the federal presence was barely visible.[8]

The concept of the local board originated in New England, where citizens at first controlled the schools directly through town meetings. By 1826, however, Massachusetts had already created a separate school committee divorced from the rest of local government, and the Massachusetts model spread throughout the nation. Horace Mann, a founder of the American school system, proclaimed that "the common school was to be free, financed by local and state government, controlled by lay boards of education, and mixing all social groups under one roof."[9] The school board was to be nonpartisan and nonsectarian.

In the 1800s, schools were controlled by hundreds of thousands of local board members. As late as 1890, 71 percent of Americans lived in rural areas, where the one-room school was typical.[10] By the turn of the twentieth century, however, as society moved into the modern era, big changes were in store for school boards.

Research evidence supports a view that teachers and administrators in the twentieth century were gradually socialized into a political orientation featuring the following norms: Education is a unique function that must have its own separate and politically independent governance structure. The operation of the schools should be uninvolved in politics, and professional unity of teachers and administrators should be observed in political action.[11] Overt involvement in political conflict is to be avoided, alignment with political parties is undesirable, and collective action in electoral campaigns and pressuring of public officials is not appropriate professional conduct. Supporting this viewpoint, which Iannaccone called "the politics preferred by pedagogues," were the values of professionalism, efficiency, and bureaucracy combined with a fear of community sanctions for many types of overt political action.[12]

Data on political behavior demonstrate that these political orientations in fact restricted the political activities of teachers and administrators.[13] In effect, political attitudes and behavior were consistent.[14]

TURN-OF-THE-CENTURY REFORM

A pressing public education issue during 1890–1910 was the role of the alleged unscrupulous party politician.[15] It was not uncommon in large cities for teachers to use political influence to get positions and, sometimes, later to be fired when their political patron lost an election. Frequently, members of the board of education were supported by major parties and elected on a decentralized ward basis. For instance, Pittsburgh had 222 members of local boards, and Boston had thirty subcommittees with a total membership of 142 elected on a political ward basis.[16] The Board of Education was often used as a political stepping stone, and consequently party nominations for school board were hotly contested. To gain control of the situation, reformers wanted to divorce policy making and management from the politician through centralization under a professional superintendent. This implied a divorce of school management from other municipal services, which would always be controlled to a significant extent by politicians. Moreover, teachers wanted an end to the spoils system in determining their careers.

Urban school reform was part of a broader pattern of social elites galvanizing municipal change at the turn of the century.[17] Although the surface rhetoric pitted the corrupt politician against the community-oriented citizen, the reformers' underlying motives have been questioned by several historians. The reform resulted in a professional culture that tends to be less diverse than the cultures represented in the ward boards. For instance, Hays emphasized that financial and professional leaders deplored the decentralized ward system in large part because it empowered members of the lower and lower middle class (many of whom were recent immigrants). Reformers wanted not simply to replace bad men with good; they proposed to change the occupational and class origins of decision makers.[18] Tyack expressed this viewpoint in stronger language: "Underlying much of the reform movement was an elitist assumption that prosperous native born Protestant Anglo-Saxons were superior to other groups and thus should determine the curriculum and the allocation of jobs. It was the mission of the schools to imbue children of the immigrants and the poor with uniformly WASP ideals."[19] Here we see clearly the use of change in institutional choices as a way to change policy. The watchwords of the reform movement in the city schools became centralization, expertise, professionalization, nonpolitical control, and efficiency. The most attractive models of organization for education were the large-scale industrial bureaucracies rapidly emerging in the 1880–1910 age of consolidation.[20]

The reformers contended that the board members elected by wards advanced parochial and special interests at the expense of the needs of the school district as a whole. What was needed to counter this atomization of interest was election at large. Professional expertise rested upon the assumption that scientific school administration would be independent of the particular values of particular groups. A good school system is good for everyone, not just a part of the community. This unitary-community idea would help protect schools from influences of local political parties and interest groups.[21] By 1970, social and ethnic minorities realized that, to gain representation, they needed to elect local board members by sub-district.

The 1900–1920 reformers charged, moreover, that, since the larger school boards worked through numerous subcommittees, their executive authority was splintered. No topic was too trivial for a separate subcommittee, ranging from ways to teach reading to the purchase of doorknobs. At one time, Chicago had seventy-nine subcommittees and Cincinnati had seventy-four.[22] The primary requisite for better management was thought to be centralization of power in a chief executive who had considerable delegated authority from the board. Only under such a system would someone make large-scale improvements and be held accountable.

It was sometimes a very small group of patricians who secured new charters from state legislatures and thereby reorganized the urban schools

without a popular vote in the cities.[23] This turn-of-the-century school reform was implemented by a policy issue network composed of the owners
of big business, university leaders, and municipal reformers; this network
later created concepts like the city manager.[24]

Counts's classic study in 1927 demonstrated that it was upper-class
professionals and business people who made up the centralized boards of
education.[25] For instance, in St. Louis after the centralization reforms in
1897, professional men on the board had jumped from 4.8 percent to 58.3
percent, big businessmen from 9.0 percent to 25 percent; small businessmen dropped from 47.6 percent to 16.7 percent and wage-earning employees from 28.6 percent to none (10 percent were of unknown earlier occupation). These board members in turn delegated much of their formal powers
to certified school professionals, who had the flexibility to shape the
schools to the needs of industrial society.

The doctrine that public education is "above politics" demonstrated
impressive popularity and longevity among the general public. But there
are advantages for education in the maintenance of this folklore, including
the view that education is different from other local government functions
and is run by professionals rather than politicians.[26]

The realignment in influence further enhanced what Callahan called
the "cult of efficiency" in school operation.[27] This "cult" played down the
desirability of political influence, conflict, or pressure groups and favored
scientific management. Leading academicians, for example, concentrated
on researching a specific set of tools for the administrative activities of
school management and created a merit system bureaucracy based on
university certificates.

School administrators and teachers became successful in attaining their
reform goal of "boundary maintenance," or freedom from most external
political constraints, to a greater degree than most other public programs.
Prominent characteristics of educational governance became political isolation from partisan politics and other local government institutions, tight
organizational boundaries, and a slow rate of internal change that exem-
plifies social systems generally defined as "closed systems."[28] This closed
system operated within a value system of leadership, from politically neutral competence through certified professional administrators. To keep
political parties out of school policy making, school elections remained
unaligned with political parties and ballots were nonpartisan. Moreover,
board members were elected at large as "trustees" rather than from subdistricts as "representatives."

The political attitudes of teachers reflected the political operation of the
schools. Harmon Ziegler's study of the Oregon Education Association in
the mid-1960s concluded that "there is a fairly strong feeling among teachers that being a member of a profession (which teachers strive so desper-

ately to achieve) makes it necessary to develop an organization which is 'above politics.' There is some belief that the professional stature of the teacher will suffer if the professional organization gets involved in the rough and tumble world of politics, especially electoral politics."[29]

A 1957 national survey of teachers' opinions on seven types of civic-political attitudes supplies support for Ziegler's assertion. A large majority of teachers thought teachers should not persuade others to vote for teachers' candidates in school board elections, serve as party precinct workers, conduct partisan elections, or give speeches for teachers' candidates outside of school.[30]

Roscoe C. Martin's 1962 survey of suburban schools and Robert Salisbury's analysis of city districts stressed that the political values, attitudes, and norms of school administrators with regard to the issues highlighted in this chapter paralleled those of teachers.[31] Martin's conclusions concerning the school political environment were as follows:

> Thus, is the circle closed and the paradox completed. Thus, does the public school heralded by its champions as the cornerstone of democracy, reject the political world in which democratic institutions operate. Thus is historical identification with local government accompanied by insistence on complete independence of any agency . . . of local government, lip service to general citizen activity attended by mortal fear of general politics, the logical and legitimate companion of citizen action.[32]

THE EVOLUTION OF THE ROLE OF THE SCHOOL BOARD

After the turn-of-the-century reforms, board influence was restricted by a lack of time and independent staff. Board members usually held demanding full-time jobs and could meet at night only once or twice a month. They rarely received objective criteria by which to question the professional judgments of the superintendent and his staff. Moreover, elections seldom provided board members with a specific mandate or policy platform.[33]

Before the mid-1960s, a description of the board's function would be something like this: School boards most often mediated major policy conflicts, leaving the determination of important policy issues to the professional staff; even in mediating, they might do little; in the process, they often simply legitimized the proposals of the professional staff, making only marginal changes.[34]

Although board members spent the bulk of their time on details, they did establish a policy "zone of consent" that made clear to the superintendent what was and what was not acceptable.[35] For example, a superintendent who tried in 1950 to introduce bilingual education in a rural, conservative California district would discover that this program was outside the board's zone of consent.

Not surprisingly, smaller districts with little population growth and a narrow spectrum of values and philosophies created more citizen satisfaction than did larger units. Larger, more diverse districts often featured conflict between the locals, who had lived in the district for many years, and better-educated parents who moved into suburbs far from the central city.[36]

The centralization that occurred in city school boards did not much change rural boards. Rural boards, however, were greatly affected by a rapid school consolidation process that created larger schools with the capacity to offer a wide range of curriculum options. What was once an archipelago of districts in America—with each island having a board and community in harmony—was fused into a system of larger, more varied districts. The 89,000 districts of 1948 became 55,000 five years later, 31,000 by 1961, and 15,020 by 1991.[37] During the 1970s, on any given day, three districts disappeared forever between breakfast and dinner. Earlier, in the 1960s, that many had evaporated between breakfast and the morning coffee break, with another seven gone by dinner.

Educators, who believed bigger must be better, found that these larger districts offered more options but also created more conflicting viewpoints about school policy. And, while districts grew larger, boards grew smaller; there were fewer board members available to handle complex issues and represent a diverse citizenry. In the 1930s, a typical school board member represented approximately two hundred people; by 1970, he represented three thousand constituents.

A nationwide study of school boards in the early 1970s yielded the following conclusions:

> We can say that the recruitment process implies that the potential resources of boards—representative capacity and legal authority—are underutilized. It is not surprising that school boards are WASP-ish; what does bear directly upon resource utilization is the low-keyed, self-perpetuating selection process which minimizes conflict. Such a selection process subverts the notions of lay control and hence the "public" orientation of board members. Orthodoxy and tradition are cherished; controversy is not. There is little intensive lay, or group, involvement in elections. Thus boards emerge as relatively impermeable.
>
> The early education reformers have succeeded too well; politics (i.e., partisan) and education are normally separate. Thus, the superintendent's basic resources—technical skills, information skills, information monopoly, expertise—are not matched by an equally

resourceful board. As we continue to describe the decisional culture of school systems, the lack of a balance of power between board and superintendent will become apparent.[38]

Moreover, the composition of school boards did not keep pace with the changing racial and ethnic constituency. A 1989 survey conducted by Emily Feistritzer at the National Center for Education Information in Washington, D.C., revealed that, of school board presidents, 97 percent were white and 71 percent were male, were in their late 40s, and had children at home. School board presidents have more education, make more money, and are more conservative politically than the average American.[39]

Since the 1930s, the major change in the composition of school boards as a whole has been the dramatic increase in female members from 12 percent in 1930 to 33 percent in 1991.[40] A national study of the roles of male and female school board members found that women were more involved in curricular and other educational program issues than were men; women also were less likely to delegate decisions to the superintendent. Men focused more on fiscal, contract, and management issues.[41]

For superintendents, expertise has become not only a resource but a way of life learned early and essential for occupational survival. Lacking staff, information, and linkages to the community, school boards found themselves reacting to a superintendent's agenda that highlights expertise and routine as much as possible. But the board does select and fire the superintendent, so it may not need to restate its policy orientation for every issue.[42]

What groups did school boards hear from during the reform era 1920–65?[43] The results of several surveys show that the most active voice was the Parent-Teacher Association (PTA). Almost two-thirds of the board members in the Jennings and Ziegler study of 1968 cited the PTA; the next most-often-mentioned voice, cited by one-third of the members, was that of teachers' groups. After that, contact dropped off rapidly: civil rights groups (20 percent), business groups (13 percent), right-wing groups (13 percent), and labor organizations (3 percent). In short, in-house and supportive groups (the PTA and teachers) had the most intense interaction with board members. Two-thirds of the board members and three-fourths of the superintendents thought that the board's role should not be that of a representative of the public desires—instead they stressed the trustee role.

TEACHERS AND COLLECTIVE POLITICAL ACTION

As recently as 1970, teachers were reluctant to use collective action to enhance their political influence within or outside the schools. Local school administrators preferred to deal with individual teachers, not teachers as they are collectively organized today. Indeed, a 1961 survey of the doctrines of educational administration discovered little attention to formal, organized groups of teachers.[44] The National Education Association (NEA), the dominant national organization of teachers, paid scant attention to the local scene and concentrated its efforts on research and national legislation. The tenets of educational administration stressed group activity, and unions would lead to unnecessary and harmful conflict among educators, who needed to stay united.[45] The schools stressed the harmony of interests and agreements on goals among all types of professionals, including teachers and administrators. Moreover, school administrators anticipated correctly that, once employee organizations became viable political interest groups, teacher leadership would have a survival instinct to seek out and maintain conflict over issues in school governance.[46] Even a September 1965 NEA national survey found that only 22 percent of the teachers favored collective bargaining.[47]

This internal stance on collective organization was mirrored in teacher and administrator conduct in local, state, and national elections. In 1961, organizations of teachers and administrators had not accepted the political necessity of giving money or endorsements to candidates.[48] Ziegler found that the membership of the Oregon Education Association was far more supportive of "defensive" activities (if teachers were attacked by the community) than they were of "offensive" political activities. Electoral activities were considered much more unprofessional than legislative lobbying—but lobbying is not very effective if the incumbents do not support the teachers' viewpoint.[49] Formal alliances with political parties were not considered seriously by professional educational organizations.

Political action among teachers involved sharp differences between the majority of female teachers (69 percent in 1960) and the minority of men (31 percent in 1960). A 1965 survey sampling all teachers revealed that campaign work by teachers in national elections was favored by 60 percent of the men but only 46.5 percent of the women.[50]

In sum, the political behavior of teachers and administrators in 1960–61 is characterized by nonpartisanship, a reluctance to engage in public conflict, and a minimal use of collective political action and bargaining. This supported a governance system dominated by administrators with poorly organized interest groups. In rural areas, however, the school board could be a transmitter of community demands without the need for organized groups because rural board members could discuss issues with citizens in many informal settings, like shopping centers and clubs.

THE EFFECTS OF COLLECTIVE BARGAINING

The late 1960s was the beginning of an intense period of implementing collective bargaining based on the industrial union model. Between 1965 and 1980, in most states except those in the Southeast and Mountain regions, teachers realized that they needed collective bargaining. This was a major movement away from administrative dominance of governance.

The outcome of collective bargaining is a written and time-bound agreement covering wages, hours, and conditions of employment. As well as involving the specifics of the contract, major disputes can occur over the scope of bargaining and grievance procedures. The negotiated contract, however, is not felt by teachers until it is implemented in the work setting. At the school site, the board's contract language must be interpreted to apply to specific circumstances. This means that the site principal, teachers, and union building representative must become very familiar with the contract's terms. Yet even familiarity does not forestall many disputes about specific teaching arrangements. These disputes can lead to grievances whose settlement can clarify the contract.

Thus, teacher influence varies by district *and* site. Teachers at school sites sometimes permit exceptions to the district contract if they seem warranted by specific school conditions. Teachers' unions have the most difficulty enforcing such contract provisions as pupil discipline, building maintenance, and security because grievance procedures are less effective with these problems. On the other hand, seniority and teacher transfer clauses are the most commonly implemented. The unions' long-run effectiveness, however, may come more from influencing decisions at state and federal levels that then percolate down to the local school system. As close students of this subject pointed out, lobbying by teachers in state capitals had a significant effect on traditional school governance.[51] Teachers were able to pass state legislation that regulated school policy in areas where they could not obtain contract provisions. The NEA has a much stronger presence at the state level because the American Federation of Teachers (AFT) has primarily big-city members.

What happens to administrator authority, particularly among principals, when contracts filter down through the loosely coupled school system? A major study found that, although some provisions tightly limit the principal's freedom of action, others get redefined to fit the particular requirements at the school site. That is, "such factors as teacher interests, educational consequences, administrative leadership and staff allegiance were balanced and counterbalanced."[52] How the principal works with the contract also affects teachers' respect for administrators. In short, having standards and expecting much of teachers earns principals tolerance and even respect from teachers in interpreting the contract; for teachers, a good school is more important than union membership, close observance of a contract, or control of the schools. As one administrator observed, "Teachers like to be part of a winning team."[53]

The ultimate effect of collective bargaining may not be as great as was once thought. Johnson stressed that the effects of collective bargaining are deep and pervasive but not so extreme nor uniform as critics often suggest.

Collective bargaining has not been shown to have increased teachers' commitment to their work or enhanced their standing as professionals, but neither has it destroyed the schools. Caricatures of straitjacketed principals, Kafkaesque school bureaucracies, or schools under siege by militant teachers scarcely represent the experiences of these sample districts. Overall, the organizational effects of collective bargaining appear to be both moderate and manageable.

This is not to suggest, though, that labor relations practices look the same in all districts of all schools. In fact, negotiations, contract language, and administrative practices are remarkably diverse.[54]

Understanding of these consequences is confused by diverse practices in local systems. No single factor accounts for this diversity in local practices, but certain important variables include the history of local labor practices, the local political culture, and—most important—the people at the center of negotiations and contract management. In California, the same districts have strikes or acrimonious labor disputes near the expiration of every contract. Some of this is caused by personalities, styles, and relationships, and some is caused by a long and bitter history of labor-management relations. However, in other districts, both sides prefer cooperation over a long period. No simple predictive model can account for these factors.

It is clear that collective bargaining has increased the complexity of the principal's job because he or she cannot apply the contract in a routine and standard manner. Moreover, there are some overall effects of bargaining, including "the movement of the locus of decision making to central offices within school systems and to locations outside of school systems, including legislatures, courts, and public administrative agencies that govern collective bargaining procedures."[55] Increasingly, local educators work within a power-sharing context where educational leadership is still possible but is surrounded by more complex requirements.

TURN-OF-THE-CENTURY REFORM RETHOUGHT IN THE 1970S

As an antidote to the lack of political participation and the dominance of the professional priesthood, several scholars advocated injecting more politics into educational governance. This movement supplemented collective bargaining in its assault on the predominant governance influence of local administrators.

Herbert Kaufman posited three competing governance values or objectives: representativeness; technical, nonpartisan competence; and leadership.[56] The first objective refers to the election of public officials, the use of referenda, and the preferred effectiveness of the legislative branch in determining education policy. The second refers to the demand for officials to be trained and qualified for their jobs and a preference for education decisions based on technical and professional considerations rather than on partisan political premises. The third value refers to executive coordination through some central mechanism that ensures reasonably consistent and efficient education programs.

The literature of educational politics in the 1970s advocated a stronger emphasis on governance structures and processes for representation.[57] A reorientation of priorities from the turn-of-the-century reforms of centralization, depoliticization, expertise, and civil service competence would be a first step toward this goal. The new priorities would be increased representation, the school as the unit of governance, decentralization, and lay control. The values conflict inherent in education would be highlighted, not obscured behind a facade of professional expertise. Some writers wanted a dismantling of the reforms of 1900–1920 through

— board elections by subcommunity districts rather than at large;
— all members of a school board running at once; and
— optional use of partisan endorsements.[58]

The effectiveness of a school board would be enhanced by its having its own independent staff. In large districts, decentralization and community control would accompany the establishment of an independent board staff. School board members would receive salaries in large districts and be expected to surrender part of their outside activities. These central school board members would be buttressed by elected citizen/staff advisory councils (including community members) *for each school.*

This type of governance plan recognizes that it is the school, rather than the entire district, which is the critical nexus between the child and the substance of education.[59] The school site is also large enough to have relevance for state aid formulas. We need to know whether money for special federal and state programs is reaching the schools with the most needy pupils. Moreover, we need to know whether these needy schools are receiving an equitable share of the local district's budget for "regular" programs. Even in small school districts, it is the school site that is the biggest concern to the parents. If community participation is not high at all school sites, this plan might have beneficial effects. In addition to what is done in government, how things are done and how people feel about their governance are crucial.

The 1970s reformers contended that the United States should rethink the assumption that the community is a unity for educational policy and that, consequently, there should be a uniform educational program in all schools.[60] With safeguards to prevent racial and economic segregation, school-site emphasis can be linked to the concept of parent-choice clusters. Schools in the same geographic area could feature quite different programmatic approaches—open classrooms, self-contained classrooms, schools without walls, and so forth—and parents could choose their preferred approach. All alternatives could be within the public sector to avoid the difficulties of an unregulated voucher scheme. A plan with choices would provide greater leverage over school policy by parents.

There was some movement based on the advocacy for governance reforms in the 1970s. By 1991 more than half of urban school boards were elected by subdistricts,[61] and school-site decision making was a major component of the restructuring rhetoric.[62]

THE MARKET ALTERNATIVE TO POLITICAL GOVERNANCE

The main 1980s intellectual challenge to the pattern of institutional choice was advanced by market theorists. This argument is exemplified by Chubb and Moe's *Politics, Markets and America's Schools*.[63]

> One of their major points is that the . . . system's familiar arrangements for direct democratic control do indeed impose a distinctive structure on the educational choices of all the various participants . . . and that this structure tends to promote organizational characteristics that are ill-suited to the effective performance of American public schools. This social outcome is the product of countless individual decisions, but it is not an outcome that any of the major players would want or intend if acting alone. It is truly a product of the system as a whole, an unintended consequence of the way the system works.[64]

In short, the political web surrounding U.S. schools was so complex, fragmented, inclusive, and incoherent that it drastically restricted school-site autonomy and school effectiveness. Chubb and Moe used data from *High School and Beyond* to imply that school autonomy is a crucial determinant of pupil achievement. Consequently, they recommended drastic changes in the institutional structure of schools, including federal, state, and central office deregulation, plus scholarships for each student, who could then choose any deregulated school (public or private) that meets a very minimal standard.

If we believe Chubb and Moe, the major politics of the education "problem" have changed 180 degrees during the last forty years. In the 1960s the consensus was that education suffered from too little politics—education was a relatively closed political system controlled by professional educators with an underdeveloped interest group structure. School support groups like the PTA dominated, and the superintendent and principals were "in charge."[65] There was a need for more interest groups, higher election turnouts, and more candidates for school board elections. In the mid-1960s, the state level was viewed as a minor player oriented to serving rural schools. This view culminated when two political scientists (Ziegler and Jennings) published *Governing American Schools,* based on a nation-wide survey.[66] They criticized the schools for a low level of "representative democracy," with particular emphasis on school boards.

> It is patent that, when measured against the yardstick of a classic democratic theory of leadership selection, school district governance hardly comes through with flying colors. There are, indeed, certain board prerequisites which might well be considered discriminatory. Competition is limited, sponsorship and preemptive appointments common. Challenges to the status quo are infrequent; incumbents are but rarely challenged and more rarely still defeated. There are often no issue differences at all in an election . . . Communication is sparse, often one-sided in either the supportive or nonsupportive mode, and ad hoc. For its part the board feels threatened when any but harmless group activity flourishes because that has come to mean that all is not well in the district, that the natives are restless.[67]

Ziegler and Jennings went on to extol the "salutary effects of politics." They argued that the apolitical stance of the 1900–1920 school governance reformers created an institution with an ethos that was "above politics." They called for proposals to provide more representative democracy and "large doses of politics."[68]

Well, sixteen years later, along came Chubb and Moe claiming that the political doses and numbers of fragmented organized interests were too large and had caused political gridlock. Had the political web of U.S. schools changed so much in sixteen years, or was the database faulty? Chubb and Moe claimed that the large and stultifying bureaucracy merely reflected numerous political winners who had enshrined their gains in incoherent school policies and structural homeostasis. They did not address the numerous small local school districts below 500 or 1,000 pupils where bureaucracy was minimal. They argued that, under a system of democratic control, the public schools are governed by an enormous, far-flung constituency in which the interests of parents and students carry no special status or weight. When markets prevail, parents and students are thrust onto center stage, along with the owners and staff of schools; most of the rest of society plays a distinctly secondary role, limited for the most part to setting the framework within which educational choices are made.[69]

Unlike Jennings and Ziegler, Chubb and Moe used secondary sources, including *Schools in Conflict* by Wirt and Kirst,[70] to substantiate their claims. School administrators may build rolling coalitions of different interests to obtain their goals. But Chubb and Moe believe that these coalitions can make only minor changes and do not represent parents and students. The politics of gridlock are overwhelming change, and rolling coalitions can only make very marginal policy changes.

THE EVOLUTION OF THE STATE ROLE

Under the U.S. Constitution, education is a power reserved to the states. The basis for state control over education was well established as early as 1820 by constitutional and statutory provisions. Most state constitutions contain language that charges the legislature with the responsibility for establishing and maintaining a system of free public schools. The operation of most schools is delegated by the state to local school boards.

Historically, the states have controlled local education through several means.[71] The state may, for example, establish minimums of curriculum, teacher qualifications, and facilities below which local school operations cannot fall. States may encourage local schools to exceed minimums and often share some of the costs if local districts provide higher salaries or extend the school year. Most states have specified or encouraged reorganization of school districts. In the 1940s, states began to require consolidation of school districts and eliminated so many that, where there were nine school districts in 1932, only one existed in 1978. The total number decreased from 128,000 to 16,000.

States have required local provision of services, such as education for the handicapped. Indeed, a major argument for state control is that it can ensure equality and standardization of instruction and resources.[72] Local control advocates, however, assert that local flexibility is desirable because the technology of education is so unclear. In essence, the argument over local control focuses on the trade-off between two values—equal (and adequate) treatment and freedom of choice. Moreover, the influence of laymen is more likely to be enhanced by the availability of local discretion for decentralized governance units like school boards. State centralists argue, however, that state minimums do not restrict local discretion. Over time, such requirements are transformed into a low level of school services, which is exceeded substantially by districts either with greater wealth in taxable property or with a greater willingness to levy taxes or both.

In sum, equality, efficiency, and choice are three state policy values that often compete.[73] The first two have been growing in public acceptance, and the state role has increased. Local options, on the other hand, have been curtailed over the past forty years.

VARIATIONS IN STATE CONTROL

States differ markedly with respect to historical patterns of control over objects of governance such as curriculum, personnel administration, and finances, depending on whether the state follows a centrist or a localist policy. In New England the local schools enjoy an autonomy from state controls that may have its roots in resentment against such centralized authorities as the colonial English governor. By contrast, textbooks and courses of instruction in the southern states are often centrally determined.[74]

State curriculum mandating has both historical and political causes. Often newer subjects, such as vocational education and driver training, have needed state laws to gain a secure place in the curriculum. These subjects were introduced into the curriculum after 1920 amid great controversy, whereas mathematics and English never required political power to justify their existence. Consequently, the standard subjects are less frequently mandated by state laws.

Lying behind the interstate variation in local control is a concept called *political culture*, which refers to the differing value structures that manifest themselves in the characteristic behavior and actions of states and regions.[75] Political culture ranges widely in its objects—political rules, party structures, government structures and processes, citizens' roles, and attitudes about all these. In short, political culture is a constraint helping to account for major differences among states in local versus state control. It affects policy feasibility. It also helps to determine whether state control will expand and the inclinations of local officials to evade state influence.

The capacity of state education agencies (SEAs) to intercede in local school policy has also increased dramatically in the last twenty years. Ironically, the federal government provided the initial programmatic and fiscal impetus for this expansion. The Elementary and Secondary Education Act (ESEA) of 1965 and its subsequent amendments required state agencies to approve local projects for federal funds in such diverse areas as innovation and education for disadvantaged, handicapped, bilingual, and migrant children. In each of these federal programs, 1 percent of the funds were earmarked for state administration. Moreover, Title V of the ESEA provided general support for state administrative resources, with some priority given to state planning and evaluation. By 1972, three-fourths of the SEA staffs had been in their jobs for less than three years.[76] All of the expansion in California from 1964 to 1970 was financed by federal funds. In 1972, 70 percent of the funding for the SEA in Texas came from federal aid. The new staff capacity was available for SEA administrators or state boards that wanted a more activist role in local education.

Advocates of local control, such as teachers' unions, school boards, and administrators' associations, feud among themselves and provide a vacuum that activists for state control can exploit. These education groups cannot agree on common policies with their old allies, such as parent organizations, the American Association of University Women, and the League of Women Voters. The loss of public confidence in professional educators and the decline of achievement scores have created an attitude among many legislators that local school employees can no longer be given much discretion.

STATE ACCOUNTABILITY AND PROGRAM MANDATES

Between 1966 and 1976, thirty-five states passed accountability statutes and fourteen claimed to have "comprehensive systems" with several components. Despite a lack of common definition and concepts, four thousand pieces of accountability literature were published. In effect, the desire for accountability has focused state control on school outcomes in addition to state-defined minimum inputs. Some of the areas where state accountability control has expanded are requirements for new budget formats (including program budgeting), new teacher evaluation requirements, new state tests and assessment devices that reorient local curriculums to the state tests, state-mandated procedures for the setting of local educational objectives, parent advisory councils for school sites, and state-specified minimum competency standards for high school graduation.

The demand for equal opportunity spawned new state programs for populations with special needs.[77] States now classify children in several ways and mandate services and standards for the various categories of students. Some of these pupil classifications are students in vocational education and career education, the mentally gifted, disadvantaged migrants, underachievers, non–English speaking students, American Indians, pregnant minors, foster children, delinquent children, and twenty or more different categories of handicapped children.

In sum, some of the major policy areas that show the dramatic increase of state influence during the last two decades are state administration of federal categorical grants, the state role in education finance, state requirements for educational accountability, state specifications and programs for children with special needs, and state efforts to increase academic standards. Substantive changes have become possible in large part because of an increase in the institutional capacity of states to intervene in local affairs. Thus, most state legislatures have increased staff substantially and added research capacity. They also now meet annually and / or for more extended sessions than in the 1970s.[78] The academic reform that began in 1983 galvanized a significant increase in state testing and curricular experts, and state staff increased in the mid-1980s to implement new teacher policies, including increased entry requirements.

Another factor increasing state influence is increased conflict among traditional supporters of local control. Local control advocates—such as teachers' unions, school boards, and school administrators' associations—

frequently feud among themselves and provide a vacuum that state control activists can exploit. These education groups cannot agree on common policies with their old allies such as the PTA. The loss of public confidence in professional educators and the decline of achievement scores also cause many state legislators to feel that local school employees should no longer be given so much discretion.[79]

As a means to implement state influences, key structural changes leading to the growth and diversification of state tax sources have developed.[80] From 1960 to 1979, eleven states adopted a personal income tax, nine a corporate tax, and ten a general sales tax. Thirty-seven states used all three of these revenue sources in 1979, compared with just nineteen states in 1960. State income taxes provided 35 percent of all tax revenue in 1978, compared with 19 percent in 1969. This diversification of revenue systems provided the states with a capacity to increase services that was further enhanced by numerous tax increases to fund reforms after 1983. The favorite tax to increase was the sales tax, either through rate increases or extension of the sales tax base to services. Even states with slow economic growth raised the sales tax from 1983 to 1986, including Arkansas, South Carolina, and New Mexico.

STATE REFORMS IN AN ERA OF ACADEMIC EXCELLENCE

The extent of state education reform after 1983 is startling even when one acknowledges that states have been on the move since 1965. By July 1984 the Education Commission of the States reported that 250 state task forces had sprung up to study every aspect of local education and to recommend changes in local control. The state legislative output by 1985 was prodigious and can be categorized as follows:

— teachers: career ladders, incentive pay systems, and training / certification measures
— the academic experience: curriculum / graduation requirements, testing, enrichment programs, academic recognition, and minority programs
— financing: state support, tax increases, changes in funding formulas, and improvements in quality
— organization and structure: academic calendar, articulation, corporate-school partnerships, and academic bankruptcy

These categories do not, of course, include all changes states have enacted, but they do cover the most popular types of reform.[81]

Change in general government's view of an appropriate SEA role can be traced to legislative concern that dollar equalization did not always lead to equal education services because of fundamental differences in local capacity, to gubernatorial assertion that state economic interests were allied with state reputations for educational quality, and to legislative response to citizen complaints that local officials were not meeting their responsibilities and that state standards or assistance was required. Conversely, where general government actors have not modified their view of an appropriate state education role, state-level decision makers believe, as a Nebraska legislator put it, that "the local schools are doing a pretty good job" or that the state's entrenched local control mores (e.g., in Maine and Oregon) make substantive state involvement politically infeasible.[82]

What is striking about the 1983–87 state reform era are (1) the rapidity of the spread of similar policies among the states and (2) the tendency for the reforms to affect similar states with highly dissimilar political cultures. Traditional bastions of local control like Maine and Arizona were extremely active in this round of reform along with more centralized states like Florida and California. The rapidly spreading reforms also penetrated the technical core of local instruction—curriculum, testing, and teacher performance—in a way that expanded dramatically on state school improvement programs before 1983.

STATE TECHNIQUES FOR CURRICULUM CONTROL

What did these general considerations mean when states turned to implementing curricular reforms? Margaret Goertz prepared a matrix of instruments that states use to influence local academic standards and overcome local resistance to state-imposed curriculums. She distinguished among state (1) *performance standards* that measure an individual's performance through tested achievement and observations; (2) *program standards* that include curricular requirements, program specifications, and other state requirements affecting time in school, class size, and staffing; and (3) *behavior standards* that include attendance requirements, disciplinary codes, homework, and so forth.

Her fifty-state survey demonstrated dramatic increases from 1983 to 1986 in state specification and influence in all of these types of standards. A closer analysis, though, reveals that these reforms only accelerated a state policy trend that began over fifteen years ago in such areas as compensatory and special education. But the 1983–86 state initiatives were focused on the core academic subjects rather than on special services for target groups.[83]

Although the scope of state activity is very wide, the effectiveness of state influence on local practice has been questioned. Arthur Wise thinks it is quite potent, whereas John Meyer sees the reverse through "loose coupling" between state and local organizations.[84] Curriculum alignment is one concept states are using to control local curriculum more tightly and overcome the local capacity to thwart implementation. The key is to have the same curricular content emphasized and covered across the state: curricular frameworks, tests, textbook adoption criteria, accreditation standards, university entrance content expectancies, and criteria for teacher evaluation. Identical content coverage must be a single strong thread woven through all of these state policy instruments, binding all to certain standards. Advocates for local control will be appropriately concerned about such a strategy, but local authorities usually have some latitude to choose what they will emphasize.

THE EVOLUTION OF THE FEDERAL ROLE

In 1950, when the U.S. Office of Education was transferred to the Federal Security Agency—forerunner to the Department of Health, Education, and Welfare (HEW)—it had a staff of three hundred to spend $40 million. Growth was slow and largely unrecognized. By 1963 forty-two departments, agencies, and bureaus of the government were involved in education to some degree. The Department of Defense and the Veterans Administration spend more on educational programs than do the USOE and the National Science Foundation combined. The Office of Education appointed personnel who were specialists and consultants in such areas as mathematics, libraries, and school transport; these specialists identified primarily with the National Education Association. Grant programs operated through deference to state priorities and judgments. State administrators were regarded by the USOE as colleagues who should have the maximum decision-making discretion permitted by categorical laws.

The era 1963–72 brought dramatic increases in federal activity, but the USOE's essential mode of delivering services remained the same. The differential funding route was the key mode, seeking bigger and bolder categorical programs and demonstration programs. The delivery system for these categories continued to stress the superior ability of state departments of education to review local projects. Indeed, the current collection of overlapping and complex categorical aids evolved as a mode of federal action that a number of otherwise dissenting educational interests could agree on.[85] It was not the result of any rational plan for federal intervention but rather an outcome of political bargaining and coalition formation. Former USOE head Harold Howe expressed its essence:

> Whatever its limitations, the categorical aid approach gives the states and local communities a great deal of leeway in designing educational programs to meet various needs. In essence, the Federal government says to the states (and cities) "Here is some money to solve this particular program; you figure out how to do it . . ." But whatever the criticisms which can in justice be leveled against categorical aid to education, I believe that we must stick with it, rather than electing general aid as an alternative. The post-

war period has radically altered the demands we place on our schools; a purely local and state viewpoint of education cannot produce an educational system that will serve national interest in addition to more localized concerns.[86]

An incremental shift in the style of USOE administration also came with expanded categories. The traditional provision of specialized consultants and the employment of subject matter specialists were ended in favor of managers and generalists who had backgrounds in public administration rather than professional education. These newer federal administrators were more aggressive, creating a political backlash against federal regulation that Ronald Reagan was able to highlight in his 1980 campaign.

MODES OF FEDERAL INFLUENCE

Since the 1950s there have been basically six alternative modes of federal influence upon state and local education organizations:

1. General aid: Provide no-strings aid to state and local education agencies or such minimal earmarks as teacher salaries. A modified form of general aid was proposed by President Reagan in 1981. He consolidated numerous categories into a single block grant for local education purposes. No general-aid bill has ever been approved by the Congress, and this issue died in 1964 with the defeat of President Kennedy's proposals.

2. Stimulate through differential funding: Earmark categories of aid, provide financial incentives through matching grants, fund demonstration projects, and purchase specific services. This is the approach of the Elementary and Secondary Education Act and the dominant mode.

3. Regulate: Legally specify behaviors, impose standards, certify and license, and enforce accountability procedures. The bilingual regulations proposed by the Carter administration (and rescinded by President Reagan) are a good example.

4. Discover knowledge and make it available: Commission research studies, and gather and make other statistical data available. The National Science Foundation and OERI perform the first function, and the National Center for Education Statistics the second.

5. Provide services: Furnish technical assistance and consultants in specialized areas or subjects. For example, the Office of Civil Rights will advise school districts that are designing voluntary desegregation plans.

6. Exert moral suasion: Develop vision and question assumptions through publications and speeches by top officials. Thus, President Reagan's Secretary of Education William Bennett advocated three C's—content, character, and choice—in numerous speeches and articles in the popular media. This mode of federal influence is termed the *bully pulpit* by the press.

THE REAGAN AND BUSH ADMINISTRATIONS

The Reagan administration endorsed a tuition tax credit to reimburse parents who send their children to private schools. Although various members of Congress have pushed this idea for decades, this was the first time a president had endorsed it. Reagan's plan was defeated, but federal aid to private schools will continue to be a major issue during the 1990s, although vociferously and unanimously opposed by public education interest groups.

Overall, the Reagan administration promoted five other basic changes in federal educational policy in addition to assisting private schools, moving

1. from a prime concern with equity to more concern with quality, efficiency, and state and local freedom to choose;
2. from a larger and more influential federal role to a mitigated federal role;
3. from mistrust of the motives and capacity of state and local educators to a renewed faith in governing units outside of Washington;
4. from categorical grants to more unrestricted types of financial aid; and
5. from detailed and prescriptive regulations to deregulation.

The Bush administration increased federal categorical aid more than Reagan did but was unable to enact any bold new proposals. The federal role is larger than its 6 percent of finance share (state 50%, local 44%). Before 1990, federal influence relied on categorical grants, research and development (R&D), and the bully pulpit. The regulations around categorical grants provide some leverage over state and local funds. After 1990, however, federal policy shifted to accomplishing national goals and helping to create national curriculum content standards and exams. These nationalizing influences on curriculum could presage a major shift in U.S. education governance with effects similar to those of the Scholastic Aptitude Test (SAT) and the American College Testing (ACT) program, but with higher standards. National exams and standards are *not* part of the federal government, but rather are promoted by voluntary organizations like the National Education Goals Panel and the National Board of Professional Teaching Standards. This quasi-governmental style has a long tradition in the United States.

AN OVERVIEW OF THE HISTORY OF EDUCATIONAL GOVERNANCE

This historical overview has traced the changes in educational governance since the turn of the century. There have been profound changes since 1900, when one-room rural schools predominated, with governance dominated by superintendents and boards. The superintendent and school board have become more of a reactive force, trying to juggle diverse and changing coalitions across different issues. Many school reforms (such as new math) have disappeared, but some left structural changes that could be easily monitored and that created a constituency. Consequently, a partial legacy from the 1960–80 era was tremendous growth in the specialized functions of the school, including administrative specialists in career education, bilingual education, nutrition, health, remedial reading, and so on. Many of these new structural layers diluted the superintendent's influence because the specialists were paid separately by federal or state categorical programs. They were insulated from the superintendent's influence by separate financing and the requirements of higher levels of government.

THE SQUEEZE FROM THE TOP

One element that today is very different for local authorities is the intensity and scope of recent state policy actions. The most striking feature of state-local relations during the last twenty years has been this growth in state control over education. Today organizations of professional educators and local school boards are making suggestions for only marginal changes in proposed new state policies. And under the Reagan administration, new federal initiatives were restricted to rhetoric, data collection, and the sponsorship of small pilot programs.

These trends cede considerably more control of education to the states. However, there will be enormous variation in how states take control—from the highly aggressive states, such as California and Texas, to the more passive, such as New Hampshire and Colorado. Dangers attend aggressive, broad-based state education policy. States change policy through statutes and regulations, which have a standardizing effect. Also, the focus of state policy making is no longer on categorical groups, such as handicapped or minority students. Instead, it is aimed at the central core of instructional policy, including what should be taught, how it should be taught, and who should teach it. State-level political actors leading the current wave of reform are legislators, governors, and business interests. The traditional education interest groups—teachers, administrators, and school boards—have been used primarily in pro forma consultative roles.

Increasing state control has not been limited to such traditionally high-control states as California and Florida. The high tide of state intervention in local instructional policy is washing over Virginia and Connecticut—longtime bastions of local control. National movements and widespread media coverage have played a crucial role in the current reform wave, just as they did with the 1970s issues of school finance reform and minimum competency testing. Some state initiatives, such as high school graduation standards, moved through the states without any federal mandate or organized interest-group lobbying.

THE SQUEEZE FROM THE BOTTOM

As a result of these changing internal and external forces, the discretionary zone of local superintendents and boards has been progressively squeezed into a smaller and smaller area. The superintendent's discretion is squeezed from the top by increasing regulations from the legislative, administrative, and judicial arms of the federal and state governments. In addition, there has been the expanding influence of private interest groups and professional reformers, such as the Ford Foundation and the Council for Basic Education. Moreover, interstate groups, such as the Education Commission of the States, increased their influence, as did nationally oriented organizations, such as the Council for Exceptional Children. All over the nation, networks of individuals and groups sprang up to spread school finance reform, competency testing, increased academic standards, and other programs.

Superintendents and local boards also found their decision-making powers squeezed from the bottom by the growth of local collective bargaining contracts reinforced by national teacher organizations. A national study documented the incursion of these organizations into educational policy.[87] And, as noted, the last three decades have seen the growth of local interest groups, often resulting from national social movements.

A yet-unstudied question is whether these constraints and forces external to local settings have been more influential and effective than those of the 1920–50 era, for example, the Progressives and professional societies.

CONCLUSION

Current social movements differ from those of the nineteenth century, exemplified by Horace Mann, which were interested in building institutions like the schools. Today social movements challenge public institutions and try to make them more responsive to forces outside the local administrative structure. Some would even assert that these movements help fragment school decision making so that schools cannot function effectively. The litany of the media portrays violence, vandalism, and declining test scores as the predominant condition of public education.

In California, for example, this situation has become so serious that the schools increasingly suffer from shock and overload characterized by loss of morale and too few resources to operate all of the programs that society expects schools to offer. The issue then becomes how much change and agitation a public institution can take and still continue to function effectively. Californians are confronted with numerous successive initiatives such as proposition 13, vouchers, spending limits, and an extreme version of all the other forces sketched above. Citizens there and elsewhere go to their local school board and superintendent expecting redress of their problems only to find that the decision-making power is at the state or some other nonlocal level. The impression grows that no one is "in charge of" public education.

All of this does not mean that local school authorities are helpless. Rather, it means that they cannot control their agenda or shape decision outcomes as they could in the past. The superintendent must deal with shifting and ephemeral coalitions that might yield to the superintendent some temporary marginal advantages. But many of the policy items on the local agenda arise from external forces, such as state and federal governments, or from the pressures of established local interest groups, including teachers.

The earlier 1920–60 era of the "administrative chief" has passed with profound consequences; the new school politics are much more complex and less malleable.

Despite these cumulative institutional choices to move away from local control, there are indications that U.S. citizens are unhappy with the changes. Coombs gave a vigorous case for more local control:

1. Public opinion still supports more local influence and less influence for higher governments.
2. Local school politics tend to be more democratic in several important ways than are decisions made at higher levels.
3. While there will be tension between state and local policy makers, the result is policy that is better adapted to diverse local contexts.
4. Further erosion of the local role risks diminishing public support for the public schools.[88]

In support of the first point, Coombs cited relevant 1986 Gallup poll data in table 2.2. The biggest loser in this public referendum is the federal

TABLE 2.2 Public Views about Who Should Control Schools

Should have:	Federal Government	State Government	Local School Board
More influence	26	45	57
Less influence	53	32	17
Same as now	12	16	17
Don't know	9	7	9

Source: Gallup Poll, 1986.

government, but local school board influence is preferred much more often than is state government.

Despite these public preferences, the 1992 national policy debate focused on national standards and national exams. This would shift governance even more away from the local context. A counter move would be to strengthen the local school board. Several reports recommend that states recharter school boards as educational policy boards that surrender board operational oversight and expenditure control and prohibit board hiring below the level of the superintendent.[89] School boards would focus on strategic planning and curriculum standards rather than operational details. Without such a change in the local boards to restore confidence in local governance, the probable outcome is a continued flow of influence to nonlocal levels. Americans have made an institutional choice over many years to alter drastically the once preeminent value of local control by a school board and professional administrative staff.

ADDITIONAL READING

Margaret Goertz, *State Educational Standards* (Princeton, N.J.: Educational Testing Service, 1986).

Lorraine McDonnell and Anthony Pascal, "National Trends in Teacher Collective Bargaining," in *Education and Urban Society* (1979): 129–51.

National Education Association, *A Pocketful of Ideas* (Washington, D.C.: National Education Association, 1965).

Policy Analysis for California Education, *Conditions of Education in California* (Berkeley, Calif.: Policy Analysis for California Education, 1989).

Frederick Wirt and Michael Kirst, *Schools in Conflict*, 1st, 2d, and 3d eds. (Berkeley, Calif.: McCutchan, 1982, 1989).

NOTES

1. William Clune, *Institutional Choice as a Theoretical Framework* (New Brunswick, N.J.: Center for Policy Research in Education, 1987).

2. Ibid., 4–5.

3. David Tyack, *One Best System* (Cambridge: Harvard University Press, 1974).

4. U.S. Department of Education, *A Nation at Risk* (Washington, D.C.: Government Printing Office, 1983).

5. Frederick Wirt and Michael Kirst, *Schools in Conflict* (Berkeley, Calif.: McCutchan, 1992).

6. John Chubb and Terry Moe, *Politics, Markets and America's Schools* (Washington, D.C.: Brookings Institution, 1990).

7. Ellen Lageman, *The Politics of Knowledge* (Chicago: University of Chicago Press, 1989).

8. Lawrence Iannaccone and Peter Cistone, *The Politics of Education* (Eugene: University of Oregon, 1974), 41–49.

9. Michael Kirst, "School Board: Evolution of an American Institution," *American School Board Journal*, Special Issue (November 1991): 11–13.

10. Tyack, *One Best System*, 66.

11. Robert Hess and Michael Kirst, "Political Orientations and Behavior Patterns," *Education and Urban Society* 3, no. 4 (February 1971): 453–77.

12. Lawrence Iannaccone, *Politics in Education* (New York: Center for Applied Education, 1967), 19–29.

13. Hess and Kirst, "Political Orientations."

14. L. Harmon Ziegler and M. Kent Jennings, *Governing American Schools* (North Scituate, Mass.: Duxbury Press, 1974).

15. David Tyack, "Needed: The Reform of a Reform" in *New Dimensions of School Board Leadership* (Evanston: National School Boards Association, 1964): 29–51.

16. Tyack, *One Best System*, 88–97, 155–70.

17. Samuel Hays, "The Politics of Reform in Municipal Government in the Progressive Era," *Pacific Northwest Quarterly* 55, no. 163 (1963).

18. George Counts, *The Social Composition of Boards of Education* (Chicago: University of Chicago Press, 1927).

19. Tyack, *One Best System*, 35.

20. Tyack, *One Best System*.

21. Robert Salisbury, "Schools and Politics in the Big City," *Harvard Education Review* 37 (Summer 1967): 408–24.

22. Tyack, *One Best System*, 129–67.

23. Ibid.

24. Ibid.

25. Counts, *Social Composition of Boards*.

26. Lee Browder, "A Suburban School Superintendent Plays Politics" in *The Politics of Education at the Local, State, and Federal Levels*, ed. Michael Kirst (Berkeley, Calif: McCutchan, 1970), 191–94.

27. Raymond Callahan, *Education and the Cult of Efficiency* (Chicago: University of Chicago Press, 1962).

28. Iannaccone, *Politics in Education*, 82–98.

29. Harmon Ziegler, *The Political World of the High School Teacher* (Eugene: University of Oregon, 1966), 57–58.

30. National Education Association, *Practice and Opinion of Teachers on Civic-Political Activities* (Washington, D.C.: National Education Association, 1957).

31. Salisbury, "Schools and Politics."

32. Roscoe Martin, *Government and the Suburban School* (Syracuse: Syracuse University Press, 1962), 89.

33. Kirst, "School Board."

34. William Boyd, "The Public, the Professionals, and Education Policy: Who Governs?" *Teachers College Record* 77 (1976): 556–58.

35. Ibid.

36. Ibid.

37. Wirt and Kirst, *Schools in Conflict*.

38. Ziegler and Jennings, *Governing American Schools*, 33.

39. Emily Feistritzer, *Survey of School Boards* (Washington, D.C.: National Center for Education Information, 1989).

40. Wirt and Kirst, *Schools in Conflict*.

41. Feistritzer, *Survey of School Boards*.

42. Boyd, "Public, Professionals, and Education Policy."

43. Harmon Ziegler and Kent Jennings, "Response Styles and Politics: The Case of School Boards," *Midwest Journal of Political Science* 15 (1971): 290–321.

44. Alan Rosenthal, *Pedagogies and Power* (Syracuse: Syracuse University Press, 1969), 2–4.

45. Ibid., 9–13.

46. Ibid., 9–17.

47. National Education Association, *Survey of Teacher Opinion* (Washington, D.C.: National Education Association, 1965), 1.

48. Ziegler, *Political World of the Teacher*, 50–58.

49. Ibid.

50. National Education Association, *Survey of Teacher Opinion*, 1.

51. James Guthrie and Patricia Craig, *Teachers and Politics* (Bloomington, Ind.: Phi Delta Kappan, 1973).

52. Susan Moore Johnson, *Teachers in Schools* (Philadelphia: Temple University Press, 1984), 162–63.

53. Ibid., 163.

54. Ibid., 164–65.

55. Anthony Cresswell and Michael Murphy, *Teachers Unions and Collective Bargaining* (Berkeley, Calif.: McCutchan, 1980), 201.

56. Herbert Kaufman, *Politics and Policies in State and Local Government* (Englewood Cliffs, N.J.: Prentice-Hall, 1963).

57. Edith Mosher and Jennings Wagoner, *The Changing Politics of Education* (Berkeley, Calif.: McCutchan, 1978).

58. Michael Kirst, *Governance of Elementary and Secondary Education* (Aspen: Aspen Institute, 1976), 25.

59. James Guthrie, "School Based Management," *Phi Delta Kappan* (December 1986): 305–9.

60. Henry M. Levin, ed., *Community Control of Schools* (Washington, D.C.: Brookings Institution, 1970).

61. National School Boards Association, *Urban Dynamics: Lessons in Leadership from Urban School Boards* (Washington, D.C.: National School Boards Association, 1992), 5–6.

62. Jane David, *Restructuring in Progress: Lessons from Pioneering Districts* (Denver: National Governors' Association, 1989).

63. Chubb and Moe, *Politics, Markets and America's Schools*.

64. Ibid., 14.

65. Martin, *Government and the Suburban School*.

66. Ziegler and Jennings, *Governing American Schools*.

67. Ibid., 244–45.

68. Ibid., 246–54.

69. Chubb and Moe, *Politics, Markets and America's Schools*, 2–56.

70. Wirt and Kirst, *Schools in Conflict.*

71. Tyll Van Geel, *Authority to Control the School Program* (Lexington, Mass.: D.C. Heath, 1976).

72. Frederick Wirt, "State Policy Culture and State Decentralization" in *Politics of Education,* ed. Jay Scribner (Chicago: University of Chicago Press, 1977).

73. Walter Garms, James Guthrie, and Larry Pierce, *School Finance* (New York: Prentice-Hall, 1988).

74. Wirt, "State Policy Culture."

75. Ibid., 177–87.

76. Frederick Wirt and Michael Kirst, *Political and Social Foundations of Education* (Berkeley, Calif.: McCutchan, 1975), 161.

77. Patricia Anthony and Stephen L. Jacobson, *Helping At-Risk Students* (Newbury Park, Calif.: Sage, 1992).

78. Alan Rosenthal and Susan Fuhrman, *Legislative Education Leadership* (Washington, D.C.: Institute for Education Leadership, 1981).

79. Joseph Murphy, *The Education Reform Movement of the 1980s* (Berkeley, Calif.: Policy Analysis for California Education, 1991).

80. Wirt and Kirst, *Schools in Conflict.*

81. Dennis Doyle and Bruce Cooper, *Taking Charge: State Action in School Reform in the 1980s* (Indianapolis: Hudson Institute, 1991).

82. Milbrey McLaughlin, "State Involvement in Local Educational Quality" in *School Finance and School Improvement,* ed. Allan Odden (Cambridge, Mass.: Ballinger, 1985), 65.

83. Margaret Goertz, *State Educational Standards* (Princeton: Educational Testing Service, 1986).

84. Arthur Wise, *Legislated Learning* (Berkeley and Los Angeles: University of California Press, 1979); John Meyer, "Organizational Factors Affecting Legalization in Education" in *School Days, Rule Days,* eds. David Kirp and Don Jensen (Philadelphia: Falmer Publishing, 1986), 256–75.

85. James Sundquist, *Politics and Policy* (Washington, D.C.: Brookings Institution, 1968).

86. Harold Howe, *National Policy for American Education* (Washington, D.C.: U.S. Office of Education, 1967), 3.

87. Cresswell and Murphy, *Teachers Unions.*

88. Fred Coombs, "The Effects of Increased State Control in Local District Governance" (Paper presented at the annual meeting of the American Education Research Association, Washington, D.C., April 1987), 8.

89. Jacqueline Danzberger, Michael Kirst, and Michael Usdan, *Governing Schools: New Times, New Requirements* (Washington, D.C.: Institute for Education Leadership, 1992).

3 ATTITUDES, CHOICES, AND BEHAVIOR: SCHOOL DELIVERY OF HEALTH AND SOCIAL SERVICES

MICHAEL W. SEDLAK

Pressure has mounted since the mid-1980s to revitalize and deepen the provision of health and social services through the schools.[1] This pressure has been building in response to two primary developments. First and most generally, there has emerged the conviction that children in this country have had to bear the costs of unprecedented levels of adult self-indulgence, thoughtlessness, incompetence, and, perhaps most importantly, misfortune. A vast array of physical, emotional, and social problems that are battering the lives of schoolchildren seem to be caused by the inability of adults to live productive, healthy lives, to build and maintain families able to comfort and nurture children, or to organize communities that protect the young from emotional stress and physical harm. There has emerged a sense that today children really do face harder, more dangerous lives than in the past. And, this argument concludes, since children are ordinarily incapable of responding to serious problems in healthy ways that ensure even their survival—let alone their ability to flourish—the schools should provide health and social services to help students because no one else is willing or able to rescue them.

Second and more specific to the educational enterprise, one of the criticisms of the school reforms that followed the release of the U.S. Department of Education's *A Nation at Risk* in 1983 was that the first wave of initiatives concentrated exclusively on tightening the screws on students to get them to improve their academic performance. The reforms, this argument runs, have consisted largely of state-level efforts to tighten grad uation requirements and institute competency tests for students and many new teachers. The reforms' thrust is thought to narrow the definition of the function of schools and to focus resources on improving traditional measures of academic achievement. Narrowing the function of schooling seems to neglect many of the broader social purposes of education that had captured the imaginations of activists for a generation or more. An excessively narrow aspiration of attempting to achieve academic excellence, this argument concludes, could lead to the delegitimation—and ultimately to the divestment—of many of the social services (and related social service curriculums) that many came to see, by 1980, as essential to developing the whole child.

Over the past seven years, these two trends have converged to inspire a new generation of enthusiasm for delivering health and social services through the schools (i.e., maintaining comprehensive health clinics, providing dental services, offering counseling and social work services to suicidal adolescents or prepubescent anorexics) and for expanding the associated social service curricular areas (i.e., health education, drug abuse education, parenting classes for pregnant adolescents).

Many of these calls to action are made by people who seem unaware that American schools have provided social services for a century. There is much to be learned from reconstructing this involvement, about the sources and pattern of initiation, about the reception from families, about the influence of occupations undergoing professionalization, about the control of financial sponsors, and about the effects on students. In this interpretive overview I attempt to periodize the history of social services in schools, to examine the ebb and flow of their fortunes, and to probe their meaning for the educational enterprise.

THE FORMATIVE PERIOD, 1880–1917: THE ROLE OF PRIVATE INITIATIVE

The early history of social services in the schools was closely related to the changing role of formal education in America, particularly, but not exclusively, at the secondary level. Once primarily dedicated to serving the elite, the high school became an increasingly mass institution after the 1880s. The establishment of social services played an important part in this transformation; not only did more students attend high school, but also those who enrolled came increasingly from diverse origins: from the middle and working classes and from ethnic and racial minority groups. The attendance of these children could be assured only through sustained attention to making the schools more attractive and considerate of their aspirations and personal social circumstances. Traditional, academic programs characteristic of the earlier classical schools would neither appeal intellectually to the new constituencies nor provide the care necessary to retain those children who were willing to attend once they had actually enrolled in school. The transformed mission of secondary schooling during the late nineteenth and early twentieth centuries—to prepare the vast majority of children for life by enhancing their vocational skills, improving the efficiency of their occupational choices, preventing social maladjustment, and ensuring adequate levels of personal hygiene and public health—obligated schools to offer more than traditional classes in history, science, mathematics, and languages.

The transformation of schooling that led to the introduction of social services was rooted in several related intellectual shifts during the late nineteenth century. The first shift accepted the active intentional intervention of public institutions into traditionally private relationships and affairs. Confidence about turning to public policy and institutions replaced the ambivalence about interventionary practices that had dominated the early nineteenth century. Public policy became more aggressive and increasingly committed to ameliorating social problems by controlling the development or behavior of individuals and their institutions. Private interests sought alliances with public authorities at all governmental levels. Together they became excited about the role that educative agencies could play in improving the lives of individuals and communities. As one expression of this movement to expand the domain of legitimate public action, consequently, schools came to perform functions previously considered outside their purview, such as explicit vocational training, family rehabilitation, occupational selection and guidance, and immunization against disease.

A second shift involved the redefinition of *democracy* and *equality of opportunity* as they were applied to the role of schools in shaping both access to social and economic rewards and the ambitions of children. During the earlier era of the common schools, children from all social classes and backgrounds were theoretically and ideally to have been educated in the same classrooms and in the same curriculums, so that they might develop common values and similar aspirations and be prepared to face their lives on a fairly equal footing, with the children of privilege and of the poor able to achieve whatever they were entitled to on the basis of merit and application. This ideal vision of the common school was rather quickly undermined, however, as both affluent and ambitious middle-class parents found ways of ensuring that poorer children would attend separate schools or would abandon irrelevant classical programs to enter the work force at age twelve or so. By the end of the century, reformers were calling attention to the fact that the largely college-preparatory, classical studies offered in most schools appealed to relatively few working-class children, particularly not to those whose families lacked sufficient discretionary income to support extended education beyond the common elementary schools. It became fashionable and progressive to challenge the "unfairness" of the rigid classical academic curriculums that offered nothing of value to the vast majority of America's youth.[2] In the interests of fairness, of democratic access, and of increasing the appeal of extended schooling, reformers called for changing the education available to adolescents. To make the schools more "democratic," they endorsed a variety of non-academic, social service courses in the practical arts, domestic sciences, and health fields, as well as a limited range of direct services for children who came from less-privileged circumstances.

The final shift underlying the social service movement—a result of the first two—occurred when educators began to redefine the social functions of schooling as more ambitious than simply teaching disciplinary knowledge to privileged students. They voiced a challenge to a variety of social groups to help stir enthusiasm about the mission that the schools might play in shaping modern industrial America. Educational leaders themselves reinvented Horace Mann's brilliant marketing strategy for marshaling support for tax-supported schools by "proving" that public education was "convertible into houses and lands, as well as into power and virtue."[3] The progressives affirmed the indispensable role that schools might play in solving virtually every domestic economic and social problem: urban and labor disorder, the alienation of the lower classes, deteriorating public health and sanitation, immigrant communities in need of Americanization, spreading immorality, physical disability, and severe family disorganization that contributed to juvenile delinquency and ultimately to adult crime. Health services advocates Ernest Hoag and Lewis Terman drew one of the most expansive visions for the social services movement when they claimed that "the public school has not fulfilled its duty when the child alone is educated within its walls. The school must be the educational center, the social center, and the hygiene center of the community in which it is located—a hub from which will radiate influences for social betterment in many lives."[4] Traditional academic machinery and methods would be inadequate to respond to this vastly redefined educational purpose. To be responsible for solving these problems, schools would, the reformers concluded, have to be granted far more authority and discretion over the lives of children and, indirectly, over the lives of their students' parents. And they would require considerably more financial and personnel resources.

Although school administrators and teachers embraced the social services movement, the initial impetus for establishing and maintaining most initiatives came from outside the schools. In particular, local women's groups, philanthropists, settlement house workers, and other private sector groups launched the movement to organize health and social services for schoolchildren. The educational establishment consistently welcomed the private efforts, particularly the considerable financial resources provided by settlements and philanthropies and the volunteer labor offered by women's clubs. Educational leaders graciously cooperated with virtually every private group that was interested in devoting labor and money to establish and maintain school-based social services.[5]

But it proved to be public service–oriented women—through their own clubs, as leaders or workers in the settlements, or as lobbyists with local urban charities and philanthropies—who were instrumental in moving the schools to adopt virtually all of the social services (and many of the other important innovations, such as the kindergarten) during the late nineteenth and early twentieth centuries. In the era before the social service fields were professionalized, volunteers from such organizations donated food to schools for the first subsidized lunch programs and often stood in line to serve the students their meals. They helped to locate and install domestic science equipment and often instructed students in gourmet cooking or fine sewing. They recruited physicians to present lectures on personal and social hygiene. When they could not actually provide the products necessary to sustain the services themselves, they cooperated with other influential civic groups interested in child welfare and juvenile delinquency to lobby for the public provision of services to children. They joined progressive organizations, for example, to press for the extension of compulsory attendance and child labor legislation, the creation of social and recreational centers and public playgrounds, and the financing of special rooms and facilities in schools for handicapped children.

Almost without exception, private and public interests cooperated in organizing health and social services in schools principally to increase the schools' holding power over the new constituencies, many of which were notoriously reluctant to have their children withdraw from the work force or remain in school beyond the age of compulsory attendance. Providing medical inspections and inoculations, eyeglasses, warm coats and hot lunches, and visits to family homes to convince an Italian father to allow his son to graduate from high school were ways of building loyalty to the schools and trust in them as responsive local public institutions. Marketing strategies for the social service fields differed, but during the formative period virtually all of them involved maximizing participation in school on the part of working-class and immigrant children. Some services were introduced to make children healthy enough to attend on a regular basis: nurses, medical inspectors, vaccinators, dentists, and an assortment of health educators and nutrition experts were recruited to improve the physical conditions of students whose lives were spent too often on the debilitating streets; special open-air or anemic classrooms were established to accommodate the needs of children whose respiratory ailments would have kept them isolated in noneducational institutions. Some programs were nurtured to provide more direct relief from poverty and unemployment—food and clothing, possibly assistance for adults in finding a job—so that children would not be too ashamed to attend school; this was often the function of the first visiting teachers (school social workers). Other programs were designed to make school more appealing to children with less academic ambition: the unbookish practical and manual arts, social service curriculums, and other personal development subject matter were offered as a diversion, if not a comprehensive alternative, to core academic experiences.

During the formative period, health and social services were organized in schools almost exclusively in the nation's larger, diverse urban centers. Although educationally progressive suburbs and smaller communities with fewer than twenty thousand inhabitants occasionally experimented with health and physical education programs, national surveys found that only a handful of larger cities exhibited any substantial commitment to maintaining nonacademic social services, except for courses in domestic science and the practical arts, which were introduced in almost every school system by 1910. From studies of the timing of the creation and spread of social services, it seems clear that the existence of a visible and demanding clientele—a critical mass of working-class and immigrant school-age children—was a precondition for the organization of school-based social services.

Such preconditions existed in Chicago, for example, but not in a group of other communities in northern Illinois whose involvement in social services and social service curriculums has been thoroughly examined.[6] The early experiences of these towns reflected the timing and pace of developments in similar communities across the nation. In Chicago, for example, to complement the practical arts and vocational programs established during the 1890s in both elementary and high schools throughout the city, during the early twentieth century the board of education approved the organization of a comprehensive array of health and welfare services, subsidized food programs, special segregated facilities for habitual truants and delinquents, vocational guidance and counseling departments, child study and diagnostic testing bureaus, social centers, playgrounds and physical education activities, continuation schools, instruction in safety and hygiene, and even an abortive series of sex education lectures. Various surveys conducted before 1922 suggest that, of the nation's eighty largest cities, perhaps 75 percent maintained some combination of similar social programs. Although Chicago led the movement to establish many delinquency prevention and remediation programs, by and large it was neither exceptionally progressive nor tardy in organizing school-based social services.

The pattern of introducing social services outside of the largest cities was irregular and haphazard. They were often established on a part-time basis by spreading a single staff member across several fields. If personnel were aggressive in promoting one area over another or if merchandising agents from manual arts or home economics supply companies convinced an administrator of the distinctive value of his or her equipment, work in those areas might be supported briefly. Investments fluctuated with the economic health of the community and the whims of administrators. When commitment existed at all, it was intermittent. And many of the social services were often opposed as inappropriate or illegal activities undeserving of public subsidy. William Reese, in particular, explored the scope and nature of resistance to school-based social services and exposed the particularly virulent political opposition in many medium-sized cities to food and medical programs that were denounced as collectivist.[7]

As one might expect, privileged suburbs devoted virtually no re- sources to providing social services through the schools (or through any other public or private organizations, for that matter). Before World War I, for example, Evanston, Illinois, spent nothing on nonacademic services or coursework, except for a few industrial arts classes after 1901 and one or two lectures on physical culture and domestic science. With one of the wealthiest and most highly regarded academic systems in the state, Evans- ton maintained no guidance or counseling, health, health education, or social welfare programs. In an elite community with a college-bound ado- lescent constituency, there were few dropouts and almost no truancy. Al- though the city was increasingly settled by working-class whites and black service workers, there was little pressure to broaden the system's rigorous but narrowly classical curriculum. Public authorities assumed that parents were fully responsible for their children, and public services beyond the municipality's park system were not necessary to ensure the health and well-being of the city's children.[8]

The pattern was similar in smaller working-class communities, like Blue Island and Waukegan, Illinois. Even though fewer than 15 percent of their high school graduates went on to college and dropouts were becom- ing a visible problem by 1910, resources were concentrated almost exclu- sively on the practical arts curricular fields. Although Waukegan at- tempted to set up a small program in physical education and hygiene and tried to maintain a lunch program at the high school, educational authori- ties in both communities were no more interested in committing local public funds to social services than were their counterparts in Evanston. In the competition for school-based resources, the core academic faculty per- sisted in defending the traditional mission of the schools, that of offering a narrow, classical education to the local academic elite. Nor, by and large, did the embryonic private sector interests have sufficient presence to coun- teract the schools' relatively narrow definition of its mission.

The role of private initiative and the struggle to secure public support for school-based social services can be illustrated by examining the process through which Chicago and Waukegan first became involved with subsi- dized school lunch programs. The movement began in Chicago during the 1890s with increasing criticism of prevailing arrangements for allowing children to secure their midday meals. At Englewood High School, for example, some students brought food from home. Others purchased waffles from a wagon parked near the school. Others patronized a local bakery, where they gorged themselves on pie, dill pickles, and cream puffs. Some repasts consisted simply of soda fountain fare. Other pupils rushed to inconvenient restaurants, where slow service forced them to gobble their lunches before running back to get to their classes on time. One student recalled that this arrangement resulted in a "pain in the stomach, an ache in the head, a zero in the teacher's classbook, and a great daub of blueberry pie on the shirtwaist." Classes during the afternoon were "lifeless." The school building was "foul with the remnants of lunch." The school yard, and most probably the adjacent streets and lawns, were "so bestrewn with paper bags, banana peels, fragments of broken meats, and decadent bones that residents and owners thereof were shaken by a chronic palsy which was due half to wrath and half to malaria."[9]

A decade of criticism led to the establishment of a school lunchroom in 1903. What was noteworthy about the Englewood experiment was the direct and extensive participation of the local women's club. The club members' voluntary contribution of time, effort, and foodstuffs enabled the school to prepare and sell nutritious meals at prices lower than students paid for inferior lunches in the vicinity. A varied menu made it possible to purchase a complete meal for eleven or twelve cents, about the cost of a lunch brought from home. Men accustomed to eating in a Chicago restaurant, one teacher observed, would agree that they would be fortunate to pay only thirteen cents for a "dish of oyster soup, a portion of chicken pie, a hot biscuit and butter, and a doughnut 'like mother used to make,' all in abundant quantity, all appetizing, and all served, not by young men who grow surly unless bribed to do their duty, but by ladies whose presence would adorn any home or grace any social function." Indeed, wholesome, inexpensive food was not the only, nor even the most obvious, benefit. The pupils were able to meet daily with many of "the best women of the community," an opportunity that was in itself "a privilege and an education." The volunteers' presence quickly proved to be a potent, yet inconspicuous, factor in assuring discipline, the school staff agreed, and their unselfish service inspired proper citizenship.[10]

The privately sponsored program was also judged an educational success in more traditional terms. Children missed fewer days of school because they developed fewer colds and less dyspepsia. Epidemics, once rampant in the neighborhood, became uncommon. Scholarship improved with better attendance. Tardiness among the afternoon classes was virtually eliminated.

Although the successes of the lunchrooms were roundly applauded, it is understandable that neighboring tradespeople, whose businesses were devastated by the schools' food programs, would be restrained in their enthusiasm. Competition forced bakers to close; the waffle man suffered; the soda fountain lost considerable revenue. The pain of such economic injury was occasionally expressed in lawsuits challenging the schools' right to construct and operate lunchrooms. Even the board's attorney advised in 1908 that the public schools had no right to spend money on any purpose other than direct education.

Despite the attorney's warning, the board explored its prerogative not only to serve lunches but also to subsidize their preparation with public funds. As evidence of malnutrition mounted during the first decade of the twentieth century, school principals had begun approaching representatives of charity organizations and women's clubs to increase their generosity toward the food programs to enable more poor children to receive the benefits of a healthy meal. The board moved aggressively to channel its own resources into the programs that were supported by the private agencies. As was often the case with special services, heavily subsidized "penny lunches" were first provided at the board's expense to pupils attending one of the system's institutions for crippled children.[11] It was not until late 1910 that the board approved a trial penny lunch program for students in regular schools, whose mental progress was thought to be "retarded by the lack of nourishing food." For schools in neighborhoods serving the city's neediest children, the district initially provided facilities and purchased ovens and other equipment to make it easier and cheaper to offer balanced meals on the school grounds. The women's clubs continued to donate some food and to serve many meals, but as the experiment broadened the volunteers were less able to provide the bulk of the service themselves, and the board assumed considerable responsibility for the lunch program generally and almost exclusive control over the subsidized penny lunch venture. The board agreed with civic leaders in Toledo, who in the same year recognized that "the brain cannot gnaw on problems while the stomach is gnawing on its empty self." Furthermore, educational administrators in Chicago were aware that children from different ethnic neighborhoods preferred different foods, a situation brought into bold relief, perhaps, by the distressing experiences in other cities where riots greeted the efforts of schools to design and enforce a uniform menu. In Chicago, Jewish children attending the Foster school, for example, were served Kosher meals; Italian students at Adams and Jackson were delighted with macaroni, bread, and syrup.[12]

The penny lunches, one of the most visible social service programs established in larger cities during the early twentieth century, were judged a successful investment for Chicago. "Although the work is still in the experimental stage," the superintendent stated just a year after the general introduction of the penny lunches, "the consensus of opinion is overwhelmingly in favor of continuing it and enlarging its scope." Children who received the subsidized meals, it was agreed, "have shown marked improvement, not only in their physical condition, but also in the character of their [school] work." The program's director enthusiastically endorsed the penny lunches in 1912. She and other school leaders were so convinced that the community had so completely recognized the advantages of "Bread as a Means of Education" that school architects would have to reckon with incorporating this progressive feature in their future designs by adding kitchens, storage rooms, and eating facilities.[13]

Although commonplace in cities like Chicago (one survey found that more than one hundred cities were serving penny lunches to needy children before World War I), such enthusiasm and confidence of public support for subsidized school lunches was relatively rare in smaller communities during this period. The abortive attempt to shift support for school-based meals from private to public coffers in Waukegan illustrates another—perhaps more common—tendency in the early twentieth century. As in Chicago, students in Waukegan were dissatisfied with their schools' lack of an organized lunch program. Three-fourths of the high school's 341 students petitioned the board of education in 1910 to establish some sort of formal facility. A local civic association, the Sesame Club, volunteered to provide the program's operating costs if the board made available a room and appropriate equipment. The board accepted the club's invitation. Within a year the lunchroom, which served meals at an average cost of a dime, was virtually self-sustaining. The club asked the board to assume full responsibility for the experimental project. Although the board agreed in principle to sponsor the program, inadequate funds postponed action, and the Sesame Club continued to support the facility. This arrangement continued until after World War I, when another local women's club assumed responsibility for preparing and serving lunches at the school. Within another year, however, club members began to complain that operating the lunchroom placed too great a burden on their organization's coffers and threatened to withdraw completely unless the board helped them financially. Initially, the board agreed to make up any deficit caused by the lunch program, but it seems that the funds were not forthcoming because the women—discouraged by the city's apparent lack of commitment to malnourished students—disassociated themselves from the project at the end of the academic year. Faced with funding the entire program, the board recommended that the district provide no main courses, but instead sell only milk, soup, chocolate, and ice cream, requiring students to bring sandwiches from home. This arrangement prevailed until the federal government made funds available for subsidized food programs after World War II.[14]

Examples of similar efforts in social work, sex education and hygiene, guidance and counseling, medical inspection, dental clinics, open-air classrooms, and other social service ventures could easily be substituted for this brief reconstruction of the subsidized penny lunch initiative. During the formative period before World War I, school-based social services were established and sustained largely through private sector efforts. Throughout most of America's communities, the progressive agenda of instituting social services in the schools died aborning or was only tentatively tolerated along with regular academic courses. The central lesson of the origins of the social services continued to shape their relationship to schools for decades. Although schools were willing to "house" the social service programs, they effectively resisted "adopting" them. As long as external financial support could be found, the schools attempted to make time and space for them. When such assistance evaporated, so did the services; at best, their scope was severely constricted, and their missions were dramatically narrowed.

THE QUEST FOR LEGITIMACY AND PROFESSIONALISM: SOCIAL SERVICES IN PROSPERITY AND DEPRESSION, 1918–1959

Although the fledgling social services continued to struggle, with at best a fragile connection to the public schools, the era following World War I witnessed a strong public drive to ensure that such efforts were accepted as legitimate and merited more than a few square feet of building space in which to serve lunch or more than thirty minutes a year for a lecture on "Kindness to All Living Things." The campaign to embed the social services and associated curriculums more deeply and genuinely in the schools got off to a booming start with the release of the National Education Association's *Cardinal Principles of Secondary Education* in 1918. The *Principles* challenged the academic functions of schooling with a relentless call for attention to using educational institutions to improve health, to make vocational choices and preparation more efficient, and to strengthen a variety of personal social and management skills. The Seven Cardinal Principles provided an influential, systematic, sustained, and coherent justification for the support of social services. The *Principles'* vision of the schools' engagement in a broad range of social functions gave inspiration and ammunition to unimaginative, or less courageous, administrators in districts with resources concentrated on traditional classical academic programs to experiment with or expand their health and social services. Although the *Principles* did not offer a new way of looking at schools, since many of its objectives were already operational in some communities, the report imposed a uniform purposefulness on a set of programs that most educators had thought of as discrete.[15]

The effect of the *Cardinal Principles* was buttressed by other events. World War I itself played a role in expanding social services over the course of the next decade. During the war, many communities increased the amount of time their schools devoted to physical education, military training, domestic science, and hygiene programs. Reserve Officer Training Corps (ROTC) and Red Cross projects were often organized in schools, with the military and volunteer associations providing instruction and most of the supplies, uniforms, and weapons. Communities supported these health programs because of the public's perception of large numbers of unfit youth, a product of reports of high rates of military disability. Most physical education programs, which were usually voluntary and no more organized or demanding than recess games, were obviously inadequate. The health of the nation's children and, implicitly, the ability of the United States to conduct a war depended upon rigorous exercise and nutritious meals, both of which could be delivered almost universally through the schools. Health and physical education programs had requirements imposed and standardized during and immediately after the war. Similarly, domestic science curriculums expanded to include first aid, nursing, and efficient shopping and cooking practices.[16]

Several educational and philanthropic ventures launched in the early 1920s focused the public's attention on the schools as appropriate institutions for the delivery of social services to children and youth. The mental hygiene movement in general, and the visiting teacher and guidance clinic experiments funded by the Commonwealth Fund and the Laura Spelman Rockefeller Memorial Foundation specifically, contributed to the momentum building to use schools to prevent delinquency and shape or control deviant behavior of all kinds through nonacademic programs. Throughout the 1920s and even into the 1930s, these sponsors directed their resources toward the prevention of social and emotional maladjustment by establishing pilot projects and clinics in an array of communities, from small rural districts to diverse urban centers. Although their direct influence was modest at best—because most communities refused to sustain the projects after the external funding was withdrawn—they did leave at least two important legacies. To complement the pilot projects, the philanthropies encouraged the training of social service staff, particularly as visiting teachers, counselors, and parent education specialists, by supporting graduate and professional school centers in several cities. In addition, the widespread publicity surrounding the projects stimulated the professionalization of the core social service fields. For decades school social workers, for example, would look back upon the Commonwealth Fund placements and clinics and the important empirical work conducted by staff members associated with the projects as the pivotal phase in the development of their professional identity, even though some cities had been employing visiting teachers since the turn of the century.[17]

Finally, changes in school enrollment strongly influenced the scope and pattern of social service delivery during the decade following World War I. As the holding power of the schools increased during the 1920s, enrollments mushroomed. If prevailing social service staff/student ratios had just remained constant, the number of providers would have increased steadily. Because many of the students who began or remained in school after the war came from families and neighborhoods strained under the pressures of urban life and poverty, however, many communities recognized that an increase in their social service investment seem justified. Consequently, both the total numbers and the proportion of nonacademic social service personnel rose during the 1920s.

The experience of the four communities in Illinois suggests the striking changes in investment that occurred after World War I. In Evanston, the number of nonacademic personnel grew from five in 1915 to thirty by 1931, and the ratio of social service to total professional staff doubled from 12 to 25 percent. In smaller, working-class Blue Island, the number increased from four to ten during the same period, as the proportion jumped dramatically from one-third to 46 percent (a figure that reflected the expansion of practical and domestic arts teachers). Similarly, in Waukegan, the number of professional staff associated with the social services and service curriculums grew from five to forty-two on the eve of the Depression, which represented a doubling of the proportion of such personnel from 22 to 45 percent. Comparable staff figures are not available for Chicago, but district expenditures reveal a parallel pattern. The practical and domestic arts budget increased tenfold during the 1920s. Costs associated with running the district's "special" schools for maladjusted youth rose quickly from $100,000 in 1915 to nearly $600,000 in 1931. Social center and related recreational services, on which virtually nothing was spent in 1915, consumed about $1 million by the end of the 1920s. The number of social workers, psychologists, child study experts, and health officers grew far faster than the overall professional instructional staff, which tripled over the decade following the war.[18]

Despite the apparent strength of the expansion of the social services movement during the 1920s, the position and security of most programs in the vast majority of districts were so weak that they could not withstand the pressure to curtail nonessential activities that accompanied the Depression of the 1930s. Investment ratios in the social service fields, which had improved steadily over the 1920s, suddenly worsened during the 1930s. Commitment to delivering social services through the schools was apparently more fragile than the staffing and funding figures of the 1920s implied. Reductions during the Depression reflected not simply the elimination of titles or despecialization of services as responsibilities were transferred to other educational personnel. Instead, public school and municipal authorities in most communities attempted to have private and public noneducational agencies perform the social welfare, counseling, recreation, and health services that were being curtailed by their schools.

Most tellingly, in spite of the theoretical benefits of a broad program of social welfare and vocational adjustment services during a period of intense social turmoil, occupational displacement, poverty, delinquency, and alienation, traditional *academic curricular fields* were protected far more successfully than were the auxiliary services. In general, the recently appended ancillary services were sacrificed to protect the interests of the regular classroom teachers. The experiences of Chicago and Blue Island illustrate this response to the financial contraction imposed by the Depression.

On 12 July 1933, the Chicago public school system was "disemboweled," according to one prominent journalist, when the board of education, after two years of gradually reducing the district's social services, voted to restore fiscal order to Chicago by, among other things, eliminating the visiting teacher and special investigator program; abolishing the guidance bureau; closing the Parental School for maladjusted children; eliminating all but one continuation school; trimming the child study staff by 50 percent; dismissing all elementary physical education, manual training, and household arts teachers; and cutting the high school physical education program in half.[19]

Pressure for such a reduction had been building for several years, as a disputed tax assessment in Cook County had impeded the collection of property taxes and a Citizens' Committee on Public Expenditures was demanding a considerable cut in the schools' levy. The problems imposed by the financial cuts were compounded by a sharp increase in the high school population, which more than doubled between 1926 and 1932. Since the district's teaching staff grew half as fast as enrollment, personnel resources were quickly stretched to the limit to cover instruction in the basic academic subjects. The committee spoke constantly of preserving only the "common schools" and obviously intended to "reduce public education in Chicago to the 'three R's.'"[20] The board of education joined the Committee in trying to convince the public that the proposed cuts were the only alternative to closing the public schools entirely. The district had "accumulated many so-called 'fads and frills' or 'extra-curricular' activities and embellishments," the board claimed. Among other extravagances, "social service activities were carried on by visiting teachers, truant officers, et cetera, with overlapping authority and duplication of activities, not only in the schools but also outside of the schools with Social

Service Agencies, maintained by other branches of the Government." Many of the system's special programs and services were too costly and benefited too few individuals to warrant their continued expensive operation. All in all, the board concluded, "there were many activities in the schools which under more prosperous conditions would be useful and desirable, but which because of existing financial conditions required reduction to a minimum or elimination, at least for the present."[21]

Rather than allow the schools to close, force the taxpayers to support a bloated program of services and activities, or cut expenses across the board, selective reductions were thought preferable. "There has been no curtailment of educational activity," argued the board. The "tool" subjects (reading, writing, mathematics) were retained. Instruction in the "cultural subjects" (literature, history, art, music, science, languages) was not reduced. Although reorganized, physical training was continued. The important vocational programs were preserved. Lunchrooms, bathhouses, and playgrounds were to be continued in neighborhoods that needed them. Those special teachers and service providers who could be retrained to conduct regular academic classes would be rehired as quickly as possible, with their tenure rights and pensions unimpaired.[22]

The local and national educational communities were outraged by the curtailment of many ancillary social services. Teachers in Chicago echoed the comments of George Zook, U.S. commissioner of education, who observed that these events constituted "an amazing return to the dark ages," in the "opposite direction" from work being undertaken "by intelligent educators everywhere." Professor Charles Judd of the University of Chicago, author of the chapter on education in President Hoover's massive study, *Recent Social Trends in the United States*, warned an audience of twenty-five thousand teachers and their supporters that, "if the city of Chicago cannot ward off this blow which has been aimed at its future, then the disaster which threatens us will become a menace to the nation." If the spirit of democracy could be so easily destroyed in Chicago, he concluded, every city and town would be forced by "reactionaries to reduce the school program to instruction in rudimentary subjects." Other educators agreed and challenged the citizens to avoid returning to "the bare bones of schooling." John Brewer of Harvard, an early leader of the guidance movement, threatened that, "just as the Chicago gangs have overflowed upon other territory, so many of the pupils now to be denied an education will later flow into other cities and states" to damage their economies and undermine their social stability.[23]

Even though local social service leaders from inside the schools and from the city's many private agencies joined the educators in expressing their deep fears about the consequences of enacting the proposed cuts, their words had no influence on the board. The reductions went into effect in the fall of 1933. Except for a brief infusion of external funds from the federal and state governments (which helped Chicago to establish the nation's first driver education program in 1936), the retrenchment policies enacted by the board continued to limit the effort to deliver social services through the schools.

Despite the teachers' claims of a conspiracy between the board and the business community to restrain public expenditures, it seems as though Chicago's mass of taxpayers supported the curtailment of programs that most agreed served relatively few children. And many of the students who benefited most from the auxiliary services were from among the weakest, most disorganized elements of the city. Tax-paying parents of parochial school students (about one-third of the city's children) consistently pressed for the retrenchment of the public school system, since they hated paying twice for their children's education. The public school services to which students from the Catholic schools were entitled were left relatively intact, such as the attendance department. Although they were able to get 350,000 signatures on a petition challenging the board's decisions, Chicago's teachers were unable to marshal sufficient support among the general public to reverse the thrust of the plan to retrench the social services while expanding core academic instruction.

This interpretation is reinforced and clarified by reconstructing the Depression experience of Blue Island, a community in which there was no suggestion of a business conspiracy such as that which obscured the character of the public's vision of Chicago's schools. The economic collapse that confronted the nation in general and the peculiar financial problems associated with the Cook County tax collection fiasco of the early 1930s severely aggravated conditions in Blue Island, already one of northeastern Illinois' poorest communities. Compounding the fiscal difficulties prevalent in the area were Blue Island's responsibility for educating the children of nearby Robbins, an impoverished black community that included a large percentage of families unable to pay any taxes, and the existence of a large number of cemeteries, which had been withdrawn from the tax rolls. Reflecting the national pattern, high school enrollment doubled between 1928 and 1932 and increased another 50 percent to 1,400 by 1939. The school's faculty did not increase at all until 1936, and then annual additions never kept pace with rising enrollments. This explosive expansion, combined with one of the area's weakest tax bases, caused instructional expenditures to drop sharply from $120 per student on the eve of the Depression to approximately $50 by the mid-1930s. Blue Island's economic and personnel resources were stretched to the limit.[24]

The burden of responding to the deteriorating financial condition was not spread evenly over all programs but was concentrated on the social services and associated curricular fields. The pure services were discontinued, and the social service, physical education, and practical arts curriculums were severely curtailed. The special rooms were converted to regular classroom use. In 1936 the state visitor was concerned about Blue Island's selective response and was particularly disturbed that "much of the non-academic work" had been dropped early in the Depression. The district's superintendent complained that financial pressures were "stupendous," and he could not see a way of restoring the programs when he had to keep the schools open for a year on six months' worth of income. The following year the state investigator's indictment was even more scathing. The students' scholarship, he argued, was far poorer than it should have been, attributable, he maintained, to the "unsuitability of the present rather narrow, traditional curriculum." The course of study offered in this working-class community was "entirely traditional, academic, and college preparatory," even though only one in eight graduates went on to college. He was flabbergasted. "Why should a school teach Latin, German, and French each for three or four years, ancient history, and advanced mathematics, when it is greatly indebted, and at the same time provides no work in shop, household arts, and fine arts, and curtailed courses in commerce, physical education, and remedial reading?" What would happen to the 85 percent who did not go on to college? The very work that Blue Island stopped, he argued, should have been increased during the 1930s, and "many of the college preparatory courses eliminated entirely or shortened." He recommended that Blue Island restore the programs it had curtailed and establish an array of health, counseling, and social services for the children of the town's working-class families.[25]

Although levies continued to fail and the state visitor returned the following year to raise similar objections to the superintendent's policies, it was learned that the district had not only refused to expand the service sector but also actually expanded the academic curriculum by adding several new classes in the foreign languages and mathematics. The annual criticisms began to have a small but evident effect on Blue Island; by the Depression's end, commercial classes were slowly being added, and new facilities were constructed. By 1941 Blue Island high school was offering six credits annually in commercial classes, a half-credit in hygiene, and two credits in home economics. In that same year it also offered twelve credits in foreign languages, six in science, seven in the social sciences, and four in mathematics.[26]

These events illustrate the complexity of interests and aspirations that were shaping public educational investments at the time and particularly the continuing struggle to secure the place of the social services in the schools. Blue Island's case reveals the ability of the entrenched academic faculty to protect their subject matter interests despite the minuscule attention given to the core disciplines in the *Cardinal Principles*. Most employees in the nonacademic and social service programs had joined the system relatively recently, at least in contrast to the basic academic faculty. It was relatively easy to terminate the recently hired, least defensible elements of the staff when the public was not vocally and visibly enthusiastic about the social services.

These events also reveal the residual appeal of the classical model of secondary education in a working-class community. This model that was sustained by an established, predominantly classically trained faculty and administration engaged in fueling the community's aspirations for a college-preparatory curriculum even though fewer than one graduate in eight actually attended college.

The Blue Island and Chicago experiences also illustrate the extent to which the process of professional takeover of the social service movement was irregular, haphazard, and riddled with intragroup competition and conflict. For example, the state visitors, representing the progressive expansion of professional hegemony over the social welfare of the public, used what few resources they possessed to encourage local citizens to rely on their educational institutions for ever more social services. They encountered pockets of resistance from citizens still disturbed by the intervention of schools into concerns and privileges traditionally beyond the prerogative of the schools and from entrenched classical academic teaching staffs committed to preserving their fields from the steady encroachment of social service personnel.

Social services were not reduced or eliminated everywhere. The case of Evanston reveals, first, that access to services depended in part on one's social class and economic status and, second, that social service providers were beginning to redefine *need* to justify and legitimize their efforts in even privileged communities. During the Depression Evanston expanded its social service and practical arts programs despite a financial crisis without precedent in the community's history, even though it was not nearly as severe as the fiscal collapse experienced in Chicago, Blue Island, or most other towns in the United States. With the Cook County tax problems compounded by rising enrollments, per pupil instructional allocations fell from $170 to $110 between 1932 and 1935 before climbing back to $140 by 1939. The superintendent protected instructional and social service programs during the Depression by cutting back capital improvement projects and trimming teachers' salaries by a total of 30 percent over four years.[77]

Superintendent Francis Bacon defended symmetrical reductions in the face of citizens who called for the elimination of targeted programs, such as those in health and physical education, which they believed were expensive to maintain. Bacon claimed that these fields were among the cheapest to staff (costing only $11.56 per pupil per year, compared to the Greek department, which cost $113.33 per student). Even if health and physical education had been more costly, he would have done everything possible to retain them because they were considered "by the best educational authorities" to be "the most important of educational activities." The overall educational program was already too narrow, he argued, especially in the social service curricular areas, which he called "unusually meager." Visitors found that Evanston was "woefully lacking in many of the modern school subjects," which Bacon maintained included the practical arts, health, and safety education. A curriculum designed exclusively for the "professional classes has not satisfied the needs and abilities of all the children of all the people." A "truly democratic school will not exist until there is suitable education for all youth," Bacon stated. At a time when this middle- and professional-class community was witnessing an upsurge in juvenile delinquency, the superintendent was disinclined to selectively cut the vital social service and related nonacademic curriculums in which Evanston had just recently begun to invest.[28]

As a self-consciously "progressive" school district, Evanston possessed an unfaltering commitment to serving the individual interests of all of its children. And as an affluent community, it had the wealth to expand its programs and services to address the needs of an increasingly diverse student body.

The expansion of social services during the 1930s in communities like Evanston also illustrates a considerable change in thinking about the causes of social problems facing children and the role of school-based social services in their prevention or remediation. Beginning in the late 1920s, professional social service providers associated with a variety of public and private agencies, including school-based social and mental health workers, cooperated in popularizing new concepts and definitions of the causes of delinquency and maladjustment. Briefly, they articulated and promoted the notion that such problems of youth were only rarely caused by common forms of environmental deprivation or hereditary deficiencies. They rejected both of these traditional explanations of human misery and substituted the concept that successful personal adjustment was a complex, lifelong process requiring the continual attention and intervention of the helping professions. Fundamental tensions endemic to modern society and family life produced stresses that surfaced in their most acute form during adolescence. Successful adjustment depended upon regular evaluations, counseling, and social work supervision.

Social welfare professionals capitalized on these concepts by moving to expand the market for their services. They took advantage of the unprecedented and massive contributions of state and federal public agencies in providing relief assistance to the poor and unemployed during the Depression to reorient many agencies toward serving *middle-class* families and the attendant long-term, complicated process of individual psychological and emotional adjustment. The mental hygiene movement, a strong influence on the evolution of social work during the 1920s, stressed the opportunity of the helping professions to prevent potential behavior and maladjustment problems by identifying "nervous," "anxious," and "emotionally disturbed" children through scientific testing and treating them individually in therapy-oriented clinics.

Simultaneously, school-based social workers and counselors turned from their initial role as advocates for the improvement of children's environmental conditions to more "professional" preoccupations, such as individual psychological casework and testing. Historically, school social workers had been closely identified with coercive attendance, truancy, and delinquency services; they dealt primarily with the most visible and discouraging behavior problems, most of which were rooted in poverty and violence. During the 1930s, they reoriented their role to serving all children and successfully penetrated markets in affluent and professional communities to disassociate themselves from the stigma of exclusive association with the impoverished, criminal, and otherwise most intractable problem youth.[29]

Progress was steady but slow during the 1930s and 1940s, in large part because many unsuspecting members of the middle class needed to be convinced that they suffered from serious emotional problems of the sort that warranted prolonged professional attention. This task was aided by the appearance of several national policy studies that examined the condition of children and youth and the potential for school-based social services to counteract growth in delinquency, primarily in the larger cities but disturbingly among middle-class adolescents. The reports called for schools to accept responsibility for providing physical and mental health programs and a full complement of guidance, counseling, and occupational adjustment services for all children.[30]

In 1942 the American Council of Education's American Youth Commission issued its report, *Youth and the Future*, another document that strengthened the campaign to expand school-based social services to all children. The commission challenged America's schools to prepare youth to confront and resolve personal problems and vocational maladjustment, as well as to read and develop a civic consciousness. The commission expressed concern over the "tattered remnants" of the classical academic curriculum but concluded that, in practice, these studies tended to serve no greater purpose than "to provide mental furniture for the members of the professional and leisure classes."[31]

Fueled by such rhetoric, school-based counselors and social workers joined their professional counterparts associated with state departments of education after World War II in lobbying legislatures to invest in psychological and counseling services in public schools, particularly in the highly desirable, explosive suburban markets, where the psychological model exposed a vast reservoir of middle-class adolescent problems. With direct financial assistance from the state of Illinois for the identification and treatment of emotionally disturbed children, for example, Evanston increased its staff of social workers from one in 1950 to five in 1960, a pace that dwarfed the expansion in enrollment. As "truancy" became transformed into "school phobia" by the late 1950s, it is clear that the social work community had completed the shift from their earlier advocacy focus on external, environmental conditions in urban communities and the troubled poor to a clinical orientation dedicated to easing the emotional adjustment of introspective, suburban children.[32]

Building on the successful lobbying efforts of the social workers and counselors, the social service movement in general capitalized on a number of circumstances after World War II to revitalize their fields, which had continued to languish during the Depression. Safety programs and courses were brought together and expanded during the 1940s and 1950s because of changes in state school codes that mandated school-based driver education and classes in safety education. Such mandates owed much to the lobbying efforts of the American Association of School Administrators, which devoted its 1940 yearbook to the subject of safety education. The movement spread rapidly. The number of schools offering classroom instruction in driving increased sharply after 1937, when Chicago and Evanston began conducting classes to combat the "sinister threat of the automobile in fatalities and accidents." By 1947 four out of five Wisconsin high schools provided driver education. North Dakota required all high school students to pass an examination in the subject before graduation.[33]

Similarly, health and physical education programs were strengthened by state mandates to raise participation standards. The standard in Illinois, for example, was raised to 200 minutes per week, spread over three or four days. Medical inspections were made mandatory. Credit for much of the legislation was given to state-level physical education associations. In Illinois, the state association helped to prepare a pamphlet for school administrators and board members to explain their responsibilities to support their students' physical health. One result of the activity was a sharp rise in the number and proportion of physical education teachers (student/teacher ratios in this field fell from 400:1 to 250:1) and health personnel in general, as many districts hired nurses and placed physicians and other medical specialists on retainer for the first time.

And, of course, the most visible effort reflecting the expansion of public investment in nonacademic services was the federally funded school lunch program, which survived a grisly legislative controversy to be enacted in 1946. The U.S. government had been donating surplus agricultural produce to schools since the mid-1930s. By 1944 several representatives

pushed an appropriations bill that would have contributed federal revenue directly to schools to augment the surplus food. This initiative sparked
an intense controversy, however, and raised fundamental questions about
the legitimacy of public schools providing social and health services to
their students. Although little opposition to feeding "needy children" was
apparent in the vigorous debate over the proposals, some senators attacked the lunch bill principally on the grounds that it was not a proper
federal function and because the bill's supporters had "drawn a false picture of under nourishment in the schools." If the federal government is to
feed schoolchildren, objected Senator Robert Taft (R-Ohio), "we might as
well give every school child a pair of shoes." Congressman Bushfield (R-
S.D.) reminded his colleagues that the lunches were never intended to
relieve hunger problems but were originally supported to "get rid of surplus farm products and hire W.P.A. labor." With these reservations in
mind, nevertheless, both the Senate and the House were willing to continue the food subsidy program as a "temporary war measure" for two more
years.[34]

In late February 1946, Congressman Flannagan (D-Va.) calmly introduced a measure to appropriate $65 million for subsidized lunches,
launching what was remembered as one of the most "hectic" periods of
debate in congressional history. Flannagan made his intent simple: to
make the federal lunch contribution permanent by providing matching
funds to the states to subsidize nutritional lunches for needy students.[35]

The discussion that followed Flannagan's measure was not at all calm.
Supporters of the bill demanded permanent relief for hunger in America
and applauded the federal lunch program as an appropriate tool with
which to begin to approach this objective. A flood of postcards, purported-
ly written by children, carrying such pleas as "Don't take my lunch away
from me!" began to swamp the legislators. One representative recalled
Commerce Secretary Wallace's comment that "the pigs in Iowa were better
fed than a large proportion of the children in Washington." Debate, originally scheduled to last two hours, consumed three days. The opposition
denounced the bill, claiming that the establishment of a federal lunch
program was the first step in a campaign to make all children "wards of the
state." The most vociferous exchanges accompanied Congressman Adam
Clayton Powell's (D-N.Y.) amendment that forbade discrimination on the
basis of race, color, or creed. Southern Democrats saw "Communist Dynamite" in Powell's brief amendment, noted one influential newspaper, since
Powell was generally assumed to be a "protégé of the New York Daily
Worker," an official communist paper. Enraged by the implications for their
region, the southerners threatened to form a bipartisan coalition with Republicans, critical of the federal effort, to defeat the bill.[36]

They were unsuccessful. On 21 February 1946, the House approved the appropriations bill by a vote of 276 to 101, thereby sending it to the Senate. After some controversy and slight revision, the Senate approved the legislation and sent it on for President Truman's signature. On 4 June 1946 the National School Lunch Act became Public Law 396. Powell's amendment was itself amended to force states to spend their funds equally on children of all races but continued to permit them to spend the funds in racially separate schools.[37]

Although the federal (and state) lunch programs encountered continual criticism throughout the 1940s and 1950s, they expanded rapidly. By 1957, for example, applications for reimbursement for subsidized lunches were submitted by more than twelve hundred separate institutions in Cook County alone, including public and parochial schools, local community child care organizations, and neighborhood councils.[38]

By the end of the 1950s, consequently, social service efforts were thriving. Relative enrollment stability and generally good financial conditions, coupled with increasingly aggressive professional lobbying, stimulated demand in communities that had never felt much need to invest public school resources in providing health and social services to their children.

SOCIAL SERVICES AND THE DISADVANTAGED, 1960–1986: FEDERAL POLICY AND THE PRACTICE OF NEUTRALITY

The momentum behind the expansion of the social service movement so visible during the late 1940s and 1950s continued through the 1960s and early 1970s. Following enrollment trends, staffing in many social service fields began to decline slightly after 1974. Total revenues available to most districts increased in parallel with enrollment growth. Sources of revenue began to change, however, as the share raised through local property taxes declined and the share derived through direct targeted aid from the state and federal governments increased. A portion of the growth of state funding (through income, sales, and vice taxes) was attributable to equalization initiatives that attempted to reduce differences in per pupil expenditures across districts. But much of the state and federal share was dedicated to specific programs, intended for targeted student populations. Many such programs were created to provide compensatory aid for disadvantaged children, often in the form of additional services for needy and exceptional students.

As a result, communities of all kinds created or expanded their social service programs. In Blue Island, for example, the number of counselors tripled from 7 to 23 between the early 1960s and the early 1970s; the number of health professionals increased from 2 to 11. Comparable growth in staff occurred in Evanston and Waukegan as well. In Chicago the professional social work staff, which began to be rebuilt in the 1950s and consisted of only 2 members in 1958, grew gradually to 9 in 1964, after which it exploded to 133 by 1975. The truant officer force expanded from 177 to 250 during the 1960s. Expenditures on all attendance services rose from $750,000 during the late 1950s to $3.3 million by the early 1970s. Total annual costs of recreational and social center programs jumped from $2 million to $7 million between 1960 and 1972. During the late 1960s Chicago began to operate several family living centers for pregnant adolescents, at an annual cost of $1 million. The system's other special schools for delinquent and maladjusted children nearly tripled in cost to $5 million over the decade of the 1960s. Despite such dramatic growth, the proportion of educational expenditures devoted to the social service fields remained relatively stable during the 1960s and 1970s, largely because the entire educational enterprise grew so enormously and because the regular academic fields sustained their efforts to retain their share of the school budget. Indeed, because so much of the expansion in social services was stimulated by "new" external money from the federal and state governments, the core academic fields actually slightly increased their share of the traditionally funded instructional budget.[39]

The social service experience of the decades after 1960 reflect at least one persistent theme and several new ones. In part the compelling issues of this period were rooted in changes in the funding of services and the influence of federal policy. In part they were shaped by important changes in the helping professions.

In contrast with the efforts of the 1950s to "universalize" services by expanding markets to include middle-class and affluent students, many leaders of the initiatives of the 1960s were determined to redirect their focus to disadvantaged populations. Many of the new thrusts, therefore, were cast as mechanisms for removing the barriers to learning that confronted children of the poor or those who suffered racial or economic discrimination. Advocates believed that the problems facing such children were largely material and relatively more easily identifiable than the widespread psychological maladjustment thought to be prevalent during the early 1950s. Their response focused on improving the economic conditions of the poor through employment training, work-study, and counseling programs; nutrition experiments that included provisions for breakfast in addition to free or subsidized lunches; and improved health services.

State funds intended to address problems of maladjustment, combined with revenue from the Elementary and Secondary Education Act of 1965 (ESEA) and contributions from businesses and private agencies, underwrote a vast array of imposing new programs dedicated to reducing truancy, recovering dropouts, and ensuring efficient vocational training and placement for urban minorities and working-class white youth. Investment in these new programs for the disadvantaged was fundamentally fueled and shaped by federal education, job training, social welfare, and health spending, particularly that associated with manpower development (1962) and vocational education (1963) legislation, and by the anti-poverty components of the ESEA. The funds were typically earmarked for specific groups of children, and the lengthy list of projects supported with ESEA or Model Cities revenues undertaken by many school districts after 1965 reflects the social service movement's changed ambitions and concerns.

The schools became preoccupied with using federal funds for attacking problems of truancy and nonattendance in particular. Once schools began to enroll the vast majority of children and youth, it became possible to define those unwilling to attend as "deviant" and targeted for attention. And since it became increasingly common for school revenues to be tied to some sort of measure of average daily attendance, administrators had a strong financial incentive to establish programs to keep adolescents in school.

The fashion in which many social service programs were introduced, particularly those initiated or expanded through state and federal mandate, left a legacy of administrative and financial problems for many districts. Although school systems graciously received programs that were accompanied by state and federal reimbursement funds during the 1960s and 1970s, administrators and school board members found that the levels of external support only rarely kept pace with the costs of delivering the services. They became highly critical of being forced to provide social programs under legislative mandate without the financial assistance to cover all of their direct and administrative expenses.

This led to an unprecedented defection of many educational administrators as a constituency that was historically committed to preserving and expanding nonacademic social services. Once enthusiastic about the opportunities inherent in the expansion of their schools' function to include the delivery of social services, administrators began to cringe under the financial burdens accompanying programs that were constantly attacked as diversionary, wasteful, subversive, ineffectual, or even illegitimate.

Despite the growth of social service investments during the 1960s and 1970s, there seems to have been little intention to integrate most of the programs fully. As long as external funding was available, experimental projects flourished but, to protect themselves wherever possible, boards of education refused to make them permanent. Once external funds diminished or enrollments declined, many services and nonacademic programs were curtailed. Part of the attractiveness of some of the initially well-funded programs was that they could be established without significant capital investment and therefore could be dismantled as funding declined. Such arrangements made it relatively painless to eliminate personnel who existed largely on the periphery of the schools and often averted confrontations with school employee unions.

In addition, financial support for social services during the 1960s and 1970s, particularly federal antipoverty aid, encouraged the development of different forms of professional relationships, including an intriguing inversion of the prevailing historical pattern of professional dominance. Federal policy deepened an antiprofessional ethos that had evolved from cultural observers like Paul Goodman and community organizers like Saul Alinsky, who stressed the value of local self-determination. For a variety of reasons, public policy during the Kennedy and Johnson administrations emphasized the importance of enhancing the authority, responsibility, and role of paraprofessionals, nonprofessionals, and clients, the "maximum feasible participation" of the recipients of social services. The movement was determined to empower service recipients by demystifying expertise and undermining professional hegemony by placing the poor and racial minorities in positions of autonomy and authority in the administration of many federally funded programs.

This movement influenced the delivery of school-based services in several ways. To get funds, boards of education had to demonstrate that parental or "community" interests were represented, an obligation that usually resulted in the formation of community councils that advised school administrators on local and neighborhood matters. More directly, however, new projects often attempted to draw heavily upon noncertified, indigenous personnel, individuals assumed to be in a better position to establish rapport with disaffected students than were tenured, white, middle-class professionals. Such funding arrangements, consequently, were occasionally used to circumvent local professional social service providers.

The results were riddled with tension, jealousies, and suspicion. Scholars have demonstrated that success on the part of indigenous nonprofessionals threatened the legitimacy of existing public institutions. They have provided examples of educational and social welfare professionals and municipal authorities attempting to undermine the efforts of community leaders and noncertified personnel. Occasionally, the conflicting interests were brought into relief by the movement to organize social services through purchase of service contracts or other forms of cooperative agreements with private agencies or individuals. This pattern of cooperation has been common in most urban communities since the late 1890s. As long as regular school resources were not depleted, few administrators resisted, and indeed administrators often welcomed the participation of community groups, especially if they brought outside funding.[40]

Social service professionals assigned either to individual schools or to central pupil service bureaus, however, have been less receptive to this arrangement. Chicago's experience during the late 1960s and 1970s with one private counseling and social work agency in particular, Youth Guidance, illustrates the troubling issues inherent in organizing competing social service programs under the guise of promoting cooperation. Youth Guidance was founded in 1924 as the Church Mission of Help, an evangelical social service agency for unwed mothers and young women in danger of moral corruption. During the 1950s the staff diversified their efforts by introducing counseling programs for young men and women and occasionally operated on the periphery of the schools. In cooperation with the board of education, Youth Guidance in 1969 established Project Step-Up, an effort to prevent delinquency among students by providing intensive social work and counseling services in several schools characterized by disruptive behavioral problems, uncommonly high truancy and dropout rates, a demoralizing number of underachievers, and predominantly minority student bodies.[41]

Youth Guidance moved quickly to recruit African-American and Hispanic counselors so that a comfortable rapport could be established with the alienated students, something which middle-class, white social workers and guidance personnel had presumably found difficult. Within a short time Youth Guidance came to devote virtually all of its efforts to the lucrative public school program. Participating schools made space available to the agency's teams, who worked with students referred by classroom teachers or administrators. Convinced of the program's success with students, various public and private sources, including particularly the United Way of Metropolitan Chicago and the state's Department of Human Services, underwrote the agency's expansion over the next dozen years.

Shortly after Youth Guidance officially entered the schools, however, tensions developed between the certified social workers employed by the Chicago public schools and the agency's young field workers, who the system's professionals occasionally criticized as "street people." The professional staff feared that the Youth Guidance workers would inevitably overidentify with the demanding, disruptive students and subvert whatever respectability and legitimacy had been achieved in the troubled targeted schools. They were genuinely concerned that the young workers would be taken in by the manipulative students. Familiarity with such erosion of control led the certified social workers to emphasize the importance of appropriate professional education and experience.

As resources for such services diminished after 1972, competition between the two groups intensified. Although the district's superintendent made it clear that Youth Guidance could not receive direct financial payments from the board of education—forcing it to develop other sources of income—the system's social service professionals were convinced that the

continued presence of the agency threatened their hard-won but still fragile employment security. As long as the board could rely on Youth Guidance and other agency personnel who were virtually free, the system's staff
worried about the district's commitment to maintaining a large, permanent force of professionals, a sentiment that was aggravated by the dis-
missal or reassignment of several hundred social service personnel after
1972. Although the presence of the Youth Guidance workers in many
respects validated the role of the school social workers, the professional
staff was disturbed by the implications of cost differentials between the
two programs. Youth Guidance served each of its clients for approximately
$200 annually. Special projects initiated by the board with regular staff
similar to those undertaken by Youth Guidance often cost thousands of
dollars per student served. A substantial portion of such program expenses, however, reflected essentially administrative or bureaucratic cost,
a fact that distressed many of the school social workers, who worried that
the public assumed that they could not compete on a cost basis with
private agencies on purchase of service contracts or federal grants.

Exacerbating the tension over competing for scarce resources and job
security, the Youth Guidance experience revealed a conflict over the
changing nature of the "pure" social services delivered through the
schools. Professional social workers and counselors employed by the
school system came to believe that the character of their work had been
redefined and diminished through a radical transformation since the late
1960s. Outside funding was accompanied by stiff bureaucratic requirements that forced the system's professionals to devote their time not to
service delivery but to the flow of paperwork and administrative detail
that consistently threatened to consume them. They began to feel that their
therapeutic expertise was increasingly directed toward diagnostic and re-
ferral tasks. Many became jealous of the hands-on services that the paraprofessionals and Youth Guidance staff were customarily allowed to perform and resented the relative independence afforded to community
workers and project counselors.

Because of such competition and resentment, many of Chicago's professionals resisted the extension of institutionalized, allegedly cooperative,
joint ventures with private agencies. One director of social work for the
schools, for example, used his authority over an internship program to
deny stipends to Youth Guidance staff who were working in the Chicago
system. At one time at least twenty positions were left unfilled when they
could have been made available to students enrolled at local social work
schools who wanted to gain experience with the Youth Guidance program.
Professional school social workers also lobbied at the state level to have
certification requirements tightened to the point of denying Youth Guidance staff who were not trained specifically in "school social work" the

opportunity to work with students in a school setting. They pursued these objectives in an effort to consolidate control over every component of the school's social service delivery system under public authority and to reduce or eliminate the opportunity of the private agencies to develop competing programs.

The transformation of another group of social service programs—those intended for pregnant adolescents—illustrates a final set of issues that continue to affect educational policy and practice. Over the past two decades or so, many helping professionals associated with educational institutions have intentionally adopted an ethos of neutrality and techniques of therapy that have not challenged destructive youthful behavior and have made it difficult for students seeking service to make fully informed decisions about their lives (or the lives of those around them in many cases). Such a transformation can be readily explored by reconstructing the recent history of programs for unwed mothers.

Until the mid-1960s the private sector—through maternity homes, "erring women's refuges," and evangelical Christian organizations—provided virtually all of the services that were typically available to pregnant adolescents. Established as part of the urban charities movement of the late nineteenth century, institutions serving "wayward girls," as they were often called, intentionally used a strategy of enforced motherhood (by forcing pregnant adolescents to retain custody of their out-of-wedlock infants) as a therapeutic strategy of rehabilitation. By 1870 virtually all of the homes and shelters enforced strict rules against permitting young women to place their babies up for adoption. Supervisors were convinced that "nurturing the maternal bond" was one of the most potent methods of guaranteeing that the women would conduct themselves responsibly and avoid relapses once released from the homes. The trustees of Chicago's Erring Women's Refuge, for example, claimed that their antiadoption policies resulted in striking "success" rates in excess of 90 percent (fewer than 10 percent delivered another child out of wedlock). The staff attributed the stability that the women had achieved in their lives to the "sacredness of maternity, the sense of obligation to helpless infancy, the clinging arms around the mother's neck, the lisping of the sweetest name to childhood—mama," which developed the best qualities in each resident's nature. One supervisor distributed a letter she had received from a former resident who claimed that her baby had given her a "purpose in life and keeps me good." During the 1920s, officials of Chicago's Florence Crittenton Anchorage accused local delivery hospitals of conspiring to steal their residents' newborn children and sell them into the sordid black-market baby system.[42]

As the industry professionalized between 1930 and the early 1960s, the institutions' approaches changed dramatically. Leadership of the movement shifted fairly rapidly as the federated charities organizations (predecessors of the United Way) forced local institutions to replace the religious volunteers who had run the homes for the previous half century with professionally trained social workers. The leaders of the federated charities pressed for this change relentlessly, and during the hard times of the Depression of the 1930s the income raised through the Community Chests' consolidated giving campaigns proved to be so irresistible that organization after organization capitulated to the professionals' demands for staffs of psychiatrically trained social workers with experience in the problems of emotionally disturbed adolescents.

The professional caseworkers who assumed control of the institutions by the 1940s confronted the rehabilitation programs common to the evangelistic homes and found them undesirable in virtually every respect. To the outgoing matrons, all of the residents were in the same situation, all had been unable to handle temptation in a Christian fashion, all had been seduced and abandoned by predatory men, and all simply needed to forget their past downfall and face the future with the confidence that both faith and motherhood would bring. In contrast, the professional social workers stressed individual, case-by-case evaluations and psychiatric profiles, intelligence tests, and family studies and offered a unique therapy for each woman. They substituted a medical, psychiatric model for the prevailing moral model. The homes were "not prisons for culprits, but shelters and schools for the crippled," argued one social worker; the young women were not admitted "because of their *sin*, but because of their *need*."[43]

The professionals subsequently launched an onslaught against the home's treatment strategies, particularly against the practice of forcing the residents to retain custody of their children. Enforced motherhood undermined whatever opportunities the women might ever have for further education or economic independence. It was essential for the residents to be unencumbered and able to relocate, impossible feats for adolescents who kept their babies. The changed attitude can be seen by contrasting the opinions of the director of the Crittenton Anchorage. Just before the federated takeover, the outgoing matron insisted that, "if the girls do not stay in the home [often for two to four years] and take responsibility for their babies they would be apt to return 'to their old haunts and habits' and it would be too easy for them to have another baby." The new director offered a fundamental reconceptualization in 1951, when she argued flatly that "the baby must be given in for adoption for [the] protection of himself and [the] mother." Retention records indicate that the Anchorage's policies were not simply rhetorical. Before World War II, more than 80 percent of the young mothers had kept their children. By the early 1950s approximately 80 percent were released for adoption, almost all while the mothers were still in the hospital.[44]

As urban black unwed parenthood became increasingly visible during the late 1950s and early 1960s and as young white women were less in need of residential maternity care because of public toleration of their condition, the private maternity homes began to lose business. As families had grown to see the maternity homes as adoption agencies and as liberal views permitted the retention of children born out of wedlock, young women stopped turning to the residential, custodial, secretive institutions. Black youth rarely sought admission to maternity homes, since few institutions welcomed them, and it was assumed that there existed virtually no African-American adoption market. The softening of the maternity market during the 1960s caused most of the homes to close or to reorient their social work staff to serving adolescents with other emotional and health problems.[45]

In their place, the public schools began to establish programs for pregnant adolescents, a movement that was launched with direct funding from the federal government. Since the residential facilities were reluctant to serve minorities and pregnancy was no longer seen as a problem requiring intensive isolated treatment out of the public's view, activists pressed to have community-based comprehensive care centers organized in public schools. The first, and most famous, was established at the Webster School in Washington, D.C., in 1963 with financial support from the Children's Bureau Welfare Research and Demonstration Grants Program. As obstacles to their expansion declined over the balance of the 1960s, the school-based comprehensive care centers (often called schools for girls with special needs and funded with ESEA money after 1965) became the dominant model for serving pregnant adolescents.[46]

Most concern about the special schools focused on the relatively weak educational programs that they typically offered, imbalanced as they were toward parenting and child care skills and away from regular academic classes in history, mathematics, science, and language arts, courses that would prepare them for higher education. Districts were caught in a variety of tensions. Parents rebelled at the notion of transferring the "mature" unwed mothers into regular classrooms, where they could "contaminate" the development of luckier adolescents. Few young women pressed for full academic integration, although several high-profile court decisions won that right for young women in the early 1970s. And, as in the case of many other categories of special students, the pregnant young women were more financially valuable if they were isolated in their special programs. Ironically, the availability of external financial support made it easier for local school administrators to circumvent the public mandate to integrate the young women.

More recently another concern has emerged about practices that are common to the comprehensive care centers for pregnant adolescents. Even a brief exposure to the operation of the facilities reveals the extent to which they quickly came to be based upon an assumption that the young participants will retain custody of their children. Many of their most prominent features try to minimize the young women's concerns about the burdens of retention or to stimulate and reinforce their fantasies about mothering. Many centers added child care services for students who delivered and tried to return to school or to locate employment. The nurseries have been staffed by pregnant adolescents participating in child care and parenting classes, and some have encouraged them to experience motherhood vicariously. Courses in family life education began to include components on family budgeting and to offer advice on establishing an independent household or acquiring public welfare funds as a single parent.[47]

Beyond attempting the laudable task of trying to improve the parenting of expectant adolescents, some individuals have called attention to the extent to which such admirable efforts may have contributed to the decision of young women to raise their children alone. Sincere and well-intentioned policies to protect innocent adolescents and children from the consequences of unfortunate behavior may have returned to exacerbate the serious problems of unwed motherhood for young women and their infants. Challenges have been brought against policies that might inadvertently increase the retention of children born out of wedlock while attempting to protect infant health.

Everyone agreed that public toleration of adolescent pregnancy and even unwed motherhood for teenagers had the greatest influence on the decisions of young women to retain custody of their babies while refusing to get married. Public policies made it less painful or inversely more attractive, but general social tolerance was more important. But it has also been suggested that public policies and institutional practices have contributed inadvertently to the shift in behavior and therefore merit some examination.

Complementing the coursework that the centers made available, most of them established group counseling sessions as the primary therapeutic strategy for working with the young women. Group counseling reinforces the effect of peer pressure. Indeed, it was introduced to take advantage of the role that the peer norm enforcement process played in shaping decisions and building self-esteem (which the helping professions had come to view as essential to the recovery of pregnant adolescents). By design, group or peer counseling programs for adolescents inevitably enforced conformity to the dominant posture of the group. When a young woman's values conflict with those of a group established to strengthen her self-esteem, two remarkably candid social workers admitted in their defense of the therapy for pregnant adolescents, "she must change her values if she wants to be identified with the group." Only young women with extraordinary ego strength possess the self-confidence to resist the "consolidated opinion of her peers."[48]

Unfortunately, by the late 1960s, adolescent opinion had begun to endorse retention aggressively, even outside the intense, group counseling cauldron. Some leaders in the adoption field recognized this. One commentator recently noted that the young woman "who shares with friends that she is planning adoption may be subjected to unsolicited advice of how she should try to parent the child and suggestions that she is less than caring if she does not."[49]

Adoption and, later, abortion were choices rarely discussed in the counseling sessions. Group sessions encouraged both participants and the counselors and social workers who led them to pursue comforting, supportive sessions that mutually validated one another's experiences and aspirations without facing the tense, divisive, painful confrontations that would have invariably accompanied the discussion of unpopular or repugnant pregnancy resolution options, such as relinquishment. Leaders were too often deluded into believing that they were professionally competent when they were offered the *illusion* of success that was associated with eager participation, enthusiastic consensus, and smooth sessions. Everyone would have been seduced by the immediate counseling process into pursuing attractive, immediate rewards while abandoning the opportunity to ensure that pivotal decisions were able to be based on a thorough understanding and appreciation of all of the potential costs of retention.[50]

If the helping professions had not abandoned their earlier commitment to relinquishment that had infused the homes of the 1940s and 1950s in favor of an ethos of neutrality—a therapeutic strategy of nonintervention —they might have been able to confront the intimidating peer group pressure in favor of retention. But they had adopted an intentionally neutral stance toward all forms of behavior which precluded standing against the thrust of peer pressure. It had become unacceptable to intervene in most client decisions. Issues were cleansed of their moral overtones. Problems, consequently, became technical. The professional community simply tried to make already-formed decisions as painless and inexpensive as possible. Social work leaders began to recognize the potential for great harm that this transformation made possible.[51]

The resulting delivery system retreated from controversy and confrontation in a variety of ways, far beyond the tendency to pursue smooth counseling sessions. Many of the programs were organizationally marginal, a fact of life that led staff members to avoid the sort of attention that challenging student preferences would have created. During the late 1970s and 1980s, when supplementary federal funds were in jeopardy, few center directors were committed enough to exposing all young women to the entire range of pregnancy resolution options to risk becoming embroiled in disputes that might rile an entire community. And as public acceptance of unwed motherhood among adolescents became even more widespread, young women became even less dependent on the care centers. The authority of service providers weakened relative to the power of young pregnant women. As the delivery system came to need the young women more than the pregnant adolescents believed that they needed the services, the providers became even more *passive*, afraid to jeopardize their diminishing market power. Fewer providers were willing to risk alienating prospective clients by imposing or even mentioning distasteful decisions. It is not surprising that changing market conditions helped to fashion a delivery system committed to accommodating and reinforcing adolescents' fantasies of motherhood over the genuine pain of relinquishing one's child for adoption.

These trends converged to leave the school-based centers of the 1980s as closely identified with retention as the maternity homes of the 1950s had been identified with adoption. Of the 879 students served in a sample of model programs in the state of Michigan in 1981, for example, only one elected to relinquish her child for possible adoption. A recent evaluator of an alternative program for pregnant adolescents in Fremont, Michigan, concluded that the services did "little to address the needs" of young women willing to consider placing their children for adoption. It was, to her, "a problem which needs more consideration." Of more than a score of large programs in Michigan, only one—a private agency—offered classes in decision making that addressed the realities of retention and introduced the possibility of relinquishment by bringing in representatives of adoption agencies. Although his interests are clouded, the president of the National Committee for Adoption recently echoed these concerns when he argued that "our concern is that the emphasis on making teens good parents may short-circuit the decision-making process and may inadvertently push teens, who may not be willing or able, into parenting." He cautioned all agencies that served unwed mothers to examine "their policies and the services which are offered to pregnant teens to determine whether they may be subtly encouraging single parenting over adoption."[52]

Have we come full circle in our treatment of unwed motherhood: from the efforts of matrons in private refuges a century ago to force motherhood on young women to more recent school-based programs which, by default, leave adolescents to decide to care for their babies alone? The intentions may have changed as the providers became more professional, but the effect on the young women and their children remains the same. Because the sources of sponsorship have shifted from private to public agencies, coupled with vast increases in the problem's scope, unwed motherhood has come to affect the entire community, not just the adolescents and their children.

The situation illustrates how critical it has become for helping professionals of all sorts—educators, social workers, therapists—to adopt an ethos of professionalism that does not impede their ability to communicate the true costs of bad choices. Our failure to grasp the influences of recent changes in professional ideology and practice in the social service fields has caused our educational enterprise to squander crucial opportunities to shape attitudes, choices, and behavior at a time when the consequences of bad choices are particularly harsh.[53]

NOTES

1. David B. Tyack, "Health and Social Services in Public Schools: Historical Perspectives," *The Future of Children* 2 (1992): 19–31. In addition, my interpretation of the history of school-based social services draws heavily from Michael W. Sedlak and Robert L. Church, *A History of Social Services Delivered to Youth, 1880–1977,* Final Report to the National Institute of Education, contract 400-79-0017, 1982; Michael W. Sedlak and Steven L. Schlossman, "The Public School and Social Services: Reassessing the Progressive Legacy," *Educational Theory* 35 (1985): 371–83; Michael W. Sedlak, "Young Women and the City: Adolescent Deviance and the Transformation of Educational Policy, 1870–1960," *History of Education Quarterly* 23 (1983): 1–28; idem, *Aunt Martha's Decline: The Shift from Private to Public Sector Services for Adolescent Mothers, 1960–1986,* Report to the Program on Non-Profit Organizations, Institution for Social and Policy Studies, Yale University, 1987; Steven L. Schlossman, JoAnne Brown, and Michael W. Sedlak, *The Public School in American Dentistry* (Santa Monica, Calif.: Rand Corp., 1986); David B. Tyack, "The High School as a Social Service Agency: Historical Perspectives on Current Policy Issues," *Educational Evaluation and Policy Analysis* 1 (1979): 45–57; William J. Reese, *Power and the Promise of School Reform: Grass-roots Movements during the Progressive Era* (Boston: Routledge & Kegan Paul, 1986); idem, *Case Studies of Social Services of the Schools of Selected Cities,* Final Report to the National Institute of Education, contract 400-79-0018, 1981; Eleanor Farrar and Robert Hampel, *The Delivery of Social Services in American High Schools,* Report to the Carnegie Corp., 1985; Seymour B. Sarason and John Doris, *Educational Handicap, Public Policy, and Social History* (New York: Basic Books, 1979); and Murray Levine and Adeline Levine, *A Social History of Helping Services: Clinic, Court, School, and Community* (New York: Appleton-Century-Crofts, 1970).

2. David K. Cohen and Barbara Neufeld, "The Failure of High Schools and the Progress of Education," *Daedalus* 110 (1981): 69–89.

3. Horace Mann, *Secretary's Report to the Board of Education of Massachusetts* (Boston, 1842), 82.

4. Ernest Hoag and Lewis Terman, *Health Work in Schools* (Boston: Houghton Mifflin, 1914), 10–11.

5. Reese, *Promise of School Reform*; idem, "Between Home and School: Organized Parents, Clubwomen, and Urban Education in the Progressive Era," *School Review* 87 (1978): 3–28; Sedlak and Church, *Social Services Delivered to Youth,* 20–34.

6. Sedlak and Church, *Social Services Delivered to Youth,* 20–34.

7. William J. Reese, "After Bread, Education: Nutrition and Urban School Children, 1890–1920," *Teachers College Record* 81 (1980): 496–525; idem, *Promise of School Reform.*

8. Sedlak and Church, *Social Services Delivered to Youth,* 28–29.

9. Edwin Miller, "The Lunch-Room and the Englewood High School," *School Review* 13 (1905): 201–12; Office of the Business Manager, Chicago Board of Education, "What and How to Eat: Chicago's Public School Lunch Rooms," 1939, Board of Education Archives.

10. Chicago Board of Education, "What and How to Eat."

11. Chicago, Schools, Minutes, 21 October 1908, 10 February 1909.

12. Idem, Schools, Minutes, 16 November 1910; Chicago, Schools, Annual Report 1911.

13. Idem, Schools, Annual Report 1912, 174–75, 1913, 209; Chicago, Schools, Minutes, 1 November 1911, 28 December 1908, 11 November 1914, 15 September 1915, 31 January 1917.

14. Waukegan, Schools, Minutes, 11 November 1910, 7 November 1911, 6 June 1912, 9 September 1919, 19 January 1920, 3 August 1920, 7 September 1920; Anna Barrons, "The Lunchroom in the High School," *School Review* 13 (1905): 213–15.

15. National Education Association, Commission on the Reorganization of Secondary Education, *Cardinal Principles of Secondary Education,* Bureau of Education bulletin 35 (Washington, D.C.: NEA, 1918); Edward Krug, *The Shaping of the American High School, 1880–1941* (Madison: University of Wisconsin Press, 1972).

16. Sedlak and Church, *Social Services Delivered to Youth,* 35–36.

17. Lela B. Costin, "A Historical Review of School Social Work," *Social Casework* 50 (1969): 442–45.

18. Sedlak and Church, *Social Services Delivered to Youth,* 38–40.

19. "Disemboweling Chicago's School System," *School Review* 41 (1933): 483–91; "The Recent Situation in Chicago," *School Review* 41 (1933): 733; Chicago, Schools, Minutes, 12 July 1933.

20. "Spasmodic Diary of a Chicago School-Teacher," *Atlantic Monthly* 152 (1933): 523.

21. "Our Public Schools Must Not Close," reprinted in *Elementary School Journal* 34 (1933): 246–47.

22. Ibid.

23. "The Tragedy of the Chicago Schools," *Elementary School Journal* 34 (1933): 5–6; John M. Brewer, "A Century of Retrogression?" *School and Society* 38 (1933): 604–5.

24. Sedlak and Church, *Social Services Delivered to Youth,* 55–59.

25. Charles C. Steadman to Harold Richards, 9 June 1936, Report to the Illinois Superintendent of Public Instruction Files, Community High School District 218 (Blue Island, Ill.) Archives.

26. Community High School District 218 Report to the Illinois State Superintendent of Public Instruction, 1937; P. E. Belting to Harold Richards, 10 March 1937; Belting to Richards, 31 December 1938; Community High School District 218, Schools, Minutes, 31 December 1938; Report to the Illinois State Superintendent of Public Instruction, 1941, all located in the district's archives.

27. Sedlak and Church, *Social Services Delivered to Youth,* 40–45.

28. *Evanston Review*, 18 April 1932, 17 February 1938; Evanston, Schools, Annual Report 1940; Grace Boyd, "The Development of Non-academic Courses in the Evanston Township High School," *Education* 60 (1939): 17–24.

29. Michael W. Sedlak, "The Origins and Evolution of Social Work in the Schools, 1906–1970." (Paper presented at the annual meeting of the American Educational Research Association, Los Angeles, April 1981); Costin, "School Social Work."

30. National Education Association, Educational Policies Commission, *Social Services and the Schools* (Washington, D.C.: NEA, 1939).

31. American Council on Education, American Youth Commission, *Youth and the Future* (Washington, D.C.: ACE, 1942); idem, *What the High School Ought to Teach* (Washington, D.C.: ACE, 1940); NEA, Educational Policies Commission, *Education for All American Children* (Washington, D.C.: NEA, 1948); *Mid-Century White House Conference on Children and Youth* (Raleigh, N.C.: Health Publications Institute, 1951); National Society for the Study of Education, *Yearbook on Mental Health in Modern Education* (Chicago: NSSE, 1955); Diane Ravitch, *The Troubled Crusade* (New York: Basic Books, 1983); Christopher Lasch, *Haven in a Heartless World: The Family Besieged* (New York: Basic Books, 1977).

32. Sedlak and Church, *Social Services Delivered to Youth*, 77–79.

33. Chicago, Schools, Annual Report 1937, 140, 1938, 194–99; William A. Sears, "Teaching High School Youth to Drive," *Industrial Arts and Vocational Education* (1939): 228–30; Evanston, Schools, Annual Report 1938, 13–15; Warren P. Quensel, "A Brief History of Driver Education and Its Growth in Illinois High Schools," *Educational Press Bulletin* 49 (1958): 10.

34. *Chicago Tribune*, 8 March 1944, 3 May 1944.

35. *Congressional Record*, 79th Cong., 2d sess., 19 February and 28 February 1946: 1451–79, 1484–1508; *Chicago Tribune*, 20 and 22 February 1946.

36. *Chicago Tribune*, 21 February 1946; *Congressional Record*, 1493–98, 1537.

37. *Chicago Tribune*, 22 February 1946; *Statutes at Large*, 79th cong., 2d sess., 1946, 6, pt. 1: 230–34; *Congressional Record*, 1608–28, 1724, 5602–3, 5686, 5765, 6674.

38. *Chicago Tribune*, 31 October 1957.

39. Sedlak and Church, *Social Services Delivered to Youth*, 86–89.

40. For example, see John Hall Fish, *Black Power/White Control: The Struggle of the Woodlawn Organization in Chicago* (Princeton: Princeton University Press, 1973).

41. Church Mission of Help, Board Meetings Files, 1924–55; Youth Guidance, Board Meetings Files, 1955–72; Youth Guidance, Board of Education Files, 1969–80; Youth Guidance, Annual Reports, 1924–76; Youth Guidance, Clipping Files; all records held by Youth Guidance; interview with the director of Youth Guidance, Nancy Johnstone, 1980; confidential interviews with Chicago schools' social work staff and administration.

42. Sedlak, "Young Women and the City;" Erring Women's Refuge, Annual Report 1877, 9, 1881, 7, 1871, 12, 1874, 9, 1876, 8–9; Chicago Florence Crittenton Anchorage, Annual Report 1925, 6–9; idem, Board of Manager's Minutes, 30 November 1922, 5 December 1923, 3 January 1924, Crittenton Records, accession no. 73–35, box 6, Special Collections, University of Illinois at Chicago; Vivian Zelizer, *Pricing the Priceless Child: The Changing Social Value of Children* (New York: Basic Books, 1985), chap. 6.

43. F. Emerson, "The Place of the Maternity Home," *Survey* 42 (1919): 772; Sedlak, "Young Women and the City," on the modernization campaign.

44. Family Service Section Committee, Minutes, 19 June 1940; Florence Crittenton Anchorage, February 1951; Mary Young, Evaluation of the Florence Crittenton Anchorage, 1951–1953; all located in the Chicago Welfare Council Records, box 318, Chicago Historical Society.

45. Sedlak, *Aunt Martha's Decline.*

46. Ibid.; Gail Zellman, *The Response of the Schools to Teenage Pregnancy and Parenthood* (Santa Monica, Calif.: Rand Corp., 1981); Maris Vinovskis, *An "Epidemic" of Adolescent Pregnancy? Some Historical and Policy Considerations* (New York: Oxford University Press, 1988).

47. Sedlak, *Aunt Martha's Decline;* see the powerful meta-analysis by S. Phipps-Yonas, "Teenage Pregnancy and Motherhood: A Review of the Literature," *American Journal of Orthopsychiatry* 50 (1980): 403–29, esp. 413.

48. H. O'Rourke and F. Chavers, "The Use of Groups with Unmarried Mothers to Facilitate Casework," *Child Welfare* 47 (1968): 17–25.

49. William L. Pierce, "Adoption Issues, Trends and Networking," Address to the National Committee for Adoption, Inc., 1988: 3.

50. Sedlak, *Aunt Martha's Decline;* John Platt, "Social Traps," *American Psychologist* 28 (1973): 641–51.

51. See, for example, F. Hollis, "On Revisiting Social Work," *Social Casework* 61 (1980): 3–10; Max Siporin, "Moral Philosophy in Social Work Today," *Social Service Review* 56 (1982): 516–38.

52. See, for example, Michigan Department of Education, School Program Services, "An Information Report on Pilot School-Age Parents Projects, Model Sites" (Lansing, Mich., MDE, 1982): 12; Rosemary Moss, "An Overview: Alternative Education for Pregnant Teenage Girls—1972–1980," Report submitted to the Fremont, Mich., public schools, 1980; J. Bemis Diers and R. Sharpe, "The Teen-age Single Mother," *Child Welfare* 55 (1976): 309–18; J. Harriman, "In Trouble," *Atlantic Monthly* (March 1970): 94–98. These observations about patterns of pressure in the public school-based programs have been confirmed by the work of Gail Zellman of the Rand Corporation and Lana Muraskin, formerly of the National Institute of Education. I am indebted to both of them for sharing their considerable understanding of adolescent pregnancy policy and practice since the 1960s.

53. These concerns about adolescent pregnancy programs parallel a mounting critique of public education more generally, which has begun to recognize the problems of neutrality and passivity in the classroom, developments that have not challenged patterns of bargaining and treaty making between teachers and students; see Philip A. Cusick, *The Egalitarian Ideal and the American High School* (New York: Longman, 1983); Michael Sedlak, Christopher Wheeler, Diana Pullin, and Philip Cusick, *Selling Students Short: Classroom Bargains and Educational Reform in the American High School* (New York: Teachers College Press, 1986); and Arthur Powell, Eleanor Farrar, and David Cohen, *The Shopping Mall High School: Winners and Losers in the American High School* (Boston: Houghton Mifflin, 1985), for a sample of this work.

PART TWO

Equity and Multiculturalism

4 CHANGING CONCEPTIONS OF EDUCATIONAL EQUITY

DAVID L. KIRP

As recently as the midpoint of the present century, equity concerns had no real place on the agenda of educational policy. While there existed common schools in the rough image of Horace Mann's model, these schools were common more in form than fact. In the South, white and black schoolchildren were required by law to attend separate schools; in practice, the same was true in many parts of the North and West as well. Across the nation, handicapped children were treated as ineducable and "excused"—less politely and more accurately, excluded—from instruction. Pregnant schoolgirls were kept out of public schools for fear that their presence might be an incitement. For similar reasons, Spanish-speaking youngsters in the Southwest who spoke their home language during recess and children perceived as troublemakers by school administrators were also barred from classes.

The quality of instruction varied widely from place to place. Wealthy states spent, on average, two or three times as much for the education of each student as did poor states. Southern states, which were the last to establish public schools, were also notably stingy in financing education, particularly the education of black children. While efforts to equalize intrastate school expenditures dated to the turn of the century, these had largely failed. In many states, the poorest school districts could barely provide a rudimentary education—it was not uncommon for a district not to distribute textbooks or to operate its schools on a foreshortened year—while neighboring districts with more ample tax bases outspent them many times over. At the time, neither the states nor the federal government played a major role in resource redistribution.

To correct those gross inequities, and so to bring about "simple justice" nationwide,[1] became a theme of educational policy and constitutional law after the decision in the 1954 Segregation Cases.[2] While that campaign began in the courts, it eventually involved all three branches of the federal government. In its wake the grossest of unfairnesses to black and hand-icapped students, poor and Latino and female students, were corrected.[3]

While those events marked an important chapter in the annals of educational reform, they were hardly the final chapter. The characterization of reform has continued to evolve, generally in parallel with shifts in the national political climate. While the rhetoric of the 1960s emphasized equity, the theme of the more austere 1970s was "back to basics." Excellence was stressed during the Reagan-Bush years—a theme that had gone unheard since the crisis of national confidence brought on by the Soviets' launching of Sputnik in 1957—and with a nod to fashionable market analogies, competition and choice also became policy buzzwords.[4] With the 1992 presidential election, the pendulum of reform seems likely to swing once again, with equity assuming greater importance.

The significance of this shift should not be exaggerated. The perceived need to satisfy equity-based concerns persisted in muted form even in the heyday of excellence: assuring universal school readiness, for instance, was one of the six national goals set by the fifty governors and President Bush at the 1988 education summit.[5] Moreover, the continuing involvement of the courts in a wide variety of educational policy issues has given equity advocates an ongoing forum. Although federal judges have become less sympathetic to redistributionist arguments in recent years (partly reflecting the more conservative composition of the federal bench), state tribunals have taken up the cause.

Equity claims were initially straightforward and could readily command the support of all except the bigoted. No longer. As the nature of the asserted unfairness has become less obvious and the sought-after remedies—affirmative action, greater resources for expanding categories of disadvantage, all-minority schools, and the like—have become more controversial, equity has come to function more as a partisan rallying cry than as a guide.

The language of equity continues to be deployed by policy makers devising a new national course, state legislators crafting financing formulas, school administrators shaping an institutional mission, teachers designing a classroom environment, parents making decisions about their children's futures, and even fifth graders judging the fairness of their teacher's treatment. But so many and so conflicting are the meanings assigned to equity that the concept cannot be used as a yardstick for appraising school reform. Nor can equity even serve more loosely as a term of art, an "I know it when I see it" standard similar to Supreme Court Justice Potter Stewart's conception of obscenity.

Instead, when reference is made to equity, what's being signaled is support of a particular arrangement of educational resources, such as dollars, attention, or respect—or else support of a particular pattern of educational outcomes, such as achievement, satisfaction of needs, autonomy, or ethnic identity. There are many reasons to favor one or another pattern, but upon inspection these reasons are usually distinct from the idea of equity itself. Equity has also become an advocate's weapon, a good thing being contrasted with something less good: in the contemporary discourse on American education, it's instructive that no one favors *inequality* of opportunity, at least not out loud. Equity has this much in common with excellence, the mantra of the 1980s—it has to be appreciated as a protean and politicized concept.[6] If this chapter contributes some clarity to all that policy talk, and in so doing adds perspective, it will have done its job.

LEGAL MEANINGS OF EQUITY

In a society where, as Alexis de Tocqueville observed a century and a half ago in *Democracy in America*, "scarcely any political question arises which does not, sooner or later, become transformed into a legal question," lawyers and judges have given equity its most powerful modern meanings. For that reason, the legal configurations of equity offer a useful starting point.

The benchmark issue, of course, is the quintessentially American dilemma of racial equality, and the benchmark case is *Brown v. Board of Education* (1954). In overturning state-mandated school segregation as a denial of equal educational opportunity, *Brown* emphasized the racial dimensions of equality. Blacks and whites were to be treated equitably; this meant, at the least, that students could not formally be assigned to public schools on the basis of their skin color.

The justices could have outlawed segregation without at the same time emphasizing the importance of education. Subsequent Supreme Court rulings which undid segregation of public facilities such as parking lots and restrooms were not premised on the constitutional significance of these facilities. They relied instead on a constitutional theory of racial insult that could have been applied equally persuasively to segregated schools.[7] But the fact that *Brown* concerned education is hardly incidental. For one thing, the strategy of the National Association for the Advancement of Colored People (NAACP), which orchestrated the segregation litigation over a period of decades, was to concentrate the Supreme Court's attention on forms of segregation in higher education. By the time *Brown* came to the high court, the justices had already ordered the dismantling of "separate but equal" instruction for law students at the University of Texas and for graduate students at the University of Oklahoma and in the state of Missouri.[8] In a formalistic sense, then, the plaintiffs in *Brown* were asking the Court to do no more than apply these precedents to public schools.

The Supreme Court also made much of the fact that this case concerned education, "perhaps the most important function of state and local governments . . . the very foundation of good citizenship." The opinion declared that "it is doubtful that any child may reasonably be expected to succeed in life if he is denied the opportunity of an education" and added that the harm of segregation "generates a feeling of inferiority that may affect [black children's] hearts and minds in a way unlikely ever to be undone." In a famous footnote, the Court turned to available social science evidence on child development, including psychologist Kenneth Clark's famous black doll-white doll experiment and a survey of social scientists' opinions, to bolster the constitutional contention that, for schooling at least, separate means "inherently unequal."[9]

Viewed nearly forty years later, these paeans to education are best appreciated not as subtle constitutional reasoning but instead as a rhetorical strategy, a way to marshal popular support for the abolition of Jim Crow regimes. But at the time, it was widely believed that the constitutional importance of education constituted an independent legal justification —that desegregation, while constitutionally required, was not the only constitutionally relevant aspect of educational equity.

Give reform-minded lawyers an inch and they'll take a mile; that aphorism describes the course of subsequent litigation over the constitutional meanings of equal educational opportunity.

With respect to race, the proscription against formal color barriers was broadened, both judicially and legislatively, during the two subsequent decades. Immediately after *Brown*, commentators made much of the supposed difference between desegregation, which the law required, and integration, which was said to lie outside the pale of the law;[10] in the face of Southern resistance, however, that distinction collapsed. In school districts where segregation had been required prior to *Brown*, the justices declared that the only satisfactory guarantee of nondiscrimination was to dismantle racially identifiable schools—to produce "a system without a 'white' school and a 'Negro' school, but just schools," as the Supreme Court declared in 1968.[11] The 1964 Civil Rights Act was read similarly by the Johnson administration and in the first years of the Nixon administration as well.[12]

Yet if equal opportunity seemed a matter of simple justice after *Brown*, soon enough confusion about the meaning of equity began to surface, as allegations of racial inequity became more nuanced in character and proposed remedies for discrimination became more ambitious in their scope. In a residentially segregated southern school district that had formally abandoned racial distinctions, was widespread busing required to achieve "just schools"? If so, the justices were asked (as recently as 1991), for how many years was the district legally obliged to keep busing students?[13]

Public schools in many communities outside the South were segregated in form if not in fact. Judges pondered the legal significance of whether segregation in a particular locale came about innocently or deliberately—whether it was *de jure* or *de facto*.[14] (A different argument that was put forward is that, since government assigns all students to schools, any segregation that exists is by definition *de jure* and so impermissible.) Judges also assessed the constitutionality of practices that promoted segregation, such as race consciousness in assigning teachers or the drawing of school attendance boundaries with the effect of maintaining racially identifiable schools. Did such common practices amount to official segregation, officially created inequity?

Such questions splintered the Supreme Court, even as they became matters of widespread public debate. During the deliberations in the 1971 Charlotte, North Carolina, case,[15] a suit involving substantial student busing in an urban-suburban community, a majority of the justices reportedly favored abandoning the *de jure–de facto* distinction and adopting a single nationwide constitutional standard of racial equity. Before a decision was handed down, the majority retreated from this position to maintain the unbroken line of unanimous opinions which the Court had long regarded as critical to its credibility.[16] But this tradition of judicial unanimity could not withstand changes both in the composition of the Supreme Court and in the inequities being asserted. Nor could that tradition survive in a political climate which made opposition to "massive busing" a national campaign theme.[17]

The first time the justices considered the constitutionality of northern segregation, in the 1973 Denver case,[18] a divided Supreme Court relied more on the legalistic arcana, burdens of pleading and proof, than on the kind of broadly understandable principles set out in *Brown*. Lower court judges struggled to interpret these technical rulings; not surprisingly, in the name of racial equity they imposed different legal obligations on seemingly similar communities. Then, a year later in the Detroit case, a bare majority of the justices drew a sharp legal line between segregation within a school district and segregation that crossed district lines, all but declaring that district boundaries were immune from judicial scrutiny.[19]

This decision, coupled with the increasing migration of whites from the cities to the suburbs, made racial equity a term of legal art rather than an educational reality for students. Small wonder, then, that, in the name of equity, school districts such as Detroit and Milwaukee have proposed setting up separate schools for young black males who are not succeeding in the mostly minority mainstream. Small wonder, as well, that the challenges to such proposals, made by both integrationists and those concerned about the needs of female students, have also relied on the rhetoric of equity.

BEYOND RACE

Attention to and confusion about equity proliferated far beyond the confines of race. Blacks were classically regarded as a "discrete and insular minority,"[20] prone to irrational victimization at the hands of a hostile majority, and for that reason entitled to special solicitude in the courts. In the second half of the century, other groups would draw constitutional parallels between their treatment and the treatment of blacks.

Advocates for the handicapped have been most successful at establishing the analogy in the courts. Historically, handicapped children had been warehoused in day-sitting programs or else excluded from schools as ineducable. That changed when federal courts,[21] and later Congress in the 1973 Education for All Handicapped Children Act,[22] recognized that all children are educable—that is, capable of moving from greater to lesser dependence on others—and are entitled to an "appropriate education." By law, this requirement meant instruction that was both suited to the special needs of the handicapped and as closely linked as possible to the educational mainstream.

The meaning of *appropriate education* soon became disputed terrain. Did changing a catheter for an otherwise physically able child count as education, and hence something that school personnel had to do? Did handicap include emotional upheaval? learning disabilities? language deficits? an "at-risk" childhood? In the name of equity, was it sufficient to provide an educationally *plausible* setting, which was the most appropriate among the district's limited range of offerings—or did the educational regime have to be the *most* appropriate, even if that meant spending public dollars for private school tuition? How were conflicts to be resolved between equity understood primarily in terms of handicap-specific needs, on the one side, and, on the other side, equity understood in terms of a child's proximity to the educational mainstream?[23]

Other claimants for educational equity raised different, though equally vexing, concerns. Advocates for female students focused on sex-based inequities. These included the distribution of resources in athletics—although not in extracurricular activities generally, where more was spent on girls than boys. They emphasized the relative paucity of attention that girls received in the classroom—though not classroom performance, where girls typically outdid boys. And they questioned the permissibility of all-boys' schools—even while defending all-women's colleges.[24]

Limited English speakers pushed for equity as well.[25] This meant, variously, total English language immersion, or else programs to ease the transition to English, or else distinct linguistic and cultural tracks, running from kindergarten through twelfth grade, designed to maintain group identity—separate but equal programs, if you will, the very arrangement that *Brown* had struck down as inequitable.

Like African Americans before them, these claimants turned to Congress and the administrative agencies, as well as to the courts. They won official recognition in landmark judicial rulings and in legislation such as the Education for All Handicapped Children Act and Title IX of the 1972 Education Amendments. But advocates of equity have spent the better part of the past two decades in the shadows as educational reform efforts increasingly focused on maintaining minimum educational standards, reducing the incidence of violence and drugs, and promoting excellence. While there have been a handful of equity-enhancing rulings—notably the Supreme Court's 1982 decision that children whose parents entered the country illegally are nonetheless entitled to a free public education[26]—the hope of massively boosting the educational resources delivered to blacks, ethnic minorities, and other have-less groups, which figured prominently in policy pronouncements a generation ago, has gone mostly unrealized.

INPUTS AND OUTCOMES

Attention to equity has focused not only on the claims of disadvantaged *groups* but also on the distribution of educational *resources* generally. Historically, this meant a universal and free system of education, a common curriculum, and equal access to teachers and texts.[27] But there existed sizable variations in per pupil expenditure and services to children from one state to another, within states, within school districts, and within schools. In the past thirty years, all these differences have been challenged by equity-minded reformers.

Beginning in the 1960s, there were modest attempts to deploy the new federal presence in the schools as a way of encouraging the equalization of resources. Some communities initially distributed the billion-plus dollars made available through Title I of the 1965 Elementary and Secondary Education Act (now Chapter 1) in the belief that poorer school districts should benefit. But the intention of the legislation was really to add poverty to the list of individual differences that warranted equitable treatment; states and school districts that sought to use Title I funds for general aid were dissuaded by administrative and judicial orders.[28] A federal advisory commission appointed by President Nixon recommended a more direct role for Washington in resource redistribution, proposing that federal dollars flow to states that had equalized spending. But that idea went nowhere, as states prevailed against what they regarded as Washington's meddling.

Equity advocates focused more energy on rewriting the formulas for distributing a state's resources among its school districts. Because localities relied primarily on the property tax to support their schools, richer communities were able to spend far more on schools than were their poorer cousins. Reformers had long campaigned for bigger state grants to benefit poor and urban districts, but with only limited success, because the wealthy suburban districts could usually block substantial resource redistribution in the state legislature.[29]

In the wake of *Brown v. Board of Education*, these reformers began looking to the courts for help. From the outset, though, the conceptual puzzle posed great difficulties: What does equity mean in the context of educational resources or inputs? In a 1969 case, it was argued that the state of Illinois had a constitutional obligation to apportion funds according to the needs of students.[30] But the problem, as the federal court saw things, was that *need* was not a judicially manageable standard. It provided no meaningful way of choosing between the claims of the ablest and the claims of the least prepared, no meaningful criterion at all. A very different principle of equity, requiring equal funding of all schoolchildren, was put forward as a possible alternative. That equation of equality with sameness is a familiar enough formulation, but not one that makes much educational sense. Was it really wrong for a state to respond to variations in cost of living, for example, or to attend to the higher costs of educating handicapped students? Not surprisingly, the federal trial court concluded that these were policy questions, better addressed to a legislature than the judiciary; and the Supreme Court summarily affirmed that ruling.

The critical moment in the attempt to secure resource equity through the courts came in *San Antonio Independent School District v. Rodriguez*, a 1973 Supreme Court case.[31] The legal challenge to Texas' finance scheme was couched in a manner more coherent than needs and less strait-jacketing than sameness: the quality of public education may not be a function of wealth, other than the wealth of the state as a whole. This approach to equity stressed fiscal neutrality: what was objectionable was the correlation between the per pupil wealth of a school district and the dollars spent for each pupil. Any scheme for distributing resources that was fiscally neutral, including a plan premised on needs or equal dollars, satisfied the proposed constitutional standard. The plan favored by the reformers who promoted fiscal neutrality was district power equalizing; under this approach, equal tax rates would guarantee equal dollars for schoolchildren, regardless of a district's wealth.[32]

The Supreme Court accepted the argument that the Texas school finance law (and by implication, the law in every state except Hawaii, which operates a single school district) was inequitable—"chaotic and unjust," as Justice Potter Stewart wrote in his concurring opinion. Nonetheless, by a 5–4 majority, the Supreme Court upheld the constitutionality of the statute.

"Nothing this Court holds today in any way detracts from our historic dedication to public education," insisted the justices, but the message of the decision was otherwise. Education did not occupy a preferred constitutional place. Rather, it was a form of social welfare which could be provided, more or less, as the state saw fit, much as the state had broad leeway in distributing food, clothing, and shelter. The Supreme Court intimated there might be a minimum entitlement to education—perhaps the constitutional meaning of equity required states to offer basic schooling. But as the justices saw things, the existing system more than met that standard of entitlement.

At the federal level, the *Rodriguez* decision marked an end to the push for equity in school financing. The possibilities for further judicial consideration of the matter had apparently been exhausted, and Congress and the White House appeared uninterested in the issue. But the issue flourished in the states; school finance came to illustrate the idea of a federal system as laboratories of policy experimentation. A number of states chose to rewrite their school finance laws to bring about greater equality among districts. Legal challenges were brought in almost half the states, based on state equal protection clauses or else on the language in many state constitutions that mandates a "thorough and efficient system of public education." In some states, notably California, these lawsuits prompted substantial equalization of funding; other states, such as New Jersey, resurrected the idea that states had to respond to students' needs or to the special needs of cities; elsewhere, as in Texas, the matter has been almost continuously in the courts. The range of legislative and judicial views on what is required to bring about fair school financing reflects the breadth and diffuseness of the meanings of equity.[33]

Other equity advocates have taken a different tack, arguing that meaningful equity has to do not with inputs but with the *outcomes* of education.[34] Throughout the 1960s, the dour conclusions of the *Equal Educational Opportunity Survey*, popularly if misleadingly summed as "nothing works," dampened reformers' enthusiasm for strategies to equalize outcomes.[35] But the effective schools research undertaken in the past two decades, with its emphasis on what makes for successful schools, suggested a possible line of constitutional argument.[36]

As with efforts to redistribute inputs, in the discourse on outcomes uncertainty has focused on what standard to propose in the name of equity. Advocates have called for a rule mandating equal outcomes for all students—or, differently, for a rule requiring equal outcomes across racial and class lines, so that the distribution of, say, sixth grade reading scores would be identical for black and white (or rich and poor) schoolchildren. Others argued that, at the least, schools have an obligation to mandate minimum levels of educational success for all students. By this view, a student who graduates without being able to read has a constitutional grievance against the system.[37]

These many understandings of equity have created the kinds of puzzles beloved only by philosophers and law professors. Consider: In town A, a child with a particular handicap gets private school tuition underwritten; meanwhile, town B places an identical student in a regular public school classroom for most of the day and provides modest supplementary help. Do *both* students have a legal grievance? Or, to take another example, town C scrupulously balances the assignment of minority teachers among its schools, only to encounter the complaint that it is failing to offer role models to black students and so is dooming them to failure. Town D's philosophy, which emphasizes the concept of role models, runs into objections from blacks, who claim that they are getting a segregated education—and from whites, who claim an entitlement to integrated instruction. (The constitutionality of creating a school for black male students presents similar issues.) And what about this situation? Town E makes sure that the dollar / student ratio is the same in all its schools, while Town F deliberately spends more on those who, in its judgment, need more—the handicapped, perhaps, or the gifted, or children from at-risk families. How does a court handle the raft of court cases filed by unhappy parents in these towns?

Such examples can be endlessly multiplied, which is one reason why *Educational Policy and the Law*, the 860-page casebook I co-authored, has required three wholesale revisions and two supplements in less than two decades. While it would be cheering to report that the judicial opinions, the scholarly commentary, and the many statutes that purport to define equal opportunity provide a path through this confusion, it would also be untrue.

The concept of needs has one meaning for the handicapped and another for those with deficits that aren't accepted as a handicap. Courts quarrel over when a once-segregated school district has become "unitary" and so can set school attendance boundaries to coincide with the boundaries of neighborhoods that have become segregated. Whether the preferences of the black families living in those communities have any bearing on the matter is itself debatable. Meanwhile, legislators who believe that classic notions of racial equity have become outmoded threaten to deny judges the authority to make such rulings. In disputes over equity between boys and girls on the athletic field, girls are sometimes said to be entitled to identical treatment (a single coed team), sometimes to different treatment (sex-segregated teams). And so it goes.

The present Supreme Court is unlikely to contribute much to our understanding of educational equity anytime soon. Nor will it have the chance, for wise advocates have learned to keep such issues out of the federal courts, instead addressing their pleas to state tribunals. But even at the height of equity consciousness, clarity was in short supply. Though the Court usually had principles in mind, it paid little attention to conflicts among those principles. When the idea of equity became inexpedient to pursue, notably in the Texas school finance case, the justices backed off.

Nor has Congress done much better. The definitions of equity in various pieces of federal legislation—Chapter 1, Head Start, the Education for All Handicapped Children Act, and the like—don't attempt consistency or even coherence. Usually they represent political responses to interest group pressures. Sometimes bureaucratic pressures are the driving force. Consider, for example, the widespread use of pullout programs for slow learners financed by Chapter 1, adopted not because this makes educational sense but because it leaves a tidy paper trail for the auditors. But whether politics or bureaucratics is regnant, the pull of equity on policy is fairly weak.

INSIDE THE CLASSROOM

The most significant differences in treatment of students may well be found *within* schools, in the dollars spent on, and the quality of teachers assigned to, different classes.[38] During the Supreme Court argument in the remedy phase of *Brown*,[39] NAACP attorney Thurgood Marshall responded to a question from the bench about the permissibility of ability grouping by declaring that it was acceptable "to put all the smart ones together and all the dumb ones together," so long as the basis for assignment was not racial. Barely a decade later, though, in perhaps the most ambitious judicial definition of educational equity, a federal judge in Washington, D.C., ordered an end to segregation that resulted from ability grouping, abolishing tracking based on students' tested ability and ordering that expenditures among schools be equalized.[40]

Inequities are endemic even within classrooms, in the ways teachers respond to different students. Yet as sociologist Christopher Jencks pointed out in an elegant essay, within classrooms as among school districts, there is no one right standard of fair treatment to impose.[41] Jencks asked a hypothetical teacher—whom, with a nod to *Pygmalion*, he called Ms. Higgins—how she would go about equitably treating the students in her third grade reading class. "What [did] her belief in equal opportunity impl[y] about the distribution of the main educational resources at her disposal, her time and attention?"[42] He took Ms. Higgins through five possible responses: *democratic equality*, giving everyone equal time and attention; *moralistic justice*, rewarding those who make the most effort; *weak humane justice*, compensating students who have been shortchanged at home or in earlier schooling; *strong humane justice*, compensating youngsters who have been shortchanged in any way; and *utilitarianism*, focusing attention on the ablest.

Several of these ideal-type approaches have their approximate counterparts in such macrostrategies as Head Start, Title I (now Chapter 1), and
former Education Secretary William Bennett's "excellence" agenda. But
Jencks pointed out the tensions among them and the practical difficulties in
implementing any of them. Identity of treatment, while intuitively appealing, makes for hard going in the real world of differently attentive students. Though moralistic equality means to focus on that attentiveness, as
a practical matter it cannot, and so it winds up rewarding achievement,
including effortless achievement, which is not at all the intention. Humane
theories of justice, while more attractive, are hard to put into action, for
how can "Ms. Higgins take account of *all* the factors that influence an
individual's choices, including subjective costs and benefits" which influence a child's opportunities to learn? How can she even know, for instance,
which parents encourage learning and which do not—and what can she
do about the difference?

Moralistic theories of classroom justice assume that children can be
held accountable for their failures because they have free will; humane
justice assumes that the settings in which kids wind up determine their
choices. Moralistic justice awards prizes, while humane justice encourages
Ms. Higgins to act as a coach who makes all her students into prize winners. With "every moment in our lives . . . both an ending and a beginning," said Jencks, both world views are sometimes right, and there is no
ready way out of this quandary. Utilitarianism, which is supposed to maxi-
mize the overall welfare levels of students, requires knowledge about the
relationship between Ms. Higgins' time and pupils' eventual success—
specifically, about whether a teacher can have more of an influence on the
ablest or least able readers—that the empirical literature does not provide.

One response to these uncertainties, Jencks concluded, is for Ms. Higgins to revert to her original intuition and treat all students identically.
None of the arguments for an unequal distribution of time and attention is
really compelling—and none of the principles, neither virtue nor disadvantage nor benefits, is really usable in Ms. Higgins' classroom. "Democracies typically put the burden of proof on those who favor unequal treatment, and in practice this burden is so heavy that the egalitarian 'null
hypothesis' can always carry the day." Equity, Jencks concluded, "is an
ideal consistent with almost every vision of a good society," whether centered on markets or rights or social programs. It is a "universal solvent,"
compatible with the dreams of almost everyone. Jencks sees these attri-
butes of equity, not as signaling a fatal weakness of the concept but rather
as revealing its peculiar strength. In this formulation, equity becomes one
of those conflict-muting aspirations, the kind of common ideal without
which social ordering is impossible. But it could be said with equal justification that focusing on equity—or, more typically, on inequity—serves

mostly to maintain dissatisfactions, senses of injustice, in the face of an impossible-to-satisfy aspiration of policy.

EQUITY AND EQUITIES

What might be the nature of equity-driven policy initiatives to come? Advocates for equity have typically pushed their causes as if equity existed in a sphere of its own, apart from the aspirations of other reformers and other reforms. When the unfairnesses were glaringly obvious, and readily definable in constitutional terms, this made sense. But efforts to promote educational equity affect other contemporary proposals for systemic change, and other reform aspirations, whether for greater choice or a re-design of the governance of schools, for multiculturalism or the invocation of a national identity, need to be assessed in the light of equity. This trans-formation of the nature of equity-based arguments has institutional ram-ifications as well. In the decades following *Brown*, the Supreme Court, that "least dangerous branch" of the federal government, took the lead in de-fining equity, with the coordinate branches mostly implementing stan-dards set by the judiciary. In the present era, though, equity is fully entan-gled in the policy give-and-take, the political give-and-take too, which surrounds educational policy making. That means equity concerns will no longer primarily be the province of judges and lawyers but will arise wherever policy is being fashioned.

Equity has often been equated with sameness. But a hundred flowers can bloom in the equity garden, since very different kinds of schools take seriously all the aspects of equity that emerge from the judicial and legisla-tive record as well as from the annals of good practice. No single philoso-phy of education or pedagogical strategy is uniquely synonymous with equity claims.

Equity entails both maintaining uniform standards and paying individ-ual attention to students' talents and desires. Common rules have the advantage of offering a sustaining structure of fairness, and rules make it plain that the locus of authority in schools is not subject to debate, although the form that rules take will depend on the pedagogical philosophy of the school. Interest in promoting equity must take account of significant differ-ences in students' backgrounds. In the increasingly heterogeneous urban public schools across the country, paying attention to cultural differences is neither a frill nor a matter of political correctness but a necessity. How else can teachers recognize styles of learning or sense what there is to be drawn out from individual students? How else can schools convince parents, some habitually timid toward authority and others angry about their own treat-ment as students, to involve themselves in their children's education? Equity means different things to children, teachers, and parents. Partly these differences are developmental. They reflect other things as well, including gender-based and race-based variations in treatment. The role one occupies in the school hierarchy matters also. Ask a teacher or a child if she is being treated fairly, ask the child's parents too, and the criteria for fairness will, understandably, vary.

To be meaningful, the aspiration to promote equity requires more resources than urban and poor rural school systems are typically able to muster. The argument about whether boosting financial support for schools or encouraging innovation matters most is similar to the beer commercial in which one side shouts "tastes great" while the other responds "less filling." The equitable distribution of a pittance embodies a grudging form of fairness. It is also a morally unsatisfactory form of fairness, because of the extent to which differences in the resources devoted to a child's education still depend on the wealth of a child's family and the community in which he or she resides.

Only the narrowest understanding of equity focuses exclusively on achievement tests or any other fixed measure. In day-to-day school life, as Christopher Jencks' account of Ms. Higgins' classroom reveals, equity has more to do with paying attention to the broad array of claims—some based on need and others on effort or performance—that students advance. It also entails attending to the concrete choices that teachers and administrators make on a day-to-day basis; what deserves attention, in the name of equity, is the content of teachers' exchanges with students, teachers' conversations with one another and with parents after school, and professional dialogue as well.

As these observations suggest, equity—or, more precisely, *the equities*—are necessarily in conflict. Public schools are regularly called upon to be what no other institution in the society even aspires to becoming: nonracist, nonsexist, nonclassist, open places; palaces of learning, enclaves of joy which respond equally well to a range of children's talents and desires which would fill a modern-day Noah's Ark. How could expectations be otherwise, given the pulls and tugs of the society—and how could any school *not* fail at this mission?

This view of the equities—as significant, particularized, in conflict, and in flux—is consistent with the larger aims of contemporary educational reform. It is a conception that confirms both the protean nature and the breadth of aspiration that the idea of educational equity entails.

NOTES

1. The phrase is taken from Richard Kluger, *Simple Justice* (New York: Alfred A. Knopf, 1975).

2. 349 U.S. 483 (1954).

3. See Mark G. Yudof, David L. Kirp, and Betsy Levin, *Education Policy and the Law* (St. Paul, Minn.: West Publishing, 1991), chaps. 5 and 6, for a thorough compendium of the cases and law review articles on equal educational opportunity.

4. Ibid., at chap. 7. See also David Kirp, "What School Choice Really Means," *Atlantic Monthly* 20, no. 5 (November 1992): 119–24.

5. See David Kirp, "The 'Education President' " in *Eyes on the President: History in Essays and Cartoons*, ed. Leo Heagerty (Occidental, Calif.: Chronos, 1993).

6. See, e.g., Thomas Timar and David Kirp, *Managing Education Excellence* (Philadelphia: Falmer Publishing, 1988); Leon Botstein, "Education Reform in the Reagan Era: False Paths, Broken Promises," *Social Policy* 3–11 (Spring 1988).

7. See, e.g., Watson v. Memphis, 373 U.S. 526 (1963); New Orleans City Park Improvement Ass'n v. Detiege, 358 U.S. 54 (1958).

8. Missouri ex re. Gaines v. Canada, 305 U.S. 337 (1938); McLaurin v. Board of Regents of the University of Oklahoma, 339 U.S. 637 (1950); Sweatt v. Painter, 339 U.S. 629 (1950).

9. See, e.g., Edgar Cahn, "Jurisprudence," *New York University Law Review* 30, no. 150 (1955).

10. See, e.g., Robert McKay, "With All Deliberate Speed—A Study of School Desegregation," *New York University Law Review* 31, no. 991 (1956).

11. Green v. County School Board of New Kent County, Virginia, 391 U.S. 430 (1968).

12. See Harrell Rodgers, Jr., and Charles Bullock III, *Law and Social Change* (New York: McGraw-Hill, 1972); Gary Orfield, *The Reconstruction of Southern Education* (New York: John Wiley, 1969).

13. Board of Education of Oklahoma City Public Schools v. Dowell, 498 U.S. 237 (1991).

14. See, e.g., Paul Brest, "The Supreme Court, 1975 Term—Foreword: In Defense of the Antidiscrimination Principle," *Harvard Law Review* 90, no. 1 (1976); Frank Goodman, "*De Facto* Segregation: A Constitutional and Empirical Analysis," *California Law Review*, 60, no. 275 (1972); Owen Fiss, "Racial Imbalance in the Public Schools: The Constitutional Concepts," *Harvard Law Review* 78, no. 564 (1965); U.S. Civil Rights Commission, *Racial Isolation in the Public Schools* (Washington, D.C.: Government Printing Office, 1968).

15. Swann v. Charlotte-Mecklenburg Board of Education, 402 U.S. 1 (1971).

16. Dennis J. Hutchinson, "Unanimity and Desegregation: Decision-Making in the Supreme Court, 1948–1958," *Georgetown Law Journal* 68, no. 1 (1979).

17. See generally Gary Orfield, *Must We Bus?* (Washington, D.C.: Brookings Institution, 1979).

18. Keyes v. School District No. 1, 413 U.S. 189 (1973).

19. Milliken v. Bradley, 418 U.S. 717 (1974).

20. U.S. v. Carolene Products Co., 304 U.S. 144 (1938).

21. Mills v. Board of Education, 348 F. Supp. 866 (D.D.C. 1972); PARC v. Commonwealth of Pennsylvania, 334 F. Supp. 1257 (E.D.Pa. 1971).

22. 29 U.S.C.A. SS 1401-61.

23. See generally Yudof, Kirp, and Levin, *Education Policy and the Law*, 719–40.

24. Ibid., 760–93.

25. Ibid., 793–816. See also Lau v. Nichols, 414 U.S. 563 (1974).

26. Plyler v. Doe, 457 U.S. 202 (1982).

27. James Coleman, "The Concept of Equality of Educational Opportunity," *Harvard Educational Review* 38, no. 1 (1968): 7–22.

28. See *Report on Changes under Chapter 1 of the Education Consolidation and Improvement Act*, prepared for the Subcommittee on Elementary, Secondary, and Vocational Education of the Committee on Education and Labor of the U.S. House of Representatives (Washington, D.C.: Government Printing Office, 1985).

29. See Walter Garms, James Guthrie, and Lawrence Pierce, *School Finance: The Economics and Politics of Public Education* (Englewood Cliffs, N.J.: Prentice-Hall, 1978).

30. McInnis v. Shapiro, 93 F.Supp. 32 (N.D.Ill. 1968), *aff'd sub nom.* McInnis v. Ogilvie, 394 U.S. 322 (1969). The needs principle was first articulated in Arthur Wise, *Rich Schools, Poor Schools: The Promise of Equal Educational Opportunity* (Chicago: University of Chicago Press, 1968).

31. San Antonio Independent School District v. Rodriguez, 411 U.S. 1 (1973).

32. John Coons, William Clune, and Stephen Sugarman, *Private Wealth and Public Education* (Cambridge: Harvard University Press, 1971).

33. See Richard Lehne, *The Quest for Justice: The Politics of School Finance Reform* (New York: Longman, 1978); John Coons, "Recent Trends in Science Fiction: *Serrano* among the People of Number," *Journal of Law and Education* 6, no. 23 (1977); William E. Thro, "To Render Them Safe: The Analysis of State Constitutional Provisions in Public School Finance Reform Litigation," *Virginia Law Review* 75, no. 1639 (1989).

34. Mark Yudof, "Effective Schools and State Constitutions: A Variety of Opinions," *Texas Law Review* 63, no. 865 (1985).

35. Christopher Jencks, "The Coleman Report and the Conventional Wisdom" in *On Equality of Educational Opportunity*, ed. Frederick Mosteller and Daniel Moynihan (Cambridge: Harvard University Press, 1972), 69–115.

36. Stewart Purkey and Marshall S. Smith, "Effective Schools: A Review," *Elementary School Journal* 83 (1983): 427–52.

37. See generally Gershon Rattner, "A New Legal Duty for Urban Public Schools: Effective Education in Basic Skills," *Texas Law Review* 63, no. 777 (1985).

38. See Edward Pauley, *The Classroom Crucible* (New Haven: Yale University Press, 1992).

39. 349 U.S. 294 (1955). See generally Mark Yudof, "Implementation Theories and Desegregation Realities," *Alabama Law Review* 32, no. 441 (1981); Robert Carter, "The Warren Court and Desegregation," *Michigan Law Review* 67, no. 237 (1968).

40. Hobson v. Hansen, 269 F.Supp. 401 (D.D.C. 1967); see generally David Kirp, "Schools as Sorters: The Constitutional and Policy Implications of Student Classification," *University of Pennsylvania Law Review* 121, no. 705 (1973).

41. Christopher Jencks, "Whom Must We Treat Equally for Educational Opportunity to Be Equal?" *Ethics* 98 (1988): 518–33.

42. Ibid., 214.

5 ETHNIC DIVERSITY AND NATIONAL IDENTITY IN PUBLIC SCHOOL TEXTS

REED UEDA

The scholastic treatment of ethnic groups in American public schools underwent a profound transformation from World War II to the 1990s. In classroom lessons, minorities turned from marginal figures into important and exemplary citizens of the American nation. This revolutionary historical change was sensitively revealed in textbooks and formal curriculum, the key forces that have driven American schooling. These pedagogical tools, in turn, reflected changing sets of external intellectual and ideological forces that redefined the character of ethnic pluralism in the nation.

For much of national history, American schools paid nearly exclusive attention to the inculcation of national identity, eschewing the cultivation of diverse group identities. History and literature lessons formed the principal vehicles for purveying formal national identity, but after 1900 social studies also assumed this function to a considerable degree.[1] These lessons transmitted a unifying code of political beliefs and symbols and shaped knowledge of the principles of democratic government and republican citizenship.[2] The schools created a shared civic world view that overarched group differences and served as a key to participation in nation building.[3]

A persistent influence on the development of a model of national identity was the nation's historical condition of ethnic pluralism. Mass immigration expanded the variety of ethnic and racial groups continuously throughout national history. Of the major immigrant-receiving nations in the world during the nineteenth and twentieth centuries, the United States absorbed by far the largest number of immigrants and the greatest variety of ethnic groups.[4] This historical condition inescapably complicated the formulation of national identity and its transmission through the schools. As a consequence, to a large extent the construction of national identity in the schools was an aspect of guided assimilation for the children of immigrants.

Nevertheless, an embryonic movement toward education for cultural pluralism began to develop. The call for appreciation of foreign cultures derived from the doctrine of liberal Americanizers such as Jane Addams contending that immigrants brought cultural contributions that would enrich American society.[5] An approach called *intercultural education* began as early as the 1920s to urge teaching about ethnic diversity.[6]

As World War II approached, educators grew increasingly interested in how schools could positively reflect the historical ethnic diversity generated by the forming of a nation out of waves of international migration. They sought to make learning about the nation's minorities a path toward creating greater democracy among individuals of different ancestry.

THE RISE OF DEMOCRATIC PLURALISM

The World War II years witnessed the emergence of a growing need to identify the international dimensions internal to American group life and external to the involvement of the United States in world affairs.[7] Educational theoreticians began to reevaluate the notion of the melting pot as a model for social evolution. They reinterpreted the melting pot as a coercive and homogenizing social design. In 1945, the yearbook of the National Council for the Social Studies presented a critical view of the melting pot as "an unwholesome standardization" detracting from "the continuation of the foreign heritage."[8] Educators began to call for the adoption of cultural pluralism in ethnic relations. A notion of democracy underlay their proposals. Cultural pluralism, they felt, was more consistent with democratic ideals because it endorsed the freedom of groups to determine their own cultural way of life.

The intellectual shift toward validating and encouraging cultural pluralism intertwined with wider movements toward decreasing prejudice and discrimination. World War II was a turning point in official attitudes toward ethnic and racial barriers. Government gradually increased efforts to promote intergroup toleration. Multinational cultural events occurred in several states to celebrate the ethnically diverse sources of national strength during the war.[9] After the war, various states founded government commissions to combat discrimination.[10] Antidiscrimination was predicated on a confidence that social policy science could attack prejudice as a learned behavior that could be unlearned. Shortly after the war, a series of psychological studies identified prejudice as a socially constructed pathological condition that could, to a degree, be treated or prevented.[11]

In a climate disposed toward encouraging intergroup tolerance, textbook writers entered into the business of educating for intergroup awareness and mutual understanding. The publisher Ginn and Company inaugurated the Tiegs-Adams Social Studies Series, which included titles such as *Your People and Mine* and *Your Country and Mine: Our American Neighbors*. Published in 1949, *Your People and Mine* provided an overview of American history from the colonial era to the mid–twentieth century. It emphasized the joint effort of different social groups in the building of the American nation.[12]

The central theme of these texts—how national identity arose out of the immigrant character of all Americans—reflected the positive vision of American ethnic history developing in the postwar decades. American intellectuals endorsed the view that immigration was a social good and was a defining ingredient of nationhood. Some discussed the validity of a pan-immigrant model to account for American national identity. The major social historian of the era, Oscar Handlin, charted the pivotal role of the immigrant experience in all group histories, including those of blacks and Puerto Ricans. He argued that the latter were united with the descendants of European immigrants in the common experiences of migration from a stagnant rural order to a modern urban world.[13] Nathan Glazer, perhaps the era's most influential sociologist of ethnic relations, viewed blacks and Puerto Ricans as the latest groups to follow the pathway taken by European immigrants.[14]

The history and social studies textbooks of the 1950s and 1960s began to express a benign form of democratic cultural pluralism that scholars such as Handlin and Glazer articulated.[15] Whereas the melting pot described by policy makers in the early twentieth century stressed unidirectional and progressive melting toward Anglo-conformity, the democratic pluralism model tolerated multidirectional intergroup assimilation and voluntary ethnic identification. New textbooks showed that the American nation was defined by the mixture of different groups. They emphasized that, despite dissimilar ancestries, all Americans were equal as citizens. Ethnic diversity was one aspect of the complex social character of the nation. It testified to the freedom under democracy given to groups to pursue their own way of life. Many texts still supported the melting pot model, but the cutting edge of innovation was the concept of cultural pluralism.[16] An observation by Frances FitzGerald described the mixing of old and new ideas in the transitions of textbook writing: "[New] scholarship trickles down extremely slowly into the school texts."[17]

Despite new efforts to portray diversity in its relation to nation building, the role and history of ethnic groups remained a very small part of curriculums and textbook treatments in the years after World War II. Blacks appeared chiefly in the institutional history of slavery, and Indians had a minor role in the account of colonization and westward expansion. Most textbooks devoted only a small amount of attention to immigration.[18]

To the extent that cultural pluralism was pictured in the texts of the 1950s and 1960s, it was seen as an aspect of the health of civil society under American democracy, where government permitted the private right of voluntary ethnic identification. Confidence in free pluralism drew on the feeling in the early cold war era that the American institutions proven superior in the Second World War would also prevail against communism because of their democratic character. The free pluralism model complemented the growing political movement of antidiscrimination. The elimination of prejudice and discrimination would create an arena in which tolerant and pluralistic ethnic relations could grow. Government would guarantee equal opportunity for individuals; it would not protect the privileges, the power, and the cultural interests of particular groups. History and civics texts envisioned the creation of free ethnic pluralism in the United States as an unfolding of the nation's destiny as a democracy.

FROM DEMOCRATIC PLURALISM TO MULTICULTURALISM

The free pluralism ideology began to be discussed in a sharper key in the 1960s as a result of pivotal historical events. Educators began to express dissatisfaction with the limited coverage of ethnic groups found in textbooks. They explored possibilities for enlarging the representation of ethnic diversity. In 1963, Vincent R. Rogers and Raymond H. Muessig complained in *The Social Studies* about the failure of textbooks to address the need for a deeper understanding of the social and ethnic diversity shaping American life. They noted that "too many texts are filled with slanted 'facts,' stereotypes, provincial and ethnocentric attitudes, and superficial, utopian discussions which skim over conditions as they actually exist in life today." They decried the presence of too many "characters in text" having "first names like Bill, Tom, and John, rather than Sid, Tony, and Juan and last names like Adams, Hill, and Cook rather than Schmidt, Podosky, and Chen." Rogers and Muessig deplored the portrayal of Americans as "white, Anglo-Saxon, Protestant, white collar, and middle class," giving the impression that "all Americans live on wide, shady streets in clean suburban areas, occupy white Cape Cod style houses, drive new automobiles, have two children (a boy and a girl, of course) and own a dog."[19]

An optimistic and homogeneous image of American life seemed out of touch in the political climate of the 1960s when the crisis of war and racial revolution revealed the shortcomings of American society. The Vietnam War and the black power movement combined to undermine the positive conception of American institutions that supported the workings of free pluralism.[20] Antiwar critics and black power advocates portrayed American society as enduringly flawed by racism and capitalist exploitation. These developments prepared the way for the radicalization of opposition to the institutional foundations of American nationhood. Among these foundations was the idea of the melting pot.

As the radical social critique unfolded, the melting pot model was seen in increasingly negative terms.[21] In the most extreme attacks, it was treated either as an efficient and coercive dissolver of ethnic groups or as an abject failure because groups remained unmelted and unequal.[22] Spokesmen for the descendants of European immigrants at hearings for the Ethnic Heritage Studies Act in 1970 attested to the harmful ways in which the dominant melting-pot ideology had stripped away their ethnic identities.[23] While representatives of European ethnic groups decried the cultural self-denial imposed by the melting pot, minority groups announced that the melting pot was inapplicable to their historical experiences. Black, Hispanic, Asian, and Native American militants conceded that the assimilation model or the melting pot may have worked for European immigrants but was irrelevant to their group experiences. Rejecting all assimilationist models, these advocates called for the adoption of a victimization-oppression model based on the theory of "internal colonialism."[24] They repudiated the view that blacks were on the same path to assimilation that the European immigrant population had traveled earlier. From the radicals' perspective, Asians and Hispanics were primarily seen not in terms of their social identity as immigrants but rather in terms of their racial identity as minorities. Studies that emphasized ethnocultural persistence, often represented in the form of resistance to oppressive assimilation under the hegemony of capitalism, gained prominence in the world of scholarship.[25]

The circles of debate over educational policy quickly joined the escalating attack on the melting pot and the mounting efforts to sharpen cultural pluralism. In a 1970 volume on elementary school social studies, William W. Joyce wrote, "Our nation's experiences in minority group relations demonstrate that the proverbial American melting pot has been a colossal fraud, perpetrated by a dominant majority for the purpose of convincing society at large that all cultural groups, irrespective of race or ethnic origin, were in fact eligible for full and unrestricted participation in the social, economic, political, and religious life of this nation."[26] In 1972, the American Association of Colleges for Teacher Education (AACTE) issued a manifesto endorsing what can be called a strong model of multicultural education. Called "No One Model American: A Statement on Multicultural Education," it was a remarkably prophetic and influential document expressing many tenets of strong multiculturalism that would be discussed and refined by educationalists during the subsequent two decades.[27]

"No One Model American" began by denouncing assimilation. It demanded that schools "not merely tolerate cultural pluralism" but "be oriented toward the cultural enrichment of all children and youth through programs rooted to the preservation and extension of cultural alternatives." The statement defined four goals of multicultural schooling: "(1) the teaching of values which support cultural diversity and individual uniqueness; (2) the encouragement of the qualitative expansion of existing ethnic cultures and their incorporation into the mainstream of American socioeconomic and political life; (3) the support of explorations in alternative and emerging life styles; and (4) the encouragement of multiculturalism, multilingualism, and multidialectism." These goals viewed multiculturalism primarily as a means of cultural empowerment, not as an academic tool for improving scholastic and civic knowledge. The manifesto stressed that "multicultural education reaches beyond awareness and understanding of cultural differences" and aims at "cultural equality."

To follow up on its multicultural statement, the AACTE's *Journal of Teacher Education* published a "multicultural" symposium in 1973 to advocate a social studies approach that would heighten appreciation of group identity and culture.[28] The symposium opened with a guest editorial from William A. Hunter, president of the association, declaring that "America's culture is unalterably pluralistic." Hunter charged that "historians and educators have either omitted or distorted the facts regarding American cultural diversity." He repeated the call sounded in "No One Model American" for social reconstruction and transformation through multicultural approaches:

> The multicultural philosophy must permeate the entire American educational enterprise. To this end, we—the American people—must reclassify our entire societal and institutional objectives, rethink our educational philosophy. Assessment in light of these concepts will lead to conceptualizing, developing, and designing restructured educational institutions. Curriculums, learning experiences, the competencies of teaching professionals, whole instructional strategies—all must adjust to reflect and encompass cultural diversity.

By the early 1970s, influential figures in the world of education had fully articulated an oppositional ideology toward assimilationist models of schooling in ethnic diversity. It demanded that schools teach about ethnic identity and culture as part of their institutional transformation that would subserve social transformation. The components of this ideology maintained a powerful shaping influence over models of multicultural schooling proposed from the 1970s to the 1990s. They usually included the following tenets: The melting pot was not only a historical inaccuracy, but also a deceptive invention to gain acquiescence from ethnic minorities while concealing their domination by white elites. Minorities had to recover a knowledge of their true historical past, buried by the privileged focus on the melting pot. They could achieve this only if schools were equipped to enlarge knowledge and appreciation of ethnic identity. Without this service, students would be deprived of their cultural heritage. They would lack the self-esteem and self-knowledge that would aid them in organizing for individual and group empowerment.

The strong version of multiculturalism based on heightening group identities to effect social transformation was not translated immediately and wholesale into teaching or the curriculum. Frequently, textbooks and guides for teachers supplied a kind of weak multiculturalism in which schooling provided greater knowledge of the ethnic diversity underlying American life to increase scholastic understanding about society's character. Furthermore, even in the late 1970s, the range of ethnic diversity portrayed in some of the most popular secondary history textbooks was fairly modest. In these volumes, American Indians and black slave society received increased treatment, but the handling of immigration hardly achieved greater depth than that found in the textbooks of the 1950s. Asians and Hispanics received very minor attention. European immigration was discussed with little examination of specific ethnic groups or even the historically important differences between northern and western Europeans and southern and eastern Europeans. Secondary American history books continued to highlight the traditional achievements and turning points of nation building. They treated at length the political and institutional effects of the American Revolution and the Civil War.[29] Civics textbooks continued to concentrate on explaining the primary mechanisms and institutions of the American polity. They devoted little space to affirmative action and racial inequality.[30]

The 1980s, however, comprised a watershed in which ethnic-based curriculums became a central force in curricular reform. In 1987 California adopted a social studies-history framework that portrayed the integral roles of ethnic minorities in the evolution of the state and nation.[31] New York State in 1991 adopted a new social studies-history framework reflecting the centrality of ethnic differences.[32]

An enormous impetus toward inventing and installing multicultural curriculums also came from a crucial social change, the return of mass immigration. Since the 1970s, annual totals for immigration climbed to levels that had not been reached since the late nineteenth century. For the first time in history, most of the immigrants came from outside Europe, especially from Latin America and Asia. Policy makers felt pressure to equip the schools with new lessons and texts suitable for guiding the assimilation of students who came from every part of the world.

Educational scholars embracing the strong multiculturalism model first advocated in 1972 by the AACTE's "No One Model American" formatted it to the opportunities for institutionalizing ethnic curriculums growing from the 1970s to the 1980s.[33] Elementary social studies was particularly susceptible to this development. Geared toward teaching for simple awareness, it casually verged upon celebration and stereotyping of ethnic differences. An example of how elementary teaching could construct simplistic group identities is found in the "Illustrative Learning

Activities" of John U. Michaelis's *Social Studies for Children,* a teacher training text. Michaelis urged the adoption of these types of lessons because of the "high priority" to "developing an appreciation of one's own and other cultures and to eradicating racism, classism, sexism, ethnocentrism, prejudice, and discrimination."[34]

Michaelis's teacher handbook went further to propound the need to transform the entire school milieu to accomplish this task. "The school environment and the hidden as well as the visible curriculum," he urged, "should be attuned to ethnic pluralism, learning styles and cultures of children from various groups, local conditions and resources, and ethnic group languages." The consequences of this institutionalized transformation would go far beyond improvement in scholastic knowledge to the heightening of ethnic consciousness and the empowering of group difference.[35]

Michaelis's lessons were indicative of the path educators were paving to deal with ethnic diversity in the classroom. It was built on an idealized and uncritical view of the consequences of cultivating ethnic or racial consciousness. Michaelis's lessons to nurture ethnic awareness were examples of pedagogical tendencies criticized by a historian and editor of *The Harvard Encylopedia of American Ethnic Groups,* Stephan Thernstrom, when he pointed out in 1985 that the "current fashion of asking students 'who they are' and encouraging them to explore their ethnic roots can also be carried too far. Too often, it is assumed that we all are or should be ethnics." Indeed, a romantic, idealized view of the benign qualities of ethnic or national identity affected early multiculturalism. The extent to which it could be a force contributing to guilty, aggressive, or divisive feelings was not examined by multiculturalists in a rigorous, self-critical way. Thernstrom cautioned, "As the example of Lebanon reveals so clearly, ethnic awareness is not necessarily benign and colorful. It can be enormously destructive if cultivated to the point at which a sense of the ties that bind a nation together is lost."[36]

Overlooking these issues educationalists took to new heights the methods for transforming the school into a multicultural vehicle. A scholar at the University of Washington, James A. Banks, led the way. In numerous articles and books, Banks presented an organizational plan to install the strong multicultural agenda for social transformation earlier announced by AACTE in 1973.[37] Multicultural schooling, he found, had a cardinal role in worldwide "ethnic revitalization" movements. Banks advised a "multifactor, holistic paradigm," a "change strategy that reforms the total school environment in order to implement multicultural education successfully." He envisioned a total reconstruction of the school staff, its attitudes and values, institutional norms and values, assessment and testing procedures, curricular and teaching materials, linguistic modes, teaching and motivational styles, and the relative status of cultures. The widespread acceptance of multicultural totalism was shown in an announcement in the American history syllabus for the City of New York for 1990: "In the final analysis, all education should be multicultural education."[38]

The plans for institutionalizing multiculturalism in the 1980s assumed the primacy of ethnic and racial experience in shaping personal development. Frequently this premise was couched in terms of declarations of the inevitability of diversity. The New York State elementary social studies program advised teachers to help students acquire "a growing capacity to accept diversity as inevitable and natural."[39] Multicultural educators urged schools to make students aware of ethnic differences and identities, as a top priority. They contended that students—particularly those who were white—would learn about the diversity of other group experiences and perspectives, thus lessening the formation of prejudice and intolerance. New York State's *Curriculum of Inclusion* announced that, as a result of multicultural education, "children from European cultures would have a less arrogant perspective."[40] Furthermore, the cultivation of ethnic identity in the schools had beneficial effects on learning. The therapeutic character of multicultural schooling would enable students to gain self-esteem that in turn would produce confidence and interest in learning.

Because the goals of multiculturalism had a subjective character, they unavoidably involved inner effects that were hard to deal with rationally or empirically, such as group pride, sensitivity, resentment, and oppressor guilt. The endeavor to increase knowledge of other cultures easily slipped into demands for competence in other cultures and respect for their equality. These basically subjective criteria encouraged education that dwelled on eliciting feelings and sensitivity from both cultural insiders and outsiders rather than the attainment of objective scholastic knowledge.

The notion that schooling should raise self-esteem had roots in the privileging of subjective and psychological states that supplied a sense of group security, a widely noted development in American culture after World War II. The subjective quest for peer-group acceptance and dependency examined by such cultural critics as David Riesman shaped the socialization experiences of the generation growing up in middle-class communities and postprogressive schools in the 1950s and 1960s.[41] Members of the baby boom generation took from their upbringing a view that feeling part of a group was necessary for a positive sense of identity. Although it is difficult to demonstrate precise patterns of cause and effect, those who entered the field of education seem to have taken a deep sensitivity to group-identity issues into their efforts to deal with ethnic diversity in the classroom. To many of them it made personal sense that schooling should properly cultivate group identity and self-esteem. In addition, minority radicals began to criticize assimilationist or integrationist identity as

based on a sense of inferiority. They began to call for psychological liberation from a "colonized" self-image and to urge the strengthening of racial
identity and pride.[42]

The cultural quest for self-esteem had complex and nebulous origins,
but it crystallized easily as a form of simple justice on the political agenda
of minority liberation politics. The necessity for it was regarded as self-
evident. Ethnic leaders advocated the equality of group esteem as a cardinal aspect of empowerment and welfare.[43] So did the major organizations
influencing the teaching of history and social studies in the schools. The
Organization of American Historians issued a "Statement on Multicultural
History Education" announcing that, "because history is tied up with a
people's identity it is legitimate that minority groups, women, and working people celebrate and seek to derive self-esteem from aspects of their
history."[44] The view that schools had a duty to cultivate group-centered
feelings and sensitivities reflected an intensifying subjectivism in race relations. In its most extreme forms, this heightened subjectivity was receptive
to new mythic themes hinging on Manichean moral judgments. The movement assailing the Columbian quincentenary spawned new anti-Western
themes predicated on the moral elevation of American Indians and Africans over Europeans.[45] Asa Hilliard, an educational psychologist, and
Leonard Jeffries, the head of the Afro-American program at City College of
New York, created a mythic source of black cultural and ethical superiority
in their Afrocentric model of ancient Egyptian civilization.[46]

Perhaps the change in the political climate having the most important
influence on the evolution of multicultural education was the rise of official
minority-group identity. Official group identity, to the extent that it has
evolved since the 1960s, represented a movement away from inclusive
citizenship in a unitary political community toward separate subnational
status. Individual opportunity and private rights in the sphere of civil
society were to be replaced by official group rights in a politicized domain
of ethnic identities and relations. The division of the nation into separate
official groups gained ground in various ways. The adoption of preferential policies, variously labeled affirmative action and including bilingual
education, necessitated the formulation of official identities as an entry key
to programs.[47] The census bureau and government agencies began to
count and classify groups to preserve the permanent and separate identity
of Asians, blacks, and Hispanics.[48] The recentering of ethnic identity
around official and political status required reductionist shortcuts where
subgroups and nationalities were oddly homogenized. Such incongruent
combinations included the merging of Koreans and Samoans into an Asian
Pacific bloc and the molding of Hispanics of a variety of racial origins into a
unitary Hispanic bloc. Advocates justified official identity as "people of
color" on the grounds of common victimhood. The creation of official

nonwhite groups implicitly defined an official white group with exaggerated historical unity. The official minority viewpoint tended to overlook the history of racial discrimination against European immigrants.[49] European ethnic groups were homogenized into a white racial bloc with separate and conflicting interests from those of nonwhite minorities. The movement toward official groups sharpened boundaries between all groups, but especially between whites and nonwhites, and reduced their inherent heterogeneity into a category.[50] This racial typology and the official identities it fostered deeply influenced the reconceptualization of ethnicity in multicultural education.

REWEAVING THE ETHNIC STRANDS

In the midst of these developments, history and social studies textbooks in the 1980s stepped up their coverage of ethnic groups. *The American Dream*, by Lew Smith, adumbrated this trend. The 1980 edition consisted of a sketchy chronological presentation of traditional American history joined to a set of readings illustrating the social experiences of different groups. It devoted a large portion of pictures and text to Indians, slaves, and immigrants.[51] The multiauthored textbook, *Civics: Citizens in Action*, supplied discussions of affirmative action and ethnic discrimination; it included many minorities in pictures of Americans engaged in their roles as citizens.[52] The enlargement of group roles and identities often portrayed ethnicity in terms of inclusion and integration, as merely one ingredient in the wider processes of community building and nation building. Margaret Branson's *America's Heritage* gave immigrants and racial minorities coverage to locate the roles they held in common with all groups in the achievements of national history.[53] The innovative Houghton Mifflin social studies series likewise supplied detailed treatment of American Indians, African slaves, and immigrants from worldwide homelands as part of a nationalizing experience.[54] Elementary social studies also reflected an enormous enlargement of the presentation of diversity. Illustrations, photographs, and stories portraying diverse minorities emphasized their involvement in universal roles and activities. The new presence of minorities in texts portrayed the United States as a harmonious multiracial society.[55]

One formula that produced an inclusive framework for group history in the era of multiculturalism was the further extension of the pan-immigrant model. *A More Perfect Union* by David A. Bice announced that "all Americans are immigrants or the descendants of immigrants." Even Native Americans were immigrants. Like the waves of migrants who came afterward, they were drawn by the magnetic forces of "push and pull." They left an unsatisfactory situation for better opportunities in North America. Bice explained, "Finding food was difficult in Asia, so prehistoric people were pulled to North America by following animals who had found better feeding grounds. A long time later these Americans were joined by people on the move from the continent of Europe." Blacks were immigrants, too, according to Bice, but they were forced to emigrate, the "exception to the idea that people move because they are pushed from one place and pulled to another."[56] Lew Smith's *The American Dream* indicated that all Americans were immigrants by a reference to all waves of migrants from English colonization onward as "non-Indian immigrants." According to Smith, the "first non-Indian immigrants to the United States came in groups of a hundred or two at a time in the early 1600s."[57] In the pan-immigrant approach to American ethnic history exemplified by Bice's and Smith's texts, all groups (including Indians and slaves) were united by the common experiences of immigration, settlement, and the joint effort of building communities and the nation's institutions.

The expansion of immigrant identity reflected the search for a new unifying model of national identity. It sought to teach youngsters that they were all Americans because they were united by experiences held in common as immigrants and their descendants. In a sense, this was a pedagogical revisioning of Oscar Handlin's insight that "the immigrants were American history."[58] This theme had been invoked in a more limited way by textbooks in the 1950s, such as the aforementioned *Your People and Mine*, but the social studies-history curriculums of the 1980s and 1990s magnified its articulation through a vast expansion of historical information and symbolic representation of ethnic groups.

Another formula to organize the various ethnic strands of American society flowed out of the repudiation of the melting pot model. The decline of the melting pot prepared the way for recharting the image of American society as a mosaic of separate and discrete ethnic elements. This ethnic model generated tendencies toward proportional group representation in the teaching of history and social studies. The establishment of group representation as a historiographic principle was due indirectly to a pivotal change in historical scholarship that began in the 1960s, emphasis of the need to rewrite history "from the bottom up."[59] This intellectual movement inaugurated a wave of scholarship on the working class, women, and ethnic minorities which powerfully expanded knowledge of the evolutionary dynamics forming American society.[60] In the hands of those interested in pedagogical utilitarianism, the new social history was vulnerable to degeneration into a form of mechanical tokenism. Proportional ethnic representation in texts and curriculums became a kind of historiographic quota or equity principle used to counteract the omission or marginalization of non-European groups as causative agents in traditional historical accounts. As George W. Maxim explained the situation to be corrected in

Social Studies and the Elementary School Child, "Although America has been known as a great *melting pot,* the virtues and achievements of the dominant Anglo-American sector of society were historically revered, while those of the Afro-American, the Native American, the Chicano, and the Oriental were neglected."[61]

Many textbooks by the late 1970s seemed to rest on a hierarchy of textual and visual space quotas. Blacks received the most coverage, Indians were second, European immigrants followed, and Asians and Hispanics received the slimmest treatments. Ethnic studies by proportional representation had built-in intellectual limitations. It substituted for a probing analysis of ethnicity a mechanical and token listing of group role models and homogenized group profiles that usually stressed victimization. Moreover, this approach to maintaining different ethnic presences in history obscured the dynamic relations of groups to each other and to larger historical patterns.[62]

Perhaps the greatest problem with proportional representation, however, was its potential to encourage the treatment of history as a group possession. Entitlement to a place in history led to demands for historical equity, which groups began to see as a right, as something they should control. Insiders had a special claim to authority about group history, and they competed against outsiders to construct and transmit it in their own way. American history underwent parceling according to ethnicity, and race turned into a battleground on which groups defined and asserted for political purposes their own visions of group history. Advocates of multiculturalism used the revision of the history-social studies framework for New York State in 1989 as a drive to empower minority cultures.[63] In California, advocates of a history defined and controlled by internal group perspective protested the state's adoption of the Houghton Mifflin history-social studies textbooks that dealt saliently with ethnic groups but in the framework of a nationalizing and inclusive experience.[64]

The cultivation of multicultural identities possessed a functionalism within the developed forms of group-identity politics, although teachers of multiculturalism often treated diversity as an aspect of individual student identity and neglected a systematic theory of pluralism in which it would play a vital role.[65] Strong multicultural education complemented social policies and political agendas predicated on group identity, such as preferential policies labeled affirmative action. Since preferential policies organized access to opportunity and status according to group identities and representations, to the extent that multicultural education cultivated them it helped reconfigure power along pluralistic lines. Multicultural education possessed the potential to form the building blocks of identity necessary to enrolling future generations as members of official groups. This outcome can be described as the pluralistic functionalism of multicultural education. Multiculturalism seems to have already assumed this role in schools in various localities. In many communities, the teaching of group identities and cultures is under way or being installed.[66] The New York State Social Studies Program in 1988 advised teachers to "stress ethnic customs and traditions that are learned and passed down from generation to generation."[67] The history course of study for the New York City public schools in 1990 instructed, "Multicultural education first requires that students build an awareness of their own cultural heritage."[68] In the most extreme applications of multiculturalism, pluralistic functionalism spilled over into a separatist functionalism that nurtured exclusive group cultures.[69]

THE CONTESTED TERRAIN OF DIVERSITY

Some of the problematic qualities of strong multicultural education can be probed by a set of comparisons with the Americanization movement and progressive education. Strong multiculturalists and Anglo-Saxon Americanizers shared a belief in the existence of reductionist collective identities. While the latter urged adherence to a superior Anglo-Saxon cultural ideal, the former endeavored to formularize and celebrate ethnic identities. In other words, strong multiculturalists, like conservative Americanizers, endorsed a filiopietistic view of group identity. As a consequence, both sought to enhance self-approving and uncritical orientations in education. For example, the former urged sensitivity and self-esteem and the latter patriotism and Americanism. In another area of comparison, strong multiculturalists resembled progressive educators in subordinating intellectualism to presentism, making learning subserve the concern with current social problems.[70] They also resembled progressives in anticipating that the implementation of their programs would produce a reconstructed society harmonizing all factors, which the historian Richard Hofstadter criticized as the utopian fallacy of progressive schooling.[71] Whereas progressive educators endeavored to achieve a harmonized society by expanding citizenship, multiculturalists aimed at social transformation through intensification of group identity. However, in contrast to the centered transformation produced by national identification under Americanization and civic identification under progressivism, strong multiculturalism encouraged a decentered transformation through subnational identification.

Many scholars were troubled by these qualities of multicultural education. Critics early on found the ethnocultural quest for self-esteem unattainable or unproductive of better learning. In a *Saturday Review* article in 1968, Larry Cuban asserted that whether the installation of ethnic content "will raise self-esteem or invest youngsters with dignity is debatable."[72]

Albert Shanker, head of the American Federation of Teachers, doubted that schooling in group pride and perspectives would enhance learning and worried about its divisive effects.[73]

The most trenchant examinations of multicultural education came from scholars concerned with its influence on the cohesion of a multiethnic and multiracial nation. Many of these thinkers found it useful for students to study the various ethnic strands in American history. Some could accept a weak multiculturalism based on a nationalizing and inclusive vision to improve a student's knowledge of the complex character of American society. The educational historian Diane Ravitch in 1990 endorsed this form as "pluralistic multiculturalism."[74] These scholars worried about strong multiculturalism—what Ravitch called "particularistic multi-culturalism"—because of its emphasis on ethnic differences, separatism, relativism, and subjective elements like self-esteem and filiopietism. They were troubled by how easily multiculturalists crossed into the area of inventing cultures and identities, how willingly they substituted a nebulous relativism (the New York State "Curriculum of Inclusion" assumed that all cultures were arranged in "a round table") for unifying and ordered relations. They saw a danger that schools would further the division of society into separate cultures, producing the loss of community and heightening ethnic conflict. Frances FitzGerald worried that the message of multicultural texts would be that "Americans have no common history, no common culture, and no common values, and that membership in a racial or cultural group constitutes the most fundamental experience of each individual."[75] Hazel Hertzberg likewise was concerned in 1981 that the installation of "the New History" of social groups undermined the coherent understanding of national history.[76] Arthur M. Schlesinger, Jr., criticized in 1991 the multicultural social studies framework of New York State as a step toward the "decomposition" of the nation through the cultivation of separate group identities.[77]

Perhaps the most far-seeing criticisms came from two Harvard scholars who worried about the way multicultural schooling could artificially harden and rigidify a historical matrix of fluid ethnic relations. While approving the New York framework, the sociologist Nathan Glazer gravely warned that "we fall into the danger, by presenting a conception of separate and different groups fixed through time as distinct elements, in our society, of making our future one which conforms to our teaching, of arresting the processes of change and adaptation that have created a common society, a single nation."[78] The historian Stephan Thernstrom saw schooling in group identities as analogous to schooling in religious identities, a problematic and controversial operation in a culturally diverse nation. Adopting an international perspective, Thernstrom suggested that to let schools privilege ethnic identities was incongruent with the historical weakness of ethnic boundaries in America and would superimpose sharp and hard group boundaries more characteristic of Lebanon or Yugoslavia.[79]

Recent events indicated that even some of the earliest proponents of multicultural education have begun to criticize their own policies somewhat along the lines laid out by its various critics. In California, in the wake of numerous racial clashes in public schools and the Los Angeles riot, educators and scholars felt the need to call for a reappraisal of multicultural education. They acknowledged the evidence that multicultural schooling intensified ethnic divisions by stressing group pride and exclusive identities. Various students exposed to the prevailing multicultural curriculum described these effects. Educators felt reluctant to abandon multiculturalism but considered how it could be revised to emphasize more inclusion and cross-group experiences. Their remarks indicated a new interest in finding ingredients for a broader form of taught identity.[80]

Nevertheless, on the eve of the twenty-first century, schools have come to treat the cultivation of ethnic diversity as equivalent in importance to the guided development of national identity. This situation reflects a historical trend in the wider society toward the deconstruction of nationhood and national identity and the recentering of ethnic and cultural identities around official group categories. The new diversity education has helped to lead the country toward state pluralism—a kind of mosaic or rainbow state—whose outlines have been emerging since the 1970s. The view that essential group differences should be recognized and enhanced by the state has underlaid the installation of multicultural curriculums. It has shifted the emphasis in schools from building a common education for national citizenship to the creation of diverse cultures and identities.

The educational officialization of group identity may bring more group recognition and a stronger sense of ethnicity, but at the possible cost of eroding, at the foundation of liberal democracy, the freedom of individuals to define their identities irrespective of inherited factors or homogeneous group identities superimposed upon them. A multicultural education that creates separate and fixed identities rather than showing the intermixing and overlapping areas among groups can encourage students to develop a deterministic, stereotypical, and exclusionary way of seeing themselves.

A growing state pluralism will probably affect the role of schooling in the future integration of the children of immigrants in the American nation. The students in our classrooms will be encouraged to see themselves according to official identity categories not as individual citizens whose ancestry is adventitious, but as Latinos, Asians, and Africans. If this pattern expands, assimilation will no longer work as in the past, when it was a force for a more open society. Ethnic boundaries could close and the United States could become a more divided society prone to xenophobia.

To avoid this path, educators should recognize that the world melting-pot culture emerging in the United States is rapidly blurring cultural boundaries. The educational mechanisms of modernization inventing state ethnicity are at odds with the deeply rooted universalizing and globalizing forces at work in the nation. Those who would homogenize and separate culture into an ethno-centered possession should ponder the thoughts of the Harvard sociologist, Orlando Patterson. "Once an element of culture becomes generalized under the impact of a universal culture," Patterson pointed out, "it loses all specific symbolic value for the group which donated it. It is a foolish Anglo-Saxon who boasts about 'his' language today. English is a child that no longer knows its mother, and cares even less to know her. It has been adapted in a thousand ways to meet the special feelings, moods and experiences of a thousand groups." Patterson therefore announced that "ethnic WASP culture is no longer the culture of the group of Americans we now call WASP's." Jim Sleeper, who cited these insights by Patterson in his book on liberalism, *The Closest of Strangers*, recalled how, when he was a teacher in a New York high school, "the Chinese-American students in my class were [not] interested in adopting 'white' culture as much as they were interested in becoming part of the larger 'universal' culture of constitutional democracy and technological development."[81]

Whether democratic universalism can survive the hardening of ethnic identities in an age of expanding pluralism is already a vital question. In the 1990s, xenophobia, nativism, and isolationism resurged; group-identity politics continued to produce conflict and division. The new educational efforts to construct national identity and diversity will defuse these tendencies only insofar as schools focus on showing students *how* to think about ethnicity rather than *what* to think about it. It is useful for students to know about the ethnic strands, but they must know that a higher understanding can come only from exploring how they were woven into the fabric of a much greater and democratic whole.[82]

NOTES

1. Charles E. Merriam, *The Making of Citizens* (Chicago: University of Chicago Press, 1931), 211.

2. Bessie Louise Pierce, *Civic Attitudes in American School Textbooks* (Chicago: University of Chicago Press, 1930), chap. 12; Charles E. Merriam, *Civic Education in the United States* (New York: Charles Scribner's Sons, 1934), x–xi.

3. Frank V. Thompson, *Schooling of the Immigrant* (New York: Harper & Brothers, 1920), 15–17.

4. William S. Bernard, ed., *American Immigration Policy* (New York: Harper & Brothers, 1950), chap. 10.

5. Jane Addams, *Twenty Years at Hull House* (New York: New American Library, [1910] 1961), chaps. 11–12, 14–16.

6. Nicholas V. Montalto, *A History of the Intercultural Educational Movement, 1924–1941* (New York: Garland Publishing, 1982).

7. Frances FitzGerald, *America Revised: History Schoolbooks in the Twentieth Century* (Boston: Little, Brown & Co., 1979), 55–56; Alexander Alland, *American Counterpoint* (New York: John Day Co., 1943).

8. Hilda Taba and William Van Tils, eds., *Democratic Human Relations: Promising Practices in Intergroup and Intercultural Education in the United States* (Washington, D.C.: National Council for the Social Studies, 1945), 346–47, cited in Hazel Hertzberg, *Social Studies Reform: 1880–1980* (Boulder, Colo.: Social Science Education Consortium, 1981), 75.

9. Richard Polenberg, *One Nation Divisible: Class, Race, and Ethnicity in the United States since 1938* (New York: Penguin Books, 1980), chap. 2.

10. Morroe Berger, *Equality by Statute: Legal Controls over Group Discrimination* (New York: Columbia University Press, 1952); Leon H. Mayhew, *Law and Equal Opportunity* (Cambridge: Harvard University Press, 1968).

11. T. W. Adorno, Else Frenkel-Brunswick, D. J. Levison, and R. N. Sanford, *The Authoritarian Personality* (New York: Harper & Brothers, 1950); Abram Kardiner and Lionel Ovesey, *The Mark of Oppression: A Psychosocial Study of the American Negro* (New York: Harper & Brothers, 1951); N. W. Ackerman and Marie Jahoda, *Anti-Semitism and Emotional Disorder* (New York: Harper & Brothers, 1950); Gordon W. Allport, *The Nature of Prejudice* (Cambridge: Harvard University Press, 1954).

12. Josephine McKenzie (with Ernest W. Tiegs and Fay Adams), *Your People and Mine* (Boston: Ginn & Co., 1949), 6–7.

13. Oscar Handlin, *The Uprooted* (Boston: Little, Brown, & Co., 1951); idem, *The American People in the Twentieth Century* (Cambridge: Harvard University Press, 1954); idem, *The Newcomers: Negroes and Puerto Ricans in a Changing Metropolis* (Cambridge: Harvard University Press, 1959); idem, *A Pictorial History of American Immigration* (New York: Crown Publishers, 1972).

14. Nathan Glazer and Daniel P. Moynihan, *Beyond the Melting Pot: The Negroes, Puerto Ricans, Jews, Italians, and Irish of New York City* (Cambridge: MIT Press, 1963).

15. Oscar Handlin, "Historical Perspectives on the American Ethnic Group," *Daedalus* (Spring 1961), 220–32; idem, *Out of Many: A Study Guide to Cultural Pluralism in the United States* (New York: Anti-Defamation League of B'nai B'rith, 1964), chaps. 3, 4.

16. FitzGerald, *America Revised*, 80–81.

17. Ibid., 43.

18. Mabel B. Casner and Ralph H. Gabriel, *The Story of American Democracy* (New York: Harcourt, Brace & Co., 1949); Ralph Volney Harlow and Ruth Elizabeth Miller, *Story of America*, rev. ed. (New York: Henry Holt, 1953); Henry W. Bragdon and Samuel McCutcheon, *History of a Free People* (New York: Macmillan Co., 1954); Glenn W. Moon, Don C. Cline, and John H. MacGowan, *Story of Our Land and People* (New York: Henry Holt, 1955); Gertrude Hartman, *America: Land of Freedom*, 2d ed. (Boston: D.C. Heath & Co., 1957); Fremont P. Wirth, *United States History*, rev. ed. (New York: American Book Co., 1957).

19. Vincent R. Rogers and Raymond H. Muessig, "Needed: A Revolution in the Textbook Industry," *Social Studies* 54 (October 1963), 169.

20. Morris Janowitz, *The Reconstruction of Patriotism: Education for Civic Consciousness* (Chicago: University of Chicago Press, 1983), 106–12.

21. Stanley Coben, "The Failure of the Melting Pot" in *The Great Fear: Race in the Mind of America*, ed. Gary B. Nash and Richard Weiss (New York: Holt, Rinehart & Winston, 1970), 144–64.

22. Diane Ravitch, *The Schools We Deserve: Reflections on the Educational Crisis of Our Times* (New York: Basic Books, 1985), 219–20.

23. Arthur Mann, *The One and the Many: Reflections on the American Identity* (Chicago: University of Chicago Press, 1979), 37–38.

24. Robert Blauner, *Racial Oppression in America* (New York: Harper & Row, 1972); Nathan Glazer, *Ethnic Dilemmas, 1964–1982* (Cambridge: Harvard University Press, 1983), 79–93.

25. Herbert G. Gutman, "Work, Culture, and Society in Industrializing America, 1815–1919," *American Historical Review* 78 (1973): 531–88; Virginia Yans-McLaughlin, *Family and Community: Italian Immigrants in Buffalo, 1880–1930* (Ithaca: Cornell University Press, 1977).

26. William W. Joyce, "Minority Groups in American Society: Imperatives for Educators and Publishers" in *Readings in Elementary Social Studies: Emerging Changes*, 2d ed., ed. Jonathan C. McLendon, William W. Joyce, and John R. Lee (Boston: Allyn & Bacon, 1970), 289–90.

27. AACTE Commission on Multicultural Education, "No One Model American: A Statement on Multicultural Education," *Journal of Teacher Education* 24 (Winter 1973), 264–65.

28. "Symposium on Multicultural Education," *Journal of Teacher Education* 24 (Winter 1973). The symposium included these articles: Normand R. Bernier and Richard H. Davis, "Synergy: A Model for Implementing Multicultural Education"; Charles F. Leyba, "Cultural Identity: Problems and Dilemmas"; Thomas R. Lopez, Jr., "Cultural Pluralism: Political Hoax? Educational Need?"; Carl J. Dolce, "Multicultural Education—Some Issues"; Hilda Hidalgo, "No One Model American: A Collegiate Case in Point"; Gwendolyn C. Baker, "Multicultural Training for Student Teachers."

29. Nathan Glazer and Reed Ueda, *Ethnicity in History Textbooks* (Washington, D.C.: Ethics & Public Policy Center), 4–5, 41–42.

30. Marcel Lewinski, *American Government Today* (Glenview, Ill.: Scott, Foresman & Co., 1980); John Patrick and Richard Remy, *Civics for Americans* (Glenview, Ill.: Scott, Foresman & Co., 1980).

31. California State Board of Education, *History-Social Science Framework: For California Public Schools Kindergarten through Grade Twelve* (Sacramento: California Department of Education, 1988).

32. New York State Social Studies Review and Development Committee, *One Nation, Many Peoples: A Declaration of Cultural Interdependence* (Albany: New York State Board of Education, 1991).

33. Lauren S. Young, "Multicultural Education: A Myth into Reality," 127; Harry N. Rivlin, "General Perspectives on Multiculturalism," 121–22; Rupert A. Trujillo, "Multiculturalism," *Journal of Teacher Education* 26 (Summer 1975): 125–26;

William J. Stewart, "Infusing Multiculturalism in the Curriculum through Broad Themes," *Education* 98 (March–April 1978): 334–36; "Multicultural Education," special issue, *Journal of Teacher Education* 28 (May–June 1977).

34. John U. Michaelis, *Social Studies for Children: A Guide to Basic Instruction*, 7th ed. (Englewood Cliffs, N.J.: Prentice-Hall, 1980), 205.

35. Ibid., 199–205.

36. Stephan Thernstrom, "The Humanities and Our Cultural Heritage" in Chester E. Finn, Jr., Diane Ravitch, and Holley Roberts, *Challenge to the Humanities* (New York: Holmes & Meier, 1985), 77.

37. See especially James A. Banks, "Multicultural Education: Development, Paradigms and Goals" in *Multicultural Education in Western Societies*, ed. James A. Banks and James Lynch (New York: Praeger, 1986). Also see by Banks, "Cultural Pluralism and the Schools," *Educational Leadership* 32 (December 1974): 163–66; "Ethnic Studies as a Process of Curriculum Reform," *Social Education* 40 (February 1976): 76–80; *Multiethnic Education: Practices and Promises* (Bloomington, Ind.: Phi Delta Kappa Educational Foundation, 1977); (with Ambrose A. Clegg, Jr.) *Teaching Strategies for the Social Studies: Inquiry, Valuing, and Decision-Making* (Reading, Mass.: Addison-Wesley Publishing Co., 1977); *Teaching Strategies for Ethnic Studies*, 2d ed. (Boston: Allyn & Bacon, 1979); (with Cherry McGee Banks) *Multicultural Education: Issues and Perspectives* (Boston: Allyn & Bacon, 1989).

38. New York City Public Schools, *United States and New York State History: A Multicultural Perspective*, grade 7, vol. 1 (New York: New York City Board of Education, 1990), vii.

39. New York State Education Department, *Social Studies Program*, Kindergarten, updated ed. (Albany: Bureau of Curriculum Development, 1988), 9.

40. New York State Commissioner of Education, *A Curriculum of Inclusion* (Albany: New York State Education Department, 1989), iv.

41. William H. Whyte, Jr., *The Organization Man* (New York: Simon & Schuster, 1956), pt. 7; David Riesman, with Nathan Glazer and Reuel Denney, *The Lonely Crowd: A Study of the Changing American Character* (New Haven: Yale University Press, 1950), chap. 3; Christopher Lasch, *The Culture of Narcissism: American Life in an Age of Diminishing Expectations* (New York: W. W. Norton & Co., 1979), 122–27, 379–91.

42. Malcolm X, *The Autobiography of Malcolm X* (New York: Grove Press, 1965); Stokely Carmichael and Charles V. Hamilton, *Black Power: The Politics of Liberation in America* (New York: Vintage Books, 1967), chap. 2.

43. See, for its historical emergence, J. R. Pole, *The Pursuit of Equality in American History* (Berkeley and Los Angeles: University of California Press, 1978), 335–46.

44. *Organization of American Historians Magazine of History* 6 (Summer 1991): 61.

45. C. Vann Woodward, "The Fall of the American Adam: Myths of Innocence and Guilt," *Social Studies Review* (Fall 1992): 9–11.

46. Arthur M. Schlesinger, Jr., *The Disuniting of America: Reflections on a Multicultural Society* (Whittle Direct Books, Whittle Communications L. P., 1991): 35–36; Eric Pooley, "Dr. J," *New York Magazine* (2 September 1991): 32–37.

47. The most probing examinations of preferential policies can be found in Nathan Glazer, *Affirmative Discrimination: Ethnic Inequality and Public Policy* (New

York: Basic Books, 1976); Abigail Thernstrom, *Whose Votes Count? Affirmative Action and Minority Voting Rights* (Cambridge: Harvard University Press, 1987); Terry Eastland and William J. Bennett, *Counting by Race: Equality and the Founding Fathers to Bakke and Weber* (New York: Basic Books, 1979); Linda Chavez, *Out of the Barrio: Toward a New Politics of Hispanic Assimilation* (New York: Basic Books, 1991); Thomas Sowell, *Preferential Policies: An International Perspective* (New York: William Morrow & Co., 1990).

48. Stephan Thernstrom, "American Ethnic Statistics" in *Immigrants in Two Democracies: French and American Experience,* ed. Donald Horowitz and Gerard Noiriel (New York: New York University Press, 1992), 80–111.

49. The pioneering studies of the role of racial attitudes toward European immigrants are John Higham, *Strangers in the Land: Patterns of American Nativism, 1860–1925* (New Brunswick, N.J.: Rutgers University Press, 1955); Barbara Solomon, *Ancestors and Immigrants: A Changing American Tradition* (Cambridge: Harvard University Press, 1956). Well-known attacks on the "inferior" racial subgroups among European immigrants can be found in Madison Grant, *The Passing of the Great Race: Or the Racial Basis of European History* (New York: Charles Scribner's Sons, 1918); Lothrop Stoddard, *The Revolt against Civilization: The Menace of the Under Men* (New York: Charles Scribner's Sons, 1923).

50. Ravitch, *The Schools We Deserve,* 259.

51. Lew Smith, *The American Dream* (Glenview, Ill.: Scott, Foresman & Co., 1980).

52. Mary Jane Turner, Cathryn J. Long, John S. Bowes, and Elizabeth J. Lott, *Civics: Citizens in Action* (Columbus: Charles E. Merrill Publishing Co., 1986).

53. Margaret Branson, *America's Heritage* (Lexington, Mass.: Ginn & Co., 1982).

54. The series included Beverly J. Armento, Gary B. Nash, and Christopher L. Salter, *A More Perfect Union* (Boston: Houghton Mifflin, 1991); idem, *America Will Be* (Boston: Houghton Mifflin, 1991). See David L. Kirp, "Textbooks and Tribalism in California," *Public Interest* (Summer 1991): 20–36.

55. Dorothy J. Skeel, *Others* (New York: American Book Co., 1979); John Jarolimek, Elizabeth H. Rowell, and Thomas B. Goodkind, *People and Neighborhoods* (New York: Macmillan Co., 1987); idem, *Families and Friends* (New York: Macmillan Co., 1987); Barbara Radner Reque, *Homes and Neighborhoods* (Lexington, Mass.: D.C. Heath & Co., 1987).

56. David A. Bice, *A More Perfect Union: United States History and Geography to 1850* (Marceline, Mo.: Wadsworth Publishing Co., 1991), 464–67.

57. Smith, *The American Dream.*

58. Handlin, *The Uprooted,* 3.

59. Barton J. Bernstein, *Towards a New Past: Dissenting Essays in American History* (New York: Alfred A. Knopf, 1967), xi–xii.

60. David H. Fischer, "Introduction" in *Albion's Seed: Four British Folkways in America* (New York: Oxford University Press, 1989), vii–xi.

61. George W. Maxim, *Social Studies and the Elementary School Child* (Columbus: Charles E. Merrill Publishing Co., 1983), 402.

62. Glazer and Ueda, *Ethnic Groups in History Textbooks,* chap. 2; Robert Lerner, Althea K. Nagai, and Stanley Rothman, "History by Quota?" *Academic Questions* 5 (Fall 1992): 69–83.

63. New York State Commissioner of Education's Task Force on Minorities: Equity and Excellence, "A Curriculum of Inclusion," July 1989; Diane Ravitch, "Multiculturalism: E Pluribus Plures," *American Scholar* 59 (1990): 337–54; Schlesinger, *The Disuniting of America*, 33–36.

64. Armento, Nash, and Salter, *A More Perfect Union* and *America Will Be*.

65. Michael R. Olneck, "The Recurring Dream: Symbolism and Ideology in Intercultural and Multicultural Education," *American Journal of Education* 98 (February 1990): 147–74.

66. Ravitch, "Multiculturalism," 342; Nathan Glazer, "In Defense of Multiculturalism," *New Republic* (2 September 1991): 18–22. Also see Michael R. Olneck, "Terms of Inclusion: Has Multiculturalism Redefined Equality in American Education?" (unpublished paper), which refers to the teaching of group identities reported in an unpublished study by Richard M. Merelman, "Black History and Cultural Empowerment: A Case Study," University of Wisconsin-Madison, 1992.

67. New York State Education Department, *Social Studies Program*, grade 1, updated ed. (Albany: Bureau of Curriculum Development, 1988), 46.

68. New York City Public Schools, *United States and New York State History: A Multicultural Perspective*, grade 7, vol. 1 (New York: New York City Board of Education, 1990), vii.

69. Kirp, "Textbooks and Tribalism," 30–31.

70. Hazel Hertzberg, "History and Progressivism: A Century of Reform Proposals" in *Historical Literacy: The Case for History in American Education*, ed. Paul Gagnon (Boston: Houghton Mifflin, 1989), 96.

71. Richard Hofstadter, *Anti-intellectualism in American Life* (New York: Alfred A. Knopf, 1962), 388.

72. Larry Cuban, "Black History, Negro History, and White Folk," *Saturday Review* (21 September 1968): 64–65.

73. See among Albert Shanker's regular editorials in 1991 called "Where We Stand": "The Danger in Multiple Perspectives"; "Sacrificing Accuracy for Diversity"; "Courting Ethnic Strife"; "Don't Stop Teaching the Common Heritage." These are published in *The New Republic* (1991).

74. Ravitch, "Multiculturalism," 340.

75. FitzGerald, *America Revised*, 104.

76. Hertzberg, *Social Studies Reform*, 145–46.

77. Schlesinger, *The Disuniting of America*, chap. 4.

78. Nathan Glazer, "Additional Comments" in New York State Social Studies Committee, *One Nation, Many Peoples*, 35–36.

79. Stephan Thernstrom, "The Humanities and Our Cultural Heritage" in Finn, Ravitch, and Roberts, *Challenge to the Humanities*, 77.

80. Sharon Bernstein, "Multiculturalism: Building Bridges or Burning Them?" *Los Angeles Times*, 30 November 1992, A1.

81. Jim Sleeper, *The Closest of Strangers: Liberalism and the Politics of Race in New York* (New York: W. W. Norton & Co., 1990), 232–34.

82. Gary B. Nash, "History for a Democratic Society: The Work of All People" in Gagnon, *Historical Literacy*; Harry S. Broudy, "Cultural Pluralism," *Educational Leadership* 33 (December 1975): 173–75.

6   AMERICAN HISTORY RECONSIDERED: ASKING NEW QUESTIONS ABOUT THE PAST

GARY B. NASH

"The civil rights battles of the '50s and '60s were fought in the courtroom," wrote David Nicholson of the *Washington Post*, "but in the '90s the struggle for cultural parity will take place in the classroom as blacks and other minorities seek to change what their children are taught."[1] The swirling multicultural debate around the country during the past few years is proving Nicholson correct. But the debate has gone far beyond the subject of what is taught and has led to some remarkable—and sometimes troubling—notions of what we are as a people and a society.

Often lost in the present furor is even an elementary sense of how far the writing and teaching of history has moved away from the male-oriented, Eurocentric, and elitist approaches that had dominated for so long at all levels of the American educational system. New calls for change often ignore what has already occurred in the rethinking and rewriting of history and, in so doing, sometimes prescribe new formulas that contain hidden dangers.

RETHINKING THE PAST

Among academic historians, agreement is widespread today that history has been presented—whether in school textbooks, college courses, museum exhibits, or mass media—in a narrow and deeply distorted way, not just in the United States but in every country. In the 1930s, when he was writing *Black Reconstruction*, W. E. B. Du Bois wrote: "I stand at the end of this writing, literally aghast at what American historians have done to this field . . . [It is] one of the most stupendous efforts the world ever saw to discredit human beings, an effort involving universities, history, science, social life, and religion."[2] Few white historians would have agreed with Du Bois at the time, for in fact he was attacking their work. But a half century later, the white president of the Organization of American Historians,

Leon Litwack, agreed with this assessment. In his presidential address in 1987, Litwack charged that "no group of scholars was more deeply implicated in the miseducation of American youth and did more to shape the thinking of generations of Americans about race and blacks than historians."[3]

Such charges of miseducation can be readily confirmed by looking at a few of the most widely used textbooks in American history. David Muzzey's various American history textbooks for the schools, probably the most widely used throughout the nation from the 1930s through the 1950s, made African Americans completely invisible. As Frances FitzGerald wryly commented, slaves "appeared magically in this country at some unspecified time and had disappeared with the end of the Civil War."[4] Slavery was a political problem for white men to worry about, but slaves and free blacks were neither a social group with their own history of struggle and survival nor an economic and cultural force that helped shape American society.

Though most textbooks followed Muzzey in making slaves and free blacks disappear, a few college textbooks, beginning in the 1930s, introduced Africans in North America as a distinct people with their own history. But, through a fortuitous combination of European and African cultural characteristics, the slaves turned out to be centered workers. European masters, coming from enlightened cultural stock, were generally considerate of their slaves; Africans, coming from a retrograde cultural stock, were pleased to trade barbaric Africa for the civilized European colonies in the Americas. Oliver Chitwood, publishing his college textbook on American history in 1931 and leaving it virtually unchanged through the 1960s, informed students that,

> generally, when the master and slave were brought into close association, a mutual feeling of kindliness and affection sprang up between them, which restrained the former from undue harshness toward the latter . . . We find that there were always some brutal masters who treated their black servants inhumanely, but they were doubtless few in number . . . Good feeling between master and slave was promoted in large measure by the happy disposition or docile temperament of the Negro. Seldom was he surly and discontented and rarely did he harbor a grudge against his master for depriving him of his liberty. On the contrary, he went about his daily tasks cheerfully, often singing while at work . . . The fact that he had never known the ease and comforts of civilization in his homeland made it less difficult for him to submit to the hardships and inferior position of his condition. In this respect, the American Negro was better off than the slave of ancient Rome,

who was often the intellectual equal and sometimes the superior of his master.[5]

Chitwood's message for college undergraduates took some time to percolate down to the precollegiate textbooks, but at least as early as 1947 it had appeared in *My Country*, a fifth grade textbook published by the state of California. For years thereafter, thousands of children learned about slavery and slave life from these passages:

> The Negroes were brought from Africa and sold to the people of our country in early times. After a while there came to be thousands and thousands of these Negro slaves. Most of them were found in the southern states. On the southern plantations, where tobacco and cotton and rice were grown, they worked away quite cheerfully. In time many people came to think that it was wrong to own slaves. Some of them said that all the Negro slaves should be freed. Some of the people who owned slaves became angry at this. They said that the black people were better off as slaves in America than they would have been as wild savages in Africa. Perhaps this was true, as many of the slaves had snug cabins to live in, plenty to eat, and work that was not too hard for them to do. Most of the slaves seemed happy and contented.

As for slave children, life was a bowl of cherries:

> Perhaps the most fun the little [white] masters and mistresses have comes when they are free to play with the little colored boys and girls. Back of the big house stand rows of small cabins. In these cabins live the families of Negro slaves. The older colored people work on the great farm or help about the plantation home. The small black boys and girls play about the small houses. They are pleased to have the white children come to play with them.[6]

The narrow and clouded lenses through which historians looked for years—which in the main reflected the dominant biases of white, Protestant America—extended far beyond the history of black Americans. Du Bois would surely have been equally dismayed if he had read one of the most widely used books in Western Civilization courses in the 1960s, where the much-honored British historian, Hugh Trevor-Roper, magisterially proclaimed that it was useless to study African history (or presumably the history of several other parts of the world outside Europe) because this would only be to inquire into "the unrewarding gyrations of barbarous tribes whose chief function in history . . . is to show to the present an image of the past from which, by history, it has escaped."[7]

Similar mental constructions prevailed in regard to Native American history. In 1958, introducing Douglas Leach's history of King Philip's War in 1676, the bloodiest Indian war of the seventeenth century in North America, Samuel Eliot Morison instructed readers about the parallels between seventeenth-century European-Indian relations and the decolonization movements in the Third World after World War II: "In view of our recent experiences of warfare, and of the many instances today of backward peoples getting enlarged notions of nationalism and turning ferociously on Europeans who have attempted to civilize them, this early conflict of the same nature cannot help but be of interest."[8]

Embedded in the controlling idea that European–Native American relations revolved around the confrontation of savagery and civilization lay the idea that conflict between higher and lower cultures was inevitable and that the outcome was foreordained. Muzzey's books, the historical primers for millions of American children for two generations, asserted that "it was impossible that these few hundred thousand natives should stop the spread of the Europeans over the country. That would have been to condemn one of the fairest lands of the earth to the stagnation of barbarism."[9] Dozens of other books followed the same basic formula that neatly placed the responsibility for what happened in history upon impersonal or superpersonal forces, eliminating the notion of individual or group responsibility because what happened, and the way it happened, was presented as the result of forces that mere man could not alter. As Isaiah Berlin told us, historical explanations that stress inevitability are the victor's way of disclaiming responsibility for even the most heinous chapters of history. Once inevitability has been invoked, "our sense of guilt and of sin, our pangs of remorse and self-condemnation, are automatically dissolved . . . The growth of knowledge brings with it relief from moral burdens, for if powers beyond and above us are at work, it is wild presumption to claim responsibility for their activity or blame ourselves for failing in it . . . Acts hitherto regarded as wicked or unjustifiable are seen in a more 'objective' fashion—in the larger context—as part of the process of history."[10]

The paradigmatic shift in the writing of history is far from complete, but some of those who currently protest about Eurocentric or racist history take little account of how resolutely the present generation of historians—scholars and teachers alike—have come to grips with older conceptualizations of history. Academic historians, most of them detached from what is going on in the primary and secondary schools of the country unless they have school age children enrolled in public schools, are often puzzled by the furor over the question of "whose history shall we teach" because they have watched—and participated in—wholesale changes in their own discipline during the last thirty years or so. African and African-American history, women's history, and labor history are taught in most colleges and universities; Asian-American, Hispanic-American, and Native-American history are taught in many. These courses are built on an outpouring of scholarship in this generation.

African-American history can be taken as an instructive example. Even fifteen years ago, John Hope Franklin, author of the leading textbook in African-American history, wrote of "a most profound and salutary change in the approach to the history of human relations in the United States." He noted that in the process of this change "the new Negro history has come into its own."[11] Since 1977, this blossoming of black history has continued unabated. In compiling a bibliography of African-American history about just the period from 1765 to 1830 for the forthcoming *Harvard Guide to Afro-American History*, I tracked down over two hundred books and more than twelve hundred articles published since 1965. The proliferation of scholarship for the period after 1830 is even greater. When the *Harvard Guide* is completed, it will list thousands of books, articles, and doctoral dissertations on African-American history and race relations—an enormous outpouring of scholarship that has wrought fundamental changes in the basic contours and emphases of American history.

In women's history, the amount and range of scholarship—and sophisticated courses built upon it—is equally impressive. The biannual Berkshire Conference of Women's Historians is a flourishing enterprise that draws hundreds of historians together and serves as a showplace of exciting new scholarship. In African-American and women's history, younger scholars are building on the work of a few old hands to create the knowledge for a thorough understanding of the history, literature, art, music, and values of Hispanic Americans, Native Americans, Asian Americans, and other groups. It is a measure of how the historical profession has changed that so many of the book prizes awarded by the Organization of American Historians in recent years have gone to books about the struggles of racial groups and women in the making of American society.

In the current atmosphere of heated debate, it is worth some reflection on why and how such wholesale change has occurred in the writing of history. Four developments have intersected to cause a major transformation. First—and largely forgotten in the current debates—is the change in the recruitment of professional historians, the people who do historical scholarship, teach at the collegiate level, and, ultimately, are responsible for the textbooks used in the schools. Before World War II, professional historians were overwhelmingly drawn from the ranks of white, male, Protestant, and upper-class American society. From the perspective of this first professional cadre of historians, it was entirely fitting that they should be the keepers of the past because they believed that only those of the highest intellect, the most polished manners, and the most developed aesthetic taste could stand above the ruck and look dispassionately at the annals of human behavior. Such a view conformed precisely to the centuries-old view of the elite that ordinary people were ruled by emotion and only the wealthy and educated could transcend this state and achieve disinterested rationality. Pitted against this thoroughly dominant group since the early nineteenth century was a small number of women, African Americans, and white radicals who worked without much recognition as they tried to create alternative histories.

Small cracks in the fortress of the historical profession began to appear in the 1930s as Jews struggled for a place in the profession. Peter Novick's book on the historical profession, *That Noble Dream: The "Objectivity Question" and the American Historical Profession*, gives a vivid picture of the way the profession grudgingly yielded to Jewish aspirations. When applying for his first teaching job, Richard Leopold—who would emerge as a major historian of diplomacy—was described by a graduate mentor at Harvard as "of course a Jew, but since he is a Princeton graduate, you may be reasonably certain he is not of the offensive type." Bert Lowenberg was described in a letter of recommendation as follows: "by temperament and spirit . . . [he] measures up to the whitest Gentiles I know."[12]

Not until after World War II would more than a handful of Jews gain admission to the historical profession. By that time, the G.I. Bill was opening the doors of higher education to broad masses of Americans. This enormous expansion, which created a majority of the college campuses existing today, rapidly enlarged and diversified the historians' guild. Religious barriers continued to fall, and class barriers began to fall as well, though not without creating consternation in some quarters. At Yale, George Pierson, the chairman of the history department, wrote the university's president in 1957—during a period when the growth of American universities demanded thousands of newly trained professors—that, although the doctoral program in English "still draws to a degree from the cultivated, professional, and well-to-do classes . . . by contrast, the subject of history seems to appeal on the whole to a lower social stratum." Pierson complained that "far too few of our history candidates are sons of professional men; far too many list their parent's occupation as janitor, watchman, salesman, grocer, pocketbook cutter, bookkeeper, railroad clerk, pharmacist, clothing cutter, cable tester, mechanic, general clerk, butter-and-egg jobber, and the like." Five years later, Carl Bridenbaugh, the president of the American Historical Association, lamented what he called the "great mutation" that he believed was undermining the profession. "Many of the younger practitioners of our craft, and those who are still apprentices, are products of lower middle-class or foreign origins, and their emotions not infrequently get in the way of historical reconstructions."[13]

The notion that lower-class and foreign-born backgrounds disabled apprentice historians by conditioning them to substitute emotion for reason was revived when racial and gender barriers began to fall in the 1960s. The historical profession had for many decades included a small number of notable women and African Americans and an occasional Native American, Hispanic American, and Asian American. But women began to enter the profession in substantial numbers only in the 1960s, while members of racial minority groups have increased since that time only slowly. Charges that emotions outran analytic insight were again heard from members of the old guard, none of its members more vocal than Oscar Handlin, whose Jewish background had nearly stopped him from entry into the profession a generation before.[14] But by the late 1970s, the old guard had been swamped, and social historians had surged forward to displace the traditional emphasis on male- and elite-centered political and institutional history or an intellectual history that rarely focused on the thought and consciousness of people who were not of European descent.

Given these changes in the composition of the profession, which by 1990 had made women more than 35 percent of all graduate students in the humanities, it is not surprising that new questions have been posed about the past—questions that never occurred to a narrowly constituted group of historians. The emphasis on conflict rather than consensus, on racism and exploitation, on history from the bottom up as well as from the top down, on women as well as men, on popular as well as elite culture is entirely understandable as people whose history had never been written began challenging prevailing paradigms by recovering their own histories. Step by step, new historians (including many white men) have constructed previously untold chapters of history and have helped to overcome the deep historical biases that afflicted the profession for many generations.

Sustaining and strengthening the transformation that was beginning to occur because of the different background of historians was the dramatic period of protest and reform that occurred in American society in the 1960s and 1970s. The struggles of women, people of color, and religious minorities to gain equal rights spurred many historians (many of whom were involved in these movements) to ask new questions about the role of race and gender relations in the nation's history and to examine racial minorities, women, and working people as integrally involved in the making of American society. They were not breaking new ground altogether; for many decades, reaching back to the early nineteenth century, pioneering individual scholars had tilled the fields of women's and minority history, and the events of the 1930s had spurred interest in labor history. But the professional colleagues of this avant garde offered little appreciation of their work, and certainly their efforts to recover the history of women, people of color, and the working classes rarely found a place in textbooks used at the primary, secondary, or even collegiate level. The importance of the social protest movements of the 1960s and 1970s was to legitimize the work of those who had been regarded as cranky radicals and who, in the immediately preceding years of the McCarthy witch hunts, had often been hounded out of academe.

A third development fueling the change in the writing and teaching of history has been the decolonization of the Third World and the growing interdependence of the nations of the world. The national liberation movements that erupted after World War II were accompanied by the emergence of intellectuals who began to construct the history of what Eric Wolf calls "the people without history." Both in Third World countries and in the West, historians began to insist on the integrity of the cultural practices and the venerable histories of indigenous peoples who had been demeaned by the colonizing mentality that measured all civilizations by the European yardstick. In the United States, such efforts were yoked—often uneasily—to area studies programs established by the Ford Foundation, most notably the African studies centers established at a number of major universities. In the public schools this has increased the awareness of the importance of studying the histories of many cultures and of teaching world history rather than simply the history of Western civilization. The internationalization of economic, political, and cultural affairs has driven home the point to historians and teachers that a Eurocentric history that measures all progress and renders all historical judgments on the basis of the experience of one part of the world will not equip students for satisfactory adult lives in the twenty-first century.

Last, the teaching of history has changed dramatically in recent years because teachers have been awakened by seeing the composition of their own classrooms change so swiftly during the last two decades. The public schools especially have been repopulated with people of different skin shades, different native languages, different accents, and different cultures of origin. More than two-thirds of the children in public schools in New York City, Houston, Dallas, Baltimore, San Francisco, Cleveland, and Memphis are not white. In Los Angeles, Chicago, Philadelphia, Detroit, San Antonio, Washington, D.C., El Paso, and New Orleans, children of color occupy more than three-quarters of all classroom seats in the public schools and in a few of these cities comprise more than 90 percent of all public school children.

Such a demographic revolution—accounted for by the century-long migration of rural, southern African Americans to the cities and by the immigration acts of 1965 and 1990 that opened the doors especially to people from Asia and Latin America—reminds us that this nation has always been a rich mosaic of peoples and cultures. It reminds us also that we cannot begin to understand our history without recognizing the crucial role of religious prejudice and racial exploitation in our past as well as the vital roles of people from many different ethnic, racial, and religious backgrounds in building American society and making American history. The more usable past that a new generation of historians had been creating since World War II became all the more imperative in the schools as new immigrants and people of color became numerically dominant in most of the large urban public school systems. This will continue. More than 90 percent of all immigrants—legal and undocumented—entering the United States in the 1980s were from Asia and Latin America, and the pattern is holding in the 1990s.

To what extent has the presentation of history in the public schools reflected the developments in historical scholarship? In 1979, reviewing American history textbooks as they had been written for schoolchildren from the early twentieth century forward, Frances FitzGerald concluded that "the texts of the sixties contain the most dramatic rewriting of history ever to take place in American schoolbooks."[15] In FitzGerald's view, one of the largest changes was in the textbooks' new presentation of the United States as a multiracial society—a signal revision brought about, in her view, more because of the pressure of school boards in cities with a high percentage of black and Hispanic students (Newark, New Jersey, and Detroit, particularly) than because of the influence of new historical scholarship on writers of textbooks for the schools. Yet FitzGerald admitted that, by the late 1970s, textbooks were far from cleansed of Eurocentric bias and represented a "compromise . . . among the conflicting demands of a variety of pressure groups, inside and outside the school systems"—a compromise "full of inconsistencies" (among which, she noted, was an almost absolute ban on any discussion of economic life, social and economic inequality, and violence and conflict in American life).[16]

Why was it that the flowering of social history in the universities that made such important gains in breaking through Eurocentric conceptualizations of American history and world history made only limited gains for the teaching of a less nationalistic, white-centered, hero-driven, and male-dominated history in the schools? In theory, the schools might have been expected to reflect faithfully the remarkable changes in historical scholarship. This proved not to be the case for several reasons. First, most social studies teachers had only a smattering of history in their Bachelor of Arts education—a few courses or a minor for the large majority of them. Second, most teachers were trained at schools where the new scholarship was only palely represented because the 1970s were years in which new faculty appointments were few, especially in the state universities where most teachers are trained. Third, the books used in the schools, although often produced by professional historians, only cautiously incorporated the new social history of women, laboring people, and minorities because publishers who catered to a national market were far more timid than university presses about publishing history that radically revised our understanding of the past, especially the American past. Thus, by the early 1980s, the textbooks in United States history for the secondary schools reflected far less of the new scholarship than textbooks written for college survey classes.

If the 1960s and 1970s brought only a partial transformation of the curriculum, the 1980s, and especially the early 1990s, have been a period in which the reconceptualization of history, as presented in the schools, has made impressive gains, even though it has had to struggle against a resurgent conservatism, inside and outside the historical profession, that opposes even the partial reforms of the last generation. The barrage of hostile responses to the far more inclusive history presented in the last generation confirms J. H. Plumb's remark that the "personal ownership of the past has always been a vital strand in the ideology of all ruling classes."[17]

Some of the opposition to a new, more inclusive history grew out of the white backlash to the liberal programs of the Kennedy-Johnson era. It was this kind of gut-level, grassroots disgruntlement that Jules Feiffer captured in the early 1970s with his cartoon about the white hard-hat worker who complained, "When I went to school I learned that George Washington never told a lie, slaves were happy on the plantation, the men who opened the West were giants, and we won every war because God was on our side. But where my kid goes to school he learns that Washington was a slave-owner, slaves hated slavery, the men who opened the West committed genocide, and the wars we won were victories for U.S. imperialism. No wonder my kid's not an American. They're teaching him some other country's history." Feiffer's cartoon pointed up the idea that an elitist, male-dominated, Eurocentric history had considerable appeal within the white working class because, although they were largely excluded from such a history, they were also the beneficiaries of it relative to women and people of color.

In recent years, the argument over "whose history shall we teach" has caused schisms and heated debate within the historical profession.[18] Unlike the period of the 1930s through the 1950s, when opposition to a reconceptualized history was expressed in terms of the unsuitability of the outsiders entering the profession, the current debates within the historical profession focus on the kind of history that is being written. The former outsiders are now within the academic gates, and it will not do any longer to attack them as sociologically and temperamentally unsuited for the work they do; rather, it is the history they write that has come under fire. Opponents see the new history of women, laboring people, religious and racial minorities—sometimes lumped together under the rubric "social history"—as creating a hopelessly chaotic version of the past in which no grand synthesis or overarching themes are possible to discern and all coherence is lost. Of course, the overarching themes and coherent syntheses achieved in older histories derived from studying mostly the experiences of only one group of people in American society or in grounding all the megahistorical constructs in the Western experience. The contribution of the social historians is precisely to show that the overarching themes and the grand syntheses promulgated by past historians will not hold up when we broaden our perspectives and start investigating the history of all of the people who constituted American society, French society, or any other society. The new scholarship has, for example, not only provided an immensely enriched understanding of the history of women and the family but also in the process obliged all historians to rethink the allegedly coherent paradigms for explaining the past that were derived from studying primarily the male experience.

Some of the opposition to the new history stems simply from resistance to change or discomfort with the loss of comfortable, old paradigms. For example, many historians used to arguing about Turner's frontier thesis— that the frontier was a crucible where democratic ideas and values were continuously replenished and where settlers built and rebuilt democratic institutions—are finding it painfully unsettling to consider the westward movement from the perspective of the Lakota or Cheyenne who watched the wagon trains appearing from the East, from the vantage point of Mexican ranchers and miners of the Southwest who found themselves demographically and politically overwhelmed by the land-hungry white migrants, or through the eyes of Chinese contract laborers brought to the Pacific slope in the 1870s to build levees and railroads. For each of these groups, the frontier movement was anything but heroic and anything but the westward march of democracy.

The new history, in paying close attention to gender, race, and class, emphasizes that historical experiences have varied with the position and power of the participants. This premise makes it harder to tell a simple or unified story about such eras or movements as the Jacksonian Age of the Common Man, the Westward Movement, the Progressive Era, or the post-1945 Affluent Society. Such labels become only the tell-tale labels of a narrowly conceived history.

The challenge of a history built upon consideration of alternative experiences and perspectives goes beyond simply incorporating notable women or people of color into traditional narrative themes; it forces the invention of genuinely new story lines and master syntheses, based on the diverse and motley experiences of the entire society under investigation. This challenge, while liberating historians from simple, biased, and justificatory formulas about the past, also raises real perplexities about the prospects of wresting any kind of general unity out of multiple and conflicting perspectives. For example, if older historical accounts achieved a spurious unity by mostly taking the experiences of a single group—white men—as the unspoken measure of historical significance, redress does not come simply from incorporating into a revised story the newly recognized and acknowledged experiences of women, since the category of "women" itself further dissolves into multiple and conflicting perspectives arising out of racial, economic, regional, and other differences. As one feminist historian described the "seemingly intractable" problem (applied just to writing women's history): "What is the conceptual link for women's history . . . among what seems to be an infinite proliferation of different (women's) stories? . . . Is there a common identity for women and is there a common history of them we can write?"[19] If the sin of the old history was to impose a false unity on diverse experiences and perspectives, the problem for the new history is to give voice to the diversity of perspectives while still constructing overall themes and explanatory paradigms.

Notwithstanding the sharp attacks on social history in recent years, multiculturalism—defined as the integration of the histories of both genders, people of all classes, and members of all racial, ethnic, and religious groups—has proceeded rapidly during the last few years. Multicultural curriculums, "stressing a diversity of cultures, races, languages, and religions" and eliminating "ethnocentric and biased concepts and materials from textbook and classroom" have been adopted by school systems throughout the United States.[20] California has implemented an explicitly multicultural history-social science curriculum, and many other states and individual school districts are following the same path, though with many variations.

AFROCENTRISM AND MULTICULTURALISM

How do these debates among professional historians connect with and affect the current debates over multiculturalism in the schools? And how do they allow us to appraise the rise of the Afrocentric perspective—a powerful movement within the public schools of the nation's largest cities? Perhaps it is not surprising, given how long it has taken for textbooks and school curriculums to change, that, while some members of the historical profession were resisting the movement toward a history that pays attention to gender, race, and class, some school reformers, especially those who were not part of the white majority, would find the reforms of the last two decades too slow and too fragmentary. For some educators, particularly a group of African Americans, the reforms were altogether wrongheaded, so that greater speed and thoroughness toward a multicultural approach was not the desired goal.

Although textbooks changed in the 1980s—and almost without exception in the direction of including more of the struggles and contributions of women and racial minority groups (though they did much less to increase coverage of the contributions and struggles of labor and religious minorities)—much else that accounts for the rise of Afrocentrism also changed. This is a movement that, reinvoking arguments first raised before the Civil War, gathered steam in the 1980s when the rhetoric and policies of the Reagan and Bush presidencies gave most African Americans and other minority groups plenty to be disillusioned about.

To be sure, some gains have been made—and a few held onto. For example, the percentage of black Americans completing high school has risen from 36 percent in 1970 (for whites the figure was 57 percent) to about 67 percent by 1988 (as against 78 percent for whites). Smaller gains have been made in the percentage of black Americans graduating from college—from 6 to 16 percent of all 25-year-olds between 1970 and 1988. Also, the black middle class has expanded substantially, from about 6 to 14 percent of all black families between 1967 and 1989 (during the same period, the white middle class also expanded, from about 17 to 31 percent of all families).[21] But by almost every social statistic available, the lowest stratum of American society, which includes a vast proportion of African Americans, has suffered egregiously during the last decade while wealth was redistributed up the pyramid. In 1989, nearly 44 percent of all black children lived below the poverty line (compared with 14 percent of white children). Similar statistics can be marshalled regarding the growing gap between black and white America in unemployment, teenage pregnancy, violent crime, infant mortality, and incarceration. Teased in the 1960s and 1970s by the vision that the end of white supremacist America might bring racial equality, many African Americans in the early 1990s feel disillusionment, frustration, and rage. It is this soil that has proved fertile for the seeds of certain extreme forms of Afrocentrism (which at heart are cultural separatist programs) to germinate, especially in the large cities where the conditions are most desperate for young American blacks. Reaganism did not create black cultural nationalism—of which Afrocentrism is one form. It has existed for two centuries. But cultural nationalism—the withdrawing into a self-enclosed world and the absolutizing of racial difference—always has its greatest appeal in times when minority groups stop believing that the gap between America's universalist ideals and the realities of daily life can be closed. White backlash and government retrenchment on civil rights in the 1980s created conditions in which black cultural nationalism grew, just as in the past its predecessor movements grew out of frustrated hopes and shattered dreams.

While facing a situation in the urban centers of American life that has made the young black male "an endangered species" in the phrase of the

NAACP, in educational circles African-American educators and their white allies have had to confront powerful traditionalists who oppose multiculturalism or grudgingly accept only gestures toward it. Education czars like William Bennett and a growing number of academics, some of them gathered in the newly formed, ultraconservative National Association of Scholars, which claims 2,500 members, have been virulently hostile to the directions in which historians (as well as scholars and educators in literature, sociology, and other disciplines) have been moving in their interpretations of American and world history and culture. A classic case of this rearguard defense of traditional history is the brouhaha over the movement by the faculty at Stanford University to reformulate its required courses in Western Civilization. Conservatives, led by William Bennett (at the time the secretary of education) went out of their way to portray the thoughtful debate at Stanford—over broadening the readings included in the required courses and changing the title of the courses to "Cultures, Ideas, and Values"—into an all-out attack on "the great books" of Western Civilization. As described by Dinesh D'Souza, the Stanford faculty, caving in to student radicals, trashed its venerable Western culture requirement and replaced it with a program that emphasized works on race and gender issues by hardly reputable Third World authors, people of color, and women.[22]

D'Souza grossly distorted what actually occurred at Stanford—both the nature of the debate and the outcome, as can be appreciated in the report of one of the Stanford instructors teaching in the "Cultures, Ideas, and Values" program and in the account of the philosopher John Searle, an avowed cultural traditionalist.[23] In fact, the Stanford faculty was engaging in what is most valuable about the academic enterprise: thinking critically about received knowledge, challenging inherited assumptions when they seem no longer legitimate, and constructing new curricular models reflecting new scholarship. Besides revising the curriculum in an academically responsible way, the Stanford faculty gave students a case study in the kind of critical thinking that is the essence of a liberal education.

D'Souza's misrepresentations are perhaps not surprising since they come from one of the founders of the blatantly racist and anti-Semitic *Dartmouth Review*. More dismaying from the perspective of African Americans and their white allies must be the flight of some with whom they stood shoulder to shoulder in earlier days—historians such as Eugene Genovese and C. Vann Woodward—to the neoconservative side of current debates on multiculturalism and political correctness. If such attacks on multiculturalism continue to parallel the growing white opposition to group entitlements and affirmative action programs, then Pat Buchanan may have his way. "When we say we will put America first," Buchanan explained, "we mean also that our Judeo-Christian values are going to be preserved, and our Western heritage is going to be handed down to future generations, not dumped onto some landfill called multiculturalism."[24] In this discouraging atmosphere of retrogressive governmental policies on issues of race, neoconservative attacks on the opening up of such subjects as history and literature to include the experiences of huge components of the population never before thought worthy of more than token inclusion, and a condition of "savage inequalities" in the public schooling of our children, Afrocentrism has become a powerful movement in the public schools of the major cities of the country.[25]

Designed primarily to nurture self-esteem in black children by teaching them of the greatness of ancestral Africa and the contributions made by Africans of the diaspora in many parts of the world, the Afrocentric approach is mostly the work of nonhistorians. Its most widely visible and vocal leaders are Molefi Kete Asante, whose degree is in rhetoric and communications; Asa Hilliard, whose degree is in education; and Leonard Jeffries, City University of New York, whose degree is in political science. Such educators surely cannot be faulted for regarding the dropout rates, low achievement scores, and lives blighted by drugs, violence, and early pregnancies of young African Americans as a national tragedy—and one that white America is largely uninterested in addressing. For these educators, an Afrocentric curriculum that sees all knowledge and values from an African perspective is a cure. "The only issue for us," says Jeffrey Fletcher, who is part of the Black United Front for Education Reform in Oakland, California, "is how we can get out of this plight. It's like if you have someone around your throat choking you. It's nice to know about the baseball scores and other cultures, but the only thing you need to know is how to get those fingers off your neck."[26]

Afrocentrism is both an intellectual construction and a social-psychological remedy, and the two parts of it deserve separate discussion. As an intellectual construction, Molefi Kete Asante explained, Afrocentricity means "literally placing African ideals at the center of any analysis that involves African culture and behavior."[27] If this means homogenizing all of the many distinct African cultures from Mediterranean Africa to steppe and forest dwellers south of the Sahara with their multiplicity of languages, religions, and cultures and if it means blurring the wide variety of historical experiences over many centuries of culturally distinct peoples, then most scholars would have much to discuss with Asante. But if Afrocentrism means simply that any consideration of African history or the history of Africans of the diaspora must begin with the culture of the homeland and follow the way it was transmitted and maintained, at least partially, outside of Africa, then a great many scholars of the black experience—historians, ethnomusicologists, cultural anthropologists, art historians, linguistic scholars, and so forth—have been Afrocentrists for a long time.

Such a black aesthetic can be traced back at least a century—for example, to the editor of the *African Methodist Episcopal Review*, H. L. Kealing, who in 1899 wrote that "the greatest bane of slavery to the American negro is that it robbed him of his own standard and replaced it with the Grecian."[28] Certainly, in this sense, I was an Afrocentrist (and simultaneously a Eurocentrist and an Indiocentrist) twenty years ago when I wrote *Red, White, and Black: The Peoples of Early America* because the main thrust of that book was to demonstrate that eastern North America in the seventeenth and eighteenth centuries was a merging ground for distinct cultures— European, African, and Indian (each culturally various within itself)—and that each culture had to be understood on its own terms if the interaction among them was to be fully comprehended.[29] Perhaps we can agree, then, that the problem with Eurocentrism in our history has never been telling the story through the eyes of the European immigrants; the problem has been leaving other chapters of the story out and universalizing European values, institutions, and behaviors so that it appeared that the European cultural yardstick became everyone's way to measure themselves and their history because it was the superior yardstick.

Hence, Afrocentrists, in insisting on appreciating the integrity of African cultures and the persistence of many of their elements during and beyond the diaspora, are building on a decades-old movement to overturn the European colonizers' mindset—a movement to which people of many ethnic and racial identities have contributed in sometimes separate and sometimes intersecting ways. In this sense, the claim of Asante that "few whites have ever examined their culture critically" and the parallel assertion that those who have, such as the British historian of Africa, Basil Davidson, have "been severely criticized by their peers" is wholly uninformed.[30] Asante's account of what he believes is stubbornly Eurocentric scholarship on African and African-American history ignores the work of two generations of African and African-American historians, including those who are English, French, Caribbean, and American and who are of various racial inheritances.

In building on a tradition of ridding ourselves of a Eurocentric approach, Afrocentrism, as practiced by some of its proponents (virtually none of whom are historians), has produced some notable contradictions and ironies and a great many oversimplifications. For example, though striving to undermine the significance of Western culture, its most trumpeted message is that Egypt was black and African (an oversimplification in itself) and that black Egyptians taught the ancient Greeks most of what they knew, which is to presume that what the Greeks knew was highly significant. An irony in Afrocentrism is that its proponents take great pains to find great figures of Western culture, such as Alexander Dumas and Aleksandr Pushkin, who had an African ancestor and claim them as evidence of the superiority of African culture. Since white America, for more than two centuries, defined anyone with any small portion of African ancestry as black, the Afrocentrists can chortle as they discover that Beethoven's great-grandfather may have been a Moorish soldier in the Spanish army (an assertion first made by J. A. Rogers, a black journalist, a generation ago but still far from proved).[31] But if Beethoven had a black ancestor, the Afrocentrists still have to live with the contradiction of celebrating someone who has been thoroughly a part of Western culture while downgrading that culture in the interest of claiming the superiority of African culture as the place where modern science, mathematics, and other disciplines had their origin.

In their treatment of Egypt, Afrocentrists such as Asante are out of touch with most reputable scholarship on the ancient world. They also give precedence to a part of Africa with which most African Americans have little cultural connection. For Asante, the "Afrocentrist analysis reestablishes the centrality of the ancient Kemetic (Egyptian) civilization and the Nile Valley cultural complex as points of reference for an African perspective."[32] It is certainly true that most nineteenth- and twentieth-century scholars in the West have taken Africans out of Egypt and taken Egypt out of Africa, relocating it in the Middle East. But in correcting this, following the work of the Senegalese Africanist Chiekh Anta Diop and more recently using very selectively Martin Bernal's *Black Athena*, Afrocentrists who are not historians have tried to turn all of the mixed-race Egyptians into black Africans and to make most of European civilization derivative from black Egypt. Moreover, in arguing that the cultures of ancient Egypt and the Nile Valley are the main reference points for an African perspective, such Afrocentrists defy most modern scholarship on the Africans of the diaspora, whose cultures in West Africa were hardly the same as the culture of the Nile. The *African-American Baseline Essays* produced for the schools of Portland, Oregon, the most comprehensive attempt to set forth an Afrocentric curriculum, clearly follow this misleading path, urging teachers to "identify Egypt and its civilization as a distinct African creation" (i.e., without Asiatic or European influences). The social studies essay devotes more than three times as much space to the history and culture of ancient Egypt as to the history and culture of West Africa in the period before the beginning of the Atlantic slave trade.[33]

Another worrisome aspect of the Afrocentrist argument, also driven home in the *African-American Baseline Essays*, is the insistence that "African scholars are the final authority on Africa." Ironically, this statement, by the author of the social studies essay, John Henrik Clarke, is made despite his reliance on a series of studies by white archaeologists demonstrating that the origins of the human species were in East Africa and despite the fact that *Black Athena*, the work of the white Jewish scholar, Martin Bernal, has attained almost biblical importance among the Afrocentrists. As the history author of a multicultural series of books for children from kindergarten to eighth grade now in use throughout California's public schools, I have been told on many occasions by self-professed Afrocentrists that I cannot write African-American history because only someone who is African American can understand it and is entitled to speak or write on the subject. However, none of these have told me what they find wrong or insensitive about the last three scholarly books I have published—*Forging Freedom: The Formation of Philadelphia's Black Community, 1720–1840*, *Race and Revolution*, and (with Jean R. Soderlund) *Freedom by Degrees: Emancipation and Its Aftermath in Pennsylvania*. By such racially polarizing reasoning, we must blot out the work of several generations of white, Hispanic, and Asian historians who have contributed to the rich literature on African history, African-American history, and the histories of peoples of the diaspora in other parts of the world.[34]

The nonscholarly form of Afrocentrism, drawing on a long-established movement to stop measuring all things by the European cultural yardstick, has moved perilously close to holding up a new yardstick that measures all things by how nearly they approach an African ideal. When we get beyond labels and cultural yardstick waving, what will be enduringly important for those who wish to study the interaction of African peoples and Europeans, in whatever part of the world, is an ability to look through several sets of lenses. Most of us learned a long time ago that this is what good history and good anthropology are all about. It is hardly arguable that, to understand African literature or African-American history or Afro-Brazilian music, one must have an understanding of African culture as well as of the cultures with which Africans were interacting. Nor is it deniable that the stigmatizing of African culture and its derivative cultures of the diaspora has been an essential part of white supremacist thought and that it has been institutionalized in our culture and in the cultures of all societies where Europeans were the cultural arbiters. But Afrocentrism becomes a new and dangerous ethnocentrism of its own when it adopts the colonizers' old trick of arranging cultures on a continuum ranging from inferior to superior. It is this aspect of Afrocentrism that disturbs black scholars such as Henry Louis Gates, Jr., who decries such "ethnic fundamentalism" and attempts "to reduce the astonishing diversity of African cultures to a few simple-minded shibboleths."[35] As long ago as 1945, Emery Reves wrote in *The Anatomy of Peace*: "Nothing can distort the true picture of conditions and events in this world more than to regard one's own country [or culture] as the center of the universe and to view all things solely in their relationship to this fixed point."[36] We seem destined to relearn this lesson.

When Afrocentrism makes the leap from theory and scholarly perspective to a curricular prescription for the schools, its problems multiply. Asante believes that "most African-American children sit in classrooms yet are outside the information being discussed." If he means this statement to apply to modern mathematics, science, and computer skills or even to reading and writing skills and if the remedy is to learn about ancient Egyptian concepts of science and magic, then black children taught in an Afrocentric curriculum will not acquire the skills and knowledge necessary to move forward in modern society. In social studies classrooms, knowledge of African history and of the many rich and complex traditions in the period before contact with Europeans can certainly awaken the interest of African-American children (and other children too, one hopes) and can teach all children that African peoples, interacting with people from other societies, have been an essential part of the history of humankind. But getting beyond romantic notions of African history will require that they learn that ethnic and national identities have been stronger than pan-Africanism on the African continent, both before and after the long era of the slave trade and European colonization.

Equally important, African-American children, as much as any other children, need to learn about the history of many cultures and historical experiences. The ultimate goal of a multicultural education is to create mutual respect among students of different religions, races, and ethnic backgrounds by teaching them that rich cultural traditions have existed for centuries in every part of the world. "The natural inclination in people to fear and distrust what they find alien and strange," wrote Robert K. Fullinwider, "is tempered by an education that makes students' religions, languages, customs, and values familiar to each other, thereby encouraging in students a sympathetic imagination, a generosity of spirit, and an openness to dialogue."[37]

Perhaps too much emphasis has been placed, in the Afrocentrist educators' program, on the power of pride in African ancestry. In themselves, ancestral pride and group pride, when kept in bounds, are conducive to a healthy sense of one's potential. For example, there is little doubt, as Roger Wilkins wrote, that it was of great importance to the Civil Rights activists to assert "a human validity that did not derive from whites" and to understand that "the black experience on this continent and in Africa was profound, honorable, and a source of pride."[38] But ancestral and group pride cannot solve the deep social and economic problems that confront so many youth who live in black communities today. If the most radical black educators devote their energies to refashioning children's self-image through an oversimplified and often invented history, what energy will go toward fighting for structural reforms that provide jobs, equal opportunities, decent housing, and a more stable family life for millions of people trapped in poverty and despair? The historian John Bracey described the "glories of

Ancient Africa" as an understandable but sadly insufficient response "to the harsh realities of the West Side of Chicago, or BedStuy, or the gang mayhem of Los Angeles."[39]

No one doubts that a crisis has overtaken this generation of young African Americans. But the Afrocentrists' faith in the social and economic healing power of a rewritten history that teaches black pride is a Band-Aid on a massive wound. We hope that it will motivate many young learners, but other remedies related to a secure family life and neighborhood environment are also necessary in the development of able, self-confident young people. Afrocentrist educators build their case on the frail premise that the underachievement of black students is caused by a Eurocentric curriculum that teaches African-American children to think poorly of themselves. Self-esteem, however, begins at home, in the early years of childhood, and, in any event, there is more evidence in empirical studies of academic achievement that good results produce self-esteem than the other way around. For example, most Asian-American students, the recipients of the same allegedly Eurocentric curriculum as African-American students, do not have the same scholastic achievement problems and do not score low when measured for self-esteem.[40] Hence, solutions to school underachievement require thinking about factors other than a curriculum that promotes racially based self-esteem.

Many successful programs offer other solutions. At the Yale University Child Study Center, "a system of unusually intense school involvement in the lives of students and their parents" has markedly raised the achievement scores of young black children from impoverished backgrounds.[41] At a Catholic elementary school in Chicago that enrolls primarily children from one of the city's notorious public housing projects, children succeed because the principal, a black Catholic priest named George Clements, demands "hard work, sacrifice, dedication." The regimen is utterly strict. "A twelve-month school year. An eight-hour day. You can't leave the campus. Total silence in the lunchroom and throughout the building. Expulsion for graffiti. Very heavy emphasis on moral pride. The parents must come every month and pick up the report card and talk to the teacher, or we kick out the kid. They must come to PTA every month. They must sign every night's homework in every subject." The payoff of such a program, according to Clements, is considerable. "We have achieved honors as an academic institution above the national norms in all disciplines."[42] In Los Angeles, two hard-driving and talented principals have put their best teachers in the early grades, emphasized reading, and set high goals for children. "I'm not running a school for dishwashers," sputters Nancy Ichinaga, the daughter of a Hawaiian cane field worker. In her school, where most students qualify for the subsidized lunch program, third grade reading scores exceed those at three-fourths of all elementary schools in the state.[43] Local programs based on other premises, but all involving dedicated teachers, inspiring principals, curricular innovation, involved parents, and well-cared-for children, have also worked.[44]

If Afrocentrism can somehow help African Americans overcome the poverty and the pathological social situation in which so many urban children are caught, it must still come to terms with its extremist wing, which is as opposed to multiculturalism as is the neoconservative right. For extreme Afrocentrists such as Jeffries and Wade Nobles, a frequently consulted Afrocentrist in the San Francisco area, teaching black pride goes hand in hand with teaching hatred of whites and white institutions. All education for black children, Nobles advises, has to be cleansed of white Western influence. "When we adopt other people's theories, we are like Frankenstein doing other people's wills. It's like someone drinking some good stuff, vomiting it, and then we have to catch the vomit and drink it ourselves."[45] Such racial hostility and cultural separatism seems almost calculated to pour fuel on the fires of the already rampant resurgence of white racism during a decade of white backlash against affirmative action programs. John Henrik Clarke, author of the history section of the Portland baseline essays, rejects all religion and urges black Americans to turn their backs on the very religious institutions that for two centuries have been the centers of political and social struggle for African Americans. "At what point," Clarke asked the second National Conference on the Infusion of African and African-American Content in the High School Curriculum in November 1990, "do we stop this mental prostitution to a religion invented by foreigners? All religion is artificial. All the major religions of the world are male chauvinist murder cults."[46]

Leonard Jeffries, the most polemical of the extreme Afrocentrists, goes even farther. He preaches that the international Atlantic slave trade was a conspiracy of Jews and that Jews, along with the Mafia, have in modern times consciously built "a financial system of destruction of black people" and are engaged in a "systematic, unrelenting" attack on African Americans.[47] Jeffries has much more to say about how the essence of world history can be understood as a racial war of the "Ice People" against the "Sun People" and about the natural intellectual and physical superiority of blacks because of the melanin advantage over whites that they enjoy. Jeffries' pronouncements have no scholarly content and are not regarded seriously in academic circles. However, because curricular change is a highly political matter, they are taken with deadly seriousness by educators who have to worry about building interracial consensus to accomplish their goals. Jeffries may intend his inflammatory remarks to undermine cross-race reform coalitions and fan the racial hostility that is much on the increase because what interests him, apparently, is black separatism, not a multiculturalism that nurtures mutual respect among people of different cultural backgrounds. But his rhetoric and curricular prescriptions serve as warnings that even more tempered forms of Afrocentrism, if they focus too much on inculcating racial pride, may unconsciously impart a sense of difference and cultural superiority that disserves the multiculturalists' goals of creating mutual respect and an appreciation of other cultures and historical experiences.[48]

It is hard to see what good can come from the programs of the extreme Afrocentrists. If some black youth emerge from such programs with enhanced self-esteem and if that leads to improved school performance that gets them into college, then they will almost certainly have to confront in college the miseducation they will have received. They would have to ponder, for example, that if all religion is artificial, as John Henrik Clarke would have them believe, the African religious traditions that the enslaved brought with them to the Americas (which helped them endure the horrors of slavery) were artificial too. They will learn in anthropology and social history courses that cultural yardsticks have always been the weapons of those who wish to proclaim the superiority of one culture over all others rather than inculcate understanding of and respect for other cultures. In short, the curriculum being proposed in some large urban school systems looks like "a shadow dance performed at the edge of the abyss."[49]

Many African-American historians ignore or reject the simplistic formulations of the Afrocentrists, but it is not easy to step forward—in a society where white discrimination and racism are still so manifest—to say so. The report of the Committee on Policy for Racial Justice, composed of black scholars and headed by the eminent historian John Hope Franklin, however, called for a multicultural curriculum that teaches children of the historical experiences, the literature, the music and art, and all the other struggles and accomplishments of all racial and ethnic parts of society. "All children," the report argued, "need to see people like themselves express the timeless concerns of humankind and to be symbolically represented in the classroom as worthy of discourse." But the report made no calls for an Afrocentric curriculum for black children. As one assessment of the multicultural debate put it, "The growing call to do that stems largely from the same perceived 'crisis' in the education of black youth that the committee found, but it comes from outside the scholarly mainstream."[50]

Equally retrogressive is the extreme Afrocentrists' focus on great African or African-American figures. It may bolster the self-esteem of African-American students to believe that Alexander Dumas, Cleopatra, and the inventor of an important machine for mass-producing shoes named Jan E. Matzeliger were African (actually, they were all of mixed-race ancestry). But a return to a hero-driven history of extraordinary people as history makers would be an ironic abandonment of the social history of the last generation, which has demonstrated the role of ordinary people in history and showed that no major transformations in any society are accomplished without the participation of masses of people.

Still other explosives infest the minefield of extreme Afrocentrism. If the Afrocentrists are correct that their curriculum will raise self-esteem and therefore performance levels—a disputed point with little solid evidence—then it is logical to suppose that what is sauce for the goose is sauce for the gander. The logical extension of their reasoning is that a Hispanocentrist approach ought to be instituted for children of Hispanic backgrounds, children of Chinese ancestry in this country ought to receive a Sinocentrist education, a Khmercentrist approach is the best road ahead for the thousands of immigrant children from Cambodia, and so forth. Indeed, logic would require the reinstitution of a Eurocentric approach for low-achieving white children or a series of nation-specific or European ethnic group–specific approaches to help underachieving children of these backgrounds overcome their disadvantages. But what approach would be used in thousands of classrooms in large cities across the country where children of a great variety of ethnic, racial, and religious backgrounds mingle? Which ethnically specific curriculum should be taught to the growing number of mixed-race children in a society where miscegenation laws, after a long struggle, no longer exist and the rate of interracial marriage is at an all-time high and is increasing yearly? And how do teachers of ethnic pride prevent that pride from turning into ethnic chauvinism and ethnic chauvinism from turning into ethnic hostility, which is what has happened historically in the case of Anglo-Saxon, German, and many other forms of ethnic pride?

SEPARATE GROUND AND COMMON GROUND

Except among what might be called white and black racial fundamentalists, who thus far have had only limited influence on curricular change, there is little argument about the desirability of including people of all classes, colors, and conditions in our accounts of how history unfolds. This is simply sound historical analysis. Nor is there much doubt that children will find history more compelling and relevant when they recognize that people of their religion, color, region, ethnic background, or class played active roles in the making of American society. While discovering the historical relevance of gender, race, religion, and other categories that help shape their identity, however, students also need to discover the common humanity of all individuals and the ways in which many of the most important lessons from history can be learned by studying themes and movements that cross racial, ethnic, religious, gender, and class lines. To this end, whatever their origins and characteristics, we should hope that all students will find inspiring figures of different colors, genders, and social positions. Why should the lives of Harriet Tubman and Ida B. Wells be relevant only to African-American female students? Likewise, what student can fail to gain wisdom from studying the trial of Anne Hutchinson or the Lincoln-Douglas debates? Who cannot draw inspiration from the courage and accomplishments of Black Hawk, John Brown, Elizabeth Blackwell, A. Philip Randolph, Louis Brandeis, Dolores Huerta, and a thousand more who are different rather than the same as oneself? W. E. B. Du Bois knew that the history he was taught was wildly distorted and used as an instrument of white supremacy. But he also understood that he benefited greatly from reading the great writers of many cultures. "I sit with Shakespeare and he winces not. Across the color line I move arm in arm with Balzac and Dumas, where smiling men and welcoming women glide in gilded halls . . . I summon Aristotle and Aurelius and what soul I will, and they come all graciously with no scorn nor condescension. So, wed with Truth, I live above the veil."[51]

The veil of which Du Bois wrote was the color line, of course, and he is only one of a long line of brilliant black scholars who drew sustenance from all parts of humanity. Ralph Ellison, growing up in Macon County, Alabama, remembered that he "read Marx, Freud, T. S. Eliot, Pound, Gertrude Stein, and Hemingway. Books which seldom, if ever, mentioned Negroes were to release me from whatever 'segregated' idea I might have had of my human possibilities."[52] C. L. R. James, the Trinidadian historian and author of *Black Jacobins*, still after a half century the most important book on the Haitian Revolution, writes movingly of his education in the classics of English literature in the schools of Trinidad. As an adult, James came to understand "the limitation of spirit, vision, and self-respect which was imposed on us by the fact that our masters, our curriculum, our code of morals, *everything* began from the basis that Britain was the source of all light and leading, and our business was to admire, wonder, imitate, learn." But James went on to read and learn from French and Russian literary greats and to find an authentic voice of his own, much enriched by his cosmopolitan education.[53] His accomplishments are a reminder that a curriculum organized around only one vantage point for learning, whether English, European, or African, will limit the vision of students and therefore keep them from being all that they can be.

Thirteen years ago, looking at the way multiculturalism was proceeding in its earlier stage, Frances FitzGerald worried that the rise of the new social history that concerned the forgotten elements of the population would lead to a history that was a bundle of fragmented group histories. This, she said, would teach that "Americans have no common history, no common culture and no common values, and that membership in a racial cultural group constitutes the most fundamental experience of each individual. The message would be that the center cannot, and should not, hold."[54] In some urban schools today, one group boycotts another group's ethnic festivities and racial tensions flare when one holiday is celebrated over another, confirming FitzGerald's fear that ethnic pride might increase ethnic divisiveness.[55]

Today, FitzGerald's question about what holds us together, whether we have a common culture, is all the more relevant. If multiculturalism is to avoid becoming a promiscuous pluralism that gives everything equal weight and explains everything in terms of identity politics and hermetic groups defined by racial descent, it must reach some agreement on what is at the core of American culture. The practical goal of multiculturalism is to foster mutual respect among students by teaching them about the distinct cultures from which those who have come to the United States derive and the distinctive, though entwined, historical experiences of different racial, ethnic, religious, and gender groups in American history. Multicultural education, wrote Robert Fullinwider, is "the conscious effort to be sensitive, both in teacher preparation and in curriculum construction, to the cultural, religious, ethnic, and racial variety in our national life in order to (1) produce an educational environment responsive to the needs of students from different backgrounds, and (2) instill in students mutual understanding and respect."[56] But nurturance of this mutual respect and an appreciation of cultural diversity can only be maintained if parents, teachers, and children reach some basic agreement on some core set of values, ways of airing disputes, how to conduct dialogue—in short, some agreement on how to operate as members of a civic community, a democratic polity. For a democratic polity to endure, the people of a society made up of many cultures must both "be willing to forbear from forcing onto fellow citizens one proper and approved way of life, . . . must possess a certain amount of respect for one another and a certain amount of understanding of one another's beliefs, . . . and [must] want to participate in a common 'civic culture.'"[57]

If the mutual respect that is at the heart of genuine multiculturalism cannot live "in isolation of specific cultural forms and supports," what are these forms and supports?[58] They are, in essence, the central, defining values of the democratic polity. The *pluribus* in *e pluribus unum* can be upheld in all manner of cultural, religious, and aesthetic forms—from the clothes an individual or group chooses to wear to their cuisine, their artistic preferences and styles, the dialect and linguistic constructions of their internal social life, their religious beliefs and practices, and so forth. But *pluribus* can flourish in these ways only if *unum* is preserved at the heart of the polity—in a common commitment to core political and moral values. Chief among these values is the notion that under our founding political principles government is derived from the people, that the people have the

right to change their government, that church and state ought to be separated, that we live under a government of laws, that certain basic rights as
spelled out in the first ten amendments to the Constitution are a precious
heritage, and that all citizens—apart from whatever group attachments
they claim—have a common entitlement as individuals to liberty, equal
opportunity, and impartial treatment under the law.

This is, of course, a body of political ideals, not a description of political
and social reality in our history. But the ideals, nonetheless, have stood as
reference points for virtually every social and political struggle carried out
by women, religious minorities, labor, and people of color. Our entire
history can be read as a long, painful, and often bloody struggle to bring
social practice into correspondence with these lofty goals. But it is the
political and moral ideals that still provide the path to *unum*. In his classic
study of race relations, Gunnar Myrdal focused on the central contradiction of a democracy that would not extend equal rights to Jews, black
Americans, and other "outsiders" and thereby engaged in a massive hy-
pocrisy. But at the same time, Myrdal recognized that such disadvantaged
groups "could not possibly have invented a system of political ideals
which better corresponded to their interests."[59] That a struggle has
occurred—and is still occurring—is no argument against the ideal of a
common core culture. It is only a reminder of an agenda still waiting to be
completed, of what the historian Vincent Harding poignantly called
"wrestling toward the dawn."[60]

NOTES

1. David Nicholson, "Afrocentrism and the Tribalization of America," *Washing-ton Post*, 23 September 1991, B1.

2. W. E. B. Du Bois, *Black Reconstruction: An Essay toward a History of the Part Which Black Folk Played in the Attempt to Reconstruct Democracy in America, 1860–1880* (New York: Harcourt, Brace & Co., 1935), 725, 727.

3. Leon Litwack, "Trouble in Mind: The Bicentennial and the Afro-American Experience," *Journal of American History* 74 (1987): 326.

4. Frances FitzGerald, *America Revised: History Schoolbooks in the Twentieth Centu-ry* (Boston: Little, Brown & Co., 1979), 83.

5. Oliver Perry Chitwood, *A History of Colonial America* (New York: Harper & Brothers, 1931), 351–52.

6. Quoted in Gilbert Sewell, "Textbooks Past and Present," *American Educator* (Winter 1991): 18.

7. Hugh Trevor-Roper, *The Rise of Christian Europe* (New York: Harcourt, Brace & World, 1965), 9.

8. Douglas Edward Leach, *Flintlock and Tomahawk: New England in King Philip's War* (New York: Macmillan Co., 1958), ix.

9. David Saville Muzzey, *A History of Our Country* (Boston: Ginn & Co., 1937), 36.

10. Isaiah Berlin, *Historical Inevitability* (Oxford, England: Clarendon Press, 1954), 39–40.

11. John Hope Franklin, "The New Negro History" in Franklin, *Race and History: Selected Essays, 1938–1988* (Baton Rouge: Louisiana State University Press, 1989), 46.

12. Peter Novick, *That Noble Dream: The "Objectivity Question" and the American Historical Profession* (Cambridge: Cambridge University Press, 1988), 173.

13. Quoted in ibid., 366, 339.

14. Oscar Handlin, *Truth in History* (Cambridge: Harvard University Press, 1979), passim.

15. FitzGerald, *America Revised*, 58.

16. Ibid., 109.

17. Quoted in Gary B. Nash, *Race, Class, and Politics: Essays on American Colonial and Revolutionary Society* (Urbana: University of Illinois Press, 1986), xviii.

18. For a sampling of recent reflections, see the essays by Theodore S. Hamerow, Gertrude Himmelfarb, Lawrence W. Levine, Joan Wallach Scott, and John E. Toews in "AHA Forum: The Old History and the New," *American Historical Review* 94 (1989): 627–98; John Higham, "Multiculturalism and Universalism: A History and Critique" and the responses by Gerald Early, Gary Gerstle, Nancy A. Hewitt, and Vicki L. Ruiz, *American Quarterly* 45 (June 1993): 195–256; and Todd Gitlin, "From Universality to Difference," *Contention*, no. 5 (Winter 1993): 15–40.

19. Joan Scott, "Woman's History" in *New Perspectives on Historical Writing*, ed. Peter Burke (University Park: Pennsylvania State University Press, 1992), 57.

20. Robert K. Fullinwider, "The Cosmopolitan Community" (typescript, University of Maryland, 1992), 2–3.

21. Sam Fulwood III, "Blacks Find Bias Amid Affluence," *Los Angeles Times*, 20 November 1991.

22. Dinesh D'Souza, *Illiberal Education: The Politics of Race and Sex on Campus* (New York: Free Press, 1991).

23. Daniel Gordon, "Inside the Stanford Mind," *Perspectives* 30, no. 4 (1992): 1, 4, 7–8; John Searle, "The Storm over the University" in *Debating P. C.*, ed. Paul Berman (New York: Dell Publishing Co., 1992): 85–123.

24. Buchanan is quoted in the *Nation*, 6/13 January 1992, 21.

25. Jonathan Kozol, *Savage Inequalities: Children in America's Schools* (New York: Crown Publishers, 1991).

26. David L. Kirp, "The Battle of the Books," *San Francisco Chronicle*, 24 February 1991, Image section.

27. Molefi Kete Asante, *The Afrocentric Idea* (Philadelphia: Temple University Press, 1987), 6.

28. Quoted in Roger Lane, *William Dorsey's Philadelphia and Ours: On the Past and Future of the Black City in America* (New York: Oxford University Press, 1991), 278.

29. Gary B. Nash, *Red, White, and Black: The Peoples of Early America* (Englewood Cliffs, N.J.: Prentice-Hall, 1974).

30. Molefi Kete Asante, "Multiculturalism: An Exchange," *American Scholar* (Spring 1991): 268.

31. J. A. Rogers, *100 Amazing Facts about the Negro: With Complete Proof: A Short Cut to the World History of the Negro* (New York: F. Hubner, n.d.), 5, 21–22.

32. Asante, *The Afrocentric Idea*, 9.

33. Martin Bernal, *Black Athena: The Afroasiatic Roots of Classical Civilization* (New Brunswick, N.J.: Rutgers University Press, 1987); John Henrik Clarke, "Social Studies African-American Baseline Essay" (Portland, Oreg., c. 1991), SS-12–13 passim.

34. Gary B. Nash, *Forging Freedom: The Formation of Philadelphia's Black Community, 1720–1840* (Cambridge: Harvard University Press, 1988); idem, *Race and Revolution* (Madison, Wis.: Madison House, 1990); Gary B. Nash and Jean R. Soderlund, *Freedom by Degrees: Emancipation and Its Aftermath in Pennsylvania* (New York: Oxford University Press, 1991).

35. Henry Louis Gates, Jr., "Beware of the New Pharoahs," *Newsweek*, 23 September 1991, 47; idem, "Pluralism and Its Discontents," *Contention* (Fall 1992): 69–78.

36. Emery Reves, *The Anatomy of Peace* (New York: Harper & Brothers, 1945), 1.

37. Robert K. Fullinwider, "Multicultural Education," *University of Chicago Legal Forum* (1991): 80.

38. Roger Wilkins, *A Man's Life: An Autobiography* (New York: Simon & Schuster, 1982), 184.

39. John Bracey, "Facing Africa: The Price of Our History," *African Commentary* (November 1989): 12.

40. For research on the problem of esteem, see Martin V. Covington, "Self-Esteem and Failure in School: Analysis and Policy Implications" in *The Social Importance of Self-Esteem*, ed. Andrew M. Mecca, Neil J. Smelser, and John Vasconcellos (Berkeley and Los Angeles: University of California Press, 1989), 72–124, and Morris Rosenberg, Carmi Schooler, and Carrie Schoenbach, "Self-Esteem and Adolescent Problems: Modeling Reciprocal Effects," *American Sociological Review* 54 (December 1989): 1004–18.

41. Reported in Nicholas Lemann, *The Promised Land: The Great Black Migration and How It Changed America* (New York: Alfred A. Knopf, 1991), 350.

42. As quoted in ibid., 303.

43. *Los Angeles Times*, 2 February 1992, 1.

44. See, for examples, the elementary schools described in David L. Kirp, "Good Schools in Bad Times," *Los Angeles Times Magazine*, 5 January 1992, 18–19, 35–37. For academic successes at two other schools where minority students predominate and students from welfare families are common, see "2 Inglewood Schools Defy Odds, Achieve Excellence," *Los Angeles Times*, 2 February 1992.

45. Wade Nobles, quoted in Andrew Sullivan, "Racism 101," *New Republic*, 26 November 1990, 20.

46. Ibid., 25.

47. Leonard Jeffries, quoted in Jim Sleeper, "Blacks and Jews," *The Nation*, 9 September 1991, 252. For two accounts of Jeffries, see Michael Eric Dyson, "Leonard Jeffries and the Struggle for the Black Mind" in *Reflecting Black: African-American Cultural Criticism*, ed. Michael Eric Dyson (Minneapolis: University of Minnesota Press, 1993), and James Traub, "The Hearts and Minds of City College," *New Yorker* 69, no. 16 (7 June 1993): 42–54.

48. See Fullinwider, "Multicultural Education," 88, and Fullinwider, "Cosmopolitan Community," 17–18, on how "a positive sense of self may be the reverse side of a negative view of others" and how "we prize our group's cultural traits in contrast to the 'unattractive' traits of other groups."

49. Kirp, "The Battle of the Books," 25; for the debate in California over the adoption of a new series of textbooks meant to respond to the call for multicultural education, the most balanced accounts are Kirp, "Battle of the Books," and Richard Reinhold, "Class Struggle: California's Textbook Debate," *New York Times Magazine*, 29 September 1991.

50. Robert K. Landers, "Conflict over Multicultural Education," *Educational Research Reports*, 30 November 1990, 691, quoting Joint Center for Political Studies, Committee on Policy for Racial Justice, *Visions of a Better Way: A Black Appraisal of Public Schooling* (Washington, D.C.: Joint Center for Political Studies Press, 1989), 3–4.

51. W.E.B. Du Bois, *Souls of Black Folk: Essays and Sketches* (Chicago: A. C. McClurg & Co., 1903), 82.

52. Quoted in Jim Sleeper, *The Closest of Strangers: Liberalism and the Politics of Race in New York* (New York: W. W. Norton & Co., 1990), 234.

53. C.L.R. James, *Beyond a Boundary* (London: Hutchinson & Co., 1963), 38–39, 70.

54. FitzGerald, *America Revised*, 104.

55. "Multiculturalism: Building Bridges or Burning Them?" *Los Angeles Times*, 30 November 1992, 1.

56. Fullinwider, "Multicultural Education," 77.

57. Ibid., 81.

58. Fullinwider, "Cosmopolitan Community," 21.

59. Gunnar Myrdal, *An American Dilemma: The Negro Problem and Modern Democracy* (New York: Harper & Brothers, 1944), 13.

60. Vincent Gordon Harding, "Wrestling toward the Dawn: The Afro-American Freedom Movement and the Changing Constitution," *Journal of American History* 74 (1987): 31.

PART THREE

Recent Strategies for Reforming the Schools

7 THE SEARCH FOR ORDER AND THE REJECTION OF CONFORMITY: STANDARDS IN AMERICAN EDUCATION

DIANE RAVITCH

To many educators, the movement for national standards and assessments seems like a remarkable innovation, a development completely unprecedented in American history. Critics, left and right, fear that it will lead to a federal takeover of curriculum; others, aware of the basic conservatism of education, declare that it cannot work and will not happen.

Whatever the truth of these assertions, the fact is that the United States has a long history of standard-setting activities, sometimes overt and purposeful, at other times implicit and haphazard. The current movement does not come from nowhere. It is grounded in a tradition of efforts to establish agreement on what American students should know and be able to do and to determine how well they have learned.

The desire to assure that all children have access to schools that offer education of similar, high quality has been a primary reason to establish standards. Over the years, standards of various kinds have evolved— sometimes purposefully, sometimes serendipitously—to foster similarity in the quality of schooling by such means as

— the use of identical or similar textbooks;
— the specification of requirements for high school graduation or college entrance;
— the use of standardized achievement tests for promotion or college admission;
— the prescription of curriculum patterns; and
— the professionalization of teacher training, with shared norms and expectations (i.e., standards).

Although educators and educational critics periodically rebel against the constraints and stifling effects of conformity, uniformity, and standardization, a great deal of time and attention have been spent by educators and legislators trying to establish shared norms, expectations, and standards for purposes of efficiency or equality or both. This tension between the search for order and the rejection of conformity is healthy, since we value individualism and imagination far too much to embrace mechanistic prescriptions. Nonetheless, the effort to assure equal access to a good education for all students inevitably requires some form of standards.

In the earliest days of formal schooling, before the Revolution, standards existed by default, since most students learned to read from a very limited number of books, such as *The New England Primer*. For many years after the Revolution, Webster's blue-backed speller provided something akin to a national standard. Webster's spellers were used not only in school but by adults for self-education, setting clear standards for spelling and pronunciation, as Webster had hoped. And for many years, Lindley Murray's *English Reader* was the standard text in literature. As early as the 1830s, however, school reformers complained about the burgeoning numbers of textbooks in every field. Even though there was a multiplicity of titles, the content of the books was more like than unlike. And in some fields, like reading, one or two series dominated the market, like the McGuffey's reading books. When one looks at the textbooks of the nineteenth century, it is striking how similar were the history books, the readers, and others vying for market share in the same subject area. The uniformity found in the reading materials extended to classroom methods, with rare exceptions.

American schools by and large had content standards, as defined in relatively uniform classroom materials, and they even had an implicit consensus about performance standards, with a broadly shared scale that ranged from A to F, or from 100 to 60. It was not exact, but educators had a common vocabulary with which to gauge student performance.

Lacking any state or national testing systems, the only reliable standard for student performance in early America was provided by college admission requirements. Each college had its own entrance requirements, and prospective students were examined by the president of the college or members of the faculty in specific subjects. The first admission requirement to Harvard in 1642 read: "When any Scholar is able to read Tully or such like classical Latin in verse and prose, *suo (ut aiunt) Marte*, and decline perfectly the paradigms of nouns and verbs in ye Greeke tongue, then may hee bee admitted into ye College, nor shall any claime admission before such qualifications."[1] (*Suo, vestro,* or *nostro Marte* was a Latin proverb meaning by one's own exertions, without any help whatever.) The only significant addition to the college curriculum in colonial times was arithmetic, which appeared for the first time in the entrance requirements for Yale in 1745: "That none may expect to be admited into this College unless upon Examination of the President and Tutors, They shall be found able Extempore to Read, Construe and Parce Tully, Virgil and the Greek

Testament; and to write True Latin in Prose and to understand the rules of Prosodia, and common Arithmetic, and Shall bring Sufficient Testimony of his Blameless and Inoffensive Life."[2]

As time went by, college entrance requirements became both broader and more specific. That is, they expanded during the course of the nineteenth century to include more subjects, such as algebra, geometry, English grammar, science, modern foreign languages, history, and geography, but they became more specific about the literary works that students must master before their examination. Thus, Columbia College declared in 1785: "No candidate shall be admitted into the College . . . unless he shall be able to render into English Caesar's Commentaries of the Gallic War; the four Orations of Cicero against Catiline; the four first books of Virgil's Æneid; and the Gospels from the Greek; and to explain the government and connections of the words, and to turn English into grammatical Latin, and shall understand the four first rules of Arithmetic, with the rule of three."[3] Although there was some small variation in the Latin works that were required, the three constants in Latin were Cicero, Virgil, and Caesar. Students prepared themselves in accordance with these content standards and presented themselves for examination at the college of their choice.

In retrospect, the requirements seem fairly uniform, yet there was still enough variation in college entrance requirements to frustrate headmasters of academies and secondary schools. Consequently, in the late nineteenth century, several associations were created to promote closer relations between schools and colleges and, especially, uniformity of college admission requirements. The collaboration was good for the schools because it relieved them of the burden of preparing students for a wide variety of entrance examinations; it was also beneficial for the colleges because it enabled them to exert influence on the curriculum of the secondary schools.

As the last decade of the nineteenth century opened, many educators believed that the addition of new subjects had turned the high school curriculum into an anarchic mess. In 1892, in an effort to promote uniformity of curricular offerings in the high schools, the National Educational Association (NEA) established a panel called the Committee of Ten to make recommendations to improve the high school curriculum.[4] The chairman of the committee was Charles W. Eliot, president of Harvard University and one of the nation's most esteemed educators of his era. The committee included William T. Harris, the U.S. commissioner of education (and former superintendent of St. Louis), four other college presidents, and three high school principals (the tenth member was a college professor).

The Committee of Ten began its work by surveying forty high schools to learn what courses they were teaching. The survey revealed that thirty-six different subjects were offered, including five foreign languages, six mathematics courses, four science courses, and a few miscellaneous courses like stenography, penmanship, and music. To modern eyes, this menu stands in sharp contrast to the more than two thousand course titles that have been regularly reported to the U.S. Department of Education by the nation's high schools since the 1970s.

The Committee of Ten was the first national blue ribbon panel to study the curriculum of the high school; in the century that has passed since the creation of the Committee of Ten, many forests have been felled to print the reports of numberless committees, commissions, panels, task forces, and study groups on the needs or future of American education. In 1892, there was no precedent for a national body to issue recommendations to the many thousands of school districts, nor was there any mechanism to promote or require compliance. The committee had no way of knowing whether anyone would heed its proposals. Yet its report, perhaps because of the stature of its members and sponsors, as well as the novelty of the undertaking, received widespread attention and achieved some measure of influence upon the curriculums of many schools.

The Committee of Ten had to wrestle with four difficult issues: First, how to resolve the antagonism between the classical curriculum and modern academic subjects like science, history, and modern foreign languages; second, how to promote uniformity in preparation of students for college (and, conversely, how to encourage colleges to accept modern subjects as valid for college entrance); third, how to respond to demands by some educators for inclusion of practical courses like manual training; and fourth, whether the high schools should offer different curriculums for those who were college bound and those who were not.

The report of the Committee of Ten was an effort both to establish new curricular standards for high schools and to alter the admission standards for colleges and universities. And while it is true that other influences were simultaneously at work in schools and society, both complementing and subverting the proposals of the Ten, it seems clear that the report was extremely effective in changing standards at both levels of education in the years after it was issued. The committee engaged nine subject matter conferences to examine each major subject and to make recommendations on how it should be taught, how teachers should be prepared, when it should be introduced, for how many hours each week and for how many years, and so on. Each subject matter conference considered carefully the components of the course of study and how the subject should be assessed for college admission. The subjects were Latin; Greek; English; other modern languages; mathematics; physical science (physics, astronomy, and chemistry); natural history (biology, including botany, zoology, and physiology); history, civil government, and political economy; and geography (physical geography, geology, and meteorology).

The Ten recommended that the modern academic subjects should be equal in status to the classical curriculum for purposes of college entry. The report endorsed four model curriculums, which differed mainly in the amount of time given to foreign languages: *classical* (containing three languages, including Greek and Latin); *Latin-scientific* (containing two foreign languages, one of them modern); *modern languages* (containing two modern foreign languages); and *English* (containing only one foreign language, either ancient or modern). This recommendation implied certain things that seemed radical to some educators: first, that neither Latin nor Greek was absolutely necessary for college preparation and, second, that students should be permitted to choose their course of study, so long as it included English, mathematics, history, science, and foreign language.

The Committee of Ten lined up unequivocally on the side of educational equality. Demands were already being heard in the educational press for different kinds of education for the children of workers and the children of privilege, but the Ten rejected this counsel. Instead, the committee took a firm stand against differentiation between those who planned to go to college and those who did not. All nine of the subject matter conferences, and the Committee of Ten itself, agreed "that every subject which is taught at all in a secondary school should be taught in the same way and to the same extent to every pupil so long as he pursues it, no matter what the probable destination of the pupil may be, or at what point his education is to cease." The report concluded that "the secondary schools of the United States, taken as a whole, do not exist for the purpose of preparing boys and girls for colleges." They exist to prepare young people for "the duties of life," for which the best preparation is what we would today call a liberal education.[5]

Subsequent commentators complained that the Ten ignored those who were not college bound (the overwhelming majority of children at that time), instead of recognizing that the Ten meant that all children—especially those who were not headed for college—should have the benefit of a liberal education. The idea of the Ten was radical then, as it is now, for they proposed that all children had the intellectual capacity to benefit from an education that included foreign languages, mathematics, history, mathematics, science, and English. The Ten saw this not as a college-preparatory curriculum, but as a curriculum that would prepare all children for a rich and full life, no matter what their ultimate vocation.

One immediate result of the report was the creation of the Committee on College-Entrance Requirements, established by the NEA to promote the recommendations of the Committee of Ten. This committee, far less cele-

brated than the historic Ten, worked at formulating a common framework
for college preparation, consonant with the recommendations of the Ten. It
recommended that high schools adopt the use of "constants" or "units" to
provide a uniform measure for all courses. The committee recommended a
total of ten units: four units (or years) of foreign languages, two units of
mathematics, two units of English, one unit of science, and one unit of
history. In a four-year program of sixteen units, this left the student free to
elect six additional units. The consequence of this suggestion was that the
curricular discussion—previously focused by the Ten on parallel, equivalent *courses of study*—shifted to the concept of interchangeable, equivalent
units. This change not only advanced the notion of a standard unit of study,
but eventually served to promote the principle of electives and of equivalency among all kinds of subject matter. These *units*, initially proposed by
the Committee on College-Entrance Requirements, were retitled *Carnegie
units* after the Carnegie Foundation for the Advancement of Teaching
defined a unit as a course of five periods each week for one academic year.

Another product of the movement in the 1890s to establish uniform
standards for high school graduation and college entry was the College
Entrance Examination Board. Sponsored by President Eliot of Harvard, the
College Board was a fulfillment, in the words of one historian, of "Eliot's
two-fold vision of uniformity of standards and flexibility of programs."[6]
The purpose of the College Board was to organize a common examination
system for college admission. This arrangement assured colleges that they
could continue to admit whomever they chose, regardless of test scores,
without relinquishing authority to any outside body.[7] It was an ingenious
solution to a vexing problem: The private sector took responsibility for
creating a standard-setting process, which left high schools free to shape
their curriculums as they saw fit and colleges free to admit whomever they
wished.

The College Entrance Examination Board of the Middle States and
Maryland held its first examination in June 1901 in nine subjects: chemistry, English, French, German, Greek, history, Latin, mathematics, and
physics. The examinations were based on standards set by recognized
national committees—for example, the American Philological Association, the Modern Language Association, and the American Historical Association. In the second year, new subjects were added: Spanish, botany,
geography, and drawing.

The College Entrance Examination Board had to grapple with the issue
of standards in the different subject areas. Initially, it assumed that it could
rely on the various scholarly bodies, like the Modern Language Association, but these proved to be uninterested in secondary school teaching. So
the board created its own "committee of review," with responsibility to
establish requirements for the examinations in each subject. This commit-

tee regularly assembled special commissions of school and college teachers to review and revise subject standards.

Even the act of reading and grading the examinations helped to support the implementation of what might be called voluntary national standards in the different subject areas. Each year, large numbers of teachers from schools and colleges across the country would meet in New York to read the examinations. There they would talk, discuss papers, laugh about "boners," and work informally at defining performance standards for their field. In modern terms, they networked as a community of scholars and teachers. At the same time, they shaped standards and enforced them. The grading of the examinations was a professional development seminar of the highest order.

Many secondary schools prepared their students for the college entrance examinations. By reading through old examinations and by perusing the College Board's syllabus of English classics, teachers could be sure that their students were well prepared for the examinations. But these practices led to complaints about cramming and to criticism that the form of the examination tested memory power rather than the students' ability to use what they had learned. Nonetheless, the secondary schools knew what their students had to learn to prepare for college and for the entrance examinations.

The College Entrance Examination Board provided a standard for college preparation, at least for those students who wanted to apply to the selective colleges that were members of the College Board. But many educators continued to object to college domination, and in the second decade of the century, the National Education Association sponsored a Commission on the Reorganization of Secondary Education (CRSE), which established a pattern of standards that sharply diverged from the academic emphasis of the Committee of Ten and the College Board.

Unlike the Committee of Ten, which was chaired by the president of Harvard and included college presidents and secondary school principals, the CRSE was dominated by educationists. Its chair was Clarence D. Kingsley, the state high school supervisor for Massachusetts, and its members were drawn mainly from the world of professional education and colleges of education. Unlike the conferences of the Committee of Ten, which focused on academic subjects, the CRSE established committees not only for academic subjects but also for industrial arts, household arts, vocational guidance, agriculture, and other nonacademic areas. The report of this commission, published in 1918, identified "the main objectives of education," as follows: "1. Health. 2. Command of fundamental processes. 3. Worthy home-membership. 4. Vocation. 5. Citizenship. 6. Worthy use of leisure. 7. Ethical character."[8] Every academic subject was required to demonstrate its value in achieving these objectives; the emphasis was on

utility and social efficiency. Several academic subjects, especially the classical languages and history, were difficult to justify or rationalize in terms of
the seven cardinal principles. Neither history nor geography survived as a
subject; both were submerged into the new field of the "social studies." The
new standard for high schools, then, was not to be based on the intellectual
development of all youngsters, nor on a commitment to the ideal of liberal
learning, but on preparing youngsters for present and future social roles.
The goal—the standard—was social efficiency. The report endorsed differentiated curriculums, including agricultural, business, clerical, industrial, fine arts, and household arts curriculums. At the time, this seemed an
appropriate approach for schools that were suddenly overwhelmed with
large numbers of immigrant children, many of whom spoke little or no
English.

The report gave strong support to the development of comprehensive
high schools. Unfortunately, it also supported the practice of curricular
tracking, whereby school officials could guide students into appropriate
curricular experiences based on predictions about students' future vocation. These guesses tended to encourage differentiation based on social
class, race, and ethnicity. Thus, the academic track increasingly became a
preserve for the minority who were college bound—the bright, the ambitious, the children of the educated—while the other tracks were occupied
by the majority of students who were directed into programs that presumably would prepare them for their future vocational roles. From the point
of view of the commission and many other educators, college-preparatory
programs were a waste of time for these children.

The report of the CRSE was, of course, a reflection of widely shared
views in the education profession and in society. The term *academic* was
increasingly used in a derisory fashion to refer to studies that had no
practical value. Many educators, for many different reasons, converged on
certain themes that appeared in the report: that an academic or liberal
education was not appropriate for everyone; that the purposes of education should be derived from the activities of life, rather than from book
learning; that book learning was sterile, "academic"; that children had
different needs and should therefore have educations that were fitted to
their needs; that the role of the school should change to fit the needs of
society (and the needs of society were usually in the eye of the beholder).
The overriding philosophy was social efficiency, and it supported curricular tracking and a devaluation of liberal education.

The two reports, separated by twenty-five years, both claimed to be
based on the principles of a democratic society. The Committee of Ten
believed that all children should have the experience of a common academic curriculum, that all should be educated in the same way regardless
of who their parents were or what their intended destination in life; the

authors of the *Cardinal Principles* believed that the curriculum should be tailored and differentiated to meet the needs of society and of children. Beginning with similar premises, the two ended up in very different places. The compromise that was struck over time between the conflicting ideals was that the principles of the Committee of Ten applied to the academic track and the principles of the CRSE governed the vocational and general track. Or, put another way, the CRSE won. The ideas of the CRSE won out not because they were argued more persuasively but because they provided a good fit for the thorny problems that faced the schools: the problems of mass education and the problems of educating large numbers of children from poor and non-English-speaking backgrounds. Parents of these children did not demand that they be excused from the academic curriculum; what evidence exists suggests that immigrant parents did not want their children to have a curriculum different from that in the best schools. It would have been possible to educate poor and immigrant children in the way prescribed by the Ten, but to do so would have required enormous intellectual energy in the reformulation of subject matter. It was easier to teach academic subjects to academically able children than to rethink and redesign what was taught in school so that all children could learn and understand the material in the college track. To do so would have been very difficult and very inefficient in an age when efficiency was highly valued. The path of least resistance was chosen, and, in time, educators and parents came to believe that certain studies—like advanced courses in mathematics and science and history—were only for the college-bound students, a distinct minority.

At the same time that the CRSE provided the rationale for differentiation of curriculum, the availability of the new techniques of standardized testing facilitated differentiation. After the debut of intelligence tests during World War I, the testing industry mushroomed, providing a broad array of tests of ability, tests of intelligence, and tests of educational achievement.

The question of standards, as applied to the academic curriculum, was defined during most of the twentieth century by college admission requirements. These consisted of the colleges' entrance requirements—a specification of so many years or units of certain academic subjects—and the college entrance examinations. Until the development of the American College Testing (ACT) program in 1959, the only national examination for the college bound was that of the College Entrance Examination Board. The College Board, while vigilant in protecting the quality of its examinations, was sensitive to constant criticism that the examinations exerted too much influence on the high school curriculum. In the years immediately after World War I, the board took interest in the new movement for intelligence testing. Unlike the traditional college entrance examinations, which tested what students knew, the intelligence tests claimed to test students' innate intelligence or what students were capable of doing. In 1922, the College Board expressed "favorable interest" in the use of a "general intelligence examination" and its readiness to administer such examinations when practicable.[9] Since none of the members of the board was an expert on psychological testing, they appointed an advisory commission of experts, including Carl C. Brigham of Princeton, Henry T. Moore of Dartmouth, and Robert M. Yerkes of Yale. Brigham and Yerkes were, of course, pioneers in the development of intelligence testing. Brigham soon emerged as the driving force in a successful effort to reorient the college entrance examinations and turn them into tests of intelligence or aptitude.

Brigham and his team of psychological experts built upon the College Board's interest in determining a student's readiness for college-level work and used it as the foundation for a new test altogether, the Scholastic Aptitude Test (SAT). There were skeptics on the College Board and among the secondary school representatives, but the experts had a mantle of authority—the authority of science—that swept along the doubters.

The first Scholastic Aptitude Test was given in 1926 to 8,040 candidates, most of whom were applying to Ivy League colleges. The father of the SAT, Carl Brigham, became a salaried member of the College Board staff in 1930, where he continued to refine the SAT. Although the SAT did not take the place of the traditional written entrance examination until the Second World War, the College Board recognized its value immediately. The appeal of the SAT grew apace with faith in social science. The standardized, multiple choice test saved the College Board from the wrath of those who complained that the college entrance examinations had too much influence over the curriculum of the secondary schools. It was the perfect answer to the angry headmaster who supposedly muttered in 1902, "I'll be damned if any Board down in New York City, with a college professor at its head, is going to tell me and my faculty what or how to teach!"[10] The SAT tested linguistic and mathematical power and had no connection to any particular curriculum. This left secondary schools free to require whatever they chose. The literature curriculum, which had been anchored by the college entrance examinations for many years, was completely abandoned by the SAT, allowing secondary schools to teach whatever books they wished and, if they chose, to drop the traditional classics altogether.

During the 1930s credibility shifted from the old-style written tests to the new-style SAT. Although some of those on the College Board must have been uneasy about the shift to intelligence/aptitude testing in place of achievement testing, Brigham became "the policy maker" of the board, "and whatever route was taken for the next few years was charted by him."[11] Colleges began to recognize the practical value of the SAT for predicting students' ability to do college-level work, and each year the number who took the SAT increased. Then, on Pearl Harbor Day, 1941, at a meeting of representatives of Harvard, Yale, and Princeton, a decision was made to cancel the June essay examinations because of the war. Normally there would have been an outcry from conservative educators, who continued to believe that an essay examination was preferable to a multiple-choice test of aptitude. But the war emergency hastened what at the time seemed inevitable. With this decision, the SAT became *the* college entrance examination for the nation's most prestigious colleges and universities. The advent of the machine-scored examination meant, first, that the standard-setting force of the traditional (i.e., written) college entrance examination was eliminated and, second, that the standard-implementing activities of those teachers and scholars who met annually to read the examinations were terminated.

During most of the 1940s and 1950s, the College Board claimed that the purpose of the SAT was not to influence standards but to help colleges identify students who were ready for collegiate studies. However, other examinations offered by the College Board defined and supported educational standards, such as advanced placement (AP) examinations and achievement tests. Over time, it became clear that the AP exams and the achievement tests bolstered high school academic standards at the same time that the SAT undermined them. With its focus solely on mathematics and verbal skills, the SAT was virtually curriculum-free. By implying that college admission would be decided by *aptitude* rather than *achievement*, the SAT encouraged the widespread belief that innate ability, not effort, was what really counted. Although the Educational Testing Service contended for many years that scores on the SAT were not affected by coaching, students did improve their performance by attending special coaching sessions or by learning test-taking skills. Until the latter 1960s, the SAT was buttressed by high school graduation requirements and college entrance requirements. When the latter two were reduced in the late 1960s and early 1970s (in response to student demands), the SAT was left standing almost alone as the guardian of standards, a role for which it was not designed and to which it was not equal.[12]

College entrance examinations were one source of educational standards; another was mandated testing, which was introduced on a broad scale in the early twentieth century. In the 1890s, educational reformer Joseph Mayer Rice introduced what may have been the first test to be administered to a large national sample (in spelling). Edward Thorndike of Columbia University introduced many standardized achievement tests. Thorndike's colleagues at Teachers College helped to spread standardized achievement testing as part of the school survey movement, which assessed the quality of numerous school districts around the nation and reached its peak in the second decade of the twentieth century. Many schools were administering standardized achievement tests in spelling, arithmetic, reading, and other subjects before the First World War. The use of widescale intelligence testing during the war, coupled with the general admiration for science and social science, helped to popularize standardized testing in the 1920s. During that decade, hundreds of intelligence tests and achievement tests were produced for use in the schools. Both kinds of tests were used to sort children according to their ability and to place them into appropriate programs.[13]

Since the 1960s, the volume of criticism of all kinds of standardized testing has escalated rapidly. Two points should be made about the general use of standardized testing of both intelligence and achievement. First, both were used to allocate students to different kinds of educational opportunities, in keeping with the curricular differentiation advocated by the CRSE. Second, the widespread adoption of standardized achievement tests relieved states and districts of the necessity of consciously setting their own academic standards. The critical point is that educators relegated the all-important task of deciding what children should know and be able to do to the commercial testmakers.

A similar story can be told about the role of textbooks as a standardizing element in American education. Woodward, Elliott, and Nagel estimated "that from 75% to 90% of classroom instructional time is structured by textbook programs."[14] Produced for mass market sales in a highly competitive marketplace, textbooks are written to satisfy the largest buyers, especially the textbook-adoption committees in large states like Texas and California. Because the textbooks have such an important role in determining what content is taught and because they are so widely used as a basic instructional tool, they in effect determine what children learn. How do textbook writers decide what children should know? We hope that the writers include among them some scholars and teachers; the writers review the contents of the leading textbooks in the field and the requirements of the textbook-adoption committees in a score or so of states. Through this serendipitous process, the writers arrive at content standards that provide the framework for their product.

With the passage of the Elementary and Secondary Education Act in 1965, standardized achievement testing became securely entrenched because the law required regular testing in schools that receive federal funding through Title I or Chapter I. So the tests, always important, gained an institutional foothold and became a mandated element in the programs of a large proportion of public schools. New programs of statewide testing were introduced in the 1970s to meet the requirements of the minimum competency movement, which demanded proof that students had achieved basic skills before graduating or being promoted. During the same era, textbooks became more uniform than ever, as big companies gobbled up little companies and as a small number of textbooks in each field captured a large percentage of the market. By 1987–88, forty-five states and the District of Columbia were using some kind of statewide test; twenty-five of those entities were employing a commercially developed, nationally normed test.[15]

The proliferation of mass-market textbooks and standardized tests has been criticized by many educators on a wide variety of grounds, but both texts and tests continue to be widely used and enormously influential on what is taught in the classroom. The relevant point, for this narrative, is that both texts and tests are prepared on the basis of assumptions about what is worth knowing. Sometimes these assumptions are explicitly and thoughtfully arrived at, and sometimes they are derived from market research (what sells) without a lot of time devoted to debating or studying what knowledge is of most worth.

The standards that are most widely shared in American education are those that have been embedded somehow in the commercial textbooks and tests, as well as in the college entrance examinations (the SAT and the ACT). Actually, we have multiple standards, depending on the curriculum track in which students are enrolled, whether they plan to go to college, and whether they have applied to a selective college or university. Students are educated to very high standards if they expect to take advanced placement examinations and if they intend to apply to one of a relatively small number of selective colleges. Students who are not planning to go to college are probably exposed to standards that are geared to minimum competency, which they may demonstrate by checking off the correct box on a test of basic skills and by tests of simple recall. Students who intend to go to an unselective college or university, one that takes almost all applicants, will encounter standards that are not demanding; the students know, and their teachers know, that they will be accepted into the college of their choice regardless of how much or how little they work in school and regardless of how much or how little they have learned in school.

The state of educational standards became a national issue in 1975, when the College Board called attention to the fact that SAT scores had fallen steadily and sharply since 1963. A study panel appointed by the College Board concluded two years later that the score declines had first been caused by the diversification of the pool of test takers but had then been accelerated by changes in the practices of the schools, such as dilution of the academic curriculum, lower enrollments in advanced courses, social promotion, less assignment of homework, and grade inflation. The panel made clear that high schools had lowered expectations for almost all students in response to what was perceived as the needs of a more diverse student body.[16]

It was not only SAT scores that declined during the late 1960s and most of the 1970s but also scores on virtually every other standardized test in the nation. Some states began to take stock of the quality of education, and none was as active as were the fifteen states that formed the Southern Regional Education Board (SREB). In 1981, a special task force of the SREB issued a statement called *A Need for Quality*, which called for higher standards for teachers and students, as well as higher teachers' salaries. Critical of the climate of low expectations in education, the SREB called for strengthening of the high school curriculum and of college entrance requirements.[17]

In 1983, *A Nation at Risk*, the report of the National Commission on Excellence in Education, appeared. That report warned of "a rising tide of mediocrity that threatens our very future as a Nation and a people." It described numerous indicators of low educational achievement and criticized specific failings in the school, especially "a cafeteria-style curriculum," low expectations, low standards, and a widespread lack of seriousness of educational purpose. Its primary recommendation was that "state and local high school graduation requirements be strengthened and that, at a minimum, all students seeking a diploma be required to lay the foundations in the Five New Basics by taking the following curriculum during their 4 years of high school: (a) 4 years of English; (b) 3 years of mathematics; (c) 3 years of science; (d) 3 years of social studies; (e) one-half year of computer science. For the college-bound, 2 years of foreign language in high school are strongly recommended in addition to those taken earlier."[18]

The publication of *A Nation at Risk* in 1983 was followed by a frenzy of public concern about the quality of education. Many states established task forces, commissions, study groups, and the like. Many raised their graduation requirements to demonstrate that students were expected to study more academic courses. Although it became fashionable to say that the reforms of this period achieved little, this is not accurate. Student enrollments increased in core academic subjects like mathematics and science, and course taking is directly related to achievement.[19]

And something else happened. A new breed of reformer emerged, as well as a new understanding of what was needed to improve student achievement. In 1983, California elected a new state superintendent, Bill Honig, who pledged to raise standards and improve the quality of public education. While tirelessly advocating increased funding for public schools, Honig started a process of reviewing and reconstructing the curriculum in each subject field. He recognized that the starting point for reform is agreement on what to teach, and he brought together panels of teachers and scholars to rewrite the state's curriculum frameworks, which serve as guidelines for textbook publishers. Since California has 11 percent of the nation's schoolchildren and since the state adopts textbooks, the frameworks offered the state a way to influence the state (and national) textbook market. Honig also revised state testing, encouraging the development of assessments that were based on the state's curriculum rather than on national norms. In effect, Honig shaped a coherent program of systemic reform by setting new curriculum standards, procuring a new generation of textbooks and technology, and developing new tests.

The southern states had already anticipated the prescription of *A Nation at Risk* through the work of the SREB. Several governors, notably Lamar Alexander of Tennessee, Richard Riley of South Carolina, and Bill Clinton of Arkansas, took the lead in shaping reform programs that emphasized the establishment of educational standards and assessments. The organizing principle of this new state-based movement was that the focus of reform should be on results, rather than on process or inputs, and that states should press for higher educational achievement while reducing regulations and other procedural burdens on schools. In 1986, Governors Alexander, Clinton, and Riley worked together on a report for the National Governors' Association, titled *Time for Results*; on behalf of the other governors, Lamar Alexander wrote that "the Governors are ready for some old-fashioned horse-trading. We'll regulate less, if schools and school districts will produce better results."[20] Thus, the governors most actively involved in state-level reforms moved to identify standards, by which they meant *what students should know and be able to do*, and to develop assessments to provide information about whether students were making progress toward the standards.

Meanwhile, there was increasing demand by policy makers for information about student achievement. In 1986, eight southern states (Arkansas, Florida, Louisiana, North Carolina, South Carolina, Tennessee, Virginia, and West Virginia) administered the tests of the National Assessment of Educational Progress to a representative sample of students. They did so to obtain "the most current and reliable measure of how their students' achievement in reading and/or writing compares to truly national and regional results." They also wanted to establish benchmarks "to gauge their students' relative achievement levels." Winifred L. Godwin, the president of the Southern Regional Education Board, explained the southern states' interest in assessment: "The obvious question is—How will we know that we are making progress? Many measures of progress will be important, but none will surpass student achievement."[21]

In 1987, a study group led by Lamar Alexander and H. Thomas James proposed an expansion of the National Assessment of Educational Progress to include state-by-state comparisons (Hillary Rodham Clinton was a member of the study group). Explicit in this recommendation was recognition that "state and local school administrators are encountering a rising public demand for thorough information on the quality of their schools, allowing comparison with data from other states and districts."[22] Implicit in this recommendation was the suggestion that school districts ought to be allowed to participate directly in the National Assessment to learn how their students were doing compared to other districts. Congress authorized trial state assessments for 1990, 1992, and 1994 but showed little interest in expanding the assessment to the district level. Even the state-by-state assessment was controversial, since many educators saw no value in the comparisons and recoiled against the drift toward a national test.

The state-level activity by policy makers and elected officials reflected a somewhat commonsense understanding that the effort to improve education must begin with an agreement about what children are expected to learn, that is, content standards. Traditionally, this agreement had been expressed in Carnegie units, defined by states as years of science or mathematics or English needed to graduate. But Honig in California and the southern education reformers moved beyond Carnegie units to seek greater specificity, to identify what children were expected to know and be able to do. And wherever there was standard setting there was also new interest in finding some reliable means of measuring student progress toward meeting the content standards, thus increasing the search for a test or an assessment that would permit comparisons across states, districts, even schools.

As many states wrestled with the difficult process of defining their standards, the National Council of Teachers of Mathematics (NCTM) embarked on a course that would alter the national debate about standards. In response to the criticisms expressed in *A Nation at Risk* and other national reports about the state of mathematics and science education, the NCTM decided to develop a new K–12 mathematics curriculum.[23] In 1986, the NCTM created the Commission on Standards for School Mathematics, which led a broad consensus process involving large numbers of teachers, supervisors, mathematics educators, and mathematicians. Writing teams met during the summer of 1987; they reviewed state curriculum frameworks and the curriculum standards of other nations. Ten thousand copies of the draft document prepared that summer were circulated and reviewed. The writing teams revised the draft standards in 1988, and the NCTM standards were published in 1989. The chair of the NCTM Commission on Standards, Thomas Romberg of the University of Wisconsin, wrote that the writing teams were given the following charge:

1. To create a coherent vision regarding:
   a. what it means to do mathematics;
   b. what students need to do in learning mathematics;

    c. what teachers should do in teaching mathematics;

    d. what the emphasis of the curriculum should be;

    e. what it means to be mathematically literate in a world that relies on calculators and computers to carry out mathematical procedures, and, in a world where mathematics is rapidly growing and being extensively applied in many fields.

2. To create a series of standards for the curriculum and for evaluation that articulates this vision.[24]

The NCTM gave three reasons for developing standards: first, to ensure quality (i.e., to "ensure that the public is protected from shoddy products"); second, to express expectations (just as, for example, the American Psychological Association sets standards for tests to establish their reliability and validity); and, third, to establish "criteria for excellence." This last reason meant that the NCTM wanted to replace low minimum standards with a goal that would become a stimulus for change; as Romberg explained it, the standards would be "the 'flag' around which teachers can rally for support" and would serve as "an informed vision of what should be done, given current knowledge and experience."[25]

The central concept of the NCTM standards is that "knowing" mathematics is "doing" mathematics. The emphasis throughout is on active learning, problem solving, reasoning about mathematics, and communicating mathematically. The standards are intended not just for the college bound, but for all students. Their goal is to transform mathematics education so that all students are able to develop mathematical power and to apply mathematical thinking. The standards are intended to replace rote memorization and drill with thinking, estimating, questioning, and figuring things out, and they provide teachers with numerous examples of suggested classroom strategies rather than with a detailed list of requirements.

The NCTM standards had their detractors, to be sure; there continued to be educators who preferred drill and practice and believed that the NCTM standards veered too sharply away from computation. And there were no guarantees that the standards would produce higher achievement because they were untested. But the NCTM standards nonetheless had a dramatic influence on the field of mathematics. First of all, they emerged from a successful consensus process: They represented the work of the nation's leading mathematics educators. Second, as standards, they were dynamic in their reach: The full implementation of the standards required the revision of instruction, teacher education, professional development, textbooks, technology, and assessment. Within two to three years after the NCTM standards were released, significant changes could be seen in every one of these areas, as textbook publishers, schools of education, technology developers, and test makers all claimed that they were working to conform to the NCTM standards.

At the same time that the NCTM was drafting and revising and publishing its standards, education moved to the front burner as a national issue. In the fall of 1988, soon after the presidential election, President George Bush invited the nation's governors to a summit in Charlottesville, Virginia. At that meeting, the president and the governors agreed that the nation should have national goals for education in the year 2000. These goals were forged through intensive negotiations between the White House and the National Governors' Association.

In the year 2000,
1. All children in America will start school ready to learn.
2. The high school graduation rate will increase to at least 90 per cent.
3. American students will leave grades four, eight, and twelve having demonstrated competency in challenging subject matter including English, mathematics, science, history, and geography; and every school in America will ensure that all students learn to use their minds well, so they may be prepared for responsible citizenship, further learning, and productive employment in our modern economy.
4. U.S. students will be first in the world in science and mathematics achievement.
5. Every adult American will be literate and possess the knowledge and skills necessary to compete in a global economy and exercise the rights and responsibilities of citizenship.
6. Every school in America will be free of drugs and violence and will offer a safe, disciplined environment conducive to learning.[26]

To monitor the nation's progress in moving toward the goals, the National Education Goals Panel was established, consisting of governors and representatives of the White House and the Department of Education. (The initial exclusion of members of Congress from the Goals Panel alienated the legislative branch and made many members unwilling to support the work of the panel.) Goal 3 and goal 4 clearly had implications for the promotion of standards. For American students to demonstrate "competency in challenging subject matter," it would be necessary to define what kind of subject matter was "challenging" and what constitutes "competency."

To advance the new agenda based on the national education goals, President Bush appointed Lamar Alexander as his secretary of education in the spring of 1991. A former governor, Alexander was committed to collaboration with the governors on behalf of the National Education Goals. He shaped the America 2000 plan, which was not a new federal program but rather was a nationwide strategy to reach the goals. It involved, first, encouraging thousands of communities to develop their own local plans to reach the goals; second, promoting the idea of "new schools," schools that would "break the mold" by using time, technology, and resources differently and more effectively than traditional schools; third, supporting the development of national standards and a voluntary national achievement test; and, fourth, advocating means-tested vouchers to allow parents to choose among public, private, and religious schools.

Shortly after Alexander took office, he persuaded Congress to authorize a bipartisan commission called the National Council on Education Standards and Testing. The co-chairs of this council were Governor Carroll Campbell of South Carolina (a Republican) and Governor Roy Romer of Colorado (a Democrat), who also were leaders of the National Education Goals Panel. The thirty-two members of the council included members of the administration, Congress, and educators. After six months of intense deliberation, the council concluded that "high national standards tied to assessments are desirable. In the absence of well-defined and demanding standards, education in the United States has gravitated toward *de facto* national minimum expectations." The council stipulated that national standards should be voluntary, not mandated by the federal government; national, not federal; geared to high expectations, not minimal competency; and designed to provide focus and direction rather than a national curriculum.[27]

To support the recommendations of the council, the U.S. Department of Education made grants to independent scholarly and professional organizations to develop content standards in science, history, the arts, civics, geography, English, and foreign languages. The grants for science and history were made even as the council was deliberating; the other grants followed the release of the council's report in January 1992. The arts, civics, and foreign languages were not explicitly mentioned in the goals, but the secretary decided that the specification of five academic subjects was not intended to exclude other important academic subjects, especially the arts, civics, and foreign languages.[28] The NCTM standards served as an explicit model, demonstrating the importance of a broad and inclusive consensus process and the power of standards to promote reform in textbooks, tests, instruction, and teacher education. In addition, the department supported grant competitions to enable states to create new curriculum frameworks in the same subjects in which national standards were being developed, in effect, inviting a synergy between national and state standard setting.

By 1993, some $10 million of federal funds had been committed to the development of national content standards in key subject areas. With additional federal funds allocated to state curriculum development not only by the U.S. Department of Education, but also—in mathematics and science—by the National Science Foundation, both money and political momentum supported widespread activity to define the content standards and performance standards at which teachers and students were to aim.

Shortly after taking office in 1993, the Clinton administration signaled its support for the standards-based reform agenda by introducing Goals 2000 to encourage the development of content standards, performance standards, and "opportunity-to-learn" standards (i.e., measures of the conditions of teaching and learning). This legislation was passed in 1994. It creates a federal agency (the National Education Standards and Improvement Council) to certify national and state standards. In the future, standards will be both national *and* federal.

Much remains to be decided: what kind of agency, if any, will oversee the development of content standards? How will these standards be revised? Will there be assessments based on the standards? Who will prepare them? Will there be any consequences (for students) attached to the results of such assessments? Can the standards be kept free of political influence? Will the standards represent criteria for excellence, or will they be diluted to a low minimum of competence?

My own view is that the purposeful effort to construct national standards is a promising undertaking that offers the hope of promoting change in many parts of the educational system. It will be a magnet for criticism, not only from those who fear the heavy hand of government intrusion, but also from educationists who distrust any emphasis on disciplinary knowledge and who find it hard to believe that children from disadvantaged backgrounds can respond to intellectual challenge.

The promise is that we as a nation can develop a clear and fruitful consensus about what we want children to know and be able to do; that this consensus will prove helpful to students and teachers and will provide the grounds for improving teacher education, assessment, textbooks, staff development, and classroom technology. The implications for assessment are obvious: Tests should be based on what students have learned, not on their aptitude or native ability. The syllabus for examinations should be made public, so that teachers and pupils know what is expected and can study what is important. It is appropriate to "teach to the test" if the test is valid, reliable, and geared to knowledge and skills that are important. The use of curriculum-free tests for important decisions—e.g., college admission and employment—serves only to certify the unimportance and irrelevance of what youngsters study in school and of the effort that they apply to their studies. With national standards, it becomes possible to base educational tests on what children learn, instead of separating what is learned and what is tested.

It seems eminently useful to describe in plain language and with forceful example what we want children to learn and to construct educational reforms around that agreement. The idea of content standards has powerful implications for instruction and assessment. It does not mean that education will be standardized, but that the expectations that we have for children will be both higher and more transparent. The act of explaining what is needed for success is an essential component of equity; other nations establish national standards both to provide equal opportunity and to encourage higher achievement. In the absence of clear expectations for all children, curricular differentiation favors the advantaged.

We learn from history that American education does have standards and that these standards have emerged in a patchwork, higgledy-piggledy, uncoordinated manner. For much of our history, our curriculum standards have been created—almost accidentally—by those who develop commercially produced textbooks and tests. What children should know and be able to do has been decided offhandedly through a sort of consensus process that occurred at the intersection between state departments of education and publishers hoping to market their products. At the high end, performance standards were established by college admission tests and advanced placement tests; for most students, however, the minimal expectations embedded in nationally normed tests became *de facto* national standards.

The challenge before us as a nation is to develop a thoughtful process to decide what knowledge is of most worth and what knowledge is most valuable to children who will live and work in the twenty-first century. History tells us that it will not be easy to do this; in fact, we know already that the fractious politics of curriculum making guarantees controversy at almost every step of the journey. Partisans with a mission will seek centralized control, if they think they can get it, to carry their message into every schoolroom; others, fearful of centralization and loss of autonomy, will resist any coordinated effort to develop content standards. But again, the message of history is that autonomy is an illusion; standards are already in place, an accidental product of decisions made for various reasons. (Was the state-adopted textbook selected because of its educative power or because it had a strong binding, good paper stock, and plentiful graphics and "mentioned" the right list of topics and names?) Could we do better as a society if we consciously and thoughtfully decided what we want children to learn and if we purposefully redesigned the customary means of assessing whether and how well students have learned what was taught? Would more children achieve at higher levels if we were explicit about what was needed for success in school? Could we serve the ends of both excellence and equity by making expectations clearer to everyone involved in the educational process? There is also the substantial risk that a federal agency, governed by a politically appointed board, will be unable to endorse anything other than lowest-common-denominator standards.

The risk—and it is real—is that the effort will prove impossible because it is too complex, too controversial, too easily misinterpreted, and too radical a change. The critics are many; for most of this century, many American educators have been suspicious, often even hostile, to reforms grounded in subject matter, in decisions about what children should learn. A persistent strain in American education reacts negatively to any emphasis on knowledge, as though problem-solving skills, creativity, and other desirable educational goals were inconsistent with knowledge.

My training as a historian warns me not to expect too much, cautions me that educators have an unfortunate habit of making the best the enemy of the good, thus beating back any proposed reform that does not promise to solve all problems simultaneously or to lift all boats equally and at the same pace. Yet my participation in the process as a reformer keeps me hopeful that we will somehow muddle through, that the naysayers will give change a chance, and that we will aim for and continually pursue a synthesis of our twin ideals of excellence and equity.

NOTES

1. Edwin Cornelius Broome, *A Historical and Critical Discussion of College Admission Requirements* (New York: Macmillan, 1903), 18.

2. Ibid., 30.

3. Ibid., 34.

4. The National Educational Association was a forerunner to today's National Education Association. At that time, however, it was not a teachers' union; most of its members were school superintendents.

5. The report of the Committee of Ten is reprinted in Theodore Sizer, *Secondary Schools at the Turn of the Century* (New Haven: Yale University Press, 1964), or see National Educational Association, *Report of the Committee on Secondary School Studies Appointed at the Meeting of the National Educational Association, July 9, 1892; with the Reports of the Conferences Arranged by This Committee, and Held December 28–30, 1892,* Bureau of Education, document 205 (Washington, 1893).

6. Edward A. Krug, *The Shaping of the American High School, 1880–1920* (Madison: University of Wisconsin Press, 1964), 147.

7. Until the mid–twentieth century, many selective colleges routinely limited the number of Jewish and Catholic students by quotas, and they would have been

reluctant to embrace any scheme that would cause them to accept students strictly on the basis of test scores.

8. Commission on the Reorganization of Secondary Education, *Cardinal Principles of Secondary Education*, bulletin 35 (Washington, D.C.: Bureau of Education, Department of the Interior, Government Printing Office, 1918).

9. Claude M. Fuess, *The College Board: Its First Fifty Years* (New York: College Entrance Examination Board, 1967), 104.

10. Ibid., 57.

11. Ibid., 113.

12. Clifford Adelman, "Devaluation, Diffusion and the College Connection: A Study of High School Transcripts, 1964–1981" (Washington, D.C.: U.S. Department of Education, 1982).

13. Paul Davis Chapman, "Schools as Sorters: Lewis M. Terman and the Intelligence Testing Movement, 1890–1930" (Ph.D. diss., Stanford University, 1979), 165–80.

14. Arthur Woodward, David L. Elliott, and Kathleen Carter Nagel, *Textbooks in School and Society* (New York: Garland Publishing Co., 1988), 7.

15. Daniel Marks, "Statewide Achievement Testing: A Brief History," *Educational Research Quarterly* 13, no. 3 (1989): 40–41.

16. College Board, *On Further Examination* (New York: College Board, 1977).

17. Southern Regional Education Board, *The Need for Quality* (Atlanta: Southern Regional Education Board, 1981), 16–20.

18. National Commission on Excellence in Education, *A Nation at Risk* (Washington, D.C.: Government Printing Office, 1983), 5, 8–9, 18.

19. Rolf K. Blank and Doreen Gruebel, *State Indicators of Science and Mathematics Education, 1993* (Washington, D.C.: Council of Chief State School Officers, 1993), 25–26.

20. National Governors' Association, *Time for Results* (Washington, D.C.: National Governors' Association, 1986), 3.

21. Southern Regional Education Board, *Measuring Student Achievement: Comparable Test Results for Participating SREB States, the Region, and the Nation* (Atlanta: Southern Regional Education Board, 1986), iii, 2.

22. *The Nation's Report Card: Improving the Assessment of Student Achievement*, Report of the Study Group, Lamar Alexander, Chairman, H. Thomas James, Vice-Chairman, with a Review of the Report by a Committee of the National Academy of Education (Washington, D.C.: National Academy of Education, 1987), 11.

23. National Science Board Commission on Precollege Education in Mathematics, Science and Technology, *Educating Americans for the Twenty-First Century* (Washington, D.C.: NSBCPEM, 1983); Thomas A. Romberg, "The NCTM Standards as a Model for Discipline-based School Reform" in *Telecommunications as a Tool for Educational Reform: Implementing the NCTM Mathematics Standards* (Wye Center, Md.: Aspen Institute, 1992), 13.

24. Romberg, "NCTM Standards as a Model," 13; National Council of Teachers of Mathematics, *Curriculum and Evaluation Standards for School Mathematics* (Reston, Va.: NCTM, 1989), v.

25. National Council of Teachers of Mathematics, *Curriculum and Evaluation Standards*, 2; Romberg, "NCTM Standards as a Model," 16.

26. National Education Goals Panel, *National Education Goals Report* (Washington, D.C.: National Education Goals Panel, 1991), ix.

27. National Council on Education Standards and Testing, *Raising Standards for American Education* (Washington, D.C.: Government Printing Office, 1992), 2–3.

28. I served in the U.S. Department of Education during this period as Assistant Secretary responsible for the Office of Education Research and Improvement and oversaw the award of grants for developing voluntary national standards.

8   REINVENTING SCHOOLING

DAVID TYACK

Imagine a new generation of American schools that are light years beyond those of today." This was the utopian goal that the New American
Schools Development Corporation (NASDC) posed for educational reformers in the early 1990s. Chartered as part of President George Bush's
America 2000 education strategy, NASDC's task was to "unleash America's creative genius to invent . . . the best schools in the world, . . . to
achieve a quantum leap in learning." Don't be content with incremental
change, said NASDC, but "assume that the schools we have inherited do
not exist." This was no ordinary task, said President Bush; the redemption
of society was at stake: "Think about every problem, every challenge we
face. The solution to each starts with education. For the sake of the future—
of our children and the nation—we must transform America's schools."[1]

In a mission with such high stakes, many leaders thought it time to
bypass traditional educators and to turn to business and technology to
rescue and transform education. The original board of directors of NASDC
was composed almost entirely of CEOs of large corporations, including the
Commissioner of the National Football League. When Whittle Communications decided to create a network of hundreds of for-profit schools, Christopher Whittle's design team included only one experienced public educator,
but he announced that his new-model schools would provide a template of
reform for all elementary and secondary education. He called this business
venture the "Edison Project" because he believes that his schools will be as
superior to the average public school as a lightbulb is to a candle.[2]

Seventy years ago Thomas Alva Edison had similar dreams of transforming instruction. "I believe," he said, "that the motion picture is destined to revolutionize our educational system and that in a few years it will
supplant largely, if not entirely, the use of textbooks." Maybe replace the
teacher, too. Here is how one teacher of that time responded to this new
dispensation:

Mr. Edison says
That the radio will supplant the teacher.
Already one may learn languages
    by means of Victrola records.
The moving picture will visualize
What the radio fails to get across.
Teachers will be relegated to the
Backwoods
With firehorses
And long-haired women.
Or perhaps shown in museums.
Education will become a matter
    of pressing the button.
Perhaps I can get a position
    at the switchboard.[3]

Faith in electronic pedagogy has returned again and again.

The radio did not quite supplant the teacher, and both NASDC and Whittle's break-the-mold schools may also fade as reforms (both have had trouble attracting corporate financing and have greatly scaled down their plans). Such attempts to reinvent schooling have reappeared from time to time and have often resembled shooting stars that spurted across the pedagogical heavens, leaving a meteoric trail in the media but then burning up and disappearing in the denser atmosphere of institutional reality. Americans admire inventors and entrepreneurs, and some hope for technological solutions to educational problems. Part of the utopian impulse in education for over a century has been a quest for a sleek, efficient school machine "light years" ahead of the fusty schools of the time. A crisis mentality about education—the challenges of Sputnik or Toyota, for example—has abetted this search for a new beginning.

Amid the constant criticism of the public schools during recent decades, reformers have found a ready constituency when they promised major transformations of education, often in the form of a quick fix and sometimes in the hope of a quick profit. The corporate advocates of private "performance contracting" to teach basic skills to potential dropouts, for example, counseled "maximum plausible optimism" in convincing the public (this term was borrowed from the pitch of aerospace contractors to the Pentagon).[4]

Innovators proposing or supporting start-from-scratch reforms have usually been persons outside the public schools—technocrats, university professors, salespeople with products to push, politicians intent on rapid results before the next election, foundation officers, business leaders, and the like. Impatient with the glacial pace of incremental reform, free of institutional memories of past shooting star reforms, they promised to transform education.

Some of these innovators held the educational establishment in low regard. Major changes were really not that complicated, they said. Progress required that mossbacks step aside and let new reformers, sleeves rolled up, step in to set things right. The first stage in reform was to convince citizens that the present system of schooling was inefficient, anachronistic, and irrational—bash the bureaucrats, blame the teachers. This has long been a strategy of utopians who condemned existing arrangements to persuade others to adopt their blueprint of a transformed future.

During recent decades, innovators who wanted to reinvent the public schools often turned to other social sectors for inspiration or legitimation for the models of change they advocated—for example, to business, the federal policy establishment, higher education, or foundations. Appeals to the ideologies and practices of technology, business management, behavioral engineering, and new organizational forms carried weight with influential decision makers who wanted to reform schooling from the outside according to plans they considered more rational than the status quo.[5]

As in the rationale for NASDC, past reformers believed that if they could create new-model schooling—lighthouse schools or comprehensive transformations—their ideas would spread quickly across the educational landscape. This was an act of faith, for rarely did the advocates of new-model schools consult either history or practitioners. History was something to be overcome, not a source of insight. And as for practitioners, why should policy analysts and entrepreneurs consult the very people who created the mediocrity of public education in the first place? Whether educators agreed or not with the break-the-mold innovators, the publicity given to the shooting star reforms made it difficult to ignore them entirely. At least it was prudent to *seem* to respond lest practitioners simply confirm their fusty image. In the aftermath of Sputnik, for example, it was reassuring on parents' night to have a panel of flashing lights in the high school physics classroom (even though teachers might find dry-cell batteries more useful for students' experiments than finicky electronic panels).[6]

In this chapter we explore a few examples of past attempts to reinvent schooling:

— by emulating management and budgeting techniques in business or government during the 1960s and early 1970s when some reformers were entranced by new management techniques developed by corporations, the military-industrial complex, university experts, and government agencies

— by contracting instruction to innovators who claimed that private corporations could do a better job of teaching the basics than the public schools could and make a profit in the process. The city that pioneered performance contracting (Texarkana, Arkansas), became for a time "the Mecca of the educational world."[7]

— by employing technology that could, advocates said, transform instruction

— by modeling the incentives and career paths of teachers on an ideology of competition and hierarchy and a practice of unequal rewards borrowed from other organizations

What was the scoreboard of results from these attempts to remodel schooling? These differed by reform, but in the main they had little lasting effect on public schools. It is easy to trace the early trajectory of shooting star reforms, for there is a rich paper trail of such reforms in the advocacy stage, when people make grandiose claims for them. It is harder to discover what happened in the stage of attempted implementation. When reforms fade or fail, silence often ensues. Since success is often equated with survival, few people have bothered to chronicle transitory innovations. As the saying goes, success has many parents, but failure is an orphan. The volume of articles in the popular and professional press on transitory reforms rose rapidly and then fell as precipitously.[8]

Why were the break-the-mold innovations proposed by outsiders mostly short-lived? Innovators outside the schools who wanted to reinvent education were often skilled in publicity and the politics of promising and claimed to use the latest models of rational planning. But they rarely factored into their plans a sophisticated understanding of the school as an institution or insight into the culture of teachers. They tended to treat "schools as though they were made of silly putty," easily molded, whereas good schools are more like healthy plants, set in good soil and carefully tended over long periods. The break-the-mold reformers rarely understood the everyday lives of teachers, their practices, beliefs, and sources of frustration and satisfaction. Their hope that a few demonstration lighthouse schools would become models to transform all school systems rarely became reality; instead, they were more likely to become boutique schools set apart from the mainstream.[9]

THE BUSINESS OF SCHOOLING

Like their predecessors in the Progressive Era, the business-oriented reformers of the 1960s and 1970s had ready-made technocratic solutions to educational problems (and often products in search of markets). Many of them thought the current administrators of schools were incompetent as planners and unaccountable for results. One approach to reform was to make the management of schools more businesslike by adopting such new managing and budgeting techniques as management by objectives (MBO); the planning, programming, and budgeting system (PPBS); and zero-based budgeting (ZBB). Another was to treat public schools as a marketplace of instructional services in which corporations could compete and teach children effectively by using the latest technologies of instruction and behavioral engineering. Business methods of planning and budgeting, competition, incentives, new technologies—these could transform antiquated public schools into centers of efficient learning.[10]

MANAGING SCHOOLING

In the early decades of the twentieth century, business and professional elites increasingly controlled the school boards of cities. At the same time, the administrative progressives were attempting to create a "science" of educational management to counter criticisms that the schools were inefficient. As superintendents and university education experts talked about running the schools, they easily slipped into language and concepts borrowed from business.[11]

Ellwood P. Cubberley, for example, liked to propose a bank's board of directors as the template for an effective school committee and the expert business manager as a model for the "scientific" superintendent of schools. He spoke of schools as "factories in which the raw materials (children) are to be shaped and fashioned into products to meet the various demands of life." Aware of criticisms that schools were profligate with the public's taxes, city school chiefs avidly calculated the cost effectiveness of everything from a lesson in English to the purchase of school desks. They wrote detailed educational objectives and blueprints for instruction. Like efficiency experts in industry—the time and motion folk—they thought it possible for managers to plan work while workers (teachers, students) did the work.[12]

The language and imagery of business efficiency proved useful to superintendents who needed to please local elites, giving them virtue by association, but much of the emulation of business was rhetorical and did not directly translate into classroom practices. Schools were not factories, and children were not passive raw materials. Like their students, teachers were active agents, not docile workers on a pedagogical assembly line. Once the schoolroom door was shut, most teachers retained considerable autonomy to instruct the children as they saw fit. Also, the governance of education was not identical to the management of business, and school boards continued to be poitical agencies, however much they claimed to be above politics. When business leaders fell out of favor during the Great Depression, so did much of the impulse to emulate the rhetoric of business.[13]

The demand for accountability and cost-effective management in public schools revived the cult of efficiency in education during the 1960s and 1970s. Reformers urged educators to reinvent educational management and budgeting by adopting techniques developed by corporations, the military-industrial complex, university budgeting experts, and government agencies. These technocratic reformers had ready-made rational solutions in search of problems, and education seemed ripe as a place to experiment.[14]

The theory behind management by objectives derived from the work of scholars like Peter Drucker, who studied business and industrial organizations. G. S. Odiorne defined MBO as "a system in which the first step of management is the clarification of corporate objectives and the breaking down of all subordinate activity into logical subdivisions that contribute to the major objectives." The program planning and budgeting system had its origins in industry. It sought to collect and analyze data in such a way that costs of programs—or their alternatives—could be linked to short- and long-term plans and goals. As secretary of defense, Robert McNamara adapted PPBS to program planning and budgeting in the Pentagon in 1961, and in 1965 President Lyndon B. Johnson extended it to all government departments. Jimmy Carter discovered that Texas Instruments developed zero-based budgeting as a way of forcing each unit to justify its budget in terms of company objectives—starting from zero. Carter then used ZBB in governmental budgeting while governor of Georgia and president of the United States. In each case the goals were to increase the rationality of planning, to relate budgeting and management to specific organizational objectives, and to use data in the service of control (though such power was supposedly exercised in a neutral way).[15]

Scholars disagree about how effective these systems were even in businesses where there was a clear objective—profit—or in an agency like the Department of Defense that used the system in procuring expensive lethal weapons. In 1971 the federal Office of Management and Budget dropped PPBS. The first Carter ZBB budget in 1979 resulted in fewer program cuts than had previous budgets in the 1970s, and the system met its demise when he was defeated in 1980. PPBS and ZBB cost a great deal of time and money, created new layers of bureaucracy, and heaped up piles of paper. Aaron Wildavsky called PPBS "tremendously inefficient" because the "inputs were huge and its policy output is tiny."[16]

Under pressure from federal and state governments to become more accountable—especially when funding from those levels increased—school systems in many parts of the nation adopted PPBS. By 1970 about three-fourths of states either had mandated or were considering requiring reports from districts in a program budget format. The number of references to PPBS in *Education Index* displayed a rapid rise in policy talk about the reform and an equally rapid decline in articles by the mid-1970s.

In 1966 California required all districts in the state to implement PPBS. The California experience illustrates the problems of importing rational systems models into educational governance and finance. In comparison with objectives at the Ford Motor Company or the Department of Defense, educational goals were often diffuse, and specifying them could cause time-consuming controversy. One district ended up with fifty-eight separate objectives just for mathematics in the primary grades. Results were hard to measure and quantify, and the methods to achieve these objectives were frequently unclear.[17]

Many public school districts lacked staff with the analytic skills to gather and interpret the data used in PPBS, and educators questioned whether such an expenditure of time, money, and paper was worthwhile in any case—what did it contribute to instruction? While recognizing the need to demonstrate that children were learning and that money was well spent, teachers complained that "Mickey Mouse in triplicate"—their rendering of PPBS—was not the way to become accountable. In his ethnographic study of the implementation of PPBS in Oregon, Harry Wolcott argued that it created problems for educators rather than solving them.[18]

But perhaps more important, in California as elsewhere, education is intrinsically a value-laden and political enterprise. Because of its trappings of expertise, PPBS may have seemed to be neutral and nonpolitical but, like its Progressive Era predecessors, it moved decision making upward and toward the center. Many who had traditionally engaged in negotiation and compromise in the budgeting process felt excluded. Thus, it is not surprising that, in 1971, responding to powerful opposition from educators, the California State Board of Education dropped PPBS. Others followed suit, and before long PPBS and its kin would be shooting stars that had once been bright but had then disappeared from sight.[19]

PERFORMANCE CONTRACTING

At first, many policy makers outside the schools and some educators inside them believed that performance contracting might provide a solution to the difficult task of teaching basic skills to underserved students. In Texarkana in the fall of 1969, over a hundred pupils identified as potential dropouts entered rapid learning centers set up by Dorsett Educational Systems. In these carpeted, newly painted rooms, they went to pick up a folder in which the teacher—called the *instructional manager*—had put the day's assignment and a record and filmstrip for each child. Then students plugged the software into a Dorsett teaching machine, put on the headset, and logged their time onto punch cards that were used to plan the next day's assignment. When they had correctly answered all the questions on the programmed lesson, they received ten Green Stamps. If they advanced a grade level in reading or mathematics, they earned a transistor radio. The child who made the most progress for the year on achievement tests won the grand prize: a portable television set. Diagnosis, prescription, achievement, reward—it was a *learning system* coupled with extrinsic rewards. The goal: to accelerate the learning of children who were falling behind in school—and to make a profit for Dorsett, which had created the system.[20]

Texarkana represented the dawn of a bright day, some thought, when for-profit businesses would contract with school districts to use technology and scientific management of learning, well laced with extrinsic incentives, to produce RESULTS—student achievement in the basic subjects. No results, no pay. There was basically no difference between schools and industry, said a systems analyst with experience at Lockheed, when he took over as center manager at a public school in Gary, Indiana, the Banneker School run by Behavioral Research Laboratories (BRL). "I view things analytically," he said. "Keep out emotions . . . You don't have to love the guy next to you on the assembly line to make the product. He puts in the bolts, you put in the nuts, and the product comes out." A Gary teacher retorted: "There's no way a man with that attitude can succeed in a school. No way."[21]

The worlds of the technocrats and the teachers were, indeed, miles apart. BRL had developed programmed books and materials to teach reading and saw the chance to run its own learning system in a Gary public school as a way to shake up what the chairman of BRL's board called the "mindless, inefficient, hideously mismanaged" public school system. There were, in name at least, no teachers at the Banneker School; instead, it employed a center manager, a learning director, five curriculum managers, fifteen assistant curriculum managers, and twenty learning supervisors in a hierarchy of responsibility and pay. Just as students had done decades before in Gary's platoon system, the students in the BRL school circulated from room to room (called *curriculum centers*) to work on different academic subjects and fields like art, music, and physical education.[22]

Some leaders of teachers' organizations and educational policy makers protested that the systems people had radically restricted the goals of schooling to drill and practice on the basic skills and performance on standardized tests. The tests themselves, some argued, were faulty measures of achievement. Gains in test scores might be only temporary results of the Hawthorne effect—the positive influence of attention—the fanfare about the project and carpeted and air-conditioned rooms. Many teachers considered extrinsic rewards to be inappropriate bribery for learning and questioned the effectiveness of contingency management. One teacher in Texarkana said that "I wonder if the children are *really* learning or just storing a little knowledge for long enough to get the reward." Teachers complained that the prepackaging of learning robbed them of the chance to exercise their own professional knowledge and discretion. But the most fundamental criticism, and one that led people to legally challenge the BRL-run school in Gary and to close it down, was that public districts were abdicating their role in shaping public policy in education when they delegated instruction to private agencies.[23]

Dorsett and BRL were only two of dozens of corporations, large and small, that regarded performance contracts as a way to make a profit by teaching children who were lagging in academic achievement. Some of these companies saw schooling as a vast new market that might take up the slack in defense contracts that were winding down along with the Vietnam War. Many school board members, government officials, and educational entrepreneurs were eager to give businesses a chance to raise levels of academic performance among these students. In 1970 President Nixon's Office of Economic Opportunity (OEO) sponsored a performance contracting experiment in which thirty-one companies competed for performance contracts in eighteen selected school districts (this paralleled another OEO experiment with markets in education, a voucher plan).[24]

The six companies that won the contracts agreed to receive no payment if pupils did not make a year's gain on standardized tests but stood to make a good profit if they did. Under Title I the federal government also subsidized twenty other performance contracts in 1970. In most cases the companies relied on teaching machines or programmed materials, individual diagnosis and prescription of learning, and extrinsic incentives. The resulting trend, said two observers, was "not so much toward educational reform under the initiative of the public sector as it is now toward marketing and sales with the private sector setting the terms. The public may find that in the majority of cases it is simply paying a higher price to put last year's product in this year's favorite package." The chair of the House Education Subcommittee, Congresswoman Edith Green, worried about the funds flowing to defense contractors entering the education business: "It is accurate to say that anyone with a brainstorm can come to Washington and get financing from the Office of Education or the Office of Economic Opportunity."[25]

Although Dorsett's instructional system in Texarkana became the model for most other performance contracts, in one respect it became a scandal to be avoided. One day the district's project director was visiting its rapid learning centers to monitor the year-end test that would determine how well Dorsett had done its job. A boy mentioned to him that he had already seen one of the test items—about a visit to a submarine. The cat was out of the bag. It turned out that in their daily lessons just before the big examination the students had been studying items taken from the test. The centers were not just teaching *to* the test; they were teaching the test. The person responsible for this fraud explained that Texarkana had assigned too many low-IQ students to the program and the standard curriculum did not work with them. Under pressure to show results and to make a profit for the company, she wove test items into the daily lessons.[26]

The Texarkana scandal moderated but did not halt enthusiasm for performance contracting. It made government agencies like the OEO and local districts more careful about getting independent audits, however, and these reports deflated the claims of the promoters. A study by the Rand Corporation in December 1971 reported that the experiment did speed up instructional change but that it focused narrowly on basic skills and introduced tricky problems of measurement and legal responsibility. The Rand researchers found a very mixed picture of test gains. When the Battelle Memorial Institute, the agency charged with evaluating the OEO experiment, presented its findings in 1972, the air went out of the balloon. In comparing the experimental classrooms taught by the companies with similar groups taught in the traditional manner, Battelle discovered that twice as many traditional classes scored better than the experimental classes in math and that nine control classrooms did better in reading compared with six of the performance contracting groups. Overwhelmingly, there was no significant difference between the experimental and control groups. OEO discontinued its funding. By 1975, after further negative studies, *Education Daily* announced that "performance contracting has been pronounced dead."[27]

As Myron Lieberman pointed out, the brief experiment was flawed as a scientific and practical enterprise. It is not clear precisely what was being measured: performance contracting, incentive plans, differentiated staffing, new instructional technology, or what? But it did become clear that effective teaching of educationally disadvantaged children was no simple matter to be solved by business smarts, extrinsic incentives, and programmed instruction. And it was equally obvious that, even with federal subsidies, there were no rich lodes of profits for companies to mine in the serried hills of American public education. The hope for easy solutions and profits by pedagogy did not disappear, however. New reformers, salesmen, and political allies would come again to promise that the private sector could succeed where the public establishment had allegedly failed.[28]

TEACHING BY MACHINE: A FICKLE ROMANCE

Many Americans relish technological solutions to the problems of learning. It has long been so. Hear the rhetoric of another era: "The inventor or introducer of the system deserves to be ranked among the best contributors to learning and science, if not among the greatest benefactors of mankind." The time was 1841. The "system" was the blackboard, which another salesman forty years later described as "the MIRROR reflecting the workings, character and quality of the individual mind." And so it went with advocates of educational radio, film, television, and programmed learning who predicted pedagogical Nirvanas that never happened.[29]

Waves of enthusiasm for technology in education often have coincided with broader changes or concerns in society. Periods of advocacy of technology have typically had common features: worry over the costs of schooling, fear that teachers were incompetent (or at least in short supply), and some sort of domestic or external threat (the Depression, Sputnik, the Japanese economic challenge) that gave special urgency to education. In troubled times some people want to find a quick fix.

The people who promised educational moonshots through technology were an assorted lot. Not surprisingly, many were business people who wanted to market their wares to the schools. Some were scholars and academic entrepreneurs—psychologists, for example, who thought that programmed instruction would rationalize pedagogy. Foundation officials seeking a quick effect on schooling sometimes saw the new media as a way around the briar patch impeding educational change. Some educational administrators who wanted their schools to be up to date embraced new technologies. A new specialist appeared in colleges, state departments of education, and school districts—the audiovisual expert—who had a vested interest as well as a faith in technology.[30]

In the top-down process of advocating and implementing technology, teachers were rarely consulted, though it was mainly their task to make it work. A small minority of teachers welcomed electronic learning, believing that it would motivate their reluctant students and make their own instruction more easy and effective, but most used the new devices minimally or not at all.

A recurring cycle of reform occurred with most forms of pedagogy by technology. They began with exaltation, a conviction that a new invention could transform education. Next came studies to document that electronic aids were at least as effective as teachers in conveying knowledge. Then arose disappointment as reports came back from classrooms about the imperfections of the reform and as surveys showed that few teachers were using the tool.[31]

The scapegoat in writings about technology has often been the teacher unwilling to climb aboard the new bandwagon. Some technologies sought to bypass classroom teachers through teacher-proof programs or electronic devices. Whatever the technologists might have hoped, behind the classroom door teachers remained the key influence on instruction. By and large, they used the technologies that fit familiar routines and classroom procedures—in other words, that helped them solve their problems of instruction. The rest they mostly ignored.[32]

Some inventions have in fact made their way into classrooms: the blackboard, cheap paper that replaced slates, books for each child made possible by sharp drops in production costs, paperbacks that supplemented textbooks, globes and maps, ballpoint pens that replaced the steelnib pens that had replaced quill pens, and, though they were controversial, cheap hand-held calculators. More complex technologies have had much less effect on everyday teaching than did the simple, durable, reliable improvements like the chalkboard that enhanced what teachers were already doing. As in other reforms, teachers have used some technologies to enhance their standard practices but rarely have used electronic aids to transform their teaching.[33]

Advocates of film as a mode of instruction saw it as the very emblem of progressive pedagogy, for it promised to breathe visual reality into the spoken and printed word and to stir minds to activity. But again the companies that wanted to sell technical solutions and the educators who were supposed to use them tended to live in different worlds. An educational researcher committed to the use of films reported that teachers "failed to make their problems articulate to the commercial producers," while business people "failed to grasp or to study the nature of instruction and the complexity of educational institutions." Many of the early free films were thinly disguised commercials for products and resented as such by teachers. Especially to blame for the cool reception of teachers to film was "the stupidity which has characterized the advertising, propaganda, and sales methods of companies" that claimed that moving pictures might supplant textbooks and even teachers.[34]

Because the early hardware was expensive and required constant maintenance and software was costly and needed to be shared by many teachers, film was first used in large cities and wealthy suburbs. Most districts had no projectors; rural schools often lacked electricity. In 1936, after a decade of florid claims about educational motion pictures, a survey of 21,000 districts (9,000 replied) found that across the nation there were only about 6,074 silent film projectors and 458 sound-film projectors in schools (it did not say how many of these were in good repair and actually in use). By 1954, when equipment was cheaper and more reliable, the NEA estimated that schools had one projector for every 415 students.[35]

But even when districts had the necessary equipment and films, most evidence suggests that teachers used educational films sparingly, except among a small cadre of enthusiasts. A study of 175 elementary teachers in New Haven, Connecticut, discovered that they ordered about 1,500 films in one year, but two-thirds of the orders came from 25 mediaphiles. When they investigated obstacles to the use of moving pictures, researchers pinpointed the teachers' lack of skills, the cost of purchase and upkeep of equipment, the inaccessibility of equipment, and the difficulty in finding the right fit between films and class lessons.[36]

On its face, radio was a simpler medium to use than film. Again, however, lack of hardware originally limited diffusion of the reform. In the mid-1930s superintendents reported only about one radio per district. An expert on educational radio estimated in 1945 that only 5 percent of children heard radio regularly in their classrooms. When principals in Ohio were asked what were the blocks to greater use of radio, they listed lack of radios (50 percent), poor equipment or reception (30 percent), and lack of coordination of radio programs with the curriculum. But advocates of radio education instead blamed teachers' "indifference and lethargy, even antagonism, toward this revolutionary means of communication."[37]

Television was going to be different, said reformers. In the 1950s, when the Ford Foundation entered the arena of electronic teaching with its subsidies and publicity, the campaign for instructional television gained momentum. Soon an airplane was circling over the Midwest beaming down programs to six states. Hagerstown, Maryland, developed a model system of closed circuit television that promised a richer curriculum at less cost. By 1961 the foundation had spent $20 million for classroom television, and the next year Congress appropriated another $32 million for that purpose.[38]

Despite unprecedented public attention and enthusiastic promotion, instructional television made slow headway. A survey of public schools in 1961 found only 1.65 television sets per district. In the mid-1960s, as federal dollars flowed into the schools, districts that had been too poor to buy adequate audiovisual equipment were able for the first time to acquire television sets along with many other kinds of machines and software. But the machines often sat idle. In the 1970s teachers reported that they showed TV programs during only two to four percent of classroom time. A decade after classroom television was introduced with a flourish, a fervent advocate lamented: "If something happened tomorrow to wipe out all instructional television, America's schools and colleges would hardly know it was gone."[39]

As with film and radio, it was primarily nonteachers who initiated and pushed instruction by television. These reformers seldom asked teachers their advice and opinions; they just told them that this was the way to go. When teachers responded enthusiastically, the technocrats were pleased. But this rarely happened. Why?

Over the course of six decades, a variety of explanations have surfaced, as Larry Cuban has shown. One already discussed is the explanation often given by the disappointed reformers: Teachers are laggard and fearful, if not incompetent. But from the teachers' perspectives, other reasons appear. One focuses on the hardware: There is not enough, or it is broken or faulty, or it takes too much time to arrange for it and use it. Another complaint is the software: It is inappropriate to the curriculum, doesn't fit the class schedule, or is of poor quality. The method of implementation from the top down—as school boards or policy makers or superintendents ordered or cajoled teachers to use a particular tool—provoked many teachers to dig in their heels or simply to put technology in the closet.[40]

But perhaps the most fundamental block to transforming schooling through machines has been the nature of the classroom as a work setting and the ways in which teachers define their tasks. The regularities of institutional structure and of teacher-centered pedagogy and discipline are the result of generations of experience of teachers in meeting the imperatives of their occupation: maintaining order and seeing that students learn the curriculum. Teachers are willing, even eager, to adopt innovations that help them to do their standard job more efficiently and that are simple, durable, flexible, and responsive to the way they define their tasks.[41]

A minority of teachers have also welcomed electronic aids to learning and have incorporated them in their standard ways of teaching. But the values that infuse the occupation have generally made teachers skeptical of learning by machine, eager to retain the patterns that work for them, and skilled at sabotaging changes imposed on them from the outside.

TRANSFORMING TEACHING

The outsiders who sought to reinvent schools through business methods, instructional systems, and technology rarely sought to see the world through the teachers' eyes. Indeed, some of them wanted to bypass teachers and to produce teacher-proof instruction. Others regarded teachers as the key to transformed schooling but, when they sought to alter the structure of teaching as an occupation and to change the incentives of teachers, they, too, rarely understood teachers' perspectives on their work; as outsiders they lacked an institutional memory of how the present system came about.

Ironically, outsiders often wanted to go directly counter to a century of efforts by teachers themselves to improve their profession. Understanding why the outsider reforms of merit pay, career ladders, and hierarchical forms of team teaching generally did not succeed requires examination of this history of educators' own efforts to create a unitary occupation with roughly equal rewards and equal status accorded to individual practitioners in cooperative but nonhierarchical relations one to another. Outsiders understood incentives in ways quite different from the perspective of teachers.

From time to time, foundation officials, business leaders, school board members, media pundits, university professors, legislators, governors, and other reformers have concluded that existing incentives and career paths in teaching made no sense. Policy talk about merit pay and differentiated staffing has been especially popular during periods when business efficiency was a popular theme and when competitive market solutions have been in favor. Treating schools as if they were ordinary market organizations and teachers as if they were employees in competitive business firms has made sense to outsiders, but teachers have often questioned the assumptions underlying the model and opposed it passively or actively.[42]

Susan Moore Johnson commented that each time merit pay became an "educational vogue . . . it was considered a novel reform." The present-day call for differentiating the roles and rewards of teachers is only the latest episode in a long history of attempts of outsiders to attract and retain the most gifted instructors, to create meritocratic standards of performance and pay, and to make schooling more efficient. In recent years many states have passed laws mandating merit pay, career ladders, master teachers, and other ways to differentiate the functions and rewards of teachers.[43]

In both the past and the present, teachers have mostly resisted such reforms. Teachers have spent decades to achieve the principle of the equality of all professionals as represented in a single salary schedule for elementary and high school teachers and equal pay for female and male teachers. Thus, it is not surprising that they have been skeptical about hierarchical models of team teaching and career ladders. Having fought to require professional training and certification of all teachers as a prerequisite for employment, teachers have opposed opening the labor market to untrained and noncertified instructors. They have not trusted the ability and fairness of administrators charged with assessing merit. They have typically regarded merit pay not as an incentive but as a bother, a threat to professional comity, and irrelevant to the chief intrinsic reward they experience—seeing their pupils grow intellectually and socially.[44]

Open conflict erupted, for example, when the school board in Kalamazoo, Michigan, decided to reward teachers differently in 1974. *American School Board Journal* trumpeted the Kalamazoo plan as the end to lockstep pay and unaccountable staff. "Take it from Kalamazoo," the *Journal* said, "a comprehensive, performance-based system of evaluation and accountability can work." This judgment was premature. The merit scheme, in which "nearly everyone evaluated everyone else," choked on paperwork and provoked frustration, not superior performance. The administrators joined the United Automobile Workers union to fight merit pay, and the teachers' union managed to recall six of the seven board members who had supported differential compensation. But repeated experiences like this one in Kalamazoo did not prevent reformers from reinventing merit pay.[45]

The history of teaching as an occupation illuminates the different values and perceptions of teachers and of the outsiders who would restructure the profession. In the nineteenth century in small school districts, hiring took place in a more or less open labor market. Local school boards basically could hire whomever they wished at whatever was the going wage, for standards of training and certification were low or nonexistent. Probably most teachers then were not even graduates of secondary schools. Farmers on school committees selected teachers rather the way they would employ a hired hand or a servant to help in the house. Teachers' salaries differed widely from place to place and even in the same one-room school when different teachers were hired to teach in summer and winter.[46]

From the point of view of those who believe in an open labor market as a guarantee of merit, this was an efficient system. In theory, at least, school boards hired the person who would provide the best service for the least money. In practice, educators complained, committee members were apt to hire inept teachers for extraneous reasons—they might be relatives, or persons in debt to a school board member, or communicants of a dominant church, or full of a manly bluster thought to be suitably cowing to the older boys in their classes. Male teachers almost always earned more than female, although there was growing evidence that women taught at least as well as men. A reform favored by educators was to make the labor market less open by restricting entry to teaching to those who were trained in pedagogy and certified. They hoped thereby to raise the quality of instruction and to hoist the miserable pay of teachers. In the twentieth century, this notion of professional training and state certification rapidly gained ground.[47]

In large cities the structure of the labor market in teaching was quite different from that in the countryside. Although there was plenty of nepotism and corruption in the selection of teachers, urban systems were much more bureaucratized. First, individual teachers generally did not bargain with lay boards in determining their salaries; instead, most districts published regular salary schedules. Second, these scales explicitly paid men more than women and secondary teachers more than elementary. This changed, however. In a series of revolts, beginning in cities like New York, women teachers organized to secure equal pay with men. Likewise, teacher organizations pressed state legislatures and school boards to adopt single salary schedules in which teachers at all levels received the same salary. Differential pay depended not on sex or level but on years of service and extent of professional preparation.[48]

As teachers tried to increase the "merit" of their occupation, then, they sought to improve training and certification so that all teachers might be considered professionals. Likewise, the NEA's (mostly female) Department of Classroom Teachers argued for a single salary scale and against differential pay by sex on the egalitarian grounds that all members of the profession—in grade school or high school, male or female—had comparable responsibilities and deserved comparable pay (in fact, one might understand the single salary schedule as a pioneer example of what today is called *comparable worth*).[49]

Such reasoning simply did not make sense to many people. At the very time when organized teachers were attempting to create more uniform compensation, in the opening decades of the twentieth century, elite school board members and some superintendents were seeking to make teacher evaluations "scientific" and to link those ratings to salary increases. How do you motivate large numbers of teachers to perform beyond the minimum expectation? How do you get more teachers to excel when they work in isolated classrooms where inspection is infrequent? These basic questions facing school boards and superintendents led many of them to emulate business by creating the earliest merit pay programs, that is, programs that would allegedly pay teachers according to performance.[50]

The history of performance-based salary plans has been a merry-go-round. In the main, districts that initially embraced merit pay dropped it after a brief trial; only a small number of districts continued to use merit pay for decades. In the 1950s merit pay became a fashionable idea and by the 1960s about 10 percent of districts had adopted some version of payment by performance. By the early 1970s, interest again declined, for just over 5 percent of districts said they had merit pay. A 1978 national survey found 115 districts (4 percent of those with more than 300 students) with provisions for payment for performance, and many of these did not in fact pay teachers differentially. When two researchers went back to those districts five years later they found only 47 still using performance-based compensation. These districts tended to be small, to have fairly homogeneous student populations, and to use merit pay in inconspicuous ways. Although there was another resurgence of interest in merit pay in the 1980s, more than 99 percent of teachers are paid on a uniform salary schedule.[51]

Richard Murnane and David K. Cohen found six districts where merit pay had been in existence for more than five years. In these schools, they said, it was voluntary, paid teachers more for extra work beyond the classroom, kept the scale of money involved low (seldom over $1,500 to $2,000), and involved teachers in shaping the rules of the plan. They argued that what kept these plans going was precisely that these districts avoided making problematic distinctions between teachers based on their classroom performance. Instead, they used the plan to solve other problems in the district, such as finding ways of bringing together teachers and administrators to discuss educational issues (e.g., the nature of evaluation in the district), finding ways of enhancing the public's perception that teachers are being held accountable, and providing chances for teachers to earn extra money by doing school-related activities.[52]

Why have so few schemes to pay teachers for their performance stuck? Murnane and Cohen argued that merit pay seldom works if its intent is to get teachers to excel because so little agreement exists among administrators and teachers over just what effective teaching is and how to measure it. In part, the complexity of the teaching act foils merit pay. Internal strife erupts over administrators' judgments that some teachers win outstanding marks and others only average.

Clearly, the outsiders who pushed merit pay have often misperceived what would in fact have motivated teachers to do a better job. This reminds us of the experience of some university professors who gave a workshop for teachers based on the principles of behavior modification. These instructors found that their incentive for completing morning tasks—a coffee break—offended rather than pleased the participants, who turned out to be Mormons opposed to caffeine.

Johnson, who actually did ask teachers about incentives and disincentives, found that teachers had good reasons for opposing competition for the extrinsic reward of merit pay:

> Promoting competition among colleagues would reduce rather than increase the productivity of schools because teachers would conceal their best ideas and pursue their own interests rather than the general good. Moreover, performance bonuses might perversely reward teachers for success with able students while discouraging efforts with those who progress more slowly. Finally, teachers resented policymakers' efforts to entice them with the prospects of one-time bonuses for a select few when many teachers held second jobs just to meet basic living expenses. By seeking to provide recognition for exemplary teachers, potentially at the expense of many others, the reforms threatened egalitarian norms that the profession supports.[53]

Teachers are not afraid of evaluation, she insisted: "they perform before exacting critics every day." What they dislike is being pitted in competition with one another or judged by arbitrary standards by people whom they do not particularly trust. The egalitarian norms shared by most teachers favor collaboration but not hierarchy of the sort represented in career ladders.[54]

Obviously, teachers care deeply about receiving adequate salaries— and rarely do—and appreciate public recognition and status, but they and the public have quite different perceptions of their sources of satisfaction and dissatisfaction. When polled about what bothered teachers the most, the general public listed poor discipline first and salaries second; teachers listed unfavorable public attitudes toward education first and salaries fourth. Over the years many studies have shown that teachers most highly value the intrinsic rewards of the occupation that come from seeing their pupils develop and that they treasure praise from students, parents, and colleagues. In 1975 Dan Lortie found that teachers in Dade County, Florida, reported that the biggest extrinsic reward they received (37 percent) was "respect from others" and the biggest psychic reward (an overwhelming 86 percent) was "knowing that I have 'reached' students and that they have learned." Johnson found a similar pattern in the 1980s among the teachers she interviewed, though such rewards of respect and praise were all too infrequent.[55]

Campaigns to create new incentives for teachers and to restructure teaching careers have rarely achieved their goals, for they have been out of synchrony with the values and practices of teachers. Like the application of business methods, systems analysis, and technology to public education, such innovations have sometimes had the unintended result of lessening, not enhancing, the very rewards that teachers find most important in their classrooms and of neglecting the "wisdom of practice" represented in their daily relationships with one another.[56]

CONCLUSION

The utopian impulses in recent decades to reinvent schooling have often been shooting stars, meteors that attracted attention but left little deposit. Some who promised Nirvana have been people eager to sell their products. Others have been activists convinced of the need for fundamental change. A few have been politicians driven by the deadlines imposed by elections. But rarely have start-from-scratch reformers really understood the character of schools as social institutions or sought to learn either from the educators who labored in them or from history.

In a society so prone to equating change with progress, it is not surprising that people who promise to reinvent schooling should attract followers. Innovators can appeal to the faith that Americans have vested in education as an engine of social betterment. Legislators, foundation officials, business leaders, social critics and others may feel compelled to do something big and new about education when schools are considered to be in crisis. Indeed, the dream of a golden age—either in past or future—has often been a vital part of campaigns to reinvent education in the present.

Schools need reform today, but the scoreboard of historical attempts to reinvent schooling suggests that starting from scratch has not been an effective strategy. What are some implications for educational policy from the history of break-the-mold reforms in recent decades?

First, don't overpromise, even if it seems advantageous in the short run. Goals and claims should be anchored both in ideals—such as equality of opportunity and intellectual excellence—and in institutional realities. Hope is a great motivator, a trigger for revitalization movements, but hype can lead to what Larry Cuban calls the "acid rain" of cynicism. In 1991 a representative sample of parents were asked if they thought that the goals of *America 2000* would in fact be accomplished in the next nine years. Only 4 percent thought that "every school will be free of drugs and violence," 14 percent believed that "every American adult will be literate," and 19 percent agreed that "American students will be first in the world in science and math." Laggard funding from the corporate sector indicates that many business leaders seem to be skeptical about the ability of NASDC to reinvent schooling.[57]

Setting high goals is an essential stage in reform, but raising expectations to a level likely to be achieved only by "schools that are light years beyond those of today" can quickly lead to discouragement or disillusionment. Perhaps even more than the average citizen, teachers tend to be allergic to utopian claims for reform, for they are the workers supposed to carry out break-the-mold reforms and often the people who are blamed when grandiose innovations fail.

Second, don't try to change everything at once but instead graft change onto what is healthy in the present system. Instead of seeking to build lighthouse schools that often stand alone for a time and then regress toward the mean, the most pressing task is to improve education where families are most in need and to increase the number of lighted schoolhouses that are centers of community. Carefully evaluate what makes such good schools in needy neighborhoods work well and make that knowledge available to educators who can adapt such practices to their own schools.[58]

Veteran school reformers concur that attempts to reform public education by creating reinvented, prefabricated schools have brought meager results. A senior program officer of the Ford Foundation, Edward J. Meade, Jr., observed that "there are lessons that can be learned from past efforts which included the development of 'new schools,' e.g. the Ford Foundation's comprehensive School Improvement Program in the 1960s and the federal government's Experimental Schools Program of the 1970s. From those examples we know that rarely do new school 'models' illuminate or instruct other schools." The demonstration schools under Title III in the Johnson administration and the experimental schools mounted during the Nixon administration produced more red tape than emulation. "The main reaction of other schools [to the Title III demonstrations]," said former U.S. Commissioner of Education Harold Howe II, "was, 'Give us some money, and we'll do it too.'" Michael Kirst declared that "the [experimental schools] program is a classic case of multiple, vague, and somewhat contradictory federal objectives . . . 'Comprehensive change' [in which all institutional forms were questioned] is more a slogan than a concept to guide operations." Model schools can easily become "boutique" schools, Milbrey Wallin McLaughlin argued, especially if they use "resources beyond the reach of most schools and classrooms." The hard and essential task is to "tackle the tough problems that characterize many of America's schools—e.g. high rates of student mobility, diverse cultures and languages, dysfunctional families and communities."[59]

Third, enlist and honor teachers as the key people in reforming schooling. A subtext in much recent policy talk about reinventing schools is that existing teachers are a drag on reform, deficient if not dim. Surveys of teachers indicate that negative images of teachers in the media and in reform discourse is a major discouragement in their lives. No informed observer would say that teachers are paragons or do not need assistance in improving instruction, but the history of educational reform makes it clear that it would be impossible to improve everyday instruction without their active participation in the planning and implementation of change. Yet the section "Who Does What?" of *America 2000* lists federal and state officials, the business community, and parents as key actors, while only mentioning teachers as one among a number of people active "at the community level."[60]

"To the extent that teachers or the education community have no effective voice in matters that affect the educational enterprise," wrote McLaughlin, "we should not be surprised if they do not accept responsibility for disappointing consequences." Reforms in education should be deliberately designed to be hybridized to take advantage of teachers' knowledge of their children, subjects, pedagogical skills, and community. Perhaps the most lasting and beneficial changes will come when reformers regard teachers as major trustees of the common good and honor their best practices and most humane values as major resources in reforming the schools.[61]

NOTES

I am grateful to the Spencer Foundation and the Stanford Center for the Study of Families, Children, and Youth for support of the research on educational reform that Larry Cuban and I are pursuing. My debt to Larry Cuban is extraordinary—the ideas here derive so heavily from his written work and many conversations that it is difficult to distinguish his contributions and my own (though he may disagree with some of my evaluations). I also am grateful for the criticisms of other colleagues on an earlier draft of this essay: Lucy Bernholz, Elisabeth Hansot, John Meyer, Daniel Perlstein, Dorothy Shipps, William Tobin, and Decker Walker. They of course should not be held responsible for my errors.

1. U.S. Department of Education, *America 2000: An Education Strategy* (Washington, D.C.: USDE, 1991), 15; New American Schools Development Corp., *Designs for a New Generation of American Schools: Request for Proposals* (Arlington, Va.: NASDC, 1991), cover, 7, 20–21 (Bush quoted p. 7); Karen DeWitt, "Bush's Model-School Effort Draws Ideas but Little Money," *New York Times*, 28 May 1992, A-9; on the millennial American faith in schooling, see Henry J. Perkinson, *The Imperfect Panacea: American Faith in Education, 1965–1990* (New York: McGraw-Hill, 1991).

2. William Celis 3rd, "Private Group Hired to Run 9 Public Schools in Baltimore," *New York Times*, 11 June 1992, A-9; David A. Bennett, "Rescue Schools, Turn a Profit," *New York Times*, 11 June 1992, A-19; Mark Walsh, "Whittle Unveils Team to Design New Schools," *Education Week*, 4 March 1992, 1, 13; Linda Darling-Hammond, "For-Profit Schooling: Where's the Public Good?" *Education Week*, 7 October 1992, 40; Jonathan Kozol, "Whittle and the Privateers," *The Nation*, 21 September 1992, 272–78.

3. Edison quoted in Larry Cuban, *Teachers and Machines: The Classroom Use of Technology since 1920* (New York: Teachers College Press, 1986), 9; Virginia Woodson Church, *Teachers Are People, Being the Lyrics of Agatha Brown, Sometime Teacher in the Hilldale High School*, 3d ed. (Hollywood: David Fischer, 1925), 59; for a more recent paean to technology, see William C. Norris, "Via Technology to a New Era in Education," *Phi Delta Kappan* 58 (1977): 451–53.

4. P. Carpenter-Huffman, G. R. Hall, and G. C. Sumner, *Change in Education: Insights from Performance Contracting* (Cambridge, Mass.: Ballinger, 1974), 54; David Tyack, Michael W. Kirst, and Elisabeth Hansot, "Educational Reform: Retrospect and Prospect," *Teachers College Record* 81 (1980): 253–69; Howard Gardner, "The Two Rhetorics of School Reform: Complex Theories vs. the Quick Fix," *Chronicle of Higher Education*, 6 May 1992, 13.

5. "Saving our Schools," *Business Week*, 14 September 1992, 70–80; Lonnie Harp, "Group Dissects Education 'Industry' with Eye to Improving Productivity," *Education Week*, 18 November 1992, 1, 13; "Saving Our Schools," special issue, *Fortune* 121 (1990); H. Thomas James, *The New Cult of Efficiency and Education* (Pittsburgh: University of Pittsburgh Press, 1969).

6. Gerald N. Tirozzi, "Must We Reinvent the Schools?" in *Voices from the Field: 30 Expert Opinions on "America 2000," the Bush Administration Strategy to "Reinvent" America's Schools* (Washington, D.C.: William T. Grant Foundation Commission on Work, Family and Citizenship and Institute for Educational Leadership, 1991), 9–10.

7. Richard Bumstead, "Performance Contracting," reprinted from *Educate* (October 1970) in *Learning C.O.D.*, ed. J. A. Mecklenburger, J. A. Wilson, and R. W. Hostrop (Hamden, Conn.: Linnet Books, 1972), 28.

8. Larry Cuban, "Reforming Again, Again, and Again," *Educational Researcher* 19 (1990): 3–13.

9. Metaphor of "silly putty" in Thomas B. Timar and David L. Kirp, *Managing Educational Excellence* (New York: Falmer Press, 1988), 127; Edward J. Meade, Jr., "Ignoring the Lessons of Previous School Reforms" in *Voices from the Field*, 46; Harold Howe II, "Seven Large Questions for *America 2000*'s Authors" in *Voices from the Field*, 27; Michael W. Kirst, "Strengthening Federal-Local Relationships Supporting Educational Change" in *The Dynamics of Planned Educational Change*, ed. Robert E.

Herriott and Neal Gross (Berkeley, Calif.: McCutchan, 1979), 275; Milbrey W. McLaughlin, "Where's the Community in *America 2000?* in *Voices from the Field,* 44.

10. Susan R. Nevas, "Analytic Planning in Education: Critical Perspectives," *Interchange* 8 (1977–78): 13–42; James A. Mecklenburger, "My Visit to BRL" in *Learning C.O.D.*, 215–18; Leon Lessinger, *Every Kid a Winner: Accountability in Education* (New York: Simon & Schuster, 1970); James, *New Cult of Efficiency.*

11. National Education Association, *In Its Own Image: Business and the Reshaping of Public Education* (Washington, D.C.: NEA, 1990), 3–40.

12. Raymond E. Callahan, *Education and the Cult of Efficiency* (Chicago: University of Chicago Press, 1962), Cubberley quoted on p. 97; National Education Association, *Business and the Reshaping of Public Education.*

13. David Tyack, Robert Lowe, and Elisabeth Hansot, *Public Schools in Hard Times: The Great Depression and Recent Years* (Cambridge: Harvard University Press, 1984), chaps. 1–2.

14. John Brackett, Jay Chambers, and Thomas Parrish, "The Legacy of Rational Budgeting Models in Education and a Proposal for the Future," project report 83-A21, Institute for Research in Educational Finance and Governance, Stanford University, 1983.

15. Odiorne quoted in S. J. Knezevich, *Management by Objectives and Results—A Guidebook for Today's School Executive* (Arlington, Va.: American Association of School Administrators, 1973), 4; Lee S. Sproull and Kay Ramsey Hofmeister, "Thinking about Implementation," *Journal of Management* 12 (1968): 43–60; Carmelo V. Sapone and Joseph L. Guliano, "Management-by-Objectives: Promise and Problems," *Educational Technology* 17 (1977): 38; Philip C. Winstead, "Managing by Objectives or Managing by Delusions?" *Educational Technology* 20 (1980): 35–37.

16. Aaron Wildavsky, "Rescuing Policy Analysis from PPBS" in *Public Expenditures and Policy Analysis,* ed. R. H. Haveman and J. Margolis (Chicago: Markham, 1970), 469; Brackett, Chambers, and Parrish, "Rational Budgeting Models in Education."

17. Michael W. Kirst, "The Rise and Fall of PPBS in California," *Phi Delta Kappan* 56 (1975): 536–38.

18. Harry F. Wolcott, *Teachers versus Technocrats: An Educational Innovation in Anthropological Perspective* (Eugene, Oreg.: Center for Educational Policy and Management, 1977), 14, 241, 244–45.

19. Kirst, "Rise and Fall of PPBS," 536–38.

20. Stanley Elam, "The Age of Accountability Dawns in Texarkana," *Phi Delta Kappan* 51 (1970): 509–14.

21. Quotations from James A. Mecklenburger and John H. Wilson, "Learning C.O.D: Can the Schools Buy Success?" reprinted from *Saturday Review,* 18 September, 1971, in *Learning C.O.D.*, 2.

22. Mecklenberger, "My Visit to BRL," 216; Roald F. Campbell and James E. Lorion, *Performance Contracting in School Systems* (Columbus: Charles E. Merrill Publishing Co., 1972), 33–39.

23. Teacher quoted in Stanley Elam, "The Age of Accountability Dawns in Texarkana" in *Learning C.O.D.*, 25; Campbell and Lorion, *Performance Contracting,* chap. 8; for a variety of criticisms, see *Learning C.O.D.*, 43–47, 391–424, and

J. Lawrence McConville, "Evolution of Performance Contracting," *Educational Forum* 37 (1973): 443–52.

24. Campbell and Lorion, *Performance Contracting*, chap. 2.

25. Richard Bumstead, "Performance Contracting" in *Learning C.O.D.*, 35; Reed Martin and Peter Briggs, "Private Firms in the Public Schools," *Education Turnkey News*, February–March 1971, in *Learning C.O.D.*, 226; Green quoted in Campbell and Lorion, *Performance Contracting*, 16.

26. Bumstead, "Performance Contracting," 34–39; Campbell and Lorion, *Performance Contracting*, 29–33.

27. *Education Daily*, 1 October 1975, 5; Campbell and Lorian, *Performance Contracting*, 111–35; Carpenter-Huffman, Hall, and Sumner, *Change in Education*, 53; Battelle Columbus Laboratories, *Final Report on the Office of Economic Opportunity Experiment in Educational Performance Contracting* (Columbus, Ohio: Battelle Memorial Institute, 1972).

28. Myron Lieberman, *Privatization and Educational Choice* (New York: St. Martin's Press, 1989), chap. 4; for a critique and analysis of performance contracting as a social experiment, see Edward M. Gramlich and Patricia P. Koshel, *Educational Performance Contracting* (Washington, D.C.: Brookings Institution, 1975); Kozol, "Whittle and the Privateers."

29. Josiah F. Bumstead, *The Blackboard in the Primary Schools* (Boston: Perkins & Marvin, 1841), viii; Andrews & Co., *Illustrated Catalogue of School Merchandise* (Chicago, 1881), 73, as quoted in Charnel Anderson, *Technology in American Education, 1650–1900* (Washington, D.C.: Government Printing Office, 1962), 18, 32; David Tyack, "Educational Moonshot?" *Phi Delta Kappan* 58 (1977): 457; Philip W. Jackson, *The Teacher and the Machine* (Pittsburgh: University of Pittsburgh Press, 1967).

30. By 1931, twenty-five states and many large cities had departments devoted to audiovisual instruction—Cuban, *Teachers and Machines*, 12; Paul Saettler, *A History of Instructional Technology* (New York: McGraw-Hill, 1968), chap. 7.

31. Cuban, *Teachers and Machines*; Anthony Oettinger and Selma Marks, "Educational Technology: New Myths and Old Realities," *Harvard Educational Review* 38 (Fall 1968): 697–717; the *Education Index* charts the rise and decline of policy talk about instruction by various technologies.

32. Larry Cuban, "Determinants of Curriculum Change and Stability" in *Value Conflicts and Curriculum Issues*, ed. Jon Schaffarzick and Gary Sykes (Berkeley, Calif: McCutchan, 1979).

33. Anderson, *Technology in American Education*.

34. Saettler, *History of Instructional Technology*, 110–11, 127.

35. Cuban, *Teachers and Machines*, chap. 1; Saettler, *History of Instructional Technology*, 302–3.

36. Mark May and Arthur Lumsdaine, *Learning from Films* (New Haven: Yale University Press, 1958), 206.

37. William Levenson, *Teaching through Radio* (New York: Farrar & Rinehart, 1945), 181; Norman Woelfel and Keith Tyler, *Radio and the School* (Yonkers-on-Hudson: World Book Co., 1945), 3, 4–5.

38. *Decade of Experiment: The Fund for the Advancement of Education, 1951–1961* (New York: Ford Foundation, 1962); Cuban, *Teachers and Machines*, chap. 2.

39. Cuban, *Teachers and Machines*, 38–39 (advocate quoted on 50).

40. Ibid., chap. 3.

41. Ibid.

42. Linda Darling-Hammond and Barnett Berry, *The Evolution of Teacher Policy* (Washington, D.C.: Center for the Study of the Teaching Profession, 1988); William R. Johnson, "Teachers and Teacher Training in the Twentieth Century" in *American Teachers: Histories of a Profession at Work*, ed. Donald Warren (New York: Macmillan Co., 1989), 237–56; U.S. Department of Education, *America 2000*, 13.

43. Susan Moore Johnson, "Merit Pay for Teachers: A Poor Prescription for Reform," *Harvard Educational Review* 54 (1984): 179, 175–85; William A. Firestone, Susan H. Fuhrman, and Michael W. Kirst, *The Progress of Reform: An Appraisal of State Education Initiatives* (New Brunswick, N.J.: Center for Policy Research in Education, 1989).

44. Johnson, "Merit Pay."

45. Richard R. Doremus, "Kalamazoo's Merit Pay Plan," *Phi Delta Kappan* 63 (1982): 409–10.

46. Wayne E. Fuller, "The Teacher in the Country School" in *American Teachers*, 98–117; Michael W. Sedlak, "'Let Us Go and Buy a School Master': Historical Perspectives on the Hiring of Teachers in the United States, 1750–1980" in *American Teachers*, 257–90.

47. David Tyack and Elisabeth Hansot, *Learning Together: A History of Coeducation in American Public Schools* (New Haven: Yale University Press and Russell Sage Foundation, 1990), 57–69.

48. David Tyack, *The One Best System: A History of American Urban Education* (Cambridge: Harvard University Press, 1974), 59–65, 255–94; Vaughan Mac-Caughey, "The Single Salary Schedule," *School and Society*, 5 July 1924, 9–13.

49. Cora B. Morrison, "Single Salary Schedules" in *Addresses and Proceedings, 1924* (Washington, D.C.: National Education Association, 1924), 480–86; National Education Association, "Teachers' Salaries and Salary Trends in 1923," *Research Bulletin* 1 (1923): 58–59.

50. Callahan, *Cult of Efficiency*; Richard J. Murnane and David K. Cohen, "Merit Pay and the Evaluation Problem: Why Most Merit Pay Plans Fail and a Few Survive," *Harvard Educational Review* 56 (1986): 2, 1–17.

51. Johnson, "Merit Pay"; P. J. Porwoll, *Merit Pay for Teachers* (Arlington, Va.: Educational Research Service, 1979); Susan M. Johnson, "Incentives for Teachers: What Motivates, What Matters," *Educational Administration Quarterly* 22 (Summer 1986): 54–79; Murnane and Cohen, "Merit Pay," 2.

52. Murnane and Cohen, "Merit Pay," 12–15.

53. Susan Moore Johnson, "Redesigning Teachers' Work" in Richard Elmore and Associates, *Restructuring Schools: The Next Generation of Educational Reform* (San Francisco: Jossey-Bass Publishers, 1990), 125, 128.

54. Susan Moore Johnson, *Teachers at Work: Achieving Success in Our Schools* (New York: Basic Books, 1992), chap. 10.

55. Jerry Duea, "School Officials and the Public Hold Disparate Views on Education," *Phi Delta Kappan* 63 (1982): 479; Dan C. Lortie, *Schoolteacher: A Sociological Study* (Chicago: University of Chicago Press, 1975), 105.

56. For discussions of the different worlds of teachers and policy makers, see Neal Gross, Joseph B. Giacquinta, and Marilyn Bernstein, *Implementing Organizational Innovations* (New York: Basic Books, 1971); Milbrey McLaughlin, "Learning from Experience: Lessons from Policy Implementation," *Educational Evaluation and Policy Analysis* 9 (Summer 1987): 172.

57. Karen De Witt, "Most Parents in Survey Say Education Goals Can't Be Met," *New York Times*, 13 November 1991, B-7; Gary Putka, "Foundation Encourages Firms to Devise a New Class of Schools," *Wall Street Journal*, 26 August 1991, B-1–2; Karen De Witt, "Bush's Model-School Effort Draws Ideas but Little Money," *New York Times*, 28 May 1992, A-9.

58. Joan Lipsitz speaks of "a 'lighted schoolhouse'" that is "reconceptualized not just as a human services center for its children, but also as a neighborhood resource for its adults"—"Scenes from the New American Civil War" in *Voices from the Field*, 36–37; Sarah Lawrence Lightfoot, *The Good High School: Portraits of Character and Culture* (New York: Basic Books, 1983).

59. Edward J. Meade, Jr., "Ignoring the Lessons of Previous School Reforms" in *Voices from the Field*, 46; Harold Howe II, "Seven Large Questions for *America 2000*'s Authors" in *Voices from the Field*, 27; Michael W. Kirst, "Strengthening Federal-Local Relationships Supporting Educational Change" in *The Dynamics of Planned Educational Change*, ed. Robert E. Herriott and Neal Gross (Berkeley, Calif.: McCutchan, 1979), 275; Milbrey W. McLaughlin, "Where's the Community in *America 2000*?" in *Voices from the Field*, 44.

60. U.S. Department of Education, *America 2000*, 23–24.

61. McLaughlin, "Where's the Community?" 43; Richard F. Elmore and Milbrey Wallin McLaughlin, *Steady Work: Policy, Practice, and the Reform of American Education* (Santa Monica: Rand Corp., 1988), 61.

THE NEW POLITICS OF CHOICE

PAUL E. PETERSON

The concept of choice is deeply embedded in the American liberal tradition, yet the educational choice movement did not begin until the 1950s. Schooling in the United States instead developed in ways quite consistent with the statist views of German idealists, as interpreted by John Dewey. But though Dewey's theories influenced American educators, judicial doctrine remained essentially faithful to the older, liberal tradition, keeping alive the possibility that schools could be established free of state control.

The choice debate moved to center stage after 1970 in response to three underlying social trends: the rising respectability of the Catholic religious tradition, the closing of the public school frontier, and the apparent deterioration of the urban school. The question of choice took a decidedly partisan twist when Republicans openly appealed for Catholic support while public educators formed close ties to the Democratic party. In the late 1980s choice advocates began focusing on the needs of racial minorities, invoking themes originally composed by Thomas Paine. It is worth starting at the beginning.

THE LIBERAL TRADITION IN AMERICA

European emigrants to the New World left behind most of the old-world trappings of crown, state, aristocracy, and established church. In their place they constructed a political language that glorified individualism, hard work, economic self-sufficiency, self-reliance, localism, and minimalist government.[1] Their liberal categories were not always consistently applied. Their belief in the right to life, liberty, and property did not necessarily restrict them from owning slaves or from conquering technologically more primitive societies. But whatever their inconsistencies, the founders of the new nation believed that they had the liberty to choose the way in which their children were to be educated. In the words of the radical Tom Paine, who made the clearest proposal for choice in education, governments should provide monies to parents to be used to send their children "to school, to learn reading, writing, and common arithmetic; the ministers of every parish, of every denomination, to certify jointly to an office, for this purpose, that the duty is performed."[2]

The Constitution written by the founders said nothing specifically about education. That was among the many matters to be left to the states. But the Constitution's First Amendment said the federal government could not intrude upon the citizen's religious beliefs: "Congress shall make no law respecting the establishment of religion, or prohibiting the free exercise thereof." Both clauses would shape the debate over school choice.

Congress did make clear in 1785 that it expected that the government would provide financial support for educational purposes; in the new territories, one section of land out of sixteen was to be set aside for "the maintenance of public schools within the said township."[3] The word *public* did not mean state controlled; it only implied communal as distinct from parental or tutorial instruction. Two years later Congress, in the Northwest Ordinance, reaffirmed that "religion, morality and knowledge, being necessary to good government and the happiness of mankind, schools and the *means of education* [italics added] shall forever be encouraged."[4]

If the commitment to education was clear, there remained ambiguity as to how these schools were to be organized. One answer was given by Benjamin Rush in his early "Plan for the Establishment of Public Schools" for Pennsylvania. He proposed that "free, public" schools be supported by letting each "scholar pay [the schoolmaster] from 1s6 to 2s6 each quarter."[5] Recognizing the ethnic and religious differences within the state, Rush suggested that "children of the same religious sect and nation may be educated as much as possible together."[6] Even Thomas Jefferson, who sought to limit the influence of the Anglican church on the educational institutions of Virginia, proposed only that "free" children be "entitled to receive tuition gratis, for a term of three years, and as much longer, at their private expense, as their parents, guardians or friends, shall think proper."[7]

Yet it remained for the English libertarian, John Stuart Mill, to articulate most convincingly the rationale for choice in education. Writing in defense of liberty against the awesome power of the state, Mill squared society's need for an educated populace with the family's right to religious liberty in a manner that has hardly been improved upon:

> Is it not almost a self-evident axiom, that the State should require and compel the education . . . of every human being who is born its citizen? . . .

Were the duty of enforcing universal education once admitted, there would be an end to the difficulties about what the State should teach, and how it should teach, which now convert the subject into a mere battlefield for sects and parties, causing the time and labor which should have been spent in educating, to be wasted in quarrelling about education . . . It might leave to parents to obtain the education where and how they pleased, and content itself with helping to pay the school fees.[8]

Mill was advocating choice as a solution to the conflicts among an established Anglican church, militant defenders of chapel, Irish Catholics, and Welsh Methodists. Since disputes among them could not be resolved, mass education in Britain evolved haphazardly and fitfully until a quasi-choice system was finally created under the Education Act of 1902. In the United States localism rescued liberalism from confronting its ambiguities. Towns, cities, counties, and churches built schools at a pace that far surpassed the rate of school construction in Europe. Yet most families had as much educational choice as they wanted. The well-to-do relied on tutors and boarding schools. The rest relied on local schools that reflected the moral and religious code of the community in which they were embedded. Choice was among localities, not within them.

THE CATHOLIC CHALLENGE TO THE PROTESTANT COMMON SCHOOL

As a fledgling public school system was being built in the early decades of the nineteenth century, it was challenged not by the dominant churches (that were often working in close collaboration with government officials) but by a swelling immigrant population from Catholic parts of Europe.[9] The changes were especially evident in Massachusetts. By 1852 over half of the 11,800 students in the Boston schools were foreign born. Distressed by the changing composition of the city's population, the Boston School Committee urged that "in our schools they must receive moral and religious teaching, powerful enough if possible to keep them in the right path amid the moral darkness which is their daily and domestic walk."[10] Horace Mann, the state's first secretary to its board of education, was no less committed to using the state-controlled common school for high moral purposes. A devout Unitarian, Mann was gravely concerned about the effects of what he regarded as papist superstitions. "How shall the rising generation be brought under purer moral influences," he asked rhetorically, so that "when they become men, they will surpass their predecessors, both in the soundness of their speculations and in the rectitude of their practice?" His public school answer to this question was so effective

that Mann won unmitigated, if rather curious, praise from the Congregationalist journal, *New Englander*: "These schools draw in the children of
alien parentage with others, and assimilate them to the native born . . . So
they grow up with the state, of the state and for the state." If the phrases
have the same ring as those Lincoln would pronounce at Gettysburg, their
meaning was hardly as grounded in the liberal tradition.[11]

Catholic leaders were less pleased with the evolution of a state-
controlled educational system than was the Congregationalist editor of the
New Englander. But neither did they want parental choice in education.
Instead, they demanded a corporatist solution in America along the same
lines that were evolving in Europe. According to long-standing Catholic
doctrine, education was the responsibility of the church, not the state.
Rome insisted on separate Catholic schools not just because the public
schools read the Protestant King James Bible but because state-
administered secular education was an imposition of the state into a realm
reserved for divine authority.

Catholics wielded sufficient local power in some cities and states to win
for a while some token state subsidies.[12] But such short-term victories only
fueled nativist, Protestant fears of immigrants and papistry.[13] The anti-
Catholic forces were so strong that in 1875 they nearly secured passage of a
constitutional amendment that explicitly forbade state aid to sectarian
institutions. Its chief sponsor, James Blaine, was nearly elected president in
1884. Although the amendment, which won approval of two-thirds of the
House of Representatives, fell one vote short in the Senate, Protestants
everywhere banned state subsidies to religious schools in state constitutions and school codes.[14]

DEWEY'S DEFENSE OF A STATE-CONTROLLED SCHOOL SYSTEM

During the ante-bellum period, the argument for state education, as made
by Horace Mann and the Boston School Board, had been muddied by a not
so hidden attempt to inculcate the Protestant faith. But in the latter part of
the nineteenth century, a more secular basis for state-controlled education
was being developed in Germany. And it was this argument, as modified
by America's greatest educational philosopher, John Dewey, which eventually became most persuasive. Discarding the liberal distinctions between
state, society, and the individual, Dewey argued that "what the best and
wisest parent wants for his own child, that must the community want for
all of its children. Any other ideal for our schools . . . destroys our democracy."[15]

Although Dewey was careful not to reject explicitly the liberal ideals
that had motivated Tom Paine and Benjamin Rush, he was quite aware that

he was rejecting an older, liberal conception of education (though he was careful to choose the German Immanuel Kant, not the English liberal John Stuart Mill, as his main antagonist). "In the eighteenth-century philosophy we find ourselves in a very different circle of ideas," he wrote in *Democracy and Education*. It was then thought that, "to give 'nature' full swing," inquiry had to be "freed from prejudice and artificial restraints of church and state." Kant opposed state education because he distrusted "rulers [who] are simply interested in such training as will make their subjects better tools for their own intentions." The rulers' interest "in the welfare of their own nation instead of in what is best for humanity, will make them, if they give money for the schools, wish to draw their plans."[16]

Recognizing the power of the liberal argument Kant had set forth, Dewey then posed what was for him the fundamental political question: "Is it possible for an educational system to be conducted by a national state and yet the full social ends of the educative process not be restricted, constrained, and corrupted?" His response drew upon the work of Georg Hegel, who provided the theoretical justification for the rising power of the German state bureaucracy. Following Hegel, Dewey portrayed the school as the transmitter of the knowledge and culture that historical processes had created. The school was special in three ways: First, it simplified the complexities of modern life so that they could be taught to young people in their parts, one at a time. Second, the school "eliminate[d], so far as possible, the unworthy features of the existing environment from influence upon mental habitudes . . . [The school was] responsible *not* to transmit . . . the whole of . . . existing achievements, but only such as make for a better future society." Finally, the school was "to balance the various elements in the social environment, and to see to it that each individual [got] an opportunity to escape from the limitations of the social group in which he was born." This third responsibility is especially important in a heterogeneous country: "The assimilative force of the American public school is eloquent testimony to the efficacy of the common and balanced appeal."[17]

A more ringing defense of the common school could not be written. This same peal of and for the public school bell was struck time and again in subsequent decades by educators convinced that public schools, properly financed, could remake society. Yet Dewey, writing in 1915 in the midst of the Great War, realized that the bell's ring was not quite true; if the state controlled the schools, could not the state pervert education for its own nationalistic purposes?

Dewey admitted two deficiencies of state-controlled education. First, the state was constrained by the "tendencies . . . which split society into classes." Second, national loyalties interfered with "a superior devotion to the things which unite men in common ends." But Dewey did not so much address these deficiencies as wish them away. To offset economic inequalities, he called for "school facilities . . . of such amplitude and efficiency as will in fact and not simply in name discount the effects of economic inequalities." Dewey expected public schools to achieve not just equality of opportunity but equality of educational and social outcomes. "Accomplishment of this end demands not only adequate . . . school facilities, and such supplementation of family resources as will enable youth to take advantage of them, but also such modification of traditional ideals of culture . . . as will retain all the youth under educational influences until they are equipped to be masts of their own economic and social careers."[18] Dewey never explained how schools would acquire the resources to undertake such a massive task, nor did he consider the threat to liberty posed by an institution so powerful it could essentially abolish the distinction between state and society.

Nor was Dewey less utopian when he examined the limitations of the nation state. "It is not enough to teach the horrors of war and to avoid everything which would stimulate international jealousy and animosity. The emphasis must be put upon whatever binds people together in cooperative human pursuits and results, apart from geographical limitations."[19] Just how schools were to eliminate rivalries among nation states by cultivating the cooperative dimension of the human spirit was left to the imagination.

Dewey's ideals were undoubtedly democratic, magnanimous, and comprehensive. Yet he showed little respect for diversity, particularity, and choice. He showed little recognition of the potential for inefficiency, corruption, or abuse. Nor, despite the Great War, did he come to grips with the potential for political perversion inherent to the institution he was creating. Most seriously, he placed no limits on the power and resources of the public school and, by extension, of the state. In the end, Dewey failed to distinguish his position from that of Hegel. If the school was to be controlled by the state, then not only must the state be good, it must be the Supreme Good, the most inclusive of all of society's institutions. In short, Dewey shifted educational thought in the United States nearly 180 degrees from the liberal grounds of the country's founders.

THE COURTS AS CARRIERS OF THE LIBERAL TRADITION

Although Dewey shaped the thinking of educators, he had only a modest effect on those judicial decisions that tried to resolve the tension between the country's liberal traditions and its rapidly developing system of state-controlled education. Although Supreme Court opinions at times iterated the argument Dewey fashioned, its doctrine, taken as a whole, has remained essentially faithful to the country's more deeply ingrained liberal tradition.

The first school-related case decided by the Supreme Court pitted the liberal and Hegelian conceptions of the proper role of the state directly against one another. Expressing a concern that hardly varied from the one Horace Mann had articulated some eighty years earlier, the state of Nebraska forbade any school, public or private, to teach students in a language other than English, on the grounds that such a law would "promote civic development by inhibiting training and education of the immature in foreign tongues and ideals before they could learn English and acquire American ideals." But the Court said Nebraska had violated the due process clause of the Fourteenth Amendment that guaranteed "the right of the individual to . . . establish a home and bring up children [and] to worship God according to the dictates of his own conscience."[20] Two years later the Court struck down on similar grounds an Oregon law compelling all children to attend a public school. Oregon, too, made the remarkably Hegelian argument that "a compulsory system of public school education will encourage the patriotism of its citizens, and train its younger citizens to become more willing and more efficient defenders of the United States in times of public danger." The Court replied that the law "unreasonably interferes with the liberty of parents and guardians to direct the upbringing and education of children under their control."[21]

Not until 1940 did the Court give signs of succumbing to the Hegelian spirit. Justice Felix Frankfurter justified a nearly unanimous decision to uphold a West Virginia statute requiring that Jehovah's Witnesses salute the flag in public school ceremonies on the grounds that such activities promoted "national unity, [which] is the basis of national security." Yet just three years later, America's liberal tradition reasserted itself, and the West Virginia law was overturned. "Compulsory unification of opinion," wrote Justice Jackson in the midst of a war against fascism, "achieves only the unanimity of the graveyard."[22] Extending this line of reasoning, the Court in 1972 disallowed the application of a compulsory attendance law to two Amish children, ages fourteen and fifteen, whose parents opposed on religious grounds their continued attendance in a public school.[23]

If the Court quite steadfastly rejected the most virulent applications of Hegelian doctrine, more subtle questions remained. What resources of the state could citizens use while engaged in religious activity? Can the state support the secular activities of religious schools? When does citizen or school use of state resources become tantamount to the establishment of religion? In responding to these questions, the Court for several decades seemed to wander through a doctrinal maze. The Court allowed sectarian schools to use state-provided textbooks but not instructional materials. It allowed state reimbursement to parents who transported their children to sectarian schools, but it denied aid for trips after the school day had begun. It allowed religious instruction during the school day in local churches but not on school premises. Some claimed that the wall between church and state that Thomas Jefferson had recommended was turning into a wall as serpentine as the one designed by Jefferson to surround the campus of his beloved University of Virginia.

This claim no longer seems accurate. Though constructed haphazardly, the church-state wall took a definitely liberal shape in the 1980s. The Supreme Court became increasingly unwilling to provide any sort of direct aid to schools operated by religious institutions. At the same time the Court allowed the resources of governments to be used by citizens for whatever purposes they preferred, regardless of whether or not these were religious. Traditional calls for aid to parochial schools have been called into question, while educational choice has been legitimized.

Perhaps the most telling decision limiting state support of parochial education came in 1975 when the Court, in *Meek v. Pittenger*, struck down all but the textbook component of a state program providing aid to sectarian schools. The decision was especially significant because it struck down much of the private school component of the compensatory education program that had been passed by Congress at the height of Lyndon Johnson's Great Society. When *Meek* was subsequently reaffirmed and extended in 1985 (*Aguilar v. Felton*), the Court made it difficult for private school supporters to expect any direct federal aid except for secular school textbooks.[24] The curves in the wall were all but eliminated.

If it was now quite certain that the state could not directly aid religious schools, what about vouchers to families who could then choose between attending a secular or a sectarian institution? The Court gave its first hint that such assistance was permissible under the Constitution in an observation made in 1973 by Justice Lewis Powell in an obscure footnote to a decision declaring that direct aid to religious schools was unconstitutional.[25] The Powell footnote became Court doctrine ten years later when the Court approved a Minnesota state income tax deduction for expenses incurred in providing "tuition, textbooks and transportation" for children attending any elementary or secondary school.[26] Although most of the benefits of the tax deduction went to families sending their children to sectarian schools, such statistical considerations were regarded as irrelevant to a determination of a statute's constitutionality. The Court decision seemed to permit tuition vouchers that gave families a choice between public and sectarian schools—even if most families preferred education in a religious setting.

THE CHANGING PLACE OF CATHOLICS IN AMERICAN POLITICS

As courts were defining more clearly the appropriate boundaries between church and state, Catholics were acquiring the respectability that gave

their educational views greater influence. The distance Catholics had traveled in American society and politics during the half century between 1930
and 1960 was little short of astounding. As late as 1928, New York Governor Al Smith had suffered a humiliating defeat in his run for the
presidency—in good part, many thought, because the majority thought a
Catholic president would obey political instructions issued by the Vatican.
Political animosity was accompanied by social snobbery. As late as the
1940s, Catholic schools were regarded as socially inferior, highly regi-
mented, intellectually restricted, scientifically backward redoubts of conformity and reaction.

These fears and sneers dissipated with the increasing prosperity and
international responsibilities of postwar America. Italian, Polish, and Irish
Catholics were incorporated into the economic, social, and political mainstream. The pope became an ally in the fight against East European Communism. John Kennedy, the first presidential candidate of Catholic affilia-
tion since Smith, not only was elected president but also became a
martyred hero. Pope John XXIII and the Second Vatican Council adapted
the Catholic religious tradition to modern realities, softening Protestant
animosities. Catholic schools not only became respectable but also, according to several national studies, performed even better than their public
counterparts.[27]

Catholic leaders sought to capitalize on their community's newly
achieved political power by renewing the demand for government aid to
nonpublic schools. Although their political strategy would in retrospect
prove faulty, their thinking at the time was not unreasonable. The emerging issue of federal aid to education seemed to open up a new opportunity
for discussion. Since early Court rulings on the constitutionality of state aid
were ambiguous and the post–New Deal Supreme Court was known to be
reluctant to declare a congressional statute unconstitutional, there seemed
to be a good chance that carefully constructed federal aid to nonpublic
schools would be considered constitutional. Also, Catholics seemed to
hold the balance of power on educational issues in the House of Representatives. Republicans and conservative southern Democrats were opposed
to any and all federal school aid for fear it would lead to federal control. No
bill could be passed without a unified northern Democratic party, and
northern Democrats could not be unified without some concessions to
Catholic interests.[28]

When Catholic demands for federal aid to private schools were countered by public school, Protestant, and Jewish cries that such aid constituted a violation of the separation of church and state, a majority coalition
could not be formed and no major education bill was passed during the
Truman, Eisenhower, and Kennedy administrations. Only when Lyndon
Johnson, the master of legislative compromise, recast federal aid to schools

as compensatory education for poor children was it possible to strike the requisite political bargain. Federal monies would go to poor children in both public and private schools.[29]

The Catholic victory was Pyrrhic. Control over the distribution of compensatory education dollars was left to state education authorities, agencies often dominated by public school supporters hostile to Catholic interests.[30] Even worse, groups of Protestants, Jews, and secularists initiated attacks on the federal programs in the courts. Instead of legitimating the corporatist philosophy espoused by Catholic leaders, federal aid spawned a legal attack in an arena where the liberal tradition was the most secure. Although the Court never declared the entire compensatory education program unconstitutional, it struck down virtually every conceivable element supporting religious schools (other than textbook provision) set up within its framework. By 1988 only 3.3 percent of private school students were receiving services under the compensatory education program, as compared to 11.1 percent of public school students.[31] It was time for Catholics to cast their political rhetoric in more liberal categories.

A liberal political argument in defense of Catholic interests had already been developed in 1958 by a Jesuit priest, Virgil C. Blum, the first scholar to write a full-length treatise on the virtues of choice in American education. Couching his argument in straightforward liberal categories (including appeals to Jefferson and Mill), Blum asserted that religious liberty was violated in a society that imposed heavy financial costs on those who wished to have their children educated within a particular religious tradition. To remedy this defect, he proposed tax credits to families who sent their children to private schools.[32] As constitutional objections to other forms of state aid continued to mount, Catholic leaders came to realize that Blum and his colleagues were correct in recasting Catholic concerns in a language consistent with the liberal tradition.

THE COST OF EDUCATION

If the demand for choice was made possible in good part by growing Catholic respectability, it was urged forward by the increasing cost of educational services. Prices were rising because education was becoming increasingly labor-intensive. While manufacturing processes were substituting capital for labor and using fewer workers to produce more and better products, schools were increasing the ratio of adults to students. Even though educational research failed to prove that class size was related to learning rates, educators continued to favor smaller, more intimate learning environments. Nationally, the average pupil/teacher ratio in public schools declined from 26.9 in 1955 to 17.6 in 1987.[33]

As a result, the per pupil cost of public education climbed steadily throughout the postwar period. Even in inflation-adjusted dollars, the increasing cost of education was staggering. Between 1950 and 1989 school costs per pupil (in 1989 dollars) increased from $1,617 to $6,180, nearly a fourfold increase after inflation. This trend affected private as well as public schools. Although per pupil costs in the private sector were less, the upward trend was actually steeper than that in the public sector.[34]

The rising costs reduced the utilization of private schools. Between 1959 and 1969 the percentage of students attending private school fell from 12.8 to 9.3 percent,[35] a fall so steep that President Richard Nixon established a National Commission on School Finance. Two years later, the commission recommended federal aid to nonpublic schools through tuition tax credits and Nixon subsequently included the tuition tax credit in his legislative agenda. Efforts to pass tuition tax credits continued in both House and Senate throughout the seventies. Private school supporters came closest to succeeding in 1978 when a school tax credit passed the House and a college tax credit passed the Senate. But the Senate members of the conference committee called to adjudicate differences between the two bills would not agree to the school tax credit, and both pieces of legislation died.

THE CLOSING OF THE PUBLIC SCHOOL FRONTIER

The rising cost of private education would not have affected public policy had not public schools undergone their own transformation. In the years immediately following World War II, the public school frontier closed. Virtually all of the major goals of public school educators had been achieved. Nearly every state required that children between the ages of six and sixteen attend school. Most young people were earning the coveted high school diploma. School teachers in all states needed at least a four-year bachelor's degree with the requisite number of pedagogical courses. School administration had been taken out of the hands of patronage-hungry school boards and placed in the hands of professionally trained administrators. The little one-room schoolhouses had been closed to make way for educational oases located in the larger towns of rural America. To accommodate the wartime and postwar baby boomers, new, updated school buildings were being opened with incredible rapidity. John Dewey's dream was becoming a reality. Schools were remaking society.

Or were they? When gaps have been closed, when bridges have been crossed, when expectations have been fulfilled, doubts almost necessarily emerge.

Conservatives were the first to express dissatisfaction. Less enamored than educators with child-centered pedagogy, Arthur Bestor called for a return to teaching fundamentals and instruction in the classical tradition.[36]

It was in this milieu that the first tuition voucher proposal was constructed by the future Nobel prize-winning economist Milton Friedman: "Governments . . . could finance [education] by giving parents vouchers redeemable for a specified maximum sum per child per year if spent on 'approved' educational services. Parents would then be free to spend this sum and any additional sum on purchasing educational services from an 'approved' institution of their own choice. The educational services could be rendered by private enterprises operated for profit, or by non-profit institutions of various kinds."[37]

Written in arcane economic language and published in 1955 in a diverse, undistinguished collection of essays, Friedman's proposal initially fell on deaf ears. Americans were too pleased with their international prowess and too concerned about the Cold War to have doubts about public schools. When Sputnik was put into orbit, the preferred solution was not tuition vouchers but more money for math and science.[38]

But concern began to spread as the new science of testing cast doubt on the progressive myth that American schools were steadily expanding and improving. The Scholastic Aptitude Test was created in the fifties to identify the most able high school students, regardless of the curriculum to which they had been exposed. Two decades later, declining SAT scores would be cited as definitive evidence that the public school curriculum was failing.[39] SAT scores, by themselves, did not provide decisive information about the state of American education. But the results from the SAT were consistent with an array of other studies of trends in student achievement. The hopefully named National Assessment of Educational Progress found very little progress in the learning of students at either the elementary or the secondary level. Comparisons with the performances of students in other countries revealed that American schools, far from being the best in the world, were hardly above average among industrialized countries. Japanese students were performing strikingly better. Finally, studies began showing that students in private schools outperformed their public school counterparts—even when results were adjusted to take into account the greater selectivity of the private school students. To the great surprise of the country's educational leaders, Catholic schools seemed to do a better job of teaching not only religious dogma but also math and English.

With each new study placing still another nail in the coffin in which the myth of public school improvement was being buried, the interest in one or another variant of Friedman's proposal quietly grew. Still, Catholics were too interested in federal aid or tax credits and Republicans too fearful of federal control to give the Friedman proposal the attention it deserved. Not until a group of left-wing reformers revamped the tuition voucher proposal would it become fit for political action.

CHOICE AND SCHOOL DESEGREGATION

As the frontier of expansion and reform was closing, a new frontier was opened by the Supreme Court's *Brown* decision declaring school segregation unconstitutional. The ensuing debate over racial desegregation and integration shaped the debate over choice in contradictory ways. It turned parental choice into a code word for racial segregation, thereby invoking implacable opposition to choice on the part of the civil rights movement. But choice also became the most promising tool for achieving stable racial integration in public schools.

In the aftermath of the *Brown* decision, most southern states adopted parental choice plans in the hope and expectation that blacks could be pressured into choosing all-black schools. When this strategy failed, four states—Alabama, Louisiana, Mississippi, and Virginia—passed legislation establishing voucherlike arrangements for children who chose to go to a private rather than a public school. Federal courts declared these choice plans unconstitutional.[40] Tax-aided systems of choice could not foster school segregation.

Instead of becoming a mechanism for segregation, choice in the form of magnet schools became one of the most powerful tools for desegregation in large central cities. Magnet schools were expected to attract both white and minority students from across the city. Magnet schools had special themes, such as the sciences, performing arts, vocational education, language instruction, or college preparation. Most received additional funding and enhanced flexibility in the recruitment of teaching staff to ensure higher quality educational services. Admission to magnets was often selective in that the performance of students in lower grades was taken into account in determining admission. Even when no formal selection criteria were applied, magnets tended to recruit the more able and ambitious students.[41]

Magnet schools seem to have assisted desegregation processes; at the very least, they seldom were more segregated than central-city schools in general. The academic performance of students in magnet schools was generally superior to that of those in other public schools, though it is uncertain whether this was due to better instruction or more able, more motivated students. Yet Denis Doyle's overall assessment in the mid-1980s reflected the judgment of most informed observers: "Magnet schools are not a panacea, . . . [but] they can and do meet the objectives set for them, including higher academic standards and greater integration."[42]

The magnet school approach was soon generalized and given the label "public school choice." Examples of public school choice ranged from a gradual extension of the magnet school concept (37 percent of all schools in Buffalo, New York, were magnet schools in 1984) to complete freedom of choice of any public school within a school district (East Harlem, New York; Cambridge, Massachusetts) to between-district choice among schools within a state (Minnesota).

Magnet schools were criticized for constituting only a token response to the problems faced by big city school systems. By concentrating resources on a few schools that were patronized by the city's more influential residents, they deflected attention away from the overall plight of central-city schools. It was argued, furthermore, that public school choice was limited choice. With choice contained within the public sector, families were unable to consider religious schools, alternative schools, single-sex schools, or schools catering to gays and lesbians.

THE CRISIS IN URBAN EDUCATION

Magnet schools were one sign that choice could be put to egalitarian as well as right-wing purposes. Other choice approaches had an ever more explicitly equalizing thrust. While they seemed to be extensions of Friedman's 1955 proposal, they owed more to the civil rights movement than to economic theory.

The civil rights movement of the late fifties and early sixties expected that a combination of lawsuits, political demonstrations, and federal intervention would desegregate big-city schools in the North as well as the South. Some (mainly white liberals) felt that interracial contact would by itself enhance the educational skills of blacks and other minorities; others (mainly blacks) felt that by bringing races together minorities could finally win for themselves the same quality services whites were enjoying. But determined white resistance to racial integration by most central-city whites frustrated both blacks and white liberals and convinced many that significant racial integration could not soon be achieved.

As important as the overt, political resistance to desegregation was the accelerating white flight from the central city. Even by 1971, seventeen years after *Brown*, whites constituted slightly more than 43 percent of the students in the schools of nineteen of the largest central cities. By 1986 the percentage of white students in these cities had fallen to 22 percent.[43]

Not only were central-city schools becoming resegregated into virtually all-minority organizations, but they were developing a reputation for extravagant incompetence. Central-city schools, it was said, were run by teacher organizations more interested in protecting seniority and staff privileges than in educating students. Big-city schoolhouses, it was asserted, were infested with neighborhood gangs, drug dealers, and ethnic hatreds. Urban bureaucracies, it was claimed, hampered principals and teachers with mindless regulations.[44]

These charges were so widely believed that they accelerated not only white flight but also the demand for choice in urban education. The most vocal critics were often associated with what was known as the New Left, who, unlike the Communists and Socialists of the Old Left, had as many doubts about the institutions created by the modern welfare state as John Stuart Mill had had about an aristocratic one. Critic Herbert Kohl reported that the bureaucratized schools of New York were destroying the lives of the children contained therein. Kenneth Clark, the black social psychologist, attacked the racism of the public schools of Harlem.[45]

Acting on these and similar criticisms, reformers in several cities were able to persuade big-city school boards to establish experimental alternative schools that would be given enough autonomy that they could explore alternative educational approaches. Between 1968 and 1971 alternative schools were established in Bellevue; Chicago; Ithaca, New York; New Orleans; Philadelphia; and elsewhere. These schools were usually small institutions that explored unconventional teaching strategies and recruited students who were failing in traditional classrooms. They frequently received outside funding from a foundation or government agency. Since no one was compelled to attend them, they became schools of choice. In most but not all cases, their student bodies were predominantly white.[46]

The alternative school concept was generalized in 1970 by a group of scholars headed by Christopher Jencks of the Harvard School of Education, who proposed that big cities construct a system of alternative schools by means of tuition vouchers. To ensure equal educational opportunity, approved schools could not ask parents to supplement vouchers with their own funds. They also had to accept all applicants or choose randomly among them, except that half of the applicants were to be chosen so as to avoid discriminating against minorities. Even though cast in egalitarian terms, the Jencks proposal was harshly condemned by liberal commentators. They criticized the plan for "shor[ing] up parochial schools, . . . [easing] the tax burden on upper-middle-class families, . . . [weakening] an already weak public educational system," and adversely affecting desegregation.[47]

Despite these criticisms and without any interest group pressure or sign of public enthusiasm for the idea, the OEO attempted a demonstration of the Jencks plan. One can hardly blame the OEO for trying. The agency was an innovative, experimental, intensely politicized organization that had been created within the Office of the President at the height of the Democratic party's War on Poverty. It was now trying to survive the animosity of Nixon Republicans committed to its extinction. Insisting that vouchers were consistent with the Republican party's rising interest in educational choice, OEO hoped it could find ways of linking its antipoverty mission with Republican doctrine.

The idea was considered in Seattle, San Francisco, Rochester, Gary, East Hartford, a group of towns in New Hampshire, and Alum Rock, California. Local opposition, not least from teacher and civil rights organizations, precluded undertaking the experiment everywhere but in Alum Rock, a fairly small school district of fifteen thousand students—55 percent Latino, 12 percent black—not far from San Jose. Here, in northern California, public school choice would get its first try, largely because a new school superintendent saw it as an opportunity to obtain federal dollars to implement his own plan for administrative decentralization.[48]

Vouchers in practice turned out to be quite different from the Jencks plan. The first thing to go was random assignment: parent groups insisted that schools first enroll applicants from the neighborhood and then admit outsiders if space was still available. Alum Rock next abandoned the efficiency principle. Teachers who lost their jobs because of falling enrollments were guaranteed jobs at district headquarters. And, just as teachers could not fail, neither could schools succeed. At the end of the first year, tight limits were placed on school enrollments, ensuring that no school would grow inordinately at the expense of the system. Finally, entry of new schools into the tuition voucher market was tightly controlled, thereby jeopardizing one of the basic principles of improvement through competition.

While the Alum Rock experiment was being implemented, law professor John Coons at the nearby Berkeley campus of the University of California was putting together, with Stephen Sugarman and William Clune III, the first statewide plan for educational choice. These scholars had been part of a prolonged, frustrating legal campaign to equalize the fiscal resources of local school districts in California and other states. By the early seventies, the three had decided that school resources needed to be equalized among families. This could be achieved, they claimed, by giving each family a tuition voucher, the value of which varied inversely with family income. Poor people would not only have as much money for education as rich people; they would have more.[49] Even John Dewey might have been pleased.

PUBLIC OPINION, PRESIDENTIAL POLITICS, AND EDUCATIONAL CHOICE

Public opinion on tuition vouchers would seem to be evenly divided. But as one of the most acute analysts of public opinion, V. O. Key, once observed, understanding the state of public opinion is tantamount to studying the Holy Ghost—its influence is everywhere present but extraordinarily difficult to identify. According to surveys of public opinion, the percentage favoring vouchers during the twenty years after the initiation of the OEO experiment averaged 45 percent while the percentage opposed averaged 42 percent. Thirteen percent had no opinion. Changes in opinion from one survey to the next did not vary by much more than what could be produced by sampling error, and no trend in public opinion over time was discernible.[50]

Analysts usually interpret such stability in public opinion as evidence that the public has solid convictions on the issue in question. Taken at face value, Americans were closely but intensely divided over tuition vouchers. Yet when efforts were made to translate these opinions into votes, the outcome, far from being closely contested, regularly resulted in resounding defeats for tuition vouchers. Michigan voters rejected vouchers in 1978 by a 3–1 margin. Supporters of the choice initiative in California were unable to secure enough signatures to put their proposal on the ballot. Oregonians defeated vouchers by an overwhelming vote in 1990, and Coloradans similarly turned down a voucher initiative by a two-thirds vote in 1992. During the 1980s bills to establish a tuition voucher plan were introduced in thirteen states, but no statewide plan won legislative approval.[51]

Public opinion is more than just the views expressed by individuals in response to pollster questions. It is also voter response to campaigns by organized groups for and against a particular proposal. Opponents of tuition vouchers were sophisticated, organized, well-financed, and politically resourceful. They included teacher organizations, public school administrators, faculty at schools of education, parent and other lay groups organized by the public schools, trade unions, and civil rights organizations. Teacher organizations, especially, viewed tuition vouchers or any other choice proposal as a fundamental threat to their very existence. As teacher leaders well knew, the transformation of a quasi-monopoly or highly regulated oligopoly into a competitive industry weakens trade union power and adversely affects employee compensation. To prevent this from happening, teacher organizations, with the help of their political allies, mobilized vast intellectual, financial, and campaign resources against any and all tuition voucher or other choice proposals.

While the interests and resources opposed to choice were substantial and well-organized, supporters of choice were few in number and lacking in resources. A few policy entrepreneurs built careers by promoting the idea. Catholics and other religious groups had much to gain in the long run, yet the benefits were too distant and uncertain to make an inordinate amount of political effort worthwhile. Poor minorities attending the worst schools in large central cities probably suffered the most from the public school monopoly, but they had few financial or other political resources with which to impress either voters or policy makers. As a result, tuition voucher proposals were defeated by decisive margins in both legislatures and referendums. Proponents had little more than an idea to peddle.

Despite the unbalanced group strength, the issue became a matter of partisan debate. Although parties are often regarded as consensus-building, issue-avoiding institutions, in this case they tended to even out what was otherwise a one-sided contest. Before 1968, neither party paid any attention to school choice; the main issue for presidential debate involved the appropriate type of federal aid that could be given to local schools. Gradually, the enthusiasm for choice swelled within the Republican ranks, while the Democratic party became increasingly hostile.

The political forces shaping these partisan positions are quite easily detected. In the wake of the Civil Rights Act of 1964, the struggle over school desegregation, and the racial turmoil in large central cities, Republicans saw the possibility of building a new political coalition that would weld together urban ethnics (many of whom were Catholic) with southern white Protestants, now seeking alternatives to the newly integrated public schools. To win urban ethnics to the coalition, Republicans became increasingly committed to tax credits, tuition vouchers, and other choice proposals. At the same time Republicans became increasingly critical of teachers' organizations, which the party identified as a vested interest inhibiting educational reform.

Meanwhile, the Democratic party, after initially expressing some support for tax aid to families with children in nonpublic schools, became ever more antagonistic to the concept of choice. The 1976 presidential nominating and electoral process may have been critical to this transformation within the Democratic party. In that year the National Education Association, the largest of the teachers' organizations, became actively engaged in partisan politics, encouraging members to participate in the presidential conventions and endorsing for the first time a presidential candidate. Public school teachers formed an important component of the Jimmy Carter coalition at the Democratic convention, and they warmly endorsed Carter's call for the creation of a cabinet-rank Department of Education. In subsequent elections, teachers' organizations remained an important ingredient in the Democratic party's primary processes, and they regularly endorsed the Democratic candidate for president. The Democratic party became the party of public education, while the Republican party became the party of choice.

THE TRANSFORMATION OF THE CHOICE DEBATE

In the late eighties, the various strands of choice politics came together, producing a new mix of issues and alliances that transformed choice policy proposals and programmatic experiments. Elements of the tuition voucher, magnet school, and alternative school approaches were brought together to focus the choice discussion on the needs of minority children in central cities.

The first hint of the new politics of choice appeared in an innovative piece of legislation introduced in the spring of 1986 by a moderate group of Republicans in the House of Representatives known as the Wednesday group. It proposed that the compensatory education program be redesigned so that each educationally disadvantaged, low-income student would be given a voucher that could be used to purchase supplementary educational services from either public or nonpublic organizations. The monies could help pay for supplemental services in public schools, but they could also help pay the tuition at a private school. When the Bush administration proposed legislation along similar lines, it made clear the Republican party's decision to emphasize choice for poor, educationally disadvantaged, inner-city minorities.[52]

The new approach to choice was politically attractive to conservative Republicans. First, it avoided the constitutional problems associated with most tuition tax credit proposals. Second, it gave Republicans an issue on which it could claim to represent broad, diffuse, and unrepresented interests, including those of the urban poor, while the Democratic party seemed to side with special interests. Third, choice gave Republicans a badly needed program consistent with party philosophy that could be presented as addressing the problems of the inner-city poor. Fourth, by focusing on choice for poor inner-city children, Republicans turned on its head the criticism that choice worked to the advantage of the well to do and educationally advantaged. Fifth, it did not disturb the workings of suburban schools to which many Republicans remained committed. Finally, the proposal highlighted the fact that upper-middle-class people had the financial resources to exercise choice, middle-class people could choose by picking their suburb of choice, but poor people living in inner cities had very little if any choice in their schools. When President William Clinton opposed private school choice for poor people while placing his own daughter in a prestigious private school in Washington, D.C., Republicans were able to denounce the presidential move as hypocritical.

Teachers' organizations, public school officials, and most Democrats roundly condemned every one of these Republican efforts to promote choice.[53] With legislatures unwilling to enact choice plans and voters casting negative ballots in referendums, choice had been reduced to a partisan staple and a political stalemate. But as the 1980s came to a close, the new politics of choice gained steam from two unlikely sources. First, two scholars at the moderate, prestigious Brookings Institution, John Chubb and Terry Moe, undertook a sophisticated, comprehensive study of a national sample of the country's public and private schools. They found that young people learned more in private than public schools. They explained their findings by pointing out that private schools, less subject to interest group and other political pressures, could more easily acquire a sense of mission. They operated more autonomously, with fewer regulations, and with a less complex bureaucratic structure. Private schools also fostered closer cooperation among staff members and concentrated their attention on enhancing the academic skills of students.[54] Their surprising endorsement of tuition vouchers captured the attention of the mass media, conservative pundits, and Republican party officials. The debate over tuition vouchers, which had slumped since the Alum Rock disaster, was suddenly reinvigorated.

Second, the first tuition voucher experiment aimed at low-income, inner-city residents was carried out in Milwaukee. A black Milwaukee state legislator, Polly Williams, unhappy with the city's public schools, proposed that state aid be given to any private school attended by a low-income student previously attending public school. Republican Governor Tommy Thompson endorsed the idea, and the country's first big-city voucher experiment began.

As with the Alum Rock experiment, compromises with antagonistic public school groups made it difficult for the experiment to succeed. The voucher, which could not be supplemented by the family's own resources, was worth only $2,500, less than one-half the amount available to the Milwaukee public schools. Sectarian schools were declared ineligible, sharply limiting the number and quality of available private schools. Voucher students could constitute only 50 percent of the private school enrollment, making the formation of new schools difficult. The number of students that could participate in the program was limited to 1 percent of the total enrollment of the Milwaukee public schools. And the program's future was challenged (unsuccessfully) in the Wisconsin state courts.

Although these design features almost certainly doomed the experiment, a two-year evaluation made available in December 1992 reported that the program seemed modestly successful. The number of students enrolled increased from 341 in 1990 to 613 in 1992; the number of schools increased from seven to eleven. Although most of the students participating in the program were very low-performing students from low-income, minority families, their parents, who had been unhappy with the learning environment provided by the public schools, were, on the whole, quite pleased with the new choice schools. Whereas only 43 percent of the parents had given the old public school a grade of A or B, 70 percent of the parents gave the new private school these higher marks.[55] Parents were particularly pleased that schoolteachers concentrated on instruction, school order was maintained, and the schools were safe. As one seventh grader reported, the new school was much better because the teachers cared and you did not have to fight. In the child's previous public school, you "really can't avoid it," he said. "They'll think you're scared."[56]

The experiment was not an unqualified success. One of the private schools closed in the first year of the program's operations. Though teachers in the private schools enjoyed their working conditions, they complained about their inadequate salaries. Initial data on student test scores coming from very small, nonrandom samples fluctuated significantly from one subject area to another and one school year to the next. As a consequence, the evaluation did not definitively show with quantitative data that small, secular private schools, operating with budgets half the size of the public schools, were better learning environments than those provided by the Milwaukee schools. Only the children's parents were convinced.

If the results of the Milwaukee experiment remained open to interpretation, there was little doubt that the debate over choice took a new turn in the late 1980s. Choice advocates had focused on the Achilles heel of the public system—the segregated, bureaucratized, expensive, ineffectual central-city schools. If middle-class families were fleeing this institution, what was the rationale for entrapping poor people within it? Despite the strong opposition to choice by the civil rights movement and most black political leaders, 57 percent of the minority population and 57 percent of those living within central cities favored school vouchers in 1991 (as compared to just half of the country's overall population).[57] In a sequel to their first study, John Chubb and Terry Moe reported that not only did average students perform better in private than in public schools, but also in private schools there was a smaller gap between the brightest and slowest students.[58]

The new debate over choice in the 1990s was not simply whether public schools were efficient but whether they were fair.[59] Tom Paine would be pleased.

NOTES

I thank Rick Hess for his research assistance and Allison Kommer and Kristin Skala for their staff assistance in the preparation of this chapter. A longer, fully documented version has been published under the title "A History of the Choice Debate in American Education," by the Educational Research and Information Center. ˘

1. Louis Hartz, *The Liberal Tradition in America* (New York: Harcourt, Brace & World, 1955).

2. Thomas Paine, *Rights of Man* (1792), 1:245, as quoted in David Kirkpatrick, *Choice in Schooling: A Case for Tuition Vouchers* (Chicago: Loyola University Press, 1990), 34.

3. "Land Ordinance of 1785" in *Documents of American History*, 6th ed., ed. Henry S. Commager (New York: Appleton-Century-Crofts, 1958), 124.

4. "The Northwest Ordinance" in *Documents of American History*, 131.

5. Benjamin Rush, "Plan for the Establishment of Public Schools" in *Essays on Education in the Early Republic*, ed. Frederick Rudolph (Cambridge: Harvard University Press, 1965), 6.

6. Ibid., 7.

7. Merrill D. Peterson, *Thomas Jefferson and the New Nation: A Biography* (New York: Oxford University Press, 1970), 147.

8. John Stuart Mill, "On Liberty" in *Educational Vouchers: Concepts and Controversies*, ed. George R. La Noue (New York: Teachers College Press, 1972), 3–4.

9. Carl F. Kaestle and Maris A. Vinovskis, *Education and Social Change in Nineteenth Century Massachusetts* (Cambridge: Cambridge University Press, 1980).

10. As quoted in Charles L. Glenn, Jr., *The Myth of the Common School* (Amherst: University of Massachusetts Press, 1987), 84.

11. Ibid., 83.

12. Paul E. Peterson, *The Politics of School Reform, 1870–1940* (Chicago: University of Chicago Press, 1985).

13. Diane Ravitch, *The Great School Wars: New York City, 1805–1973* (New York: Basic Books, 1974).

14. David Tyack and Elisabeth Hansot, *Managers of Virtue: Public School Leadership in America, 1820–1980* (New York: Basic Books, 1982), 77.

15. John Dewey, *School and Society*, 2d ed. (Chicago: University of Chicago Press, 1915), 7.

16. John Dewey, *Democracy and Education* (New York: Macmillan Co., 1916), 92, 95–96.

17. Ibid., 20–22, 28, 93–96.

18. Ibid., 98.

19. Ibid.

20. Meyers v. Nebraska, 401, 399.

21. Pierce v. Society of Sisters, 268 U.S. 528, 534.

22. C. Herman Pritchett, *The American Constitution* (New York: McGraw-Hill, 1959), 477, 478.

23. Wisconsin v. Yoder, 406 U.S. 205.

24. Aguilar v. Felton, 473 U.S. 402.

25. Committee for Public Education and Religious Liberty v. Nyquist, 413 U.S. 756.

26. Mueller v. Allen, 463 U.S. 388.

27. James S. Coleman and Thomas Hoffer, *Public and Private High Schools: The Impact of Communities* (New York: Basic Books, 1987); James S. Coleman, Thomas Hoffer, and Sally Kilgore, *High School Achievement: Public, Catholic and Private Schools Compared* (New York: Basic Books, 1982); Anthony S. Bryk, Valerie Lee, and Julia Smith, "High School Organization and Its Effects on Teachers and Students: An Interpretive Summary of the Research" in *Choice and Control in American Education, Vol. 1: The Theory of Choice and Control in Education*, ed. William H. Clune and John F. Witte (Philadelphia: Falmer Press, 1990); John E. Chubb and Terry M. Moe, *Politics, Markets and America's Schools* (Washington, D.C.: Brookings Institution, 1990).

28. Ralph Munger and Richard Fenno, *National Politics and Federal Aid to Education* (Syracuse: Syracuse University Press, 1962).

29. Philip Meranto, *The Politics of Federal Aid to Education* (Syracuse: Syracuse University Press, 1967); Eugene Eidenberg and Roy D. Morey, *An Act of Congress: The Legislative Process and the Making of Education Policy* (New York: Norton, 1969); Hugh Davis Graham, *The Uncertain Triumph: Federal Education Policy in the Kennedy and Johnson Years* (Chapel Hill: University of North Carolina Press, 1984).

30. Jerry T. Murphy, "Title I of ESEA: The Politics of Implementing Federal Education Reform," *Harvard Educational Review* 41 (1971): 35–63; Denis P. Doyle and Bruce S. Cooper, *Federal Aid to the Disadvantaged: What Future for Chapter 1?* (Philadelphia: Falmer Press, 1988).

31. U.S. Department of Education, Office of Research and Information, Center for Education Statistics, *Digest of Education Statistics 1991* (Washington, D.C.: Government Printing Office, 1991), table 351, 370.

32. Virgil C. Blum, *Freedom of Choice in Education* (New York: Macmillan Co., 1958).

33. U.S. Department of Education, *Digest of Education Statistics 1991*, table 59, p. 70.

34. Private school estimates calculated from U.S. Department of Education, *Digest of Education Statistics 1991*, table 3, p. 12; table 30, p. 34; table 36, p. 40. Public school per pupil expenditures calculated in 1989 dollars from data reported in table 158, p. 155, and table 36, p. 40.

35. Ibid., table 3, p. 12.

36. Arthur Bestor, *The Restoration of Learning* (New York: Alfred Knopf, 1955).

37. Milton Friedman, "The Role of Government in Education" in Robert Solo, ed., *Economics and the Public Interest* (New Brunswick, N.J.: Rutgers University Press, 1955), 127.

38. Paul E. Peterson, "Background Paper" in Twentieth Century Fund, *Making the Grade* (New York: TCF, 1980), 70–76.

39. Diane Ravitch and Chester E. Finn, Jr., *What Do Our 17-Year Olds Know?* (New York: Harper & Row, 1987).

40. Poindexter v. Louisiana, 275 F.Supp. 833 (1967), as quoted in *Educational Vouchers: Concepts and Controversies*, ed. George LaNoue (Syracuse: Syracuse University Press, 1972).

41. The characteristics of magnet schools are well described in Rolf Blank, "Educational Effects of Magnet High Schools" in *Choice and Control in American Education II: The Practice of Choice, Decentralization and School Restructuring*, ed. William H. Clune and John F. Witte (Philadelphia: Falmer Press, 1990), 77–110. See also Robert Dentler, *The National Evidence on Magnet Schools* (Los Alamitos, Calif.: Southwest Regional Laboratory for Educational Research and Development, February 1991).

42. Denis P. Doyle, "Magnet Schools: Choice and Quality in Public Education," *Phi Delta Kappan* 66 (December 1984): 269.

43. Paul E. Peterson, "Are Big City Schools Holding Their Own?" in John L. Rury and Frank A. Cassell, ed., *Seeds of Crisis: Public Schooling in Milwaukee since 1920* (Madison: University of Wisconsin Press, 1993), 274.

44. G. Alfred Hess, Jr., *School Restructuring, Chicago Style* (Newbury Park, Calif.: Corwin, 1991).

45. Herbert Kohl, *Thirty-six Children* (New York: New American Library, 1967); Kenneth Clark, *Dark Ghetto* (New York: Harper & Row, 1965).

46. This description is taken from Daniel Linden Duke and Irene Muzio, "How Effective Are Alternative Schools? A Review of Recent Evaluations and Reports," *Teachers College Record* 79, no. 3 (1977–78): 461–83.

47. David K. Cohen and Eleanor Farrar, "Power to the Parents? The Story of Education Vouchers," *Public Interest* 48 (1977): 73; Judith Areen and Christopher Jencks, "Education Vouchers: A Proposal for Diversity and Choice" in *Educational Vouchers*, 49–57; Christopher Jencks, "Education Vouchers: Giving Parents Money to Pay for Schooling," *New Republic*, 4 July 1970, 19–21; Eli Ginzberg, "The Economics of the Voucher System," *Teachers College Record* 72 (February 1971): 373–82, as reprinted in *Educational Vouchers*, 107; George R. La Noue, "Vouchers: The End of Public Education" in *Educational Vouchers*, 129–45.

48. Laura H. Salganik, "The Fall and Rise of Education Vouchers," *Teachers College Record* 83, no. 2 (1981): 273.

49. John E. Coons, Stephen D. Sugarman, and William H. Clune III, "Reslicing the School Pie," *Teachers College Record* 72 (May 1971): 485–93, as reprinted in *Educational Vouchers*, 59–67. See also John E. Coons and Stephen D. Sugarman, *Schools of Choice* (Berkeley: University of California Press, 1978).

50. Kirkpatrick, *Choice in Schooling*, 150.

51. Carnegie Foundation for the Advancement of Teaching, *School Choice: A Special Report* (Princeton, N.J.: CFAT, 1992), 63–64.

52. Denis P. Doyle and Bruce S. Cooper, "Funding the Individual? A Chapter on the Future of Chapter 1" in Doyle and Cooper, *Federal Aid to the Disadvantaged*, 147–65; Bruce S. Cooper, "The Uncertain Future of National Education Policy: Private Schools and the Federal Role" in William Boyd and Charles Kerchner, eds., *The Politics of Excellence and Choice in Education* (New York: Falmer Publishing, 1988), 175–79.

53. Bruce S. Cooper, "The Politics of Privatization: Policy-making and Private Schools in the USA and Great Britain," in Boyd and Cibulka, 245–68.

54. Chubb and Moe, *Politics, Markets and America's Schools*.

55. These data are taken from John F. Witte, Andrea B. Bailey, and Christopher A. Thorn, *Second Year Report: Milwaukee Parental Choice Program*, University of Wisconsin-Madison: Department of Political Science and the Robert La Follette Institute of Public Affairs, December 1992. Data on parental evaluations are in tables 12a and 12b. We have weighted each year's parental evaluation equally.

56. Carnegie Foundation for the Advancement of Teaching, *School Choice*, 69.

57. Ibid., 63.

58. John Chubb and Terry Moe, "The Question of Equality in Public and Private Schools" (Paper presented before the American Political Science Association, Chicago, September 1992).

59. Clifford W. Cobb, *Responsive Schools, Renewed Communities* (San Francisco: Institute for Contemporary Studies, 1992).

PART FOUR

The Six National Goals

10 SCHOOL READINESS AND EARLY CHILDHOOD EDUCATION

MARIS A. VINOVSKIS

President Bush and the nation's governors established six national education goals after the Charlottesville Education Summit in 1989. Perhaps one of the most widely known and highly esteemed goals is the first: "By the year 2000, all children in America will start school ready to learn." Under the three objectives of this goal, the issues of preschool programs, parent training and support, and child nutrition and health care were championed.[1]

If the specific timetable for having all American children ready for school is new, the stress on early childhood education, parental involvement, and improving the health of children has a longer history. Most educators and policy makers are familiar only with the part of the history that relates to the Head Start Program, and few analysts have made any effort to place goal 1 within a longer historical framework. This chapter analyzes efforts to promote early childhood education in nineteenth-century America, discusses the creation and development of the Head Start Program, and traces the concept, definition, and implementation of school readiness as a national education goal. This broader historical perspective about goal 1 raises some questions and issues that educators and policy makers perhaps still need to consider as they attempt to improve American education by expanding preschool education, enhancing parental assistance, and improving child health care by the year 2000.

EARLY CHILDHOOD EDUCATION DURING THE NINETEENTH CENTURY

Although most educators and policy makers view early childhood education as a rather recent phenomenon of the past twenty-five years, in fact concern about reaching and educating very young children dates back to the early nineteenth century in the United States. By examining the rise and demise of the infant school movement in this country during the first half of the nineteenth century, we will see how quickly and abruptly enthusiasm for early childhood education has waxed and waned as a means of helping disadvantaged children and reforming society.

Some historians have argued that the concept of childhood did not exist in early America. Instead, children were perceived and treated as "miniature adults."[2] More recent scholarship suggests that colonial Americans did distinguish between children and adults, but they saw children as more intellectually and emotionally capable than many Americans do today.[3] While some young colonial children were taught to read, the Puritans were not especially concerned if everyone had not mastered their letters and reading at a very early age—as long as they eventually were able to read the Bible. Moreover, the responsibility for educating young children was entrusted to the parents and not the schools.[4]

In the early nineteenth century, there was a major change in when and how young children were educated in the United States.[5] The experiences of British reformers who set up infant schools for disadvantaged youth in factory towns and large urban areas provided useful models for American reformers in the 1820s.[6] Although the reasons for creating infant schools in the United States were complex and varied, a key factor was the desire to help poor and disadvantaged urban children and their parents. Much of the rhetoric on behalf of investing in nineteenth-century infant schools sounds quite modern; claims were made as to how much money eventually would be saved by reducing the amount of welfare and crime:

> For every dollar expended on Infant Schools, fifty will probably be saved to the community in the diminution of petty larcenies, and the support of paupers and convicts. This is a serious consideration: and it may be fairly doubted, whether in the boundless range of charity, for which this city is deservedly celebrated, there is any mode in which so large a harvest of safety, goodness, and virtue can be reaped from so slender a seed.[7]

As middle-class women saw the efficacy of the infant schools for disadvantaged children, many of them wanted to send their own children to comparable institutions. The Infant School Society of the City of Boston commented that "the infant school system was designed for the poor, and for them only was it introduced into this city; but the discovery has been made, that it is equally adapted to the rich. There is now hardly a neighborhood which has not its private infant school."[8]

The early infant schools were divided on what should be taught. Some wanted to stress play activities, whereas others stressed the importance of teaching the three- and four-year-olds how to read. Since parents often wanted their young children to be taught reading, many of the infant school teachers introduced their pupils to the alphabet and to the rudiments of reading. The widespread popularity of infant schools was such that by 1840 it is estimated that 40 percent of all three-year-olds in Massachusetts were enrolled in either an infant school or a regular private or public school.[9] Early childhood education became popular not just in the larger cities, but also in the countryside as educators and parents alike sang the praises of helping young children.

The popularity of the infant schools was predicated upon the belief that children could be taught at ages three and four and that early education would be beneficial to them. Many nineteenth-century reformers assumed that children's early experiences were crucial in determining their subsequent development.[10] This assumption was certainly compatible with the earlier views of young children by colonial and early nineteenth-century Americans. Yet Amariah Brigham, a prominent young Connecticut physician, published a major treatise on early childhood learning in 1833 which warned educators and parents against infant schools. Brigham argued that overstimulating the child's mind deprived the developing brain of the essential energy necessary for growth and thereby eventually resulted in an enfeebled mind:

> Many physicians of great experience are of the opinion, that efforts to develope [sic] the minds of young children are very frequently injurious; and from instances of disease in children which I have witnessed, I am forced to believe that the danger is indeed great, and that very often in attempting to call forth and cultivate the intellectual faculties of children before they are six or seven years of age, serious and lasting injury has been done to both the body and the mind.[11]

Far from helping young children, Brigham believed that infant schools doomed them to insanity in later life.

Although many working-class parents continued to send their three- or four-year-olds to an infant or elementary school, educators and the middle-class supporters of infant schools now repudiated them. They accepted Brigham's arguments that early education was detrimental to a child's health and also agreed with teachers who believed that the presence of such young children was disruptive to a well-ordered classroom. Moreover, there was a growing feeling, thanks in part to the influence of Heinrich Pestalozzi, that young children should be nurtured in the home rather than sent to school. As a result, by the eve of the Civil War hardly any three- or four-year-old children were enrolled in school.[12]

The demise of the infant schools was so complete that most historians and policy makers are not even aware that such institutions for early childhood education predated the Head Start Program by nearly 150 years.

Interestingly, when kindergartens spread in the United States after the Civil War, their proponents were careful not to identify them in any way with the failed infant schools. By restricting these new institutions to children over age five and de-emphasizing the child's intellectual development, kindergartens were able to avoid the hostility that had developed against the infant schools. The result was that, by the end of the nineteenth century, few very young children were enrolled in any schools.[13]

THE DEVELOPMENT OF THE HEAD START PROGRAM

In the first half of the twentieth century, efforts were made to provide some early education for children through nursery schools or day care centers, but most of these were related to other, larger societal concerns than just helping the child. As part of the Works Progress Administration (WPA) in the New Deal, the federal government sponsored nursery schools to provide jobs for unemployed teachers. Moreover, under the terms of the Lanham Act during World War II, the federal government funded day care facilities for mothers working in defense-related industries. But none of these efforts left much of a lasting effect on federal policy toward early childhood education, and most of them disappeared quickly once the larger crisis had subsided.[14]

President Johnson's War on Poverty, however, was to have a major and long-lasting effect on early childhood education. Influenced by changing scholarly views of the nature of early childhood and driven by efforts to eradicate poverty, the Johnson administration created the Head Start Program, which has transformed how Americans perceive and educate preschool children.

The early twentieth-century idea that IQ was basically fixed at birth and could not be altered by the environment was challenged in the late 1950s and early 1960s by scholars such as Benjamin Bloom and J. McVicker Hunt.[15] Bloom argued that there was a "critical period" during the first five years of life and that early childhood programs could assist children from disadvantaged backgrounds. During the 1960s there was also a great increase in the proportion of articles on child rearing in the popular media that discussed the intellectual development of children.[16]

The idea that children's IQs could be improved received reinforcement from several experimental early childhood programs in cities such as Baltimore, Nashville, New York City, and Syracuse.[17] Thus, the conceptual and intellectual foundations for Project Head Start already were in place by the mid-1960s.

At the same time that ideas about the nature of childhood and IQ were changing, so too were views about poverty in the United States.[18] Poverty was rediscovered and the Johnson administration made its elimination through education one of the major goals of the Great Society programs.[19] Led by the efforts of Sargent Shriver, director of the Office of Economic Opportunity, Project Head Start was created to assist poor children overcome the disadvantages they faced when entering elementary schools.[20]

Head Start began as an eight-week summer program but was quickly converted to a full-year program. Although several key academic advisors suggested the gradual introduction of Head Start programs, Shriver insisted upon a large-scale effort starting immediately in the summer of 1965. Particularly innovative and impressive was the involvement of parents in helping their own children as well as guiding the overall program. Although the Head Start Planning Committee envisioned the program delivering a variety of services to children (including health services), the tendency of many political leaders and the media was to focus on the cognitive benefits of the program.[21] Testifying before the U.S. House of Representatives, Shriver claimed that the Head Start Program could improve the IQ of children by 8 to 10 points.[22]

There had been concerns among some advisors and analysts that the long-term effects of the Head Start Program might be limited, but policy makers and the public remained enthusiastic about these projects. A seminal but controversial evaluation of Head Start by the Westinghouse Learning Corporation and Ohio University seemed to substantiate those fears by finding that the initial IQ score gains were only temporary and faded quickly once those children entered the regular schools.

> Summer programs have been ineffective in producing any persisting gains in cognitive or affective development that can be detected by the tests used in grades 1, 2, and 3 . . . Full-year programs are marginally effective in terms of producing noticeable gains in cognitive development that can be detected by the measures used in grades 1, 2, and 3, but are ineffective in promoting detectable, durable gains in affective development.[23]

The study did go on to mention sympathetically some noncognitive and nonaffective benefits of Head Start:

> Furthermore, Head Start has been concerned with all aspects of the child: medical, dental, nutritional, intellectual, and sociopersonal. It is also a direct example of social action to help the poor; as such, it has been a facilitator of social change in the society at large. Many positive spin-off effects can be attributed to Head Start. It has pioneered in parent education and community development; it has mobilized resources for the group care of young children, stimulated research work in infant and child development, and fostered the further development of teacher competence.[24]

But the favorable statements about the program by the Westinghouse Learning Corporation generally were ignored and quickly forgotten amid the strong negative reports about Head Start in the news media. A headline in the *New York Times* proclaimed, "Head Start Pupils Found No Better Off Than Others."[25]

The release of the Westinghouse report on Head Start was met with widespread protests and criticisms from the academic community. Researchers pointed out that Head Start was not a single, homogeneous program and that certain projects may have been quite effective. Marshall Smith and Joan Bissell reanalyzed the Westinghouse data and claimed that it demonstrated that the full-year programs of Head Start had been effective—especially in urban African-American Head Start centers.[26] But the authors of the original Westinghouse report responded by rejecting the conceptual and methodological critiques of their evaluation.[27]

Interestingly, in a retrospective glance at the controversy over the Westinghouse report two decades later, Edward Zigler candidly admitted that, despite the serious methodological shortcoming of that investigation, the adverse results should not have been unexpected because of the poor and uneven quality of many of the initial programs:

> In short, there was no mystery behind the highly uneven quality of the Head Start programs in 1970. Despite the flaws in the Westinghouse report methodology, I doubt that any national impact evaluation at that time would have showed that Head Start had long-term educational benefits. Even if, as I suspected, a third of the programs were wonderful, their effects would most likely have been canceled out by an equal fraction of programs that were poorly operated.[28]

Thanks to the strong political constituency for Head Start among the parents, the program survived despite increasing doubts about its efficacy. Yet the planned expansion of Head Start under the Nixon administration was postponed, and the program basically was maintained at the same level of funding (in real dollars) for much of the 1970s and 1980s.[29]

During the 1980s interest in Head Start revived in response to an increased proportion in the labor force of mothers with young children and an increased percentage of poor children.[30] Early childhood education also gained an important boost when the longitudinal results from the highly visible but controversial Perry Preschool Program in Ypsilanti, Michigan, seemed to demonstrate that such programs significantly reduced juvenile delinquency and teenage pregnancy among at-risk students. As with nineteenth-century infant schools, the initial investment in the Perry School was frequently cited as highly cost-effective.[31]

Yet the impressive results from the Perry Preschool Program also have been challenged. Critics point out that the high-quality care provided by that program does not resemble that of most of the Head Start programs and therefore the results from the former cannot be used to judge the latter. Moreover, critics have questioned the adequacy of the statistical design of that experiment because of the significant differences between the control and intervention groups, the lack of total random assignment, and the faulty method used in the cost-benefit analysis.[32] Perhaps most disturbing is the little-noticed and belated finding that the Perry Preschool Program may not be equally effective with boys and girls. Helen Barnes, a researcher at the High/Scope Program who reanalyzed the longitudinal data, discovered that "most of the significant long-term outcome differences in the Perry study occur between the treatment and control girls. Although there are differences in long-term outcomes between the two male groups, in most cases they are not significant."[33]

The debate over the long-term effectiveness of early childhood education in general and the usefulness of the Head Start Program in particular continues.[34] Critics question the statistical rigor and methodological validity of the earlier evaluations of Head Start, while its defenders point out that children who enroll in that program are more disadvantaged than the other poor children who have not attended.[35] Ron Haskins provided one of the more balanced summaries and assessments of the vast array of studies of the effect of early childhood education:

1. Both model programs and Head Start produce significant and meaningful gains in intellectual performance and socioemotional development by the end of a year of intervention.
2. For both types of programs, gains on standardized IQ and achievement tests as well as on tests of socioemotional development decline within a few years (or even less in the case of Head Start studies).
3. On categorical variables of school performance such as special education placement and grade retention, there is very strong evidence of positive effects for the model programs and modest evidence of effects for Head Start programs.
4. On measures of life success such as teen pregnancy, delinquency, welfare participation, and employment, there is modest evidence of positive impacts for model programs but virtually no evidence for Head Start.[36]

Head Start was predicated upon the assumption that the early years of a child's life are the most crucial for long-term growth and development. Proponents of the program used the perceived plasticity and determinative importance of early childhood to justify Head Start. But some child developmentalists extended this same logic to question Head Start by arguing that the program reaches children much too late. Burton White, for example, wrote that most of the important developments occur before the age of three:

> From all that I have learned about the education and development of young children, I have come to the conclusion that most American families get their children through the first six or eight months of life reasonably well in terms of education and development; but I believe that perhaps no more than ten percent at most manage to get their children through the eight- to thirty-six-month age periods as well educated and developed as they could and should be. Yet our studies show that the period that starts at eight months and ends at three years is a period of primary importance in the development of a human being. *To begin to look at a child's development when he is two years of age is already much too late*, particularly in the area of social skills and attitudes.[37]

If scholars like White think that early childhood care and interaction must begin sooner, others like David Elkind argue against rushing young children into early intellectual activity. Repeating the mid–nineteenth-century warnings against early intellectual activity, Elkind denounces the early intellectual stimulation of children in schools (but he does not oppose all out-of-home programs for children):

> What harm is there in exposing young children to formal instruction involving the inculcation of rules? The harm comes from what I have called "miseducation." We miseducate children whenever we put them at risk for no purpose. The risks of miseducating young children are both short term and long term. The short-term risks derive from the stress formal instruction puts upon children with all its resultant stress symptoms. The long-term risks are of at least three kinds—motivational, intellectual, and social. In each case the potential psychological risk of early instruction is far greater than any potential educational gain.[38]

Other scholars implicitly raise questions about Head Start by challenging the notion that any early childhood experiences are so determinative of later developments. Work in life-span psychology and life course analysis stresses the continuity of human development and minimizes the lasting and irreversible effects of any particular events—including early childhood experiences.[39] Despite the growing popularity of life-span psychology and life course analysis, however, few scholars or policy makers have seen how the implications of this approach might affect one's support for early childhood education programs such as Head Start.

A final and still rather new attack comes from those who question the efficiency of Head Start compared to alternative expenditures for helping at-risk children. On the basis of their extensive work with at-risk children in elementary schools, Robert Slavin at the "Success for All" Program at Johns Hopkins University argues that investing in individual tutoring in the early grades is more effective than funding Head Start. Indeed, after intensive testing of the effectiveness of the "Success for All" Program, Slavin and his colleagues conclude that "the evidence presented here dispels the idea that any one year of early intervention will have substantial lasting impacts on reading achievement. There is no 'magic bullet' that sets students on the road to success . . . *Intensive* early intervention must be followed by *extensive* changes in basic classroom instructional practices if all students are to succeed throughout their elementary years."[40]

Despite some academic challenges and uncertainty about Head Start in the 1980s, most educators, policy makers, and parents continued to endorse that program enthusiastically and unequivocally. Active lobbying by the National Head Start Association (NHSA) and others helped to persuade key conservative Republican senators such as Jeremiah Denton (R-Ala.) and Orrin Hatch (R-Utah) to support the program. During the Reagan administration, Head Start was one of the very few domestic social programs that remained intact and was even endorsed by the president.[41]

EARLY EDUCATION AND SCHOOL READINESS

The election of George Bush as president in 1988 signaled a renewed interest of the federal government in education. Whereas Reagan had wanted to dismantle the newly created Department of Education and to reduce federal educational spending, Bush wanted to be seen as the "education president" and worked closely with the state governors to develop a national agenda for the improvement of education.

The National Governors' Association, reacting in part to growing criticisms of the nation's schools during the early 1980s, created seven task forces to examine the current state of affairs in education and to make recommendations for improvements. Governor Richard Riley of South Carolina headed up the Task Force on Readiness. The Task Force held three hearings in late 1985 and early 1986 and commissioned several papers on school readiness.[42] The Task Force on Readiness recommended that

> states must develop initiatives to help at-risk preschool children come ready for school. Possible state initiatives include: provide all in-home assistance for first-time, low-income parents of high-risk infants; develop outreach initiatives using community and religious organizations to assist and support young children with absentee parent(s) or guardian(s) as their sole source of nuturance;

providing high quality early childhood development programs for all four-year-old at-risk children, and, where feasible, three-year-olds; provide all parents of preschool children with information on successful parenting practices; stress continued improvement of developmental and educational programs in existing day care centers for preschool children through center accreditation, teacher credentialing, and staff development; and, finally, develop state and local structures through which various public and private agencies can work together to provide appropriate programs for young children and new parents.[43]

By building upon the initiatives of the state governors as well as his own interest in education, the president of the United States for only the third time in history called for a meeting with the nation's governors in Charlottesville, Virginia, on 27–28 September 1989 to find ways of improving American education. The objectives of the Bush administration for that meeting were broad but included the unveiling of a set of national goals in early 1990:

Objectives
1. To demonstrate the President's interest in and commitment to education as a central national priority.
2. To engage the nation's governors in a substantive discussion of the nature of the challenge we face, of alternative ways of improving our educational performance, and of those ideas for reform that seem to have the greatest promise.
3. To set the stage for a series of education proposals and national goals to be unveiled in early 1990 possibly as part of the State of the Union Address.[44]

In the briefing book for the Charlottesville Education Summit, the administration outlined six major substantive areas for the discussion: (1) Teaching: Revitalizing a Profession; (2) The Learning Environment; (3) Governance: Who Is In Charge?; (4) Choice and Restructuring; (5) A Competitive Workforce and Life-Long Learning; and (6) Postsecondary Education: Strengthening Access and Excellence. In the executive summary of the discussion of "The Learning Environment," one of the five specific items mentioned was "Early Childhood Education: We must see to it that young children are provided with early childhood and preschool experiences that prepare them for school success."[45] The specific mention of the importance of early childhood education was not surprising—almost all of the preliminary administration documents in preparation for that education summit mentioned the importance of early education, and the National Governors' Association had championed school readiness previously.[46]

Although the Bush administration did not want to commit itself to a particular set of objectives at the Charlottesville Education Summit, many of the governors wanted a more specific and conclusive joint statement at the conclusion of that meeting.[47] The resulting compromise stated that in early 1990 the president and the nation's governors would jointly establish national goals for education related to

— the readiness of children to start school;
— the performance of students on international achievement tests, especially math and science;
— the reduction of the dropout rate and the improvement of academic performance, especially among at-risk students;
— the functional literacy of adult Americans;
— the level of training necessary to guarantee a competitive workforce;
— the supply of qualified teachers and up-to-date technology; and
— the establishment of safe, disciplined, and drug-free schools.[48]

The drafting of the national education goals proceeded along two parallel tracks—one by the administration and the other by the National Governors' Association. In the administration, Roger Porter, White House domestic policy advisor, directed the activities and drew upon the staff of the Office of Educational Research and Improvement for assistance. Christopher Cross, the assistant secretary of OERI, in a set of briefing papers on the proposed education goals, provided four alternative ways of formulating the goal on early education:

— ALTERNATIVE GOAL ONE: By the year [2002], [all] children will be ready to begin first grade.
— ALTERNATIVE GOAL TWO: By the year [2002], [halve] the differences among race/ethnic groups within the population with respect to their readiness to begin first grade.
— ALTERNATIVE GOAL THREE: By [2002], disadvantaged students will participate in preschool educational programs with cognitive content [at least at the same rate] as more advantaged students.
— ALTERNATIVE GOAL FOUR: Increase the share of parents who provide positive educational experiences at home to their preschool children.[49]

The information in brackets in the above quotation was for purposes of illustration only. The year 2002 was often suggested because that would be when the children who were just entering kindergarten would graduate from high school. The other commonly used and eventually adopted alternative year for the goals was 2000.

Throughout the discussions in the administration about the proposed national goals, there was concern about how they could be measured and whether it was desirable to have more than one indicator for each goal. The goal about school readiness posed a particular challenge, since no adequate measurements had been developed to ascertain when a child was ready to enroll into a regular school. At the same time, specific recommendations for this goal could have immediate large-scale budgetary implications, since it probably would entail an expansion of Head Start. Some suggested that a scale should be developed to measure the degree of readiness of children to attend school, while others wanted to survey teachers on whether students were prepared to enter the first grade.[50]

Analysts for the Education Task Force of the National Governors' Association drafted their own set of recommendations for the national goals. They also favored having a few goals, but unlike the administration they wanted specific objectives under each of the goals and appropriate indicators to measure progress toward these objectives. One of their four general goals was that "by the time they reach school age, every American should be healthy and ready to learn." Thus, the Education Task Force of the governors highlighted the importance of early childhood development and explicitly linked health and cognitive concerns. Moreover, they proposed nine specific indicators for school readiness and set more immediate standards for the year 1995:

> Objective: All children should be healthy.
>> Target and indicator: Reduce the incidence of low birth weight children by one-half by 1995 and by one-half again by 2000.
>> Target and indicator: Reduce the incidence of children who have not received recommended inoculations by 75% by 1995 and by 100% by 2000.
>> Target and indicator: Reduce incidence of malnourished aged 0–5 children by one-half by 1995 and by one-half again by 2000.
>> Target and indicator: Reduce to no more than 1 per 1,000 the prevalence of HIV infection among women to live born infants by the [sic] 2000.
>> Target and indicator: Reduce the number of crack and cocaine addicted babies by 50% by 1995 and by half again by 2000.
> Objective: All children should be intellectually ready to learn.
>> Target and indicator: Give all four year old eligible children the opportunity to attend a year long Head Start program or

its equivalent by 1995. By 2000, provide all eligible 3 year old children the same opportunity.
Target and indicator: Provide a high quality preschool program to every disadvantaged 3- and 4-year old.
Target and indicator: All 3- and 4-year old children should be screened for potential disabilities and learning disorders by 1995. Increase the percentage of children who are identified as being at-risk who are served by one-half by 1995 and to 100% by 2000.
Target and indicator: Increase the percent of pre-schoolers who are ready to do school work upon entering school. Indicator: Need to develop a national assessment of school readiness, an assessment tool to be administered to a sample of children for the express purpose of tracking progress on this goal.[51]

In the negotiations between the Bush administration and the national governors during December 1989, much of the specificity about the goals in the earlier drafts by the National Governors' Association disappeared. President Bush announced the six national goals in his State of the Union speech on 31 January 1990. Goal 1 was simply stated as: "By the year 2000, all children in America will start school ready to learn." The text of the announcement acknowledged that no adequate assessments of school readiness existed and that it might be dangerous to develop such a scale for the purposes of determining when a child should start school:

Assessments indicating readiness for school generally are not administered by schools. Nor do the President and the Governors recommend that such an assessment, especially one that could wrongfully be used to determine when a child should start school, be developed for purposes of measuring progress toward this goal. Other current indicators of readiness may serve as proxies, and still others need to be developed.[52]

When the National Governors' Association met in February 1990, they reaffirmed the six national goals, but also expanded the specific set of objectives under each of the goals. For goal 1, the three objectives were as follows:

— All disadvantaged and disabled children will have access to high quality and developmentally appropriate preschool programs that help prepare children for school.
— Every parent in America will be a child's first teacher and devote time each day helping his or her preschool child learn; parents will have access to the training and support they need.

— Children will receive the nutrition and health care needed to arrive at school with healthy minds and bodies, and the number of low birthweight babies will be significantly reduced through enhanced prenatal health systems.[53]

Establishing indicators to measure the progress made on each of the six national goals was difficult—especially in regard to goal 1 and school readiness. In the first annual report of the National Education Goals Panel, under the heading of "what we now know," only for goal 1 did the panel state that "at present there are no direct ways to measure the nation's progress toward achieving this Goal." They went on to say that the National Education Goals Panel would be considering an early childhood assessment system to monitor this goal.[54] The four variables that they specified as important for assessing a child's readiness for school were "direct indicators of the (1) knowledge, (2) social, emotional and physical well-being, (3) language usage and (4) approaches to learning of young children."[55] To obtain this information, they proposed "student profiles of a nationally representative sample of children conducted during their first year of formal schooling. The profiles would contain four sources of information: (1) parent reports, (2) teacher reports, (3) an individually administered examination, and (4) 'portfolios' of students' performance during their first year in school."[56] The specific empirical measures of school readiness reported, however, dealt with prenatal care, birth weight, routine health care, child nutrition, parent-child interactions, preschool participation, and preschool quality.[57]

A year after creating a technical panel to work on this issue, the National Education Goals Panel acknowledged that it still had no way of measuring progress toward goal 1. It did endorse a national Early Childhood Assessment System that would obtain information on a nationally representative sample of kindergartners from their teachers, their parents, and themselves. The National Education Goals Panel now specified that the gathering of this information would occur several times during the kindergarten year. The five critical areas of a child's growth and readiness for learning were specified as (1) physical well-being and motor development, (2) social and emotional development, (3) approaches toward learning, (4) language usage, and (5) cognition and general knowledge.[58] Again, the specific indicators presented about goal 1 were the same limited information presented the year before with the addition of data on continuity of health care, availability of health insurance/Medicaid, trends in nursery school enrollment, and preschool participation of children with disabilities.[59]

Given the broad and diverse definitions of a child's school readiness and the lack of any agreement on how to measure this concept, it is not surprising that different individuals and organizations use readiness in a wide variety of ways. Even within the Department of Education, there is little coordination or discussion of how goal 1 should be defined and implemented. For example, the Office of Educational Research and Improvement has established an agency-wide task force to look at what we know about each of the six national goals and what research still remains to be done. That effort, however, has not been closely coordinated with related activities in other parts of the federal government—including those federal employees working with the National Education Goals Panel on school readiness.

Individuals and organizations outside government have also seized upon the six national education goals to further their own reform agenda. Ernest Boyer, president of the Carnegie Foundation for the Advancement of Teaching and a participant with the National Education Goals Panel, wrote a highly influential book, *Ready to Learn: A Mandate for the Nation*.[60] Boyer interpreted goal 1 broadly and used it to justify the need for such diverse programs as universal health insurance, a life cycle curriculum, neighborhood ready-to-learn centers, and a fully funded, upgraded Head Start Program by 1995. In his discussions of these issues, however, Boyer tended to cite the more positive evaluations of programs such as Head Start and ignore the more critical assessments of them. Moreover, he relied heavily upon the results of a 1991 Carnegie Foundation survey of kindergarten teachers, even though the response rate was only about one-third.[61] Thus, although almost everyone agrees that we are yet to develop any effective and reliable assessments of school readiness, this situation has not prevented many analysts and policy makers from making ambitious and expensive recommendations on behalf of this goal.

Although some have expressed reservations about the implementation and measurement of goal 1, few have challenged its overall validity or usefulness. One of the sharpest critics of the Bush administration's America 2000 Program in general and of the school readiness goal in particular is columnist Phyllis Schlafly, who fears further intrusion into education and the home:

> America 2000 has a concept of "school" that not only includes absorbing private schools into its system, but also includes expanding the public schools in order to "parent" children through their preschool years, in their after-school hours, and to provide non-school services. America 2000 wants to transform public schools into baby-sitters for pre-kindergarten kids, and into social service centers to provide meals, health care (probably including the controversial kinds), counseling and guidance. . . .
>
> Will government agents go into the homes and dictate how preschool children are raised—and then snitch on parents who reject the government's "suggestions"? This sort of thing is already be-

ing experimented with under the name "Parents as Teachers," but which many people call the "Teachers as Parents" program. Americans absolutely don't want that kind of Big Brother society.[62]

Whatever doubts some researchers had about studies of the efficacy of Head Start or measurements of school readiness or whatever misgivings some conservatives voiced about federal involvement in early education, most policy makers endorsed the program enthusiastically. Former President Bush sought a $600 million boost for Head Start for fiscal year 93 (a 27 percent increase)—the largest funding increase proposed by a president up to then.[63] President Clinton has gone even further and called for full funding of Head Start. As he stated in a major speech on education at the East Los Angeles Community College, "A country that found $500 billion to bail out the savings and loan industry can find $5 billion to full-fund Head Start."[64]

CONCLUSION

The six national education goals developed by the Bush administration and the state governors have focused public attention on the need to improve the educational system. They have also centered federal, state, and local efforts on a particular set of educational priorities and have helped to forge a broad coalition of public and private support for these objectives. Although political support for increased educational spending and innovations at different levels still has not been as strong or as consistent as that for other programs (such as assistance to the elderly), it seems to have grown in recent years.

Having all children ready to enter school is certainly one of the best-known and most popular of the six national goals. It has succeeded in attracting considerable attention and some additional resources for early education—especially for federal funding of Head Start. This is an important achievement in itself, as federal funding of Head Start in real dollars had been stagnant during the 1970s and early 1980s. Despite the broad definition of school readiness which includes concerns about children's health as well as educational reforms, however, there is little evidence to suggest that the national education goals have thus far played a major role in garnering additional political support for the noneducational components of goal 1.

This historical analysis of the development of the idea of school readiness also reveals that the United States has turned to early childhood education on several different occasions to correct what were perceived to be major problems in our society. The infant school movement addressed in large part the growing concern about urban crime and poverty in nineteenth-century America. Similarly, Head Start attempted to deal with the rediscovery of poverty in the mid-1960s. Continued concern about disadvantaged children today as well as a growing fear about America's lack of competitiveness in the global economy have spurred the recent efforts on behalf of preparing all children to attend schools. In each of these instances, there was genuine interest in helping the young children themselves; all three of these movements, however, were embedded within broader concerns about the social and economic development of this nation.

Infant schools, Head Start, and the school readiness movement all are based upon the assumption that early childhood experiences are crucial to subsequent adult development. Proponents of these reforms believed that, unless society reached at-risk children at very young ages, it would be difficult, if not impossible, to provide adequate remedial educational services later. Moreover, each of these movements was affected, in varying degrees, by the changing scientific and popular views of early childhood development. Each benefited by the emerging belief that young children were more capable cognitively and affectively than we had previously thought, but only the infant school movement was damaged irrevocably by a counter-reaction asserting that early intellectual stimulation could permanently impair the child's brain.

The reformers in each of these movements also shared the widespread belief in our society that education by itself can alleviate many if not most of the disadvantages individuals have acquired as a result of their economic or ethnic background. Although the proponents of these changes did not ignore entirely other necessary societal reforms, they often underestimated the extent to which structural problems in the economy or society acted as barriers to social and economic mobility. Thus, early education often was portrayed as a panacea for problems that might have been equally or better addressed by other programs.

While almost all of the attention was devoted to preparing disadvantaged children for regular schools, very little effort was made to change the regular schools to accommodate those children. Nineteenth-century public school teachers and administrators frequently complained about the infant schools and often joined forces with others to eventually eliminate three- and four-year-olds from the public schools. Despite early warnings that the initial cognitive gains of Head Start fade for students when they enter the elementary grades, surprisingly little effort was made to rethink and restructure the existing public schools. Although the Follow-Through Program was created in 1967 for that purpose, it has never enjoyed the visibility or support that one might have expected. Similarly, although the early drafts of goal 1 by the staff of the Office of Educational Research and Improvement in the summer of 1989 called for having all children ready for school and for having all schools ready for children, the latter part of this message was discussed and dropped in subsequent drafts in other parts of the U.S. Department of Education. Unfortunately, many public schools and teachers still have not succeeded in adapting their curriculum or teaching practices to the special needs of disadvantaged students.

After more than twenty-five years of experience with Head Start and a federal expenditure of over $21 billion to serve twelve million children, we still are not certain of the actual influence of that program on the life course of disadvantaged children. Moreover, given the diversity of Head Start programs, we also do not know which Head Start models are best suited for children in different settings. Nevertheless, most policy makers and the public are convinced of the efficacy of Head Start—though some call for improving the overall quality of the program by reducing class sizes and attracting better trained teachers by substantially increasing their salaries. Finally, very little if any effort has been made to consider whether alternative expenditures, such as more individualized tutoring in the elementary grades, might be a more effective way of helping at-risk students.

Thus, ensuring that all children are ready for school is a laudable goal and one that has ample historical precedents in this country. But the uncertainty about the actual meanings of that goal and the best ways of implementing it continues to present a serious challenge to policy makers and the public. Perhaps a pointed reminder to all of us about the importance of providing a world class education to all of our young children will help us overcome the often all-too-visible short-term difficulties and inefficiencies in having all children ready to learn when they enter school.

NOTES

1. National Education Goals Panel, *The National Education Goals Report: Building a Nation of Learners, 1992* (Washington, D.C.: Government Printing Office, 1992), 58.

2. John Demos, *A Little Commonwealth: Family Life in Plymouth Colony* (New York: Oxford University Press, 1970); John Demos, "The American Family in Past Time," *American Scholar* 43 (1974): 422–46; John Demos, *Past, Present, and Personal: The Family and the Life Course in American History* (New York: Oxford University Press, 1986); John Modell and Madeline Goodman, "Historical Perspectives" in *At the Threshold: The Developing Adolescent*, ed. Shirley S. Feldman and Glen R. Elliott (Cambridge: Harvard University Press, 1990), 93–120; Walter I. Trattner, *From Poor Law to Welfare State: A History of Social Welfare in America*, 4th ed. (New York: Free Press, 1989); Michael Zuckerman, *Peaceable Kingdoms: New England Towns in the Eighteenth Century* (New York: Alfred A. Knopf, 1970).

3. James Axtell, *The School upon a Hill: Education and Society in Colonial New England* (New Haven: Yale University Press, 1974); Carl F. Kaestle and Maris A. Vinovskis, *Education and Social Change in Nineteenth-Century Massachusetts* (Cambridge: Cambridge University Press, 1980); David Stannard, "Death and the Puritan Child" in *Death in America*, ed. David Stannard (Philadelphia: University of Penn-

sylvania Press, 1975), 3–29; David Stannard, *The Puritan Way of Death* (New York: Oxford University Press, 1977).

4. Gerald F. Moran and Maris A. Vinovskis, *Religion, Family, and the Life Course: Explorations in the Social History of Early America* (Ann Arbor: University of Michigan Press, 1992).

5. John W. Jenkins, "Infant Schools and the Development of Public Primary Schools in Selected American Cities before the Civil War" (Ph.D. diss., University of Wisconsin, 1978); Dean May and Maris A. Vinovskis, "A Ray of Millennial Light: Early Education and Social Reform in the Infant School Movement in Massachusetts, 1826–1840" in *Family and Kin in American Urban Communities, 1800–1940*, ed. Tamara K. Hareven (New York: Watts, 1977), 62–99.

6. Phillip McCann and F. A. Young, *Samuel Wilderspin and the Infant School Movement* (London: Croom Helm, 1982).

7. Mathew Carey, *Miscellaneous Essays* (Philadelphia: Carey & Hart, 1830), 314.

8. Infant School Society of the City of Boston, *Third Annual Report* (Boston: ISSCB, 1831), 9.

9. Kaestle and Vinovskis, *Education and Social Change*.

10. J. R. Brown, *An Essay on Infant Cultivation* (Philadelphia: Clark & Raser, 1828).

11. Amariah Brigham, *Remarks on the Influence of Mental Cultivation and Mental Excitement upon Health*, 2d ed. (Boston: Marsh, Capen & Lyon, 1833), 5.

12. May and Vinovskis, "A Ray of Millennial Light"; Kaestle and Vinovskis, *Education and Social Change*.

13. Carolyn Winterer, "Avoiding a 'Hothouse System of Education': Kindergartens and the Problem of Insanity, 1860–1890," *History of Education Quarterly* 32 (1992): 289–314.

14. Judith D. Auerbach, *In the Business of Child Care: Employer Initiatives and Working Women* (New York: Praeger, 1988); Victoria L. Getis and Maris A. Vinovskis, "History of Child Care in the United States before 1850" in *Child Care in Context: Cross-Cultural Perspectives*, ed. Michael E. Lamb, Kathleen J. Sternberg, Carl-Phillip Hwang, and Anders G. Broberg (Hillsdale, N.J.: Lawrence Erlbaum, 1992), 185–206; Margaret O. Steinfels, *Who's Minding the Children? The History and Politics of Day Care in America* (New York: Simon & Schuster, 1973).

15. Benjamin S. Bloom, *Stability and Change in Human Characteristics* (New York: John Wiley, 1964); J. McVicker Hunt, *Intelligence and Experience* (New York: Ronald Press, 1961).

16. Julia Wrigley, "Do Young Children Need Intellectual Stimulation? Experts' Advice to Parents, 1900–1985," *History of Education Quarterly* 29 (1989): 41–75.

17. Edward Zigler and Karen Anderson, "An Idea Whose Time Had Come: The Intellectual and Political Climate for Head Start" in *Project Head Start: A Legacy of the War on Poverty*, ed. Edward Zigler and Jeanette Valentine (New York: Free Press, 1979), 3–19.

18. Edward D. Berkowitz, *America's Welfare State: From Roosevelt to Reagan* (Baltimore: Johns Hopkins University Press, 1991); Marshall Kaplan and Peggy Cuciti, eds., *The Great Society and Its Legacy: Twenty Years of U.S. Social Policy* (Durham: Duke University Press, 1986).

19. Hugh D. Graham, *The Uncertain Triumph: Federal Education Policy in the Ken-*

nedy and Johnson Years (Chapel Hill: University of North Carolina Press, 1984); Harold Silver and Pamela Silver, An Educational War on Poverty: American and British Policy-Making, 1960–1980 (Cambridge: Cambridge University Press, 1991).

20. Edward Zigler and Jeanette Valentine, eds., Project Head Start: A Legacy of the War on Poverty (New York: Free Press, 1979).

21. Maris A. Vinovskis, "Early Childhood Education: Then and Now," Daedalus 122 (1993): 151–75; Edward Zigler and Susan Muenchow, Head Start: The Inside Story of America's Most Successful Educational Experiment (New York: Basic Books, 1992).

22. U.S. Congress, House Committee on Education and Labor, Hearings before the Subcommittee on the War on Poverty, 89th Cong., 2d sess. (Washington, D.C.: Government Printing Office, 1966), 186.

23. Westinghouse Learning Corporation, "The Impact of Head Start: An Evaluation of the Effects of Head Start on Children's Cognitive and Affective Development" (report presented to the Office of Economic Opportunity, contract B89–4536), 1:243.

24. Ibid., 255.

25. New York Times, 14 April 1969, 1, 36.

26. Marshall S. Smith and Joan S. Bissell, "Report Analysis: The Impact of Head Start," Harvard Educational Review 40 (1970): 51–104.

27. Victor G. Cicirelli, John W. Evans, and Jeffrey S. Schiller, "The Impact of Head Start: A Reply to the Report Analysis," Harvard Educational Review 40 (1970): 105–29.

28. Zigler and Muenchow, Head Start, 154.

29. Daniel P. Moynihan, The Politics of a Guaranteed Income: The Nixon Administration and the Family Assistance Plan (New York: Vintage, 1973); Gilbert Y. Steiner, The Children's Cause (Washington, D.C.: Brookings Institution, 1976).

30. Kathleen A. Clarke-Stewart, "Infant Day Care: Maligned or Malignant?" American Psychologist 44 (1989): 266–73.

31. Lawrence J. Schweinhart and David P. Weikart, Young Children Grow Up: The Effects of the Perry Preschool Program on Youths Through Age 15 (Ypsilanti, Mich.: High/Scope Press, 1980); John R. Berrueta-Clement, Lawrence J. Schweinhart, W. Steven Barnett, Ann S. Epstein, and David P. Weikart, Changed Lives: The Effects of the Perry Preschool Program on Youths through Age 19 (Ypsilanti, Mich: High/Scope Press, 1984); Lawrence J. Schweinhart, Helen V. Barnes, and David P. Weikart, Significant Benefits: The High/Scope Perry Preschool Study through Age 27 (Ypsilanti, Mich: High/Scope Press, 1993).

32. Edward F. Zigler, "Formal Schooling for Four-Year-Olds? No" in Early Schooling: The National Debate, ed. Sharon L. Kagan and Edward F. Zigler (New Haven: Yale University Press, 1987), 27–44.

33. Helen V. Barnes, "Predicting Long-Term Outcomes from Early Elementary Classroom Measures in a Sample of High-Risk Black Children" (Ph.D. diss., University of Michigan, 1991).

34. Lawrence J. Schweinhart and Gary Gottfredson, "Good Preschool Programs for Young Children Living in Poverty Produce Important Long-Term Benefits: Pro and Con," Debates on Education Issues 1 (1990): 1–8.

35. Valerie E. Lee, J. Brooks-Gunn, E. Schnur, and F. Liaw, "Are Head Start

Effects Sustained? A Longitudinal Follow-up Comparison of Disadvantaged Children Attending Head Start, No Preschool, and Other Preschool Programs," *Child Development* 61 (1990): 495–507.

36. Ron Haskins, "Beyond Metaphor: The Efficacy of Early Childhood Education," *American Psychologist* 44 (1989): 278.

37. Burton L. White, *The First Three Years of Life* (New York: Prentice-Hall, 1975), 4.

38. David Elkind, "Early Childhood Education on Its Own Terms" in *Early Schooling: The National Debate*, ed. Sharon L. Kagan and Edward F. Zigler (New Haven, Conn.: Yale University Press, 1987), 98–115.

39. Orville G. Brim and Jerome Kagan, eds., *Constancy and Change in Human Development* (Cambridge: Harvard University Press, 1980); W. Andrew Collins, ed., *Development during Middle Childhood: The Years from Six to Twelve* (Washington, D.C.: National Academy Press, 1984); S. Shirley Feldman and Glen R. Elliott, eds., *At the Threshold: The Developing Adolescent* (Cambridge: Harvard University Press, 1990).

40. Robert E. Slavin, Nancy L. Karweik, and Barbara A. Wasik, "Preventing Early School Failure: What Works?" Center for Research on Effective Schooling for Disadvantaged Students, report 26 (November 1991).

41. Zigler and Muenchow, *Head Start*.

42. National Governors' Association, *Task Force on Readiness: Supporting Works* (Washington, D.C.: National Governors' Association, 1986).

43. National Governors' Association, *Time for Results: The Governors' 1991 Report on Education* (Washington, D.C.: National Governors' Association, 1986), 14–15.

44. Roger B. Porter and Stephen M. Studdert, Memo to John H. Sununu on President's Education Summit Conference for Governors (White House, 14 August 1989).

45. White House, Briefing Paper for the Education Summit Meeting (White House, 27 September 1989).

46. National Governors' Association, *Time for Results*.

47. Julie A. Miller, "Small Group's Insider Role in Goals-Setting Provides Clues to Education Policymaking," *Education Week* (14 March 1990).

48. *New York Times*, 1 October 1989, 22.

49. Christopher Cross, Memo to John Porter (Office of Educational Research and Improvement, 30 November 1989).

50. Ibid.

51. Ray Scheppach and Michael Cohen, Memo to Governors on Education Task Force and Administration Representatives on Background for December 7 Meeting (5 December 1989).

52. Office of the Press Secretary, National Education Goals (White House, 31 January 1990).

53. National Governors' Association, *National Education Goals* (Washington, D.C.: National Governors' Association, 25 February 1990).

54. National Education Goals Panel, *The National Education Goals Report: Building a Nation of Learners, 1991* (Washington, D.C.: Government Printing Office, 1991).

55. National Education Goals Panel, *The National Education Goals Report: Building a Nation of Learners, 1992*, 191.

56. Ibid., 191.
57. National Education Goals Panel, *Nation of Learners, 1991*, 33–38.
58. National Education Goals Panel, *Nation of Learners, 1992*, 19.
59. Ibid., 59–72.
60. Ernest L. Boyer, *Ready to Learn: A Mandate for the Nation* (Princeton: Princeton University Press, 1991).
61. Ibid., 161.
62. Phyllis Schlafly, "Course Outline for a Blackboard Empire," *Washington Times*, 21 February 1992, F4.
63. *Education Daily*, 22 January 1992, 1.
64. Ibid., 15 May 1992, 1.

11 SCHOOL LEAVING: DEAD END

OR DETOUR?

JOSEPH F. KETT

In recent decades educators and policy makers have come to view dropping out of high school as a social problem of significant proportions.
Dropouts are widely believed to have bleaker job prospects than graduates
and to be more likely candidates for unemployment and casual employment. Inasmuch as Hispanics and blacks have been more likely than others
to drop out of high school, the alleged economic drain from failure to
complete high school has blended in the minds of policy makers with the
image of American society as fractured along ethnic and racial lines. In
response to these concerns, the National Education Goals Report targeted
a high school completion rate of at least 90 percent by the year 2000.

The fact that the reduction of dropouts has become one of the six
national educational goals underscores the intense interest that now surrounds the subject. Before the 1960s educators devoted much more attention to increasing the average educational attainment (or years in school) of
the American population than to the prevention of dropping out. Although these two objectives seem to be merely different sides of the same
coin, each leads to a different emphasis. Requiring publicity and programs
that were aimed at the middle of the population, the pursuit of the goal of
increasing educational attainment produced exponential gains. Inasmuch
as the great majority of young people now complete high school, making
the prevention of dropping out a major national goal sends educators on a
kind of perimeter search-and-destroy mission that by definition will yield
small numerical inceases.

Yet many of the arguments that now propel the campaign against
dropouts were developed early in the twentieth century precisely to encourage higher average attainment. An apparent consensus among educational policy makers about the value of universal secondary education
took shape before 1920, but this consensus was and remains fragile. This
fragility has resulted from several factors. First, there has long been a

difference in emphasis between educational policy makers, the kind of people who serve on national commissions, and local school officials. Each has favored "democracy" in education, but with subtly different interpretations of its meaning. During the years between the two world wars and into the 1950s, local officials thought of a democratic high school as one that drew students from all social classes of a locality, not necessarily one that reproduced the local class (or racial) distribution in any literal way. As long as some working-class teenagers attended and eagerly participated in the school's curricular and extracurricular activities, these officials were satisfied that their school was democratic. These same officials took it for granted that economic necessity would force some teenagers to leave school and would prevent others, especially farm children, from entering. But they do not seem to have been deeply troubled by this, partly because there was nothing they could do about it and partly because they wanted no part of unwilling or unmotivated students whose reluctant attendance would mar the image of wholehearted participation that they were trying to convey.

In contrast, national policy makers were more likely to doubt that economic necessity forced teenagers out of school; in their view, an appropriate curriculum, specifically one that provided vocational preparation, would induce most working-class teenagers to persist in high school. But even these policy makers doubted the value of inducing truly unmotivated students to persist. These doubts continued into the 1950s, when new attitudes toward unmotivated students began to emerge. Increasingly, educators and psychologists argued that high schools could motivate the unwilling.

Although this emphasis on motivating students continues to influence policy, during the last half century it has had to compete with an alternative approach to school withdrawal, which acknowledges that some students will drop out but which makes provisions for their later reentry into the educational system. The key institutional buttresses of this approach have been the general educational development (GED) tests and the notion of junior (later community) colleges as institutions of continuing education.

MEASUREMENTS

Concern over dropouts has intensified despite the steadily rising rate of high school completion over the last half century. Several measures testify to the rising educational attainment of the population and the increasing frequency of school completion. In 1940 more than 60 percent of all persons aged 25 to 29 had not completed high school; by 1980 only 16 percent had failed to complete high school.[1] Between 1910 and 1986 the median number of years of schooling completed by persons aged 25 or over rose from 8.1 to 12.7. Most of this change was accomplished between 1940 and 1970.[2] There has occurred, in addition, a significant convergence between the median number of years of schooling completed by whites and blacks.[3]

Although the educational attainment of the population has risen, the confluence of higher dropout rates among some minorities, especially Hispanics, and the increasing proportion of minority students in public high schools have spurred concern among policy makers, which, in turn, has focused research on measuring the dropout rate. Although dropout rates as varying as 2 percent and over 30 percent have been publicized, the dropout picture is coming into clearer focus. The National Center for Education Statistics (NCES) currently uses three measures of the extent of dropping out. First, the *event dropout rate* compares the number of students who drop out within a twelve-month period to the number at the start of the period. Second, the *cohort dropout rate* measures the experiences of a single group (or cohort) over a period of time by comparing the number of students who have left school before completion to the number present in the group at the start of the period in question. Third, the *status dropout rate*, a rough composite of the event rates summed over several years, measures the proportion of individuals in a specified age range (e.g., sixteen to twenty-four) who are dropouts by comparing the number of sixteen- to twenty-four-year-olds who have not completed high school and who are not still enrolled to the total population of sixteen- to twenty-four-year-olds.[4] Although each measure yields a different result, the three measures are ultimately compatible. Further, regression analysis has made it possible to establish trends for the first and third measures, and these trends point in a similar direction. Both event and status dropout rates have declined since the late 1970s, and this decline has included black as well as white students.[5]

None of these measures of failure to complete high school is without drawbacks, which have been fully acknowledged by researchers.[6] Collectively and individually, however, they point to both long-term and short-term increases in school completion and decreases in dropout rates. We are thus confronted with a paradox: concern with the problem of failure to complete school has risen even as the scope of the problem has contracted. Public concern over dropouts rose after World War II and, at least measured by the number of articles on the subject by researchers and policy makers, has intensified during the last two decades.

One might plausibly conclude from declining rates of dropping out that the current concern over failure to complete high school is exaggerated. From one perspective, this conclusion seems fair. A modest, even if still significant, number of students, around 348,000, dropped out of grades 10 to 12 in 1991.[7] From a different perspective, however, the persistence of dropping out gives legitimate cause for concern. First, although rates of dropping out for blacks have declined, they remain higher than those for whites, and rates for Hispanics, which consistently have been much higher than those for whites, show no trend toward decline. In addition, although an annual number of 348,000 dropouts is perhaps not alarming in itself, the cumulative effect of such annual numbers is disturbing. In 1991 nearly four million persons aged sixteen to twenty-four (12.5 percent of the age group) did not have high school diplomas and were not enrolled in school.[8] In sum, the concern of policy makers with dropouts, even at a time of rising rates of school completion, is by no means groundless. As high school completion has become the norm, the fear has heightened that dropouts will form an ever more threatening social group, disaffiliated not only from school but from society.

This fear of social disaffiliation (or alienation) has roots in the American notion of schooling as a cultural bond, a way to forge shared values. For over a century this ideal has coexisted with that of schooling as a source of economic opportunity and, although the two ideals are compatible in theory, they have often led to different emphases in practice.

ROOTS

The first flurry of interest in compulsory schooling rose as a byproduct of the mid–nineteenth-century movement for public, or common, school reform. In those days reformers were far more interested in increasing school attendance than in raising the average level of educational attainment. They feared that children who worked at early ages in factories would grow up in ignorance. They translated this simple polarity between an educated and an ignorant work force into demands that child laborers attend school for some part of the year. Without providing effective mechanisms of enforcement, legislatures consistently targeted labor in manufacturing and mercantile establishments that was so prolonged on a daily basis as to interfere with rudimentary schooling. Beyond that, the state had little interest in compelling attendance. Mid–nineteenth-century laws were far more likely to specify the minimum age at which a child could be employed in a manufacturing or mercantile establishment (usually ten or twelve) than to extend the maximum age of required schooling. When in 1873 Massachusetts rewrote its compulsory school law (first passed in 1852), it simultaneously increased the number of weeks of schooling required annually while reducing (from fourteen to twelve) the upper age limit.[9]

Odd as it may appear a century later, this lowering of the upper age limit was consistent with the importance that mid–nineteenth-century educators attached to order and regularity. Horace Mann was one among several nineteenth-century school reformers to view teenagers as a poten-tially disruptive influence in the classroom. Neither reformers nor school principals were unhappy when these "large boys" of fifteen or sixteen left school for work, for their goal was to effect more systematic schooling for those from eight to thirteen.[10]

Between 1890 and 1920 attitudes toward the schooling of teenagers underwent a sea change. To a far greater degree than in the mid–nineteenth century, educators began to emphasize the importance of edu-cational attainment or school persistence. Whereas their predecessors had bluntly contrasted the prospects of educated and ignorant workers, educa-tors now began to assemble evidence to demonstrate that those who per-sisted in school until sixteen would earn more over the long run than school leavers before that age. When in 1917 A. Caswell Ellis, a professor of education at the University of Texas, summarized various studies purport-ing to show the superior performance in the job market of those with more years of education, his bibliography included over one hundred titles, nearly all of which had been published since 1905.[11]

The movement to prolong schooling into the teens encountered consid-erable resistance. Although public high schools were established during the nineteenth century, they had not been democratic in either theory or practice, and until the late nineteenth century the legality of spending public funds on such institutions was challenged.[12] The nation contained only a quarter of a million high school students in 1890, the majority of whom were female. Nineteenth-century success mythology had cele-brated the plucky lad who left school after a rudimentary education and who rose up the ladder by his own efforts, and this view by no means evaporated after 1900.

All of this made it difficult to imagine high schools as institutions of mass education, but this is exactly what an influential body of educators began to do in the early 1900s. Published in 1918, authored by the National Education Association's Committee on the Reorganization of Secondary Education, and mainly written by Clarence Kingsley, the famed *Cardinal Principles of Secondary Education* recommended compulsory schooling until age eighteen and insisted that high school education had to become a common experience of all American youth. Although not indifferent to the economic value of added schooling, the *Cardinal Principles* essentially ap-plied the reasoning of the mid–nineteenth-century school reformers to secondary education: universal secondary schooling would act as a social bond among different classes. While advocating a diverse curriculum to accommodate the varied needs of students, the *Cardinal Principles* consis-tently emphasized the value of secondary education in creating a uniform national culture. The sundry objectives of education established by the report—health, command of fundamental processes, worthy home membership, vocation, citizenship, worthy use of leisure, and ethical character—were not conceived as independent bases for separate types of secondary schools. Rather, all students would attend comprehensive high schools and share some if not all classes. No exception was made for those whose family circumstances or individual proclivities pushed them into jobs before the age of eighteen; they too would attend, if only part-time, and, to build "social solidarity," would "share in the use of the assembly hall, gymnasium, and other equipment provided for all."[13]

Educators who favored the prolongation of schooling drew comfort from the quantum leaps in secondary school enrollments between 1890 and 1930. The proportion of seventeen-year-olds to graduate from full-time high schools rose from 3.5 percent in 1890 to 25 percent by 1926. Legal changes contributed modestly to this development; by 1918 twenty-eight states had advanced the upper limit of compulsory education beyond the age of fourteen (usually to sixteen). But nearly all of these states allowed children to leave at fourteen (in some cases earlier) if they secured work permits, and no state required attendance at high school.[14]

Although requirements that teenagers secure work permits before leaving school made their employment increasingly difficult, on balance legislation played a less important role in their removal from the labor market than did the erosion of demand for their labor. Of the various factors that contributed to this erosion, two stand out. First, the proportion of the population engaged in farming (where demand for child labor had always been keen) declined by nearly 50 percent between 1880 and 1920. Second, the introduction of machinery powered by electricity reduced the demand for unskilled labor. At the same time, the flood of immigrants in the early 1900s increased the supply of unskilled labor. To the extent that occupations still required unskilled workers, employers were more likely to employ adult immigrants than young people.[15]

The same advances in industrialization that reduced demand for unskilled labor contributed to the growth of office work, which in turn encouraged first middle-class and then working-class parents to prolong their children's education.[16] The economist Paul Douglas estimated that the ratio of clerical workers to all workers in American manufacturing dropped from one in thirteen in the decade 1890–99 to one in seven by 1924.[17] Inasmuch as the work of clerks and bookkeepers traditionally had been associated with middle-class status, the growth of office work seemed to create new opportunities for entry into middle-class work. Further, both the general and the commercial curriculums of high schools were highly compatible with preparation for office work, far more compatible, indeed, than were school shop classes with preparation for mechanical labor.[18] In sum, high school attendance increasingly seemed the ideal way to prepare for types of labor that combined cleanliness, safety, and respectability. The value of secondary education impressed working-class as well as middle-class parents. As Douglas noted, by the 1920s the manual worker, with more dollars in his Saturday night envelope, had concluded that the best way to advance his own children into the middle class was to prolong their education into high school.[19]

Many of the values that now permeate the debate over dropouts were in place by 1920: the ideal of universal high school attendance as desirable on both social and economic grounds, high school completion as a necessary objective, and the need for a curriculum that would accommodate a socially diverse population of students. In 1922 the prominent progressive educator George S. Counts asserted that "in theory we are apparently rather definitely committed to the idea" of universal secondary education and that this ideal possibly included high school completion. From Counts's perspective, practice merely had to catch up with theory, a likely development in his view. Although he recognized that the children of laborers and black teenagers were grossly underrepresented in the high schools of his day, he contended that modern industry afforded so little opportunity for adolescents that, with the encouragement of educators, universal secondary education would become the norm.[20]

For many contemporaries of Counts, however, universal secondary attendance was undesirable even in theory. Some of these dissenters resisted the introduction of any sort of vocational courses on the principle that high schools had to remain academic and selective institutions. By the 1920s this old-fashioned elitism was on the decline, but the same cannot be said for another variety of dissent, which asserted the superiority of part-time attendance. For Clarence Kingsley, the principal author of the *Cardinal Principles*, and for most mainstream progressives, part-time students were a necessary evil, but for an influential body of educators they were a positive good. Charles Prosser and David Snedden, who are usually classified as "efficiency" educators, and their many allies in the influential National Society for the Promotion of Industrial Education (NSPIE) are usually associated with the notion that vocational education should take place in separate vocational schools rather than in comprehensive high schools. The *Cardinal Principles* should be read as a response to this insistence, but what Prosser and Snedden actually favored was a rooting of job training in factory or corporation schools, with part-time continuation schools to complete general education. In their eyes systematic vocational training in the work place would always be more "real" than the make-believe vocational courses of comprehensive schools. Bullied into full-time attendance in high schools, many teenagers would always display lethargy and indifference but, given the opportunity to test themselves in the work place and to supplement their work experience with part-time schooling, these same youth would respond eagerly.

Lest we dismiss the efficiency educators as fringe eccentrics, we should remember that Prosser was the effective author of the Smith-Hughes Act of 1917, which stipulated that one-third of federal appropriations had to be reserved for separate continuation schools. In advancing their program, the efficiency educators drew not only on the experience of retraining workers for war industries during World War I but also on old-fashioned ideals about the value of work in building character. Where John Dewey, Kingsley, and Counts saw the industrial economy as a dead end for teenagers, for Prosser the world of work was still wonderful, a cornucopia of opportunity for the "plucky lad."[21]

THE INTERWAR YEARS

During the 1920s and 1930s, several factors undermined the position of Prosser and other advocates of part-time secondary education. Mainstream public educators valued the democratic socialization and moral protection of teenagers in full-time, comprehensive high schools far more than the exposure of youth to work experience, even on a part-time basis. These educators favored vocational education primarily as a way to keep teenagers in school rather than to train them for jobs. In addition, the atrophy of job opportunities for teenagers, a trend evident in 1910, became inescapable during the Depression and stunted the development of the continuation schools favored by the framers of the Smith-Hughes Act. Comprehensive high schools accounted for most of the remarkable growth of secondary school enrollments during the Depression decade, which saw a rise in the proportion of seventeen-year-olds to graduate from high school from 29.0 percent in 1929–30 to 50.8 percent in 1939–40.[22]

All of these developments brought the ideal that Counts had described in 1922 closer to achievement, but it is possible to detect in the 1920s and 1930s some subtle reservations about the ideal, even among educators ostensibly committed to democratic secondary education. For many educators, *universal* did not quite mean "everyone." When Counts said universal, he certainly meant that. Everyone except the "feeble-minded" should attend and probably should complete high school. But in the nineteenth century common school reformers also had called for the common schooling of everyone and then made so few provisions for enforcing compulsory school laws that we are left wondering about the depth of their commitment.[23] In fact, during the nineteenth century local school officials were lukewarm about compulsory schooling, which, if taken seriously, threatened to burden the schools with chronic troublemakers; they supported evening schools partly to keep rough factory children out of day schools.[24] A similar ambivalence permeated conceptions of universal secondary schooling in the 1920s and 1930s. Even those who in principle subscribed to universality indulged in unspoken but ingrained assumptions about the necessary limits of secondary education, and they would continue to do so until after World War II.

It was on the local level that this ambivalence was especially pronounced during the interwar years. Although not overtly dissenting from the ideal of democratic secondary education, school boards and principals seem to have equated democracy with the wholehearted participation of the community in the high school, not with the literal enrollment of all teenagers. The most striking feature of "Middletown's" high school, described by Robert and Helen Lynd at the end of the 1920s, was its stress on participation in extracurricular activities, especially sports. Middletown's Central High School had become a popular institution between 1890 and 1924, not only because a vastly larger proportion of its young people attended (the city's population had increased three and a half times while its high school enrollment had risen elevenfold and graduates nineteenfold), but also because the high school now had become the focal point of the city's boosters. Friday night was basketball night in Middletown, a time when the whole community seemed to be caught up in the "Bearcat spirit." Where in the 1890s high school students had mingled with adults in attending public lectures, by the 1920s adults crowded into the gymnasium to watch teenagers play.[25]

In Middletown, the sport and social clubs of the high school roughly replicated the adult social organizations that had proliferated since the 1890s. Middletown had become a city of joiners, bursting with the noisy boosterism and self-congratulatory spirit that Sinclair Lewis had satirized in *Babbitt* (1922). Generously treated by annual appropriations, Central High School had become a source of community pride. As a community institution, it seemed democratic. But not everyone belonged to the community. Not only were the city's innumerable social organizations graded by prestige, but the pecking order among its clubs was reproduced in the high school. Although the Lynds were not primarily concerned with school leavers, they paid more attention to them than did local school officials and observed the way in which social class conditioned high school attendance. By the 1920s working-class Middletowners were evidencing "great pressure toward education" in their desire "to escape to better things." But many working-class children dropped out, partly to earn money but also to escape the invidious distinctions of Central High School's social climate.[26]

Impressed by the growth and wealth of the high school, Middletown's school officials took little notice of nonattenders. The same was true of the school officials of "Elmtown," the cornbelt community of 6,500 that August B. Hollingshead studied on the eve of American entry into World War II. Elmtown's administrators were as persuaded as those of Middletown that their school democratically reflected the community, and much like Middletowners they defined the community as the participating population. Robert Hampel described the high school before 1960 as the "last little citadel," a revealing metaphor that well describes the attitudes of school administrators in the 1920s and 1930s.[27] As jewels of localities, high schools were to incarnate the community's image of its better self. Taking pride in their high school, which they envisioned as a bastion of wholesome values, Elmtown's school officials saw what they wanted to see: boys and girls eagerly coming to high school each day. What they did not see was the local lower classes and underclasses, Hollingshead's classes IV and V, the people who lived "across the canal." According to Hollingshead, school officials knew nothing about these people. When he drove with the superintendent of schools across the canal to interrogate the father of a pair of school vandals and chronic truants, the superintendent commented: "I've never been down here before. I did not know this area existed."[28]

This combination of ignorance and indifference to the local underclass permeated officials' understanding of school leavers. They confidently told Hollingshead that he would find only "a few kids" under sixteen who were out of school and not at work. When they minimized the out-of-school population of teenagers, school administrators simply did not count farm youth, especially the Norwegians. In effect, they told Hollingshead that the Norwegians did not count as part of the eligible high school population, since they were all farmers and farmers did not believe in education beyond the eighth grade.[29]

Hollingshead's own investigation revealed a more complex picture. Most school leavers were urban, not rural, and their work experience was intermittent. Not infrequently, they worked part-time while attending high school and then dropped out the moment they secured a full-time job. But even full-time work proved transient, partly because local employers took a dim view of dropouts and would employ them only in low-level work. In their middle and late teens, school leavers skipped from job to job, always in search of higher wages. Significantly, Hollingshead was sure that nothing would change this. School leavers, nearly all from classes IV and V, entered the labor force with totally unrealistic expectations, but the impulse that drove them to work was ineradicable, not economic necessity as such but their association of ready cash with the adult status they craved. High school could never provide this status, for high school students by definition were dependent and lower-class youth wanted independence.[30]

Hollingshead described school leavers as engaged in a process of adjustment, not so much to work but to their position in the class structure. Once they had reached the age of eighteen, their work experience became steadier (this was especially true of class IV youth) and they began to settle down. "Folk culture," Hollingshead found, comprehended their drifting during their middle and late teens as an inevitable "revolt of youth," but the revolt was not really threatening.[31] Rather, it was just a phase through which lower-class youths passed as they adjusted to their status as lower-class adults. Because dropping out was rooted in family psychology as much as in family economy, there was nothing that could be done to reverse it. As an urban school superintendent recollected in the 1950s, during the Depression a teenager who dropped out of high school was through with school, and the school was through with him.[32]

POLICY STATEMENTS DURING THE DEPRESSION AND WORLD WAR II

Although Hollingshead presented a more sophisticated analysis, school administrators in Elmtown voiced what might be termed the traditional view of dropouts: the requirements of family economies would always induce some children to leave school for work. Such decisions might be ill-advised, but there was little that officials could do to reverse them. The same officials complacently assumed that school leavers, especially those who persisted in school until age sixteen, would find work. But developments in the 1930s were effectively closing off teenagers' avenues of entry into the labor force. The prolongation of education, which in the early 1900s was defended as a way to increase the long-term earning power of young people, drew support from a range of policy makers in the 1930s as a way to reduce unemployment by removing young people from competition for jobs. Although implicit in earlier discussions of prolonging education, this objective became explicit in the 1930s.[33] Few justified high schools merely as custodial institutions, but trade union officials, government administrators, and school superintendents in the 1930s agreed on the value of enclosing youth apart from the labor market.

By the late 1930s studies were publicizing the relationship between prolonging education and reducing unemployment. One motif that ran through these studies was that the "youth problem," defined as the demoralization that resulted from unemployment and underemployment among those aged sixteen to twenty-four, would become a political problem in the absence of concerted attempts to address it. In *The Lost Generation*, Maxine Davis warned that boys and girls forced to enlist in "the reserve armies of industry" would become followers in the "armies of brown and black shirts."[34] In *Youth Tell Their Story*, Howard M. Bell reported that a survey of out-of-school youth in Maryland found not only widespread unemployment among young people aged sixteen to twenty-one but also signs of demoralization. In Maryland, five times as many young people wanted to work in the professions as were employed in them. Schools had equipped young people with unrealistic expectations and few skills.[35] Even worse, the more able students experienced the greatest despondency, for they were the most ambitious. Bell thought it significant that the recruits for radical youth movements in Europe during the preceding two decades had been drawn from the ranks of unemployed university graduates, and he feared a similar development among despondent high school leavers in America.[36]

The wide publicity accorded the books by Davis and Bell underscores the recurrent fear of idle youth. The early twentieth-century reformers who proclaimed the ideal of universal secondary education had reflected this fear by requiring school leavers under the age of sixteen to secure work permits. To a degree, such New Deal agencies as the National Youth Administration (NYA) and Civilian Conservation Corps (CCC) had come into existence to serve the population of out-of-school *and* out-of-work youth. But with its sundry training camps, the CCC was extremely expensive to operate. The NYA avoided this problem by allowing youth to live at home, but it could provide little more than part-time work on public projects. Inclined to view federal programs as mere stopgaps, articulate educators turned to the idea of prolonging schooling until at least age eighteen, but they did so initially without great expectations. Along with most social analysts of the 1930s, Bell did not expect a future expansion of the professions or white-collar work, and he delineated a role for schools in promoting "occupational adjustment," which meant guiding youth toward "realistic" (lower) expectations.[37]

In contrast, by the end of the 1930s the educational policy makers who gathered on the Educational Policies Commission (jointly appointed by the National Education Association and the American Association of School Administrators) were advancing more optimistic forecasts of the future of work by suggesting that technological advances would require a more highly trained labor force. In its influential report *Education and Economic Well-being in American Democracy*, this commission called for raising the minimum amount of formal schooling to ten years and the average to fourteen years. Yet, in comparison with later documents, *Education and Economic Well-being* was remarkably restrained in its assessment of the relation between schooling and earnings. While acknowledging evidence that purported to show a direct relationship between increments of schooling and wages, the authors warned that the jury was still out. Schooling would raise individual income only when a demand for skilled workers existed in a locale, and it would increase national wealth only to the extent to which it overcame "artificial" barriers to school persistence, primarily those based on class and race. This left individual ability and motivation as legitimate barriers to school persistence, and it led the commission to conclude that "the economic reasons for providing education have become largely social." That is, adequate provision for schooling would do less to raise individual or national wealth than to afford "a more equitable distribution of earned income" and "the total social income."[38]

In sum, on the eve of American entry into World War II even progressive justifications of prolonging education were still hedged by reservations. One such reservation was the continuing belief that school leavers were forced out by economic necessity. What primarily mattered to the authors of Education and Economic Well-being was that all students with the "capacity and willingness" to absorb more education, regardless of social class or race, be enabled to stay in school for at least ten years, even if income supplements were required to achieve this goal. The fact that the commission specified its target as a number of school years completed rather than the attainment of a specific age is also significant; its recommendation was compatible with an earlier proposal (which it cited) that students attend full-time until sixteen and then half-time until twenty or twenty-one years old. In addition, Education and Economic Well-being insisted that only qualified youth, those with appropriate motivation and intelligence, persist beyond the ten-year minimum. "The real source of the difficulty," the commission contended, "is that our educational opportunities are not closely enough correlated with individual abilities and social needs."[39] For all its hedging, the commission did call for the advancement of the average level of schooling to fourteen years, in other words, two years beyond conventional high school. In retrospect, it is remarkable that this proposal was put forward, for the Depression (which was still ongoing when the commission's report was approved for publication in 1939) had flattened college enrollments and had led to widespread unemployment among college graduates. But the commission drew attention to rising enrollments in junior college, an institution that would come to play a prominent role in all subsequent thinking about the prolongation of education.

Appearing first as a glimmer on the horizon at the end of the nineteenth century and widely trumpeted by a noisy minority of educators in the 1920s and 1930s, the junior college began to appeal to educators as a godsend by the late 1930s. Although still on the periphery of postsecondary education—most were housed in high schools and concentrated in a few states—junior colleges offered the promise of an upward extension of high school for two years, with the focus now primarily vocational. In this conception, civic socialization and basic education could be left to primary and secondary schools, while junior colleges and publicly funded local technical institutes addressed the need for "occupational adjustment."

This division of responsibility had the merit of preserving high schools as the common meeting grounds for different classes, an ideal articulated by the *Cardinal Principles of Secondary Education* and long threatened by the more strident advocates of vocational education and part-time schools. In addition, to qualify for federal funds under the George-Deen Act of 1936, which opened commercial or "distributive" education to Smith-Hughes appropriations, junior colleges had to specify that their vocational courses were "less than college grade," a phrase that federal education officials interpreted to include courses open to nongraduates of high schools. Thus, junior colleges seemed ideally suited to school leavers who chose to return to complete their education. This kind of continuing education proved far more appealing to American educators than had the continuation schools favored by the Smith-Hughes Act, which had been based on daily or weekly alternations between job and school. Most educators long had recognized that the United States lacked the tradition of apprenticeship that had enabled such schools to thrive in Germany. The idea of returning to school to reassess goals and to secure additional training after a few years at work seemed more suited to American conditions and ideals. In 1945 George Zook, former president of the University of Akron and president of the American Council on Education, drafted the report *Higher Education for American Democracy*, which baptized junior colleges as the vanguard of democratization, urged that they serve their entire communities (soon they would be called community colleges), emphasized their role in continuing education, and proposed making available without cost education through the second year of college for all Americans who could not afford to pay.[40]

Although most of the ideas advanced in *Higher Education for American Democracy* had antecedents in the late 1930s, developments during World War II widened the base of support for its proposals. Whereas the Depression had seemed to confirm the undeniable trend toward lower rates of youth participation in the labor market, during the war the economy revived and, as eighteen- and nineteen-year olds entered the service, jobs opened in factories and stores for younger teenagers. The number of fourteen- to seventeen-year-olds in the labor force rose from fewer than one million in the summer of 1940 to three million by the summer of 1942.[41] Demand for work permits surged among boys and girls alike, but especially among boys. In April 1944 a Census Bureau sample indicated that one in five schoolboys aged fourteen to fifteen and two in five aged sixteen to seventeen were gainfully employed.[42]

Many of these young workers continued to attend school, but as late as October 1946, six months after V-E Day, the proportion of those in their upper teens enrolled in school was lower than in 1940.[43] These developments reversed the long-term trend between 1900 and 1940 toward declining participation by youth in the labor market, and they raised some disturbing possibilities. If young people sprang at job opportunities during the war, they might continue to do so afterward, especially if the economy remained buoyant. Their quest for work would bring them into contact with demobilized veterans, with results that no one could predict with precision but which all educators feared: young people with only a single skill displaced by veterans; veterans displaced and embittered by competition with virtual child laborers. It was just this fear of a chaotic demobilization that had spurred Congress to pass the Servicemen's Readjustment Act (the G.I. Bill) in 1944. By encouraging veterans to enroll in colleges, the G.I. Bill, it was hoped, would soften pressure on jobs during the immediate postwar period.

Apprehension of chaotic demobilization and anxiety about independent, job-seeking youth coalesced to impart new urgency to the subject of dropouts. The first chapter of the Educational Policies Commission Report *Education for ALL American Youth* (1945) projected "the history that should not happen." In this hypothetical scenario the federal government would revive the NYA and CCC under the guise of a new National Bureau of Youth Service, which would bring order out of chaos by training young people for jobs at the price of federal control of education. If this occurred, the report prophesied, "the locally administered high school, for so many years the center of the American dream of equal opportunity through education, [would join] the Latin grammar school of the seventeenth century and the academy of the nineteenth in the great wastebasket of history."[44]

By 1952 a notably calmer update of *Education for ALL American Youth* was published. Subtitled *A Further Look*, this document argued that the crisis created by the war had passed, mainly because the war had given the schools the resources to solve the very problem it had created. With the demise of the NYA and CCC, the federal government had made no new effort to conduct its own parallel vocational training program. Further, the success of wartime job training programs had persuaded educators that schools could train youth for immediate employment. Industrial equipment used to train war workers under such federal programs as Training within Industry had been handed over at the war's conclusion to high schools and public junior colleges. The proliferation of junior colleges, which enrolled nearly three times as many students in 1947–48 as in 1943–44, now afforded young people opportunities to pursue vocational education at public expense beyond the twelfth grade and, in conjunction with locally sponsored vocational-technical centers, made it possible for dropouts to drop back in again. Everywhere the authors of the updated report detected a new attitude toward school retention. Increasingly, schools conducted follow-up studies of dropouts and planned programs to reduce school leaving.[45]

In sum, the experience of World War II sent educators a mixed message about school retention. The growth of junior college enrollments during the war (especially adult enrollments) and the new availability of federal surplus equipment for industrial education spurred the expectation that both school leavers and graduates could acquire job training in their late teens and early twenties, either in a community college or in a muncipal vocational-technical center. From this perspective, school leavers were not necessarily finished with education. At the same time, educators grew alarmed by the rise in youth employment during the war, feared that it might lead to a reversal of the benign trend toward lower participation by youth in the labor market, and became more persuaded than ever before of the importance of retaining young people continuously through high school.

This commitment owed a great deal to a new understanding of the reasons for dropping out and to new concepts of how to retain young people in school.

THE FRUSTRATED ADOLESCENT

During the Progressive Era and throughout the interwar years, vocational education had struck most educators as the only plausible way to retain young people who were indifferent to academic courses. But vocationalism had long been open to a variety of objections: it was expensive if rightly conducted, it was beyond the resources of small high schools, and it threatened to shatter the ideal of high school as a common experience that would forge a shared civic culture among youth. In addition, during the interwar years most educators agreed that economic necessity was the root cause of dropping out. Viewed from this perspective, a significant amount of school leaving seemed inevitable, regardless of the curriculum.

The understanding of school leaving that flowered in the 1950s, especially in connection with the life adjustment movement, portrayed school leavers and school vandals as similarly drawn from the ranks of frustrated young people, adolescents whose low self-esteem led them to engage in self-destructive behavior. A pair of articles in *Life* in the spring of 1960, entitled "Dropout Tragedies" and "A Hopeful Second Chance," embodied many of the perceptions of school leavers that marked the 1950s. The stories portrayed the effects of dropping out mainly in terms of personal tragedy and emphasized the psychological alienation of school leavers, young people for whom actual departure from school was merely the capstone of a long process of psychological withdrawal from family and peers.[46]

In this context, the task of high school therefore was not to train young people for jobs or to encourage their departure from school for job-training programs but to enhance their feelings of self-worth.[47] It was precisely their lack of self-esteem that made them want to leave school in the first instance and that left them too dispirited either to hold jobs or to succeed in training programs. In turn, low self-esteem threatened to lead youth into delinquency, a subject that evoked a barrage of publicity in the 1950s.[48] Fears of a national wave of delinquency raised the stakes, in effect, for where Hollingshead had described dropping out as initiating a painful but essentially unthreatening process of adjustment to lower-class status, social commentators in the 1950s were more likely to link dropping out to crime.

The notion that school leavers were suffering from frustration challenged and gradually subverted the traditional view of dropping out as necessitated by lower-class family economics, and it buttressed the view that school leaving had to be understood as the result of deficient motivation rather than as the product of poverty as such.[49] The difference was crucial, for where policy makers of the late 1930s had emphasized public intervention on behalf of the poor youth who was willing and capable but who lacked the means to stay in school, the new wisdom of the 1950s stressed finding ways to motivate students who were unwilling to stay in school.

The objective of raising the self-esteem of frustrated adolescents could be accomplished by guiding them into courses in which they could scarcely not succeed and by making more extensive provisions for their in-school counseling. Courses that guaranteed success were those that addressed the needs of emotionally adjusting adolescents. For example, the authors of *Education for ALL American Youth* praised a course in family living in a rural high school in which students learned "how to get along with others," how to make a wise choice of a mate, and how to meet family crises and "the economic problems of family life."[50]

The life adjustment movement lost steam in the wake of Sputnik, but it left a significant legacy to American high schools and to policy makers, who persisted long after the 1950s in the view that education had to be tailored to individual psychological needs and that ways had to be found to retain young people who loathed school. At least for frustrated teenagers with low self-esteem, the subjects taught in high school were less important than the therapies to which students brought together in a classroom could be exposed. The persistent implication of this approach was that the same psychosocial factors that propelled students to leave school would encourage, even guarantee, their social alienation.

Life adjustment also became one of the main vehicles by which new ideas about intelligence and testing entered secondary education. Tests administered to World War II inductees (tests whose basic principles had first been developed in the 1930s) overturned the pessimistic assessment of average intelligence that had emerged in the wake of the army's intelligence tests during World War I. Published assessments of the military's testing program in World War II coincided with the publication of *Higher Education for American Democracy* and contributed to the conclusion that a high proportion of the population had the capacity for one or another type of advanced (postsecondary) education. By implication, virtually anyone had the ability to profit from secondary school. As *Education of ALL American Youth* proclaimed: "All students were potential good citizens, regardless of I.Q."[51]

ISSUES OF THE 1960S

In the 1950s both educators and the public predicted that dropouts would become lawless, and in the 1960s they added jobless. World War II had silenced the fears of jobless youth voiced in the 1930s by Maxine Davis and Howard Bell, but in the 1960s the issue of unemployment rose to the top of the educational agenda and intensified concerns about dropouts. Labeled "social dynamite," school leaving increasingly became an obsession of educators during the 1960s.[52]

Rising rates of youth unemployment in the 1960s contributed to the heightened worries about dropouts, but what was most alarming were the reasons widely believed to have driven up unemployment rates among youth, the maturing of the baby boom and automation. In 1955, sixteen- to nineteen-year-olds accounted for 9.0 percent of the population; twenty years later they accounted for 12.7 percent. Policy makers may have identified the wrong villain, for, as Osterman noted, "the economy responded reasonably well to the influx of youth."[53] Nevertheless, unemployment among youth rose in the 1960s, and this was especially true of black youth, whose unemployment rates were double those of white youth. Further, as long as contemporaries blamed the baby boom and automation for unemployment, silver linings were hard to find. The baby boom would burden the economy with an apparent excess of job seekers for decades, while automation would steadily erode the kinds of jobs traditionally available to dropouts.

At first, federal policy makers saw automation as a threat to adult workers, who were targeted by the Manpower Development and Training Act of 1962 (MDTA). With the return of prosperity after 1962, the economy quickly absorbed older workers. The "problem" that the MDTA addressed virtually disappeared. But the assumption that technological advances gradually would shrink demand for low-skilled workers persisted, and by the mid-1960s it had become the basis for gloomy forecasts about the future of young workers. *Life* warned in 1963 of the loss of twenty-four million unskilled and semiskilled jobs by 1970. "All youth will have difficulty finding work," one commentator concluded; "the dropout will not stand a chance."[54]

Although inclined to substitute the global economy for automation, policy makers use much the same language now. But one difference between the mid-1960s approach to dropouts and that of the early 1990s bears noting. Today, most writers seem to assume that the primary responsibility for discouraging students from dropping out of high school lies with educational officials. For various reasons, in the mid-1960s the role of formal education was an open question. The civil rights movement and urban riots focused the attention of policy makers on black youth, who were widely perceived as victims of a "culture of poverty" that required underlying shifts in social policy, not just bandages applied by school principals.[55] In addition, although initially aimed at adult (and mainly white) workers, the MDTA and the manpower approach it represented impressed many federal officials as superior to reliance on school officials. Established under the Department of Labor, the MDTA had bypassed the vocational education establishment, which had close ties to the Department of Health, Education, and Welfare, the National Education Association, and the American Vocational Association (a powerful lobby for school-based vocational education) and which had always challenged direct federal training programs. Proponents of federal manpower programs blamed the vocational education establishment, and by implication public school administrators, for decades of failure to train workers for the jobs of today and tomorrow.[56]

Skeptical of vocational education, manpower advocates assumed that many young people would fail to complete high school. Like the framers of the NYA and CCC in the 1930s, they looked to training programs conducted by specialists (not necessarily educators) to ready youth for employment. In contrast, the NEA and the American Vocational Association insisted that schools could do the job and that vocational education's ultimate test lay in its ability to encourage school completion rather than in the quality of job training it offered.

Even before 1965 vocational educators succeeded in gaining a significant measure of control over manpower programs. An internecine struggle within the Department of Labor resulted in the turning over to vocational educators of responsibility for administering the department's training programs, a development that effectively ended any chance that the federal government would conduct its own educational system in competition with traditional school-based vocational education.[57] The Vocational Education Act of 1963 and its subsequent 1968 amendments discouraged further growth of residential training programs like the Job Corps, which had been created by the Economic Opportunity Act of 1964.

In addition, most of the funding categories established by the 1963 and 1968 legislation focused on the role of secondary schools, and virtually all provisions related to schools of one sort or another. The 1968 amendments specifically funded cooperative vocational education and work study, two measures that aimed at encouraging young people to finish school by enabling them to earn modest wages while enrolled.[58]

PERSPECTIVES OF THE 1970S

The reaction against federal manpower programs was broadly based. It included not only public school educators but also civil rights advocates, who feared that such programs would prepare black youth (who were disproportionately enrolled in most federal manpower programs) for low-level jobs; conservatives, who worried about the expense of manpower programs and who feared that the federal government would create work relief to find employment for their graduates; and many economists, who doubted that unemployment and job turnover added up to significant problems.[59] Cracks in the consensus about the value of manpower training programs raised new questions about the value of vocational education outside the work place.

Analysts have long doubted the value of vocational education as a means of occupational training.[60] But it was not until the 1970s that a sustained assault on vocational education developed as an offshoot of attacks on the theory of human capital, which had been advanced by economists in the 1950s and 1960s and which contended that increments of formal schooling yielded long-term wage gains for individuals.[61] These economists urged "investment in people" as a social strategy. In general, human-capital theory was compatible with both vocational education and manpower training because, although the latter did not depend on formal schooling, it nevertheless purported to increase the skills of workers, the same goal proclaimed by vocational educators. By the late 1960s and especially in the 1970s, human-capital theory and all of its progeny were coming under attacks that arose in the context of disillusion with manpower training programs. In contrast to those who complained about the expense of manpower programs or the evils of a federally subsidized alternative to the school, those who targeted human-capital theory as such doubted the efficacy of skill augmentation as a means of redistributing earnings. If earning depended on factors other than skill, then it made little difference who conducted programs designed to enhance skill or how efficiently they were run; vocational education and manpower training alike rested on false assumptions.[62]

Critics of the benefits of enhancing skills disagreed among themselves on many issues, but they shared the belief that dual or segmented markets characterized the American economy. In this view, occupations can be divided into primary and secondary sectors. The former offer training opportunities (on the job) and ladders of advancement; the latter provide few opportunities for acquiring skills, have no ladders of advancement, and are marked by high turnover.[63] In general, those who subscribed to the theory of segmented labor markets (SLMs) argued that the secondary market primarily was composed of teenagers and minorities (some would add women). This distinction was not entirely new. Economists since John Stuart Mill had been describing something like a secondary labor market, which they sometimes called the theory of "noncompeting groups." But SLM theory was notably boosted in the 1970s by the disillusion among liberals and leftists with the War on Poverty and the Great Society. In general, they used dual-market theory to account for the persistence of poverty and unemployment amid plenty; more specifically, they invoked it to explain why the distribution of income had failed to move toward greater equality while the distribution of education had done so.[64] This conflict among economists continues to have a variety of implications for education. Consider, for example, the issue of skills. From the perspective of human-capital theory, enhancing the skills of workers through education will yield multiple benefits. It will raise productivity, reduce competition among unskilled workers for low-skilled jobs (by increasing the pool of skilled workers), and contribute to equalizing the wages of skilled workers. All of this assumes that the demand for skilled workers is shaped by the size of the pool of skilled workers; where shortages exist, wage increases will operate to increase the number of applicants with the right skills. Schools and government training programs can contribute to the pool of skilled workers, especially if they accurately forecast trends in demand. Educational policy makers, who were partial to the assumptions behind human-capital theory even before the latter had a name, would add that modern society requires ever more complex skills, that education (schooling) must adapt to these requirements by increased vocational offerings, and that a curriculum offering marketable skills will contribute to the retention of students until graduation.

SLM theory and related strains of criticism pointed toward a different conclusion. In this alternative view, skills inhere in jobs rather than in applicants. Most training occurs after the worker gets the job. The labor market matches trainable (rather than trained) applicants with training ladders; thus, the supply of job skills is created by employer requirements, by the skills that inhere in the job the employer wants to fill.[65] To avoid wasting money training applicants who will jump to other jobs, employers make their training programs as company-specific as possible. Thus, any effort to increase skills before entry into the labor market is unlikely to succeed.

This configuration of contentions leaves open the question of how employers select trainees. Whatever their view of SLM theory, critics of human-capital theory have responded to this question by emphasizing the credentialing role of education. In the 1970s many social scientists swung toward the position that the rewards of schooling did not depend either on the occupational skills it imparted or on the general knowledge and intelligence usually associated with education. Books like Ivar Berg's *Education and Jobs: The Great Training Robbery* flatly denied any relationship between increments of schooling and higher productivity.[66] Others put forward less extreme versions of this argument by pointing to the tendency of educational levels to rise faster than job requirements for education, and they concluded that such increases as have occurred in educational requirements for jobs have reflected the expansion of the pool of educated applicants rather than any reasoned assessment of the education demanded by occupations.[67] In effect, faced with a superabundance of applicants with high levels of educational attainment, employers simply use attainment as a quick screening device for personality traits such as trainability that they believe are required for the jobs they advertise.[68] So, far from subjecting this assumed association to a test, employers merely take it for granted.

Throughout the 1970s and 1980s, this line of analysis coexisted with the more traditional argument that the value of schooling lay in the skills students learned. While conceptually antagonistic, these viewpoints agree on the importance of formal education at least through high school. Few argue with the proposition that those with superior levels of educational attainment will earn more over the long run. But the implications of the two views differ. One party conceives of high school as a time to acquire marketable skills; the other sees persistence in high school and beyond, indeed all education, as a *defensive necessity*. As Thurow wrote, "Education becomes a good investment, not because it would raise people's incomes above what they would have been if no one had increased his education, but because it raises their income above what it will be if others acquire an education and they do not."[69] To a degree, these outlooks also conflict over the prospects of teenagers in the labor market. Those who believe that schools can effectively teach marketable skills incline to the view that high school graduates will find employment in occupations that require skilled or semiskilled workers and that contain ladders of advancement. In contrast, their opponents see a gloomy market for high school graduates and an even gloomier one for dropouts. From this perspective, employers in the primary market will prefer older workers, especially those with higher education, while workers between the ages of eighteen and twenty-one will be shunted into the secondary market, regardless of whether they graduate from high school.

POLICY IMPLICATIONS

The debate over labor markets has had negligible direct effect on educators. Most educators continue to operate on human-capital assumptions, partly because human-capital theory places education at the forefront of accommodating change and partly because educators who advocate universal secondary education primarily on psychosocial grounds continue to find the economic argument for prolonged schooling an effective way to arouse public support. Although most educators have ignored the debate, it does have considerable relevance to educational policy relating to school completion. One approach to dropouts is to emphasize some combination of carrots and sticks to encourage students to persist in school until age eighteen. This approach has given rise to innumerable initiatives during the last decade. Some of these have arisen within individual schools and depend on charismatic administrators or teachers; others, like New York City's Dropout Prevention Initiative and the West Virginia program of denying driver's licenses to school leavers under eighteen, have originated with municipal or state authorities. The alternative approach has stressed that poorly motivated students should be allowed to drop out of high school on the expectation that many of them will later return to complete high school or that they will pass the GED tests (about 60 percent of high school dropouts eventually either complete high school or pass the GED tests). They also point to the expense of dropout prevention programs and question their effectiveness. Although only a few programs have been subjected to scrutiny, there is little evidence that they are cost-effective.[70] In addition, preoccupation with the prevention of dropping out threatens a return to the days of the life adjustment movement, when public schools diluted their curriculum to retain students.

Viewed from the perspective of contemporary economic theories, the first approach seems more compatible with human-capital theory, which generally emphasizes the value of acquiring skills before entry into the labor market. In human-capital theory, employers have no necessary preference for older workers; they will not go on hiring expensive university graduates if they can hire cheaper high school graduates with the right skills. The critics of human-capital theory question this assumption on empirical grounds by pointing to the inertia characteristic of large bureaucratic organizations, which discourages any empirical assessment of the value of such factors as age or credentials. For those who believe that occupational skills usually are learned on the job rather than before entry into the labor market and that industries with ladders of advancement will prefer older job applicants to teenagers, it does not make much difference whether a student persists in school until age eighteen or drops out and later reenters the educational system, for employers are less impressed by what someone claims to have learned in high school than by that person's age or credentials.

Viewed from the perspective of American educational history, a somewhat different picture emerges. The conflict between advocates of full-time versus part-time secondary education in the early twentieth century involved some of the same issues described above. The efficiency educators like Prosser and Snedden acknowledged that school leavers would encounter dead-end jobs, but they quickly added that the same was true of all teenagers. Access to better jobs depended mainly on age, not on educational attainment. In contrast, their opponents drew a direct connection between educational attainment and long-term wages. But these educators also rested their case for full-time schooling primarily on its social value. Like Horace Mann, Clarence Kingsley (the principal author of the *Cardinal Principles of Secondary Education*) cherished the ideal of *common* schooling. The achievement of social solidarity through shared educational experiences mattered more than the money value of schooling. On balance, the economic argument for schooling has always been more window dressing than substance. Even the 1940 report of the Educational Policies Commission on *Education and Economic Well-being* ultimately subordinated the economic value of schooling to its social dividends.

In sum, educators have never debated the value of schooling in quite the same fashion as have economists. Yet educators have been in conflict among themselves about the scope of universal secondary education; even progressive advocates have questioned the value of coercing the unmotivated to persist in school. In the late 1930s and early 1940s the Educational Policies Commission emphasized the need to offer all motivated youth an equal opportunity for schooling, but its attitude toward attendance by unmotivated youth was at best ambivalent. The growth of junior colleges and the invention of the GED tests during World War II put in place alternative mechanisms for dealing with those who lacked motivation during their teens.

Inasmuch as history never exactly repeats itself, the choice between encouraging continuous schooling and tolerating discontinuous schooling has never confronted successive generations in exactly the same form. The racial and ethnic correlatives of school persistence, which George Counts documented in 1922, loom larger now in the thinking of educators than the social-class correlatives that Counts also documented. Although more likely to focus on race than on class, contemporary educators share Counts's belief that schools must forge a democratic culture, that education must truly be common. It was as plausible for Counts, writing in the shadow of the great strikes of 1919, to worry about the class fissures in American society as it is for educators now to address racial fissures. Similarly, before midcentury educators were likely to emphasize economic necessity as the root cause of school leaving, while now they are more inclined to stress dropping out as a symptom of an underlying process of psychosocial alienation that begins in grade school. From this perspective, dropping out of high school is threatening rather than merely unwise, for it represents a kind of disaffiliation from society itself.

Although economists and educators have brought different emphases to the subject of school completion, these viewpoints help us to see the issue more clearly and to make some educated guesses about the likely direction of policy. Over the course of the twentieth century, educators rather than economists have been the primary shapers of policy. Economists infrequently footnote educators. Rather, educators footnote economists, especially the ones who support their belief in the value of education as the communication of skills. Whatever the descriptive value of SLM theory and its attendant stress on the attainment of credentials, economists in the neoclassical mainstream will continue to be suspicious of that theory and its implications on theoretical grounds. Educators, especially those who engage in the enterprise of formulating policy rather than in classroom teaching, will continue to advocate policies to realize the ideal of universal secondary education, even if this means muting calls for a more rigorous high school curriculum. It is also likely that they will advocate high school completion by age eighteen, a goal stated long ago by the *Cardinal Principles* and reinforced today by the fear that teenaged dropouts are more likely to graduate to the jailhouse than to the community college.

NOTES

1. Russell Rumberger, "High School Dropouts: A Review of Issues and Evidence," *Review of Educational Research* 57 (1987): 101.
2. U.S. National Center for Education Statistics, U.S. Department of Education, Office of Education Improvement and Research, *Digest of Education Statistics, 1988* (Washington, D.C.: Government Printing Office, 1988), 15.
3. Ibid. In 1950 the median for blacks was 71.3 percent of the white median; by 1986 the median for blacks had risen to 99.2 percent of the median for whites.
4. U.S. National Center for Education Statistics, U.S. Department of Education, Office of Education Improvement and Research, *Dropout Rates in the United States, 1991* (Washington, D.C.: Government Printing Office, 1992), 37–38.
5. Ibid., 7–8, 20–21. The event rate, over 6 percent in the late 1970s, fell to 4 percent in 1991. The rate for black males fell from about 9 percent in 1981 to about 5 percent in 1991. During the same period, the white male rate fell from about 5 percent to about 3 percent, and that for white females from about 5 percent to just under 4 percent. The percentage of young persons who are status dropouts declined from approximately 15 percent of those sixteen through twenty-four in 1972 to approximately 13 percent in 1991. During this period the status rate for blacks dropped from 21 percent to 14 percent, and that for whites dropped from 12 percent

to 9 percent. Hispanics make up an increasing proportion of all dropouts, in part because of their higher dropout rates and in part because of their growing proportion of the population.

6. The event and status dropout rates are based on data from the Current Population Survey (CPS), a survey conducted each October by the Bureau of the Census. Although nationally representative in theory, "the sample sizes in CPS may result in imprecise estimates of dropout and completion rates for important subgroups, including subregional areas and some minority subpopulations." See ibid., 49. Wide annual variations in Hispanic event rates may reflect the small sample size of Hispanics in the CPS. In recent years the NCES has conducted field tests to improve the CPS data.

7. Ibid., 35.

8. Ibid.

9. Forest C. Ensign, *Compulsory School Attendance and Child Labor Laws* (Iowa City: Athens Press, 1921), 61, 48–49. Richardson noted that states where enrollment levels were already high were more likely to enact compulsory school laws; see John B. Richardson, "Variations in Date of Enactment of Compulsory School Attendance Laws: An Empirical Inquiry," *Sociology of Education* 53 (July 1980): 157–63. Most scholars who have studied nineteenth-century school laws doubt that they had a significant effect on attendance; see William M. Landes and Lewis Solomon, "Compulsory Schooling Legislation: An Economic Analysis of Law and Social Change in the Nineteenth Century," *Journal of Economic History* 32 (1972): 54–87. The relationship seems to have been the other way around: high levels of attendance contributed to the passage of compulsory attendance laws partly because it was cheaper to compel attendance in states where it was already high and partly because such states were likely to have well-organized lobbies of teachers and school officials to advocate compulsory legislation; see also John W. Meyer, Audri Gordon, Joane Nagel, and David Tyack, "Public Education's Nation-Building in America: Enrollments and Bureaucratization in the American States, 1870–1930," *American Journal of Sociology* 85 (1979): 591–613.

10. Carl Kaestle and Maris A. Vinovskis, *Education and Social Change in Nineteenth-Century Massachusetts* (Cambridge: Cambridge University Press, 1980), 36.

11. A. Caswell Ellis, *The Money Value of Education*, U.S. Department of the Interior, Bureau of Education, bulletin 1917, no. 22 (Washington, D.C.: Government Printing Office, 1917), 46–52. Recent studies have undermined the assertion of revisionist historians in the 1970s that schools merely reproduced the existing class structure. Joel Perlmann demonstrated that students who attended high school in late nineteenth and early twentieth century Providence were much more likely than nonattenders with similar ethnic and class characteristics to advance into prestigious occupations; see Joel Perlmann, *Ethnic Differences: Schooling and Social Structure among the Irish, Italians, Jews, and Blacks in an American City, 1880–1935* (Cambridge: Cambridge University Press, 1988), 38–40. Racial discrimination largely negated the cash value of secondary schooling for blacks; Perlmann noted (p. 197) that "even blacks who received higher grades than whites could expect no diminution of the race handicap on jobs." For additional evidence of the economic value of

secondary schooling, see Reed Ueda, *Avenues to Adulthood: The Origins of the High School and Social Mobility in an American Suburb* (Cambridge: Cambridge University Press, 1987). Labaree found that, once admitted, working-class children did as well as middle-class children in Philadelphia's Central High School; see David F. Labaree, *The Making of an American High School: The Credentials Market and the Central High School of Philadelphia, 1838–1939* (New Haven: Yale University Press, 1988).

12. Although entry into nineteenth-century high schools was restricted by entrance examinations and graduation by opportunity costs, Vinovskis found that 19 percent of children in Essex County, Mass., in 1860 attended either a public high school or a comparable private academy; see Maris A. Vinovskis, "Have We Underestimated the Extent of Antebellum High School Attendance?" *History of Education Quarterly* 28 (1988): 551–67.

13. Committee on the Reorganization of Secondary Education, *Cardinal Principles of Secondary Education*, U.S. Department of the Interior, Bureau of Education, bulletin 1918, no. 35 (Washington, D.C.: Government Printing Office, 1917), 31.

14. Edward A. Krug, *The Shaping of the American High School*. Vol. 2, 1920–1941 (Madison: University of Wisconsin Press, 1972), 170n2.

15. Paul Osterman, *Getting Started: The Youth Labor Market* (Cambridge: MIT Press, 1980), 54–57.

16. Ileen A. DeVault, *Sons and Daughters of Labor: Class and Clerical Work in Turn-of-the-Century Pittsburgh* (Ithaca: Cornell University Press, 1990), 9–23, 102–3.

17. Paul Douglas, "What Is Happening to the White-Collar Job Market?" *System: The Magazine of Business* 50 (1926): 720–21.

18. Walter Licht, *Getting Work: Philadelphia, 1840–1950* (Cambridge: Harvard University Press, 1992), 71–72, 94–96. School-based commercial classes especially worked to the advantage of girls, for employers were more reluctant to give on-the-job training to females, who, employers feared, were more likely than boys to leave employment. See Susan B. Carter and Mark Prus, "The Labor Market and the American High School Girl, 1890–1928," *Journal of Economic History* 42 (1982): 163–71.

19. Douglas, "White-Collar Job Market," 720–21.

20. George S. Counts, *The Selective Character of American Secondary Education* (Chicago: University of Chicago Press, 1922), 150, 156, 155.

21. Charles Prosser and Charles R. Allen, *Vocational Education in a Democracy* (New York: Century Co., 1925), 53; Charles Prosser and W. A. O'Leary, *Short-Unit Courses for Wage-Earners and a Factory School Experiment*, U.S. Department of Labor, Bureau of Labor Statistics, bulletin 1915, no. 159 (Washington, D.C.: Government Printing Office, April 1915), 17.

22. David Tyack, *The One Best System: A History of American Urban Education* (Cambridge: Harvard University Press, 1974), 190; U.S. National Center for Education Statistics, *Digest of Education Statistics, 1988*, 190.

23. David B. Tyack, "Ways of Seeing: An Essay in the History of Compulsory Schooling," *Harvard Education Review* 46 (1976): 355–89.

24. Ensign, *Compulsory School Attendance*, 63.

25. Robert S. and Helen M. Lynd, *Middletown: A Study in American Culture* (New York: Harcourt, Brace & Co., 1929), 183–85, 211–12.

26. Ibid., 80, 185–87.

27. Robert L. Hampel, *The Last Little Citadel: American High Schools since 1940* (Boston: Houghton Mifflin, 1986).

28. August B. Hollingshead, *Elmtown's Youth: The Impact of Social Class on Adolescents* (New York: John Wiley, 1949), 354. Hollingshead's class IV corresponds roughly to the usual conception of the working class, people who are poor but who hold steady work and who manifest pride in their homes. His class V is an underclass composed of demoralized occasional workers, people who are looked down on as "scum" by all the other social classes of Elmtown.

29. Ibid., 329.

30. Ibid., chaps. 13–14.

31. Ibid., 349.

32. Educational Policies Commission, *Education for ALL American Youth: A Further Look* (Washington, D.C.: National Education Association, 1952), 190.

33. Osterman, *Getting Started*, 69–70.

34. Maxine Davis, *The Lost Generation: A Portrait of American Youth Today* (New York: Macmillan Co., 1936), 187.

35. Howard M. Bell, *Youth Tell Their Story: A Study of the Conditions and Attitudes of Young People in Maryland between the Ages of 16 and 24* (Washington, D.C.: American Council on Education, 1938), 187.

36. Howard M. Bell, *Matching Youth to Jobs: A Study in Occupational Adjustment* (Washington, D.C.: American Council on Education, 1941), 22.

37. Bell, *Youth Tell Their Story*, 98.

38. Educational Policies Commission, *Education and Economic Well-being in American Democracy* (Washington, D.C.: National Education Association, 1940), 121, 128–32, 119–21.

39. Ibid., 158, 131.

40. President's Commission on Higher Education, *Higher Education for American Democracy*. 6 vols. (Washington, D.C.: Government Printing Office, 1948), vol. 1.

41. James Gilbert, *A Cycle of Outrage: America's Reaction to the Juvenile Delinquent in the 1950s* (New York: Oxford University Press, 1986), 19.

42. John Modell, *Into One's Own: From Youth to Adulthood in the United States* (Berkeley and Los Angeles: University of California Press, 1989), 166.

43. Ibid., 168.

44. Educational Policies Commission, *Education for ALL American Youth* (Washington, D.C.: National Education Association, 1945), 10.

45. Educational Policies Commission, *Education for ALL American Youth: A Further Look*, 183–202, 327.

46. "Dropout Tragedies," *Life*, 2 May 1960, 106A–113; "A Hopeful Second Chance," *Life*, 9 May 1960, 102–9.

47. David Segel, *Frustration in Adolescent Youth*, Federal Security Agency, Office of Education, bulletin 1951, no. 1 (Washington, D.C.: Government Printing Office, 1951), 43–60.

48. Gilbert, *A Cycle of Outrage*, chap. 4.

49. Segel, *Frustration in Adolescent Youth*, 25–26.

50. Educational Policies Commission, *Education for ALL American Youth: A Further Look*, 360.

51. Ibid., 358. World War II also gave rise to the general educational development (GED) tests. These were the brainchild of Cornelius P. Turner, a Massachusetts school superintendent who joined the navy during the war. Assigned to the U.S. Armed Forces Institute in Madison, Wisconsin, Turner developed the GED tests so that soldiers who lacked a high school diploma could qualify for the institute's college-level correspondence courses by demonstrating that they had acquired the equivalent of a high school diploma. After the war the tests were extended to civilians, but it was not until 1959 that the number of nonveteran adults taking the tests exceeded the number of veterans; see Jackson Toby and David J. Armor, "Carrots or Sticks for High School Dropouts?" *Public Interest*, no. 106 (1992): 87–89.

52. Abraham Tannenbaum, *Dropout or Diploma: A Socio-educational Analysis of Early School Withdrawal* (New York: Teachers College Press, 1966), 1.

53. Osterman, *Getting Started*, 104. Osterman noted that the percentage of youth eighteen to twenty-four years old who were enrolled in school rose from 14.2 percent in 1950 to 31.1 percent in 1970. This development probably dampened the effect of the baby boom, for students have lower rates of labor force participation than do nonstudents.

54. Tannenbaum, *Dropout or Diploma*, 3.

55. Ibid., 19–21.

56. Garth Mangum and John A. Walsh, *A Decade of Manpower Development and Training* (Salt Lake City: Olympus Press, 1973), 49–50.

57. Mangum and Walsh, *Manpower Development and Training*, 50.

58. Dennis Nystrom and G. Keith Bayne, *Occupation and Career Legislation*, 2d ed. (Indianapolis: Bobbs-Merrill, 1979), 44–46.

59. Lloyd Ulman, "The Uses and Limits of Manpower Policy" in *The Great Society: Lessons for the Future*, ed. Eli Ginzberg and Robert M. Solow (New York: Basic Books, 1974), 95–99. Andrew Brimmer found that blacks accounted for more than half of the enrollees in the Job Corps, Neighborhood Youth Corps, and similar Great Society programs; see Brimmer, "Economic Developments in the Black Community" in *The Great Society*, 146–65.

60. Osterman, *Getting Started*, 68; Beatrice Reubens, "Vocational Education for ALL in High School?" in *Work and the Quality of Life*, ed. James O'Toole (Cambridge: MIT Press, 1974), 293–337; Licht, *Getting Work*, 92–93.

61. Douglas Adkins, "The American Educated Labor Force" in *Higher Education and the Labor Market*, ed. Margaret S. Gordon (New York: McGraw-Hill, 1974), 111–45.

62. Glen G. Cain, "The Challenge of Segmented Labor Market Theories to Orthodox Theory: A Survey," *Journal of Economic Literature* 14 (December 1976): 1217.

63. Osterman, *Getting Started*, 22.

64. Lester Thurow, "Education and Economic Equality," *Public Interest*, no. 28 (1972): 69–70.

65. Ibid., 72.

66. Ivar Berg, *Education and Jobs: The Great Training Robbery* (New York: Praeger, 1970), 85–104.

67. Adkins, "The American Educated Labor Force," 111–45; V. Lane Rawlins and Lloyd Ulman, "The Utilization of College-trained Manpower in the United States" in *Higher Education and the Labor Market*, 232. Adkins noted that in the 1930s, when demand for college-educated manpower fell sharply, no corresponding decline in the pool of college graduates occurred. He postulated that rises in educational attainment have been driven primarily by the values of parents and children rather than by observation of the labor market and, by implication, that levels of attainment will respond only slowly to changes in job requirements. Rawlins and Ulman advanced an essentially similar view.

68. Rawlins and Ulman, "Utilization of College-trained Manpower," 232.

69. Thurow, "Education and Economic Equality," 79.

70. Toby and Armor, "Carrots or Sticks," 76–90.

12 RHETORIC AND REALITY:

THE HIGH SCHOOL CURRICULUM

DAVID ANGUS AND JEFFREY MIREL

I n September 1989, President George Bush and the nation's governors issued a statement committing themselves to revitalizing American public education by establishing "clear national performance goals, goals that will make us internationally competitive."[1] Two of these goals focus on changing the basic curriculum in American schools to realize substantial educational gains by the year 2000. Goal 3 declares that "American students will leave grades four, eight, and twelve having demonstrated competency in challenging subject matter including English, mathematics, science, history and geography; and every school in America will ensure that all students learn to use their minds well, so they may be prepared for responsible citizenship, further learning, and productive employment." Goal 4 states that "U.S. students will be the first in the world in science and math achievement."[2]

The presidential and gubernatorial commitment to these national performance goals is both historic and unprecedented, but this is hardly the first time that national leaders have focused their attention on the nation's schools and sought to alter the school curriculum substantially. In this chapter we analyze the historic significance of the current reform efforts represented by goals 3 and 4 and assess their relationship to previous attempts to reshape secondary education since the end of World War II.[3] Educational historians generally have described the past half century of curricular reforms in terms of sharp swings between two diametrically opposite philosophical and educational poles, often represented as a recurring debate between proponents of the Committee of Ten report (1893) and advocates of the *Cardinal Principles of Secondary Education* (1918). In this model, the Committee of Ten position argues that "all high school students should be educated with equal seriousness in the great areas of human knowledge [i.e. traditional academic subjects], and that occupational decisions should be put off until after graduation, lest students from poorer homes lose out." The *Cardinal Principles of Secondary Education* position, on the other hand, maintains that the focus of the high school should be on the "nature and the needs of students" rather than on the often difficult and arid demands of academic disciplines.[4] From this perspective "education was considered not so much a training and disciplining of the mind as a process of developing social and civic awareness and responsibility."[5]

Indeed, historians who agree on little else accept that model of curriculum change as particularly useful in describing all of the curriculum reform efforts up to and including the current campaign to establish a core curriculum for all students. We begin this essay with a brief overview of that picture of reform and counter-reform. In the second section, however, we challenge that conventional swinging pendulum model of high school curriculum change through analyses of a series of national surveys conducted largely by the U.S. Office of Education. In the third section, we focus on science and mathematics course taking by analyzing additional surveys of enrollments in those subject areas. Finally, we assess the curriculum reforms embodied in the national goals and argue that, despite similarities to earlier back-to-basics movements, this new effort seems to mark a major break with past campaigns in two respects—in its recommended core course of study for all students and its setting of clear empirical standards for knowing if and when the reform has been a success.

CURRICULUM CHANGE IN AMERICAN SECONDARY EDUCATION, 1945–1992: THE CONVENTIONAL WISDOM

Almost every account of the modern history of the American high school describes curricular changes in terms of dramatic swings between two diametrically opposed educational and philosophical poles.[6] To demonstrate precisely how our work differs from that of other scholars, we begin by presenting this conventional model. Historians generally agree that sometime in the 1920s, as high school enrollments rose dramatically, the curricular pendulum swung away from the vision of the Committee of Ten toward that of the Cardinal Principles. High schools increased both the number and types of courses they offered, introduced curricular tracks that provided students with vocational programs that required fewer academic classes for graduation, and essentially began to shift their focus from the "needs of society" to the "needs of youth."[7] A sharp drop in educational resources during the 1930s caused a brief hiatus in this trend, even in the face of rising enrollments, as schools were forced to cut offerings in vocational education, art, and music. During World War II, despite protests from such defenders of the academic tradition as William C. Bagley and Isaac L. Kandel, the trend toward programs that stressed the practical resumed apace as educators joined the war effort by emphasizing vocational education and preinduction training over academic course work in the high schools.[8]

After the war the debate over the high school curriculum revived with the publication of two new studies, Harvard University's *General Education in a Free Society*, which reaffirmed many of the ideas espoused by the Committee of Ten, and the Educational Policy Commission's *Education for ALL American Youth*, which called for a still stronger commitment to the practical curriculums of the Cardinal Principles. Amid this debate, the U.S. Office of Education's Division of Vocational Education invited a group of educators to Washington to discuss the growing number of high school students believed by many school administrators and teachers to be ill-suited for either the college preparatory or the vocational track. The high point of this conference was the Prosser resolution, a ringing reaffirmation of the ideals of the Cardinal Principles.[9] The resolution declared that

> it is the belief of this conference that, with the aid of this report in its final form, the vocational school of a community will be able better to prepare 20 percent of the youth of secondary school age for entrance upon desirable skilled occupations; and that the high school will continue to prepare another 20 percent for entrance to college. We do not believe that the remaining 60 percent of our youth of secondary school age will receive the life adjustment training they need and to which they are entitled as American citizens—unless and until the administrators of public education with the assistance of the vocational education leaders formulate a similar program for this group.

In essence, this life adjustment education "consisted of guidance and education in citizenship, home and family life, use of leisure, health, tools of learning, work experience and occupational adjustment."[10]

Educators enthusiastically embraced this program and, historians contend, by the mid-1950s life adjustment education had been adopted in "thousands of schools throughout the land."[11] This triumph, however, did not go uncontested. As early as 1949, Mortimer Smith published *And Madly Teach*, which denounced the deterioration of academic standards in secondary education and called on the schools to reassume their "historic role as moral and intellectual teacher." Smith's book was only the first in a series of impassioned attacks by proponents of the traditional academic curriculum on the changing character of the high school curriculum. By far the most influential of these works, Arthur Bestor's *Educational Wastelands*, demanded that American high schools return to the teaching of "disciplined intelligence" and proclaimed that "schools exist to teach *something* and that this something is the power to think."[12]

Clashes between these critics and the defenders of the educational status quo dominated both the scholarly literature and, frequently, the popular press in the mid-1950s. Nothing, however, increased the intensity nor broadened the scope of these debates more than the launch of the Sputnik satellite by the Soviet Union in October 1957. Beyond its clear military and technological significance, Sputnik had a profound influence on the great educational debates of the mid-1950s. The successful launch seemed to indicate that the Soviet Union had surpassed the United States technologically, a situation that cast serious doubts on the condition and quality of American education. Indeed, Sputnik seemed to give credence to the arguments of such critics as Smith and Bestor that life adjustment and similar programs had led to a serious decline in the quality of secondary schools. Other critics of the public schools, such as Admiral Hyman Rickover, took these arguments farther and maintained that the deterioration of secondary education had contributed to our inability to compete successfully with the Soviet Union.[13]

In the late 1950s, as a result of pre- and post-Sputnik criticism, historians conventionally agree that the curricular pendulum swung back toward greater emphasis on rigorous academic standards with renewed interest in the quality of math, science, and foreign language education. In 1958, the federal government threw its weight behind these efforts by passing the National Defense Education Act, which directed money toward improving achievement in math, science, and foreign languages. In addition, early in 1959 James B. Conant, former president of Harvard University, published a best-selling book, *The American High School Today*, which called for secondary schools to reestablish strong academic curriculums and to sort students more efficiently by ability. Schools could thus train the best and brightest to realize their full potential while at the same time preparing the majority of students for suitable careers. In the next few years, these efforts to improve academic standards were aided by groups of leading scientists and scholars who received grants from the National Science Foundation (NSF) to produce new science and math curriculums, textbooks, workbooks, and other instructional aids, all designed to provide the most up-to-date knowledge in easily accessible formats. In all, these developments led historians such as Robert Church and Michael Sedlak to maintain that "the fifties and the sixties saw as profound a shift in thinking about education as had been seen since the Progressive era. The schools refocused on subject matter and intellectual discipline."[14]

This resurgence of commitment to academic excellence, however, was relatively short-lived. In less than a decade, such social and political developments as the civil rights movement, the War on Poverty, urban riots, student protests, the youth counterculture, and the long, bitter controversy engendered by the war in Vietnam combined to convince many civic and educational leaders that the previous reform effort was, at best, too limited and, at worst, irrelevant to the larger crises facing the nation. In the late 1950s, the schools had been blamed for the failure to keep pace technologically with the Soviet Union and had been recruited as a key institution in the campaign to regain our scientific and military superiority. Ten years later new national crises stimulated a similar process as the schools again were blamed, this time for contributing to the nation's problems of race, poverty, and youthful alienation. As in the 1950s, the schools were also placed in the forefront of institutions designed to ameliorate those problems. By the late 1960s, as Diane Ravitch noted, the "educational pendulum began to swing back to a revival of progressivism."[15]

Like the first wave of progressive reformers in the early years of the twentieth century, these latter day progressives sought to transform society through educational innovation. Inspired by the works of such authors as A. S. Neill, whose book *Summerhill* described a school built upon the belief that children were "innately wise," reformers in the late 1960s and early 1970s attempted to uproot the rigid, academic, and bureaucratic system that they believed was destroying the spirit of the young and contributing to their widespread alienation.[16]

Rejecting the previous reform effort that focused on raising standards and improving the teaching of content courses, this new reform campaign attempted to implement sweeping changes in every aspect of American education, including breaking down the hierarchical relationship between teachers and students, eliminating distinctions between traditional subject areas, and placing experiential learning on a par with book learning. The spearhead of this reform campaign was the open classroom movement, which rested upon literally tearing down the walls of classrooms to create expansive learning environments in which teachers facilitated student learning by guiding young people to skills and knowledge rather than lecturing them into submission. Like earlier reforms based on student needs, such as life adjustment, these innovations placed a premium on making subjects relevant to students and providing students with a wide array of choices in determining their education. Few public schools adopted the most radical of these innovations, but many districts across the country adopted important aspects of this reform movement, particularly in terms of increasing the number of electives available for students and offering courses that appealed to students' interests.[17]

By the mid 1970s, this reform movement was running on empty. There was growing public dissatisfaction with the condition of American schools, especially over what appeared to be the collapse of order and discipline within many schools and a decline in achievement levels of unprecedented proportions. In the public mind, the most telling evidence was a steady decline since 1963 in the average scores on both the verbal and mathematical sections of the Scholastic Aptitude Test and the similar (though less steady) fall over the same period in the composite scores on the American College Test. By 1975, there was a growing public demand for a return to basics, in terms of both traditional discipline and attention to fundamental academic subjects.[18]

In addition, policy makers in the federal government added their voice to the growing chorus of discontent. In the early 1970s, the Nixon administration, concerned over evidence of declining productivity in the nation's economy, launched Career Education, an ambitious, federally subsidized program designed to introduce students to "the world of work" by familiarizing them with career opportunities and helping them prepare for employment while still in school. Interestingly, Career Education, like the back-to-basics movement, also represented an attack on the amorphous general track in which most of the "student needs" courses were found. In his first report to Congress in 1971, U.S. Commissioner of Education Sidney P. Marland declared, "We must eliminate anything in our curriculum which is unresponsive to either of these goals [higher education or employment], particularly the high school anachronism called the 'general curriculum,' a false compromise between the college preparatory curriculum and realistic career development."[19]

Throughout the late 1970s and early 1980s, concerns about the condition of education in the United States continued to grow. In April 1983, the curricular trend represented by the back-to-basics movement received an enormous push in the form of a brief but powerful document published by the U.S. Department of Education, *A Nation at Risk*. In ringing terms, this report warned that "the educational foundations of our society are being eroded by a rising tide of mediocrity that threatens our very future as a Nation and a people . . . If any unfriendly foreign power had attempted to impose on America the mediocre educational performance that exists today, we might well have viewed it as an act of war." Citing such evidence as the unbroken decline of SAT scores and denouncing such common aspects of American high schools as the "cafeteria style curriculum," the authors of *A Nation at Risk* issued an educational call to arms.[20]

The report had an immediate and profound effect on educational debates. Indeed, as early as June 1983 the *New York Times* commented that *A Nation at Risk* had pushed education "to the forefront of political debate with an urgency not felt since the Soviet Satellite shook American confidence in its public schools in 1957."[21] Some recent commentators noted that many of the recommendations for improving American schools that followed *A Nation at Risk*, such as bolstering curriculum standards, raising high school graduation requirements, and improving teacher certification programs, seemed to have been recycled directly from the reports that appeared soon after the launch of Sputnik.[22]

Certainly, one area in which such comparisons seem valid is in the effort by post–*A Nation at Risk* reformers to overturn what they believed were the worst abuses of the previous wave of reform, especially the proliferation of course options for high school students. By late 1986, for example, forty-five states and the District of Columbia had raised their high school graduation requirements, forty-two states had increased math requirements, and thirty-four states had bolstered science requirements. In all, the sweeping nature of these changes and the rapid rate at which they were adopted seemed to make the current effort the most successful of any modern curriculum reform campaign.[23]

As we noted, this picture of dramatic pendulum swings in a series of great debates over the American curriculum is widely accepted by historians. We do not take issue with this general description of the debates or with the accuracy of the positions attributed to key actors and interest groups. The key question is whether these rhetorical battles actually led to the curriculum reforms attributed to them. Historians have made claims about curriculum change based largely on what people said about curriculum reform. Few historians, however, have made any attempt to analyze and interpret changes in the course-taking patterns of American high school students that have been implied by the great curriculum debates. This failure to seek empirical support for the dominant swinging pendulum model of interpretation is particularly surprising in light of the fact that the U.S. Office of Education has been collecting and publishing data on the course-taking behavior of American secondary students for nearly a century.[24] We now turn to an analysis of these data in an attempt to assess the validity of the conventional wisdom as a description of the reality of high school curriculum reform.

SUBJECT ENROLLMENT CHANGES IN AMERICAN EDUCATION, 1928–1987: INTERPRETING THE DATA

The U.S. Office of Education has shown an interest in the course enrollments of American high school students since the late nineteenth century. Enrollments in Latin and Greek were collected and reported in the 1880s, and by 1890 the list of courses had expanded to include mathematics, science, history, modern foreign languages, and so forth. This data collection on course enrollments became an annual series that continued as such until 1906. Similar surveys were carried out in 1910 and 1915, but all of these surveys reported national enrollments only for a limited list of subjects and did not fully capture the vast curriculum expansion that was actually occurring during the opening decades of the new century.[25] A much longer listing of subjects and a more detailed report of findings characterized the 1922 survey and the subsequent surveys of 1928, 1934, 1949, 1961, and 1973, the last of the series.[26] Between 1922 and 1973, the number of distinct courses reported to the USOE rose from about 175 titles to over 2,100.[27] Although it is impossible to sort out the extent to which this increase represented new courses or merely variations or elaborations on older themes, its magnitude makes it difficult to avoid the impression of curriculum expansion running amok.[28]

These surveys provide historians of the American high school with a series of increasingly detailed and trustworthy snapshots of high school course enrollments spanning the years from 1890 to 1973. In addition, researchers under contract to the National Center for Education Statistics have gathered similar data, usually from student transcripts, which can be linked to the earlier studies to provide a sweeping picture of high school curriculum development in the twentieth century. Unfortunately, these data have rarely been utilized by scholars in describing the modern history of secondary education generally or the high school curriculum specifically. Indeed, almost all of the works upon which the conventional wisdom rests have ignored these data completely.[29]

Table 12.1 presents the USOE data from 1928 to 1973 as well as data from a 1982 transcript study. It details changes in the relative share of high school course enrollments in different subject fields, compares the traditional academic subjects with nonacademic subjects, and includes the average number of courses taken per student for each survey year. Perhaps the most striking thing about this table is the degree to which it challenges the conventional account of sharp pendulum swings between the opposing curricular poles. Contrary to the conventional picture of reform and counter-reform, these data reveal one long pendulum swing toward nonacademic subjects that continues for four decades. Despite the fierce rhetorical battles about curriculum between the 1930s and the 1970s, for us the most impressive feature of these data is not change but constancy. The data reveal a steady drop in the academic share of subject enrollments that begins in 1928 and continues unabated until at least 1961. This drop includes a sharp decline in the study of foreign languages and more modest declines in mathematics and science. The growth of the nonacademic share of the curriculum can be gauged by one startling fact: in 1910, the share of high school work devoted to *each* of the five basic academic subjects— English, foreign language, mathematics, science, and history—enrolled more students than *all* of the nonacademic subjects combined. Moreover, these data do not reveal the more subtle changes within academic subjects, in which English courses were reorganized to relate "literature and life" and history and government courses were transformed into the social studies.[30] Finally, the decline in the share of academic subjects is offset by a huge increase in physical education enrollments between 1928 and 1934, an increase that continued steadily thereafter.

In addition to undercutting the swinging pendulum model of curricu-

TABLE 12.1 Percentage Distribution of Subject Field Enrollments in U.S. Public Secondary Schools, Grades 9 through 12: 1928–1982

Subject Field	1928	1934	1949	1961	1973	1982
Academic						
English	19.1%	18.6%	18.4%	17.9%	20.1%	19.9%
Foreign language	9.5	6.9	4.0	4.3	3.9	3.3
Mathematics	12.8	11.1	9.8	9.9	9.2	11.2
Science	10.6	10.1	9.7	9.3	10.0	9.4
Social studies	15.2	15.5	17.4	15.6	16.2	16.9
Computers						0.4
Nonacademic						
Industrial arts	4.0	3.5	3.7	3.7	4.2	3.4
Trade and industry	0.6	0.7	1.2	0.7	0.5	2.3
Home economics	3.3	3.3	4.3	3.6	3.5	3.4
Business	11.4	11.3	10.5	8.9	6.8	6.7
Health and PE[a]	4.9	11.5	12.4	15.9	17.5	15.9
Music	5.2	5.0	5.4	6.6	4.7	3.1
Art	2.3	1.7	1.6	2.5	3.0	3.5
Agriculture	0.7	0.7	1.2	1.0	0.4	0.5
Other	0.4	0.2	0.4	0.2	0.2	
Academic	67.2	62.2	59.3	57.0	59.4	61.1
Nonacademic	32.8	37.9	40.7	43.0	40.7	39.0
Enrollments per Student	5.02	5.09	5.61	6.42	7.00	6.97

Sources: Recoded and adapted from U.S. Office of Education (USOE), *Biennial Survey, 1926–28*; USOE, *Offerings and Registrations, 1933–34*; USOE, *Biennial Survey, 1948–50*; Wright, *Subject Offerings, 1960–61*; Osterndorf and Horn, *Course Offerings, 1972–73*; West, Diodato, and Sandberg, *A Trend Study.*
[a]Includes safety, driver's training, and ROTC.

lum change, table 12.1 challenges several other assumptions widely held by historians of the American high school. First, as we have argued elsewhere, high school curriculum changes were more rapid during the Depression years than at any other period before or since. The drop in the academic share of course enrollments was steeper between 1928 and 1934 than at any other time. We believe the impetus for that change was the sharp slope of increase in high school enrollments, higher than in any previous period, and a significant shift in the social-class makeup of the high school population. In addition, the drop in the academic share and the rise of nonacademic personal development courses in the 1930s seem to indicate that the life adjustment movement did not initiate major curriculum changes but merely justified and rationalized trends that were already under way.[31]

Second, contrary to much recent historical interpretation, the relative decline in academic enrollments was not matched by increases in vocational enrollments, except perhaps during the brief period of World War II. Rather, a large proportion of the curricular shift is accounted for by increases in such personal development courses as health, physical education, and driver's training.[32] We believe that this development was directly related to the negative assessment of both the academic and the vocational abilities of the new waves of students entering the high schools in the 1930s and after the war. Curriculum theorists from this era, such as Harl R. Douglas, routinely urged educators to design new programs to meet the needs of these new students, many of whom were "children of mediocre or inferior ability who lack interest in abstract and academic materials." What many historians fail to recognize, but the data in table 12.1 indicate, is that these students were tracked away not only from academic courses but also from vocational courses.[33]

Third, the declining share of academic courses and the growth of personal development courses continued unabated until at least 1961. In other words, it appears that the demands for increased academic coursework during the Sputnik era debates had relatively little effect on overall student course-taking patterns. Last, it appears from table 12.1 that all of these historic developments were reversed some time after 1961, a development that we will return to later.

The data in table 12.1 seem strongly to support Arthur Bestor and other critics of the 1950s, who argued that the academic seriousness of the nation's high schools had been profoundly undercut since at least the late 1920s. Defenders of the high schools, on the other hand, routinely countered these arguments by pointing out that, during the very period that the critics identified as the years of decline, the actual numbers of young people studying academic subjects rose dramatically. To take but one example, while 84 percent of high school students were enrolled in a foreign language course in 1910, this amounted to only 739,000 students. In 1949, the percentage had fallen to a mere 22 percent, but this was 1.2 million students. Table 12.2 displays the actual enrollments in the same subject fields over the same years as table 12.1. Except for foreign language, enrollments in all subject fields showed increases at every data collection point between 1928 and 1973, and even foreign language enrollments increased in every period but 1934 to 1949.[34]

The two different perspectives on the same data in tables 12.1 and 12.2 point up once more the sharp polarities in ways of viewing the purposes of the high school. If, as the 1893 Committee of Ten supposed, certain subjects are of more lasting value than others and if these are the subjects represented above as academic, then long-term declines in the *proportions* of students that are studying these subjects represent declines in educational

TABLE 12.2 Subject Field Enrollments (in thousands) in U.S. Public
Secondary Schools, Grades 9 through 12: 1928–1982

Subject Field	1928	1934	1949	1961	1973	1982
Total 9–12 Enrollment	2,897	4,497	5,399	8,219	13,438	12,661
Academic						
English	2,776	4,266	5,576	9,438	18,911	17,716
Foreign language	1,377	1,575	1,200	2,293	3,659	2,953
Mathematics	1,859	2,532	2,958	5,224	8,608	9,850
Science	1,534	2,308	2,944	4,908	9,414	8,278
Social studies	2,213	3,540	5,265	8,226	15,224	15,008
Computers						344
Nonacademic						
Industrial arts	285	798	1,127	1,944	3,921	2,980
Trade and industry	92	158	369	365	484	1,874
Home economics	477	750	1,305	1,901	3,249	3,024
Business	1,656	2,588	3,194	4,706	6,410	5,874
Health and physical education	713	2,625	3,747	8,395	16,460	14,057
Music	754	1,149	1,625	3,473	4,461	2,733
Art	340	394	486	1,335	2,795	3,061
Agriculture	106	159	364	505	346	420
Other	62	38	124	91	103	80

Sources: Same as in Table 12.1.

quality. But if, as the proponents of the Cardinal Principles seemed to be asserting, every increase in the numbers of students attending high school also represents a significant decrease in the academic abilities of the student body, then a proportionate shift away from the academic subjects is fully justified.[35] In fact, from this perspective, this shift never seemed to be rapid enough or great enough to satisfy fully the needs of the expanding secondary school student body, and this seeming insatiability of demand for more and more courses explains why the critics of these trends were not much mollified by mere increases in enrollments in science, math, and so forth.

In addition, as John F. Latimer, one of the most perceptive critics of the high school in the 1950s, argued, focusing on the increase in numbers rather than the decrease in percentages is to accept a split-level education. Because educators believed that the majority of new students were less able than previous generations, they shunted them into less challenging courses rather than searching for new and more effective ways to teach these students traditional academic subjects. This belief shaped the direction of most high school curriculum reform after the 1930s and undergirded the life adjustment movement. As table 12.2 reveals, while academic course enrollments increased, so did enrollments in less rigorous, nonacademic courses, courses that proponents of greater academic rigor did not think should be in the curriculum at all.

The terms of the debate about the high school curriculum, however, sharply altered in the early 1970s, when high school enrollment growth slowed; it finally began to drop in 1976. Instead of the constant enrollment increases in all subjects which served to soften the claims of those who decried the decline in academic course taking, there were now enrollment declines in nearly all subject fields. At the same time, however, the long-running drop in the academic share of course taking was reversed, and by 1982, even before *A Nation at Risk* appeared, the academic share had recovered to about the level of the mid-1930s (see table 12.1). Under these conditions, the debate took on a new urgency, and the question of *proportionate* enrollments, as contrasted to numerical increases, gathered more force.

Table 12.3 highlights what happened when the nation's aggregate high school enrollment reached its peak in 1976 and began to decline. This table

TABLE 12.3 Percentage of Public Secondary School Students (Grades 9 through 12) Enrolled in Subject Fields: 1928–1982

Subject Field	1928	1934	1949	1961	1973	1982
Academic						
English	95.8%	94.9%	103.3%	114.8%	140.7%	139.0%
Foreign language	47.5	35.0	22.2	27.9	27.2	23.3
Mathematics	64.2	56.3	54.8	63.6	64.1	77.8
Science	53.0	51.3	54.5	59.7	70.1	65.4
Social studies	76.4	78.8	97.5	100.1	113.6	118.0
Computer science						2.7
Nonacademic						
Industrial arts	20.2	17.8	20.9	23.6	29.2	23.5
Trade and industry	3.2	3.5	6.8	4.4	3.6	15.7
Home economics	16.5	16.7	24.2	23.4	23.1	23.9
Business	57.2	57.6	59.2	57.3	47.7	46.4
Health and physical education	24.6	58.4	69.4	102.1	122.5	111.0
Music	26.0	25.5	30.1	42.3	33.2	21.6
Art	11.7	8.6	9.0	16.2	20.8	24.2
Agriculture	3.7	3.5	6.7	6.1	2.6	3.3
Other	2.1	0.9	2.3	1.1	0.8	1.5

Sources: Same as in table 12.1.

displays the percentage of all students in grades 9 through 12 who were actually enrolled in, for example, an English or a mathematics course during each data collection year from 1928 to 1982.[36] Looked at in this way, some of the trends are consistent with those mentioned earlier, for example, the rise in enrollments in health and physical education, but others appear to be quite different. This table shows a clear effect of the 1950s concern over science, math, and foreign language. Not only the numbers of high school students enrolled in these fields but also the proportion of students increased.[37] Surprisingly, however, the growth in actual percentage enrollments in these subjects reversed over the next decade, the very period in which the new math and science curriculum designs sponsored by the National Science Foundation were being implemented in many of the nation's high schools.[38]

Another trend that appears in table 12.3 suggests that the career education movement of the Nixon years was quite effective. This movement was aimed at strengthening the vocational preparation function of the schools and focusing the attention of young people on the "world of work." It shows in these data as a dramatic increase in the proportion of high schoolers enrolled in courses in the trade and industry category, from around 4 percent to over 15 percent in less than a decade. Part of this was a shift of the orientation of courses from nonvocational industrial arts and home economics to courses with a specific vocational orientation; even when these three fields are combined, however, there was still an increase from a total of 57 percent of students enrolled in 1973 to 63 percent in 1982.

One other point to note about the trends shown in table 12.3 is the increase in the proportion of students enrolled in courses in English and social studies. We believe these are only apparent increases, artifacts of the way the USOE data were tabulated and displayed. As they are presented in tables 12.1 to 12.3, every course enrollment, regardless of the length of the course, is counted as a unit. This means, for example, that a high school offering a series of one-semester English courses such as American Literature and British Literature will appear to have twice the enrollments in English of a high school offering only year-long courses such as English 1, English 2, English 3, and English 4. In the above tables, then, subject fields in which many year-long courses have been divided into semester-long or shorter courses with different titles, such as English and social studies, are shown to have somewhat exaggerated enrollments compared to fields, such as foreign language and mathematics, in which these divisions have not occurred. This is also the most likely explanation of the increase in course enrollments per student shown in table 12.1. Rather than students in 1973 taking 40 percent more courses than students in 1928, it is far more

TABLE 12.4 Ratios of Enrollments in Year-Long Courses
to Enrollments in Semester-Long or Shorter Courses
by Subject Fields in U.S. Public Secondary Schools,
Grades 9 through 12: 1960, 1972

Subject	1960	1972
Academic		
English	93/7	63/37
Foreign language	100/0	95/5
Mathematics	90/10	91/9
Science	97/3	89/11
Social studies	81/19	58/42
Nonacademic		
Industrial arts	78/22	67/33
Trade and industry	90/10	81/19
Home economics	84/16	49/51
Business	88/12	75/25
Health and physical education	75/25	59/41
Music	100/0	79/21
Art	68/32	66/34
Agriculture	96/4	89/11

Sources: Wright, *Subject Offerings;* Osterndorf and Horn, *Course Offerings.*

likely that 20 percent of year-long courses had been split into semester-long offerings over those forty-five years.

Table 12.4 illustrates the ratios of year-long courses to semester-long or shorter courses in the fourteen subject fields for 1960–61 and 1972–73. It not only shows a significant shift toward shorter courses over the decade of the 1960s, but also illustrates that this development was quite uneven across the subject fields, with English and social studies leading the way in the academic subjects and home economics and health and physical education leading in the nonacademic subjects.

Another way to control for this distortion is to consider changes in credits, rather than course enrollments.[39] A data array based on these measures would partly rectify the distortion just described, since half-year courses in basic subjects receive only half the credit of full-year courses. Furthermore, these data provide two additional clues to curriculum change: (1) whether the assignment of credit for particular subjects has changed over time and (2) just what courses the average student or selected students have studied over the course of a four-year high school education. Data of this kind have been supplied by a series of studies of the transcripts of various cohorts of graduating seniors.[40]

The first of these transcript studies was done by the USOE in 1958 at the height of the national anxiety over the launching of Sputnik. The most recent were sponsored by the NCES in 1987 and 1993 and were designed to check the effect on high school course-taking patterns of *A Nation at Risk*. These and other transcript data are displayed in table 12.5. One point to note is that, by credits, the academic share of the distribution is considerably greater than the academic share of course enrollments, but, as we suspected, the shares represented by English and social studies are smaller. In the more recent data, differences between the distribution of credits and the distribution of course enrollments narrow considerably. It was common in the 1940s and 1950s for high schools to grant no academic credit or only partial credit for courses in health, physical education, and music; by the 1970s, however, it had become common to grant full academic credit for such courses.[41] This is also the most likely explanation for the increase in the average total credits attained by students between 1958 and 1982. It is more likely that, rather than lengthening their school days or otherwise requiring more total coursework on the part of students, high schools have increasingly granted credit for formerly noncredit activities. Clifford Adelman, whose study of changes between 1969 and the mid-1970s controlled for differences between schools in the length of periods, also noted what he called "a devaluation of time in the academic curriculum" resulting from "conscious decisions to raise the amount of credit for nonacademic courses or to mandate wholly new courses in the secondary curriculum within the same total amount of school time."[42]

Whether one considers credit distribution or enrollment distribution, the trends are the same. But the two perspectives point to different conclusions about when the low point in academic enrollments was reached. Based on enrollments, the nadir is reached some time between 1961 and 1973; with respect to credits, it seems to be reached some time in the late 1970s. Possible reasons for this difference, as mentioned earlier, are the reorganization of full-year courses into courses of a half-year or less, the increase of mandated requirements in such nonacademic fields as health and physical education, and the granting of full academic credit toward graduation for such courses.

In all, despite the variety of interpretations supported by these data, several conclusions seem warranted. First, it is quite clear that the proportion of the high school curriculum claimed by the academic subjects, whether measured by course enrollments or credits, declined significantly from the late 1920s until some time in the late 1960s or early 1970s. The available data do not permit us to date the low point of academic enrollment share more precisely. Second, it is equally clear that, up to at least

TABLE 12.5 Percentage Distribution of Credits Earned by High School Graduates by Subject Field, 1958–1990

Subject Field	1958	1969	1973	1976–81	1982	1987	1990
Academic							
English	24.2%	20.3%	18.4%	18.8%	17.9%	17.5%	17.3%
Foreign language	6.0	5.8	4.8	3.6	4.9	6.3	6.6
Mathematics	12.7	12.7	10.6	11.5	12.0	12.9	13.1
Science	11.7	11.2	12.1	10.6	10.3	11.3	11.9
Social studies	18.9	16.5	16.5	15.4	14.6	14.5	14.6
Computer science	0.0	0.0	0.0	0.0	0.5	1.7	2.0
Nonacademic							
Industrial arts	3.2	1.9	0.7	2.1	6.1	5.0	4.7
Trade and industry	0.4	5.2	5.4	5.3	3.1	2.7	2.0
Home economics	4.0	1.3	3.8	2.6	4.8	4.0	3.6
Business	8.5	7.3	7.7	8.5	4.1	3.4	2.8
Health and physical education	4.4	9.1	11.6	10.5	9.1	8.6	8.8
Music	2.3	2.5	4.6	3.3			
Art	1.1	1.9	3.2	1.6	6.5	6.2	6.6
Agriculture	0.7	0.7	0.5	0.7	0.8	0.7	0.6
Other	2.1	4.1	0.1	5.0	5.4	5.1	4.4
Academic	73.5	66.5	62.4	59.9	60.2	64.2	65.5
Nonacademic	26.7	34.0	37.7	39.6	39.9	35.7	34.4
Average credits per graduate	15.54	NA	NA	NA	21.23	23.01	23.5

Sources: Adapted by the authors from Greer and Harbeck, *What High School Pupils Study;* Adelman, "Devaluation"; Osterndorf and Horn, *Course Offerings;* Westat, *Tabulations.*

1976, both the total numbers of students and the proportion of students taking courses in academic subjects increased, except for foreign languages. The same can be said of the nonacademic subjects, and there is the rub. Whether one is dismayed or cheered by these contrasting perspectives on course enrollments depends entirely on one's view of the purpose of secondary education. For those who believe that the primary purpose of the school is to educate youth "with equal seriousness in the great areas of human knowledge," the curriculum changes of the middle fifty years of this century were a disaster. For those who see the school as responsible for meeting a wide range of youth needs and problems, as well as for "developing social and civic awareness and responsibility," the picture until recently has been much brighter. This, of course, is the long-running debate we have described throughout this chapter. What, if anything, do the data have to say about the specifics of this debate?

Perhaps the most intriguing finding here is that neither the life adjustment movement nor the conservative reaction to it in the 1950s seems to have had the profound effects on the high school curriculum usually attributed to them. Instead, the changes over the period from 1934 to 1961 seem to us to be a slow working out in practice of a basic educational philosophy that was in place long before either of these reform movements was set in motion. That philosophy asserts that the high school curriculum should be based on an analysis of the needs of the students who attend the school. Over the long period of enrollment increase, it was assumed that each new group to enter the high school represented a distinct set of different needs. In this view, then, enrollment expansion always requires curriculum expansion. Even when voices have been raised to challenge the needs-based approach to curriculum, as during the Sputnik era, the school has responded by identifying that group *within* the student body for whom it felt the proposed reforms were appropriate (i.e., in that particular case, gifted and talented children). This explains why the late 1950s reforms did not constitute a "profound shift in thinking about education" that "refocused on subject matter and intellectual discipline," but rather were both modest and short-lived.[43]

Although the life adjustment movement and the conservative reaction seem to be less potent than historians have claimed, the career education movement and the excellence movement of the 1970s and 1980s seem to have been considerably more effective than previously realized. Career education resulted in a very large increase in the share of high school students enrolled in courses in trade and industry between 1973 and 1982. The excellence movement, while considerably more complex, seems clearly to have had the result of reversing the very long trend toward nonacademic education and to have restored the academic share of course taking to about its 1930 level. Importantly, this reversal began well before *A*

Nation at Risk, though this report seems to have given considerable stimulus to it.

Finally, the data reveal at least two trends that historians have not discussed at all—the tremendous increase in school time and credit devoted to health and physical education and the decline of business or commercial courses. The conventional view of physical education enrollments has been that they rise after every war in which the nation is involved, since wars and the draft demonstrate the low levels of physical condition of the American population. The data suggest otherwise—that enrollments in physical education have been rising unremittingly since the 1930s. Historians have described the business curriculum as the most popular and effective segment of vocational education, particularly for young women, but they have not followed its development beyond the 1930s. The USOE data show that both the business share of the curriculum and the percentage of students enrolled in business courses declined quite sharply between 1934 and 1949, leveled off for about two decades, then began another sharp decline.

These conclusions are based largely on a macro-view of the high school curriculum, shifts in nationally aggregated enrollments between broad subject families. To understand more completely the interaction between curriculum reform movements on the one hand and changes in the course-taking behavior of high school students on the other, we need a finer-grained analysis. For this, we turn to a more detailed look at two subject fields, science and mathematics.

CHANGES IN SCIENCE AND MATHEMATICS COURSE TAKING, 1949–1987

Since World War II, the subject fields of math and science have received extraordinary scrutiny, both by the participants in the great curriculum debates and by USOE staffers. During the debates of the Sputnik era, enrollments and achievement levels in math and science were carefully monitored, and the National Defense Education Act provided substantial funds for the improvement of teaching and for educational resources in these specific fields. The efforts of the National Science Foundation to get university professors involved in the development of new curriculum materials and approaches were aimed primarily, though not exclusively, at these subjects. More than twenty-five years later, *A Nation at Risk* also focused considerable attention on math and science as areas of crucial importance for the country's future economic competitiveness. Today, goal 4 of the National Goals continues this trend by calling for American students to be first in the world in these subject fields.

The U.S. Office of Education has reflected the national concern for developments in science and math, and this has resulted in more frequent and vigorous efforts to track enrollment and other changes in these subjects than in other fields. The office's activities actually began much earlier than most historians have supposed. In 1948, concurrent with its endorsement of the life adjustment movement, the office carried out a small-scale national survey of the teaching of science in public high schools. This was followed by a similar survey of mathematics teaching in 1952 and joint surveys of math and science in 1954, 1956, 1958, and 1962. From its general survey of course enrollments in 1961, the office calculated a select survey of math and science offerings. In addition, tables on math and science enrollments continued to be published in the *Digest of Educational Statistics* until at least 1965.[44]

Two different rationales provided the impetus for this USOE series of studies. As the president's National Committee for the Development of Scientists and Engineers put it, "As our society depends increasingly on science and technology, it is important that all citizens have an understanding of the nature of science and mathematics. The continued security and growth of the United States in this age of technology require steady increases for many years to come in the Nation's supply of high quality engineers, scientists, and teachers of mathematics and the sciences."[45]

These rationales, the need for greater scientific literacy in the general population and the need for an increasing supply of scientists, engineers, and mathematicians, have continued to dominate debate about science and mathematics in the high schools to this day. But encouraging enrollments in science and mathematics courses can have a number of different outcomes. For example, if it is desirable that all American high school students take three years of mathematics, does it matter whether the three years consist of general math, consumer math, and remedial math or algebra, geometry, and trigonometry? And if it matters, how can reformers be certain to produce the second pattern rather than the first? More important for our purposes here, given the evidence presented in table 12.3 that math and science enrollments rose as a consequence of the late 1950s back-to-basics movement and seem to be rising again in the 1980s, how are these increases distributed within the subject fields?

The data displayed in tables 12.6 to 12.8 permit us to address this last question by focusing closely on enrollment changes within the two subject fields.[46] Table 12.6, which lists the percentage of students in grades 9 to 12 enrolled in science and math courses between 1948 and 1963, highlights the increases in these two subject areas that took place during these years. Overall math enrollment rates rose from about 55 percent of those in grades 9 to 12 in 1948 to about two-thirds in 1963. Gains in science were more

TABLE 12.6   Percentage of Students, Grades 9 through 12,
Enrolled in Science and Mathematics Courses: 1948–1963

Subject Field	1948–49	1954–55	1958–59	1960–61	1962–63
Mathematics	54.7%	55.5%	65.2%	63.9%	67.0%
General math	12.0	12.2	13.1	17.4	12.1
Elementary algebra	19.3	18.3	22.6	19.6	21.2
Plane geometry	11.1	13.6	12.5	11.7	14.5
Intermediate algebra	6.9	6.6	8.2	9.0	10.1
Solid geometry	1.7	2.2	1.4	2.1	0.7
Trigonometry	2.0	2.6	2.8	3.0	2.0
All other math	1.7	NA	4.6	1.1	6.4
Science	54.5	NA	59.6	59.7	59.9
General science	19.9	NA	20.2	22.2	18.2
Biology	18.4	19.7	21.4	21.7	24.7
Chemistry	7.6	7.3	8.4	9.1	8.5
Physics	5.4	4.6	4.8	4.9	4.0
All other science	3.2	NA	4.8	1.8	4.5

Sources: 1948 and 1960 are from the USOE general surveys of those years; 1954, 1958, 1962 are from Simon and Grant, *Digest of Educational Statistics: 1965 Edition*, 27.

modest. There were large increases in the number of students and even in the *rates* of enrollment in such rigorous courses as algebra, geometry, trigonometry, biology, chemistry, and physics. The most dramatic increases, however, were not in the most rigorous courses but in the so-called practical courses. As the author of the report comparing 1948 to 1960 noted, "Courses of a practical nature in everyday living continued to proliferate. . . . In mathematics, such courses as consumer mathematics, economic mathematics, mathematics for modern living, refresher mathematics, and terminal mathematics were reported. Science offered household biology, science for modern living, everyday physics, and consumer science, among others."[47]

In other words, science and math enrollments reveal the same trend toward an increasingly split-level education that we described in the previous section. Increases in enrollments in the rigorous science and math courses were matched and even outpaced by increases in less intellectually challenging courses. Why did this development not set off a cry of alarm in the U.S. Office of Education, which seemed to be attending closely to enrollment shifts and to be a leader in the call for a larger supply of scientists and engineers?

Careful reading of the reports of those years reveals an agency that is far more concerned with training an elite corps of scientists and mathematicians than improving scientific literacy throughout the general population. Furthermore, the office fully accepted the premise that algebra, geometry, trigonometry, and calculus were appropriate subjects for some students but inappropriate for others. There was little genuine concern for the role of science and math in the general education of a citizen.[48] Indeed, rather than supporting the efforts of such critics as Bestor to bring more rigor into high school education, the tone of the reports was more critical of the critics than of the high schools. The 1952 report acknowledged that "enrollments in mathematics for general education have increased, but the enrollments in the college-preparatory mathematics has not kept pace with the growth of the high schools," but the office failed to keep abreast of this development, not even reporting the large increases in the teaching of remedial math between 1952 and 1972.[49] The office clearly endorsed the principle of the split-level curriculum, and this principle continued to hold sway in subsequent decades.

The massive USOE and NSF curriculum projects of the 1960s provide an excellent case in point. In the wake of the Sputnik scare, the National Science Foundation set out to develop new and more challenging curriculums in the sciences, mathematics, foreign languages, and social studies. Mainly taking the form of new teaching materials designed to replace traditional textbooks, these experimental approaches were adopted by many high schools in the early 1960s. Despite the substantial amounts of money spent on these projects and the publicity they received, the NSF projects boosted enrollments only modestly at best, and they seem to have had no lasting effect.[50]

At the same time that high schools showed modest increases in some of the more rigorous math courses, they also showed increases at the other end of the difficulty spectrum, in the remedial and applied mathematics categories. In the sciences, modest declines in chemistry and physics were offset by increases in such lower level general science courses as physical science and earth/space science. Indeed, the authors of the report that considered curricular changes from 1960 to 1972 noted, "Although traditional academic courses still receive considerable emphasis, their prominence in the school curriculum has been noticeably eroded since the 1960–61 data were collected."[51]

This trend was partially caused by the shift in national priorities in the 1960s from the cold war demands for more scientists and engineers to preoccupations with domestic social problems, such as poverty and inequalities. During the decade of the 1960s, the attention of educators and policy makers alike turned away from the "needs of the talented few" to the needs of the disadvantaged child and the potential dropout. But the trend was also caused by the way in which the high schools adopted the

NSF curriculums. Schools targeted these curriculums toward the high-performing, college-bound students who probably would have taken all of the advanced mathematics and science courses the school offered regardless of the curriculum revisions.

As we argued in the previous section, the most important factor shaping the curriculum in this period was the continued growth of high school enrollments—from 8.2 million in 1960 to 13.4 million in 1972. Educators responded to these students as they had in the past by assuming that increased enrollments inevitably meant increasing numbers of low-ability students. Believing that these students weren't capable of mastering difficult course material, educators expanded the less-demanding general track and created less rigorous courses for these students. Thus, whether one looks at the humanities, the sciences, or mathematics, the dominant trend was toward rising enrollments and less challenging classes. As the authors of the report comparing 1960 to 1972 stated, "The emphasis on making a high school education available for every youth, as noted in the [1960–61] study, has continued, with added attention given to the lower ability groups. . . . Remedial courses were offered to one segment of the student population; another segment had access to advanced and college-level courses . . . Graduation requirements were relaxed in many schools, and elective courses became more prominent."[52]

These trends continued over the next decade. Enrollment rates in both science and mathematics showed sizable gains, a 12 percent increase in the overall science enrollment rate and a more than 40 percent increase in mathematics. However, in both fields these increases were concentrated in lower level courses. The non–college preparatory mathematics courses showed over three times the gains of the college preparatory sequence, and in science, except for biology, the gains were mostly in general science courses (see tables 12.7 and 12.8). While the high schools were responding to the back-to-basics pressure for increased academic course work, they did so in a time-honored fashion, designing new courses with academic titles geared to students of middling or low attainments. Over this same period of rising enrollments in science and mathematics, some studies showed a drift from the academic curriculum into the general curriculum.[53] Achievement test scores continued to decline, even for the college-bound student.[54]

During the most recent period, 1982–1990, enrollment rates in both science and mathematics continued to increase, but the pattern of these increases has been sharply different from that of previous increases. Enrollment in science increased at a faster rate than over previous years. Math increased as well, but at a slower rate. By far the most striking aspects of these changes, however, are the increases in the traditional academic courses—biology, chemistry, and physics; algebra, geometry, trigonome-

TABLE 12.7 Comparisons of Changes in Mathematics Course Taking in U.S. High Schools, 1961–1987

Subject Field	% of 9–12 Enrollment		% of 9–12 Enrollment		% of Graduates Receiving Credit		
	1960–61	1972–73	1972–73	1978–82	1982	1987	1990
College-preparatory mathematics	46.5%	45.5%	40.2%	49.8%	195.1%	250.7%	252.7%
Pre-algebra	0.0	0.4	0.2	4.3	13.2	13.5	19.7
Algebra, elementary	19.6	15.3	11.2	18.1	66.6	76.8	74.6
Algebra, intermediate	9.0	8.9	8.3	7.1	31.0	46.1	47.7
Advanced algebra / trigonometry	0.8	4.9	4.8	1.9	12.3	11.4	13.3
Geometry	13.8	11.5	11.6	11.4	45.9	56.2	59.2
Trigonometry	3.0	1.5	1.4	1.6	7.8	12.0	10.1
Advanced math[a]	0.3	2.5	2.2	4.3	16.9	26.6	26.6
Computer math	0.0	0.5	0.5	1.1	3.5	5.0	3.4
Non-college preparatory mathematics	17.4	18.5	15.0	28.2	71.0	63.3	62.7
General math	17.4	17.3	13.8	21.7	52.0	42.6	42.3
Applied math	0.0	0.9	0.9	3.7	11.0	8.9	8.9
Consumer math	0.0	0.3	0.3	2.8	7.9	11.9	11.5
Total mathematics	63.9	64.0	55.3	77.8	267.5	314.0	315.4

Sources: 1960–61 and 1972–73 are derived from Wright, *Subject Offerings,* and Osterndorf and Horn, *Offerings and Enrollments;* 1972–73 and 1978–82 are derived from West, Diodata, and Sandberg, *Trends;* 1982 and 1987 are derived from Westat, *Tabulations,* and NCES, *The 1990 High School Transcript Study Tabulations,* and represent the percentages of students in two graduating cohorts who received credit in these courses. These last two columns include private school students, since it was not possible to adjust the figures to public only at this level of detail.
[a]Includes Analysis, Functions, College Mathematics, Probability and Statistics, Calculus, and combinations of these.

TABLE 12.8 Comparisons of Changes in Natural Science Course Taking in U.S. High Schools, 1961–1987

Subject Field	% of 9–12 Enrollment		% of 9–12 Enrollment		% of Graduates Receiving Credit		
	1960–61	1972–73	1972–73	1978–82	1982	1987	1990
General science	18.9%	8.8%	5.3%	14.5%			
Biology	21.7	24.1	19.5	25.3	95.4%	113.5%	116.1%
Chemistry	9.1	7.7	8.6	7.6	35.5	49.7	54.9
Physics	4.9	3.4	2.9	1.0	16.2	21.5	23.8
Chemistry and physics, advanced			0.1	2.3			
Physical science	3.4	7.6	6.0	8.5	29.9	35.8	37.2
Earth / space science	1.0	6.6	4.5	4.9	16.2	15.9	26.0
Applied science		0.9	0.8	0.3	1.6	3.5	5.2
Other general science		6.8	3.3	0.6	30.1	23.2	18.1
Other specific science	0.8	0.3	0.2	0.4	3.0	2.1	2.1
National Science Foundation and other special programs			7.2				
Total science	59.8	66.3	58.4	65.4	227.9	265.1	283.4

Sources: Same as in table 12.7.

try, and advanced mathematics. Moreover, enrollment rates in general science courses, particularly earth / space science, seem to be on the wane.

Certainly, much of this change can be attributed to the more rigorous state-mandated graduation requirements that began in the early 1980s.[55] However, we believe that two other factors were equally, if not more important. First, reformers in the 1980s, in contrast to many of those of the Sputnik era, seem to have taken seriously the need for greater scientific literacy in the general population. Second, insofar as these reformers have also been concerned with increasing the pool of potential scientists and engineers, they have stressed the need to include women and members of minority groups in that pool. As long as these ideas hold sway, it is unlikely that the nation's high schools will be able to subvert or contain the reforms, as they have in the past, by sharply differentiating between the academic courses made available for bright, college-bound students and the so-called academic courses designed for the general track or the perceived low-ability student.

Indeed, these data seem to indicate that in the past decade a profound shift has taken place in terms of both the rhetoric of educational reform and student course-taking patterns. Where once equal educational opportunity was conceived as access to a broad range of differentiated curriculum options, an idea promoted by educators but shared by virtually all major public and private policy agencies, including the U.S. Office of Education, there is now more talk of "equalizing access to tough, academic courses" and of *all* high schools offering a rigorous "core" program of those academic courses that used to be thought of as college preparatory. If this shift in thinking takes firmer hold, reaches more deeply into the ranks of high school administrators, counselors, and teachers, and continues to influence course-taking patterns, it will constitute by far the most significant shift in educational values and behaviors since the 1930s. It will also represent the ultimate vindication of the Committee of Ten.

CONCLUSION

In 1893, the Committee of Ten asserted a vision of democratic education and of educational equality that challenged the high schools of their time—every high school student, whether bound for college or not, should follow a serious and rigorous course of study in those subjects that have proven to have lasting value in the development of our civilization. This idea did not prevail. Instead, a very different definition of democracy and a different idea of equality took hold—that a democratic education allows students to study whatever they choose and that equality consists of providing an education appropriate to each student's needs, abilities, and future destiny.

The data presented here on the long-term trends in the course-taking behaviors of American high school students illustrate the total dominance of this second set of definitions. The history of the high school has not been a long tug of war between these two conceptions, with occasional victories on either side, as many historians have suggested; instead, we see a slow but steady working out of the ideas first clearly enunciated in the *Cardinal Principles of Secondary Education*. The high school curriculum that we have, or at least had until the mid-1980s, is an amalgam of the outcomes of struggles between interest groups over control of educational policy, of the various analyses of adolescent needs that curriculum experts have produced from time to time, and of the choices and demands that students and their parents have made. It is not the consequence of a rational analysis of what knowledge will best create an enlightened citizenry educated on an equal footing.

The retreat from the ideal of the Committee of Ten has taken many forms. Most obviously, the share of course taking represented by the academic subjects drastically declined relative to the nonacademic subjects. Even within the category of academic courses, curriculum developers have given primary attention to offerings that would appeal to less able students rather than challenge the intellect. Moreover, there has been a steady trend toward courses of shorter duration and a general erosion of the notion of cumulation in learning—that the study of one subject requires prior and successful study of another. The devaluation of the coinage of academic credit is fully evident in the granting of credit for courses that were once noncredit or even extracurricular. Where the Committee of Ten recommendations sought to acknowledge the *relative* importance of subjects by varying the number of periods per week, this has proven too complicated for the modern high school, which constructs the schedule around the assumption of equal worth, equal time (five periods per week), and equal weight for all subjects.

Our analysis of the many reports on student course taking has indicated that the grip of this educational ideology may have weakened since the mid-1980s. Serious attention is being given to the old idea that all students should follow the same curriculum, whatever their career goals may be, and that to fail to require this is to deny equal educational opportunity. Supporters of this notion do not deny that there are educationally relevant differences between individuals in interests and abilities. But they argue that such differences should challenge educators to explore a host of alternative instructional methods and approaches rather than adopt the long-standing policy of split-level education. They do assert forthrightly that some subjects are inherently more important than others.[56]

This seems to be the chief significance of the National Goals, particularly goals 3 and 4. Goal 3 places English, mathematics, science, history, and geography on a level of importance somewhat higher than driver's training and personal typing, something high schools have generally failed to do. Furthermore, in the assertion that "all students [will] learn to use their minds so they may be prepared for responsible citizenship, further learning and productive employment," the operative word is *and*. Formerly, high schools represented these three aims with three different curricular tracks, the general, the academic, and the vocational, respectively, and assumed that their job was to get the right students into the right tracks. What might it mean to prepare *all* students for all three roles?

Another significance of goal 3 is its reference to students leaving "grades four, eight, and twelve having demonstrated competency." In one stroke, this goal asserts both the need to have strong vertical articulation in the curriculum between different grade levels and the need to define the grades in terms of competencies rather than merely time-in-grade.

Goal 4 may be equally revolutionary in calling for an international standard of performance. American high school educators have never doubted that our high schools are the best in the world. They are the best because they are the most democratic; i.e., they enroll a larger share of the secondary school age population than any country in the world, and they have achieved this because they have recognized that different adolescents have different curricular needs. Such thinking helped get the high schools through the 1950s without fundamental change, but it may not survive the 1980s and 1990s. We now know that several countries that have thus far rejected the concept of the differentiated high school curriculum have actually attained higher enrollment rates than ours.[57] The process of international comparison, while not likely to result in the actual attainment of goal 4, will nevertheless force us to reexamine continually some of the most cherished ideas in American educational history. One of these is surely the idea that the only way to approach universal secondary school enrollment is to make the high school curriculum less challenging and more entertaining.

Although the adoption of the National Goals and the broad support they have received are encouraging and although the data show clear signs of a significant reversal of the long trend, there are reasons to fear that the change might not be as profound and long-lasting as we would hope. First, the long declines in achievement scores recorded by the National Assessment of Educational Progress, the SAT, and the ACT have shown little reversal, despite the apparent increase in the taking of precollege math and science courses by high school students. Second, as in the 1950s, students may be taking unchallenging courses with academic titles, possibly explaining the continuously low test scores. Increases in state-mandated graduation requirements, in themselves, do not guarantee that students will be seriously engaged or that required subjects will be well taught.

Third, and most important, the most widely publicized and discussed educational reform initiatives of this decade—school choice, school-based management, politically controlled local school councils, the creation of schools committed to religious and racial fundamentalism—threaten to weaken the revolutionary potential of the National Goals. All of these assert the primacy of the particular over the universal. All argue for greater rather than less diversity in school offerings. If left unchecked by external constraints on curriculum building, they all have the potential to exacerbate the curriculum fragmentation that has characterized the very essence of the modern American high school.

The most powerful external constraint we can conceive would be the adoption of either a national curriculum or a clear set of national performance standards and assessment. Such a constraint would bring an important change to testing, since students would be tested on what they had been taught, thus making education more accountable. It would make it more difficult for educators to subvert reforms, as they have in the past, by demanding clear performance standards instead of merely requiring a particular set of courses. It would set a framework within which local experimentation in such areas as governance or teaching methods could proceed without endangering important national priorities. Finally, it might end the mockery that American high schools have made of the concept of equal educational opportunity.

NOTES

1. Bernard Weinraub, "Bush and Governors Set Goals" *New York Times*, 29 September 1989, A10.

2. U.S. Department of Education, *America 2000: An Education Strategy* (Washington, D.C.: USDE, 1991), 3.

3. We focus on developments on the high school level for several reasons. First, there is widespread agreement that secondary education is the most troubled part of the American educational enterprise. Second, almost all of the major curriculum reform movements in the last half century have sought to transform secondary rather than elementary education. Third, for almost seventy years a variety of federal agencies have been collecting data on course taking by high school students. These data, though seldom utilized for this purpose, permit in-depth analyses of curricular changes over precisely the periods during which the high school has been most under fire.

4. Arthur Powell, Eleanor Farrar, and David K. Cohen, *The Shopping Mall High School: Winners and Losers in the Educational Marketplace* (Boston: Houghton Mifflin, 1985), 241–42. For excerpts from these reports, see David B. Tyack, *Turning Points in American Educational History* (Waltham, Mass.: Blaisdell Publishing Co., 1967), 380–86, 396–400.

5. John Latimer, *What's Happened to Our High Schools?* (Washington, D.C.: Public Affairs Press, 1958), 117.

6. Robert L. Church and Michael W. Sedlak, *Education in the United States* (New York: Free Press, 1976), 288–314; Edward A. Krug, *The Shaping of the American High School, 1880–1920* (Madison: University of Wisconsin Press, 1964), 378–406; Diane Ravitch, *The Troubled Crusade: American Education, 1945–1980* (New York: Basic Books, 1983), 47–51.

7. Edward A. Krug, *The Shaping of the American High School, 1920–1941* (Madison: University of Wisconsin Press, 1972), 68–146; David B. Tyack, *The One Best System* (Cambridge: Harvard University Press, 1974).

8. Ravitch, *The Troubled Crusade*, 52–64.

9. Robert Hampel, *The Last Little Citadel: American High Schools since 1940* (Boston: Houghton Mifflin, 1986), 35–42; Ravitch, *The Troubled Crusade*, 64–69; Steven E. Tozer, Paul C. Violas, and Guy Senese, *School and Society: Educational Practice as Social Experience* (New York: McGraw-Hill, 1992), 196–97.

10. The Prosser resolution is quoted in Ravitch, *The Troubled Crusade*, 64–65. See also Lawrence Cremin, *The Transformation of the School* (New York: Alfred A. Knopf, 1961), 332–38.

11. Church and Sedlak, *Education in the United States*, 404.

12. Smith is quoted in Cremin, *Transformation of the School*, 340. Arthur Bestor, *Educational Wastelands: The Retreat from Learning in Our Public Schools* (Urbana: University of Illinois Press, [1953] 1985), 10.

13. Church and Sedlak, *Education in the United States*, 404–7; Ravitch, *The Troubled Crusade*, 69–80; Joel Spring, *The Sorting Machine: National Educational Policy since 1945* (New York: David McKay, 1976), 15–37.

14. Ravitch, *The Troubled Crusade*, 229; Spring, *The Sorting Machine*, 96–127; James B. Conant, *The American High School Today* (New York: McGraw-Hill, 1959); Tozer, Violas, and Senese, *School and Society*, 199–203; Church and Sedlak, *Education in the United States*, 407–17.

15. Ravitch, *The Troubled Crusade*, 235.

16. A. S. Neill, *Summerhill: A Radical Approach to Child Rearing* (New York: Harcourt, Brace & Co., 1960); Ravitch, *The Troubled Crusade*, 235–45.

17. Charles Silberman, *Crisis in the Classroom: The Remaking of American Education* (New York: Random House, 1970); Ravitch, *The Troubled Crusade*, 245–55; Powell, Farrar, and Cohen, *Shopping Mall High School*, 296–99.

18. Ravitch, *The Troubled Crusade*, 255–56, 263–66; Tozer, Violas, and Senese, *School and Society*, 371–72.

19. Marland is quoted in Spring, *The Sorting Machine*, 234. See also 233–36.

20. National Commission on Excellence in Education, *A Nation at Risk: The Imperative for Educational Reform* (Washington, D.C.: Government Printing Office, 1983), 5.

21. Quoted in Staff of the National Commission on Excellence in Education, *Meeting the Challenge: Recent Efforts to Improve Education across the Nation* (Washington, D.C.: U.S. Department of Education, 15 November 1983), 1.

22. Tozer, Violas, and Senese, *School and Society*, 368–83. Studies that made recommendations for improving American education include Ernest L. Boyer, *High School: A Report on Secondary Education in America* (New York: Harper & Row, 1983);

John I. Goodlad, *A Place Called School* (New York: McGraw-Hill, 1984); Powell, Farrar, and Cohen, *Shopping Mall High School*; Theodore R. Sizer, *Horace's Compromise* (Boston: Houghton Mifflin, 1984); Twentieth Century Fund, *Making the Grade* (New York: TCF, 1983); Education Commission of the States, *Action for Excellence* (Denver: ECS, 1983); National Science Board Commission on Precollege Education in Mathematics, Science, and Technology, *Educating Americans for the 21st Century* (Washington, D.C.: National Science Foundation, 1983).

23. Tozer, Violas, and Senese, *School and Society*, 378; James B. Stedman and K. Forbis Jordan, *Education Reform Reports: Content and Impact*, report 86-56 EPW (Washington, D.C.: Congressional Research Service, 1986), 12–41.

24. Hampel, *The Last Little Citadel*, 177, but see also Latimer, *What's Happened?* and Powell, Farrar, and Cohen, *Shopping Mall High School*, chap. 5.

25. For example, no enrollments were listed for such subjects as physical education and typewriting and, when these subjects first appeared in the reports in 1922, their enrollments were already greater than for many of the subjects on the earlier lists. For evidence that the subjects were being taught before they were included in national surveys, see R. B. Stout, *The Development of High-School Curriculum in the North Central States from 1860 to 1918* (Chicago: Department of Education, University of Chicago, 1921).

26. U.S. Office of Education (hereafter USOE), *Biennial Survey of Education, 1926–1928*, bulletin 1930, no. 16 (Washington, D.C.: Government Printing Office, 1930); USOE, *Offerings and Registrations in High School Subjects, 1933–34*, bulletin 1938, no. 6 (Washington, D.C.: Government Printing Office, 1938); USOE, "Offerings and Enrollments in High-School Subjects," in *Biennial Survey of Education in the United States, 1948–50* (Washington, D.C.: Government Printing Office, 1951), chap. 5; Grace S. Wright, *Subject Offerings and Enrollments in Public Secondary Schools* (Washington, D.C.: Government Printing Office, 1965); Logan C. Osterndorf and Paul J. Horn, *Course Offerings, Enrollments, and Curriculum Practices in Public Secondary Schools, 1972–73* (Washington, D.C.: Government Printing Office, 1976). To extend this series beyond 1973, the National Center for Education Statistics contracted with Evaluation Technologies, Inc. (ETI) to develop a way to transform student transcript data from the *High School and Beyond* study of the cohort of 1982 graduates into estimates of course enrollment data compatible with the 1973 data collection. See Jerry West, Louis Diodato, and Nancy Sandberg, *A Trend Study of High School Offerings and Enrollments: 1972–73 and 1981–82*, NCES 84-224 (Washington, D.C.: Government Printing Office, 1984). In our tables 12.1 through 12.3, the 1982 column is adapted from this study, although the 1973 column is adapted from the original data collection, Osterndorf and Horn, *Course Offerings, 1972–73*.

27. In the latest study available, the transcript study of the cohort of 1987 graduates by Westat, Inc., over 3,000 course titles were reported in a national sample of 22,700 student transcripts. The curriculum expansion continues apace. Westat, Inc., *High School Transcript Analysis: The 1987 Graduates*, Vol. 1, *Tabulations: 1987 High School Transcript Study, with Comparisons to the Class of 1982* (Unpublished research report submitted to NCES, November 1988).

28. To encourage greater consistency among researchers in the coding of courses, NCES contracted with ETI to develop a classification system. Clifford

Adelman did not "find the scheme to be compelling." "Devaluation, Diffusion and the College Connection: A Study of High School Transcripts, 1964–1981," Unpublished paper prepared for the National Commission on Excellence in Education, ERIC ED #228–244, March 1983. For our purposes, we did not feel that the effort of the USOE to maintain and extend a "historical table" was particularly successful, since the approach used was to try to code each new set of course enrollments into the course categories of the previous data collections. Since we were interested in changes in the relative share of enrollments in a comprehensive set of subject field categories, we recoded all of the data from the most detailed tables in these survey reports into fourteen subject fields, with as much consistency across time as possible. Any such coding is liable to a certain amount of error, and the appearance of change over time may, in small part, be the result of coding courses in one subject category rather than another.

29. There are two notable exceptions, however. First is John F. Latimer's compelling but seldom-cited book, *What's Happened to Our High Schools?* The other is David K. Cohen's outstanding essay, "Origins" in Powell, Farrar, and Cohen, *Shopping Mall High School*. Both have influenced our interpretation of high school curriculum reform.

30. Latimer, *What's Happened?* 118.

31. Even the famous Prosser resolution was presaged by his 1939 Inglis lecture at Harvard University. Charles Prosser, *Secondary Education and Life* (Cambridge: Harvard University Press, 1939). See also Jeffrey E. Mirel and David L. Angus, "The Rising Tide of Custodialism: Enrollment Increases and Curriculum Reform in Detroit, 1928–1940," *Issues in Education* 4 (Fall 1986): 101–20.

32. Recent sources have used the category "personal development courses" to group such offerings as typing, physical education, driver's education, child care, and even band. Although such categorization seems to us both logical and useful, courses that hold their place in the curriculum as a result of mandates from state governments, as is the case with physical education and driver's education, might also need to be understood as courses "in the public interest." See Adelman, "Devaluation"; Westat, *Tabulations*.

33. Douglas is quoted in Ravitch, *The Troubled Crusade*, 60.

34. Neither secondary teachers nor such national organizations representing subject matter interests as the Music Educators National Conference and the National Science Teachers Association played a very prominent role in the post–World War II curriculum debates. The reason probably lies in the enormous enrollment increases that characterized the period of 1945 to 1976. There was always a demand for more and more teachers of every subject, and classes were always adequately enrolled, if not overenrolled. From the teachers' perspective, it surely mattered very little if national enrollments in music were growing faster than those in art or if physical education enrollments were growing faster than those in mathematics. This condition has changed, however. In the fall of 1968, the national enrollment in grades 9 through 12 reached 93 percent of the 14- to 17-year-old population, and it has remained at or slightly below that figure since. In 1975, the 14- to 17-year-old population topped out at about 17,125,000, and it has been declining since. [See U.S. NCES, *Digest of Education Statistics, 1990* (Washington, D.C.: Government Printing

Office, 1991), 66.] This creates a climate in which subject matter specialists may have much more reason to be concerned about and actively engaged in debate about the high school curriculum. For example, while overall enrollment as estimated in these studies declined by about 6 percent between 1973 and 1982, enrollments in mathematics, vocational education, art, and agriculture actually increased, while enrollments in foreign language, science, and health and physical education decreased at one or two times the overall rate. We realize, of course, that it is dangerous to generalize about fields as disparate as physical education, where enrollment declines might be welcomed as an opportunity to have smaller classes in already overtaxed physical facilities, and foreign language, where enrollment loss may result in the cancellation of already tenuous third and fourth year language classes. Nonetheless, it is unlikely that, in the curriculum debates of the 1990s, teachers and subject interest groups will stay on the sidelines.

35. For sources of this idea, see Krug, *American High School, 1920–1941*, 107–17; for arguments against this view, see Powell, Farrar, and Cohen, *Shopping Mall High School*, 341–42n19, and Latimer, *What's Happened?* 73–74.

36. Remember that the 1982 column is actually derived from a set of inferences based on the transcripts of the cohort of 1982 graduates.

37. It is possible for the proportion of students enrolling in a particular subject to increase while the proportionate share of enrollment in that subject remains the same or declines only if the total number of courses elected is rising. It was, from 5.61 courses per student in 1948–49 to 6.42 per student in 1960–61.

38. See National Science Foundation, *The Status of Precollege Science, Mathematics, and Social Science Education: 1955–1975*, 3 vols. (Washington, D.C.: Government Printing Office, 1977).

39. For years, the standard measure of student course time in American high schools has been the credit or the Carnegie unit. One unit represents one academic year spent in a course meeting five times per week in periods ranging from 45 to 60 or more minutes. High school graduation requirements, whether state or local, are expressed in such units, and these units are either recorded on or can be calculated from the student's transcript or cumulative record card.

40. Edith S. Greer and Richard M. Harbeck, *What High School Pupils Study: A National Survey of the Scholastic Performance of Pupils of Various Abilities*, bulletin 1962, no. 10 (Washington, D.C.: Government Printing Office, 1962), 5–6. Other transcript studies are Adelman, "Devaluation"; Westat, *Tabulations*; and NCES, *The 1990 High School Transcript Study Tabulations: Comparative Data on Credits Earned and Demographics for 1990, 1987, and 1982 High School Graduates*, (Washington, D.C.: U.S. Department of Education, 1993). In table 12.5, the 1973 column represents estimates based on enrollments from Osterndorf and Horn, *Course Offerings 1972–73*, adjusted using credit values calculated from Adelman, "Devaluation."

41. For example, between 1961 and 1973, the share of enrollments claimed by courses in health, physical education, driver's education, safety, and ROTC increased by 10.8 percent, and the percentage of all high school students enrolled in one or more of these courses increased by 21.6 percent. Over roughly the same period (1958 to 1973), the share of credits claimed by these courses increased by 164 percent. This large difference can be explained only by a significant change in the

granting of academic credit for such courses. It is also true that, during the earlier period, some nonacademic courses met fewer than five times per week. Today, virtually all courses meet five days per week. See also Greer and Harbeck, *What High School Pupils Study*, 5–6.

42. Adelman, "Devaluation," 13–14.

43. Church and Sedlak, *Education in the United States*, 417.

44. Philip G. Johnson, *The Teaching of Science in Public High Schools: An Inquiry into Offerings, Enrollments, and Selected Teaching Conditions, 1947–48* (Washington, D.C.: Government Printing Office, 1950); Kenneth E. Brown, *Mathematics in Public High Schools* (Washington, D.C.: Government Printing Office, 1953); Kenneth E. Brown, *Offerings and Enrollments in Science and Mathematics in Public High Schools* (Washington, D.C.: Government Printing Office, 1956); Kenneth E. Brown and Ellworth S. Osbourn, *Offerings and Enrollments in Science and Mathematics in Public High Schools, 1956* (Washington, D.C.: Government Printing Office, 1957); Kenneth E. Brown and Ellsworth S. Osbourn, *Offerings and Enrollments in Science and Mathematics in Public High Schools, 1958* (Washington, D.C.: Government Printing Office, 1961); Kenneth A. Simon and W. Vance Grant, *Digest of Educational Statistics, 1965 Edition*, bulletin 1965, no. 4 (Washington, D.C.: Government Printing Office, 1966).

45. From the president's National Committee for the Development of Scientists and Engineers, cited in Brown and Osbourn, *Offerings and Enrollments in Science and Mathematics in Public High Schools, 1956*, ii.

46. Tables 12.7 and 12.8 are arranged in grouped columns, each group representing a cross-time comparison. This is necessary because differences between the studies from which these data are drawn cannot be reconciled at the desired level of detail. For example, the enrollment percentage in general math in West, Diodata, and Sandberg is 3.5 percent lower than that in Osterndorf and Horn because they omit all enrollments in remedial mathematics. There are numerous differences of this kind.

47. Wright, *Subject Offerings*, 19–20.

48. Exemplifying this, the 1958 transcript study was designed to answer such questions as Is the time of the academically able pupils being spent on appropriate subjects in our high schools? What proportion of a typical pupil's program is made up of academic subjects? The able pupils? The less able? Greer and Harbeck, *What High School Pupils Study*, 1.

49. Brown, *Mathematics in Public High Schools*, 40. Remedial math was not a reported category in the surveys of 1954, 1956, 1958, and 1962. In the general survey of 1960–61, remedial math was subsumed under "general math." There is thus no reliable information on the timing of the growth of remedial math enrollments from about 12,000 students in 1948 to over 328,000 in 1972.

50. National Science Foundation, *Status of Precollege Science*.

51. Osterndorf and Horn, *Course Offerings, 1972–73*, 4–5.

52. Ibid., 22.

53. Adelman, "Devaluation"; Donald A. Rock, Ruth B. Ekstrom, Margaret E. Goertz, Thomas L. Hilton, and Judith Potlack, *Excellence in High School Education: Cross-Sectional Study, 1972–1980, Final Report*, NCES contract 300-83-0247 (Princeton, N.J.: Educational Testing Service, 1984).

54. See Senta A. Raizen and Lyle V. Jones, eds., *Indicators of Precollege Education in Science and Mathematics: A Preliminary Review* (Washington, D.C.: National Academy Press, 1985), 114–32.

55. Thirty-six states increased requirements in mathematics and thirty-three states increased them in science between 1980 and 1984, mostly before the influence of *A Nation at Risk*. See Raizen and Jones, *Indicators of Precollege Education*, 56–58.

56. Scholars from across a broad political spectrum are coming to the view that a single curriculum is a better guarantor of equal educational opportunity than is a differentiated curriculum. See Jeannie Oakes, *Keeping Track: How Schools Structure Inequality* (New Haven: Yale University Press, 1985), 206; Mortimer Adler, *The Paideia Proposal: An Educational Manifesto* (New York: Macmillan Co., 1982), 5–6.

57. See U.S. Congress, Office of Technology Assessment, *Elementary and Secondary Education for Science and Engineering: A Technical Memorandum*, OTA-TM-SET-41 (Washington, D.C.: Government Printing Office, 1988), 15–16, and Raizen and Jones, *Indicators of Precollege Education*, 119–28.

13 LITERATE AMERICA: HIGH-LEVEL ADULT LITERACY AS A NATIONAL GOAL

CARL F. KAESTLE

Literacy has been central to the creation of American culture and government. From the Puritans' transatlantic theological discourse in the seventeenth century, to the American revolutionaries' debates about British sovereignty in the eighteenth, to the American novels of Susanna Rowson or James Fenimore Cooper in the early nineteenth century, to the vigor and scrappiness of the late nineteenth-century foreign language press, to the Palmer raids on socialist editors during World War I, to the proud, angry voices of the Harlem Renaissance, to the paperback revolution that brought Mickey Spillane to local drugstores after World War II, to the emergence of a feminist press in the 1970s—printed publications have not only told our multifarious national story but also been an important part of it.

Americans only periodically focus on the importance of literacy to the nation's fate. Reading is a mundane activity, and in the twentieth century, with nearly universal elementary schooling and very high nominal literacy rates, we have sometimes taken literacy for granted. At other times, however, our needs for literacy have become pressing and have outdistanced the abilities of American readers. At these times, literacy has become an important policy issue and a frequent topic of social commentary. We are living in such a time.

In the mid-1980s, with recession and international competition threatening Americans' economic well-being, an adult literacy reform movement began and thrived, parallel to the movement to reform public schools. Like the public school reform movement, the adult literacy movement produced books that exposed the problem and newspaper articles that described the work of local literacy agencies and dramatized the plight of low-literacy adults. There were "white papers" on television and alarming results from functional literacy tests. Sometimes this kind of reform enthusiasm fades when the problem turns out to be recalcitrant and quick solutions are not found. But the staying power of the 1980s adult literacy reform movement has been impressive. It is enshrined in the education goals set by President Bush and the nation's governors at Charlottesville in 1989, which established universal high-level adult literacy as a national goal, and in the National Literacy Act of 1991, by which Congress created a National Institute for Literacy to provide research and services at the national level and authorized funds to strengthen state literacy agencies, support work-place literacy training, and expand the Even Start program for family literacy training. These programs are aimed at a very ambitious goal. The National Education Goal for adult literacy states that, "by the year 2000, every adult American will be literate and will possess the knowledge and skills necessary to compete in a global economy and exercise the rights and responsibilities of citizenship."[1]

THE COMPLEXITIES OF LITERACY

How shall we understand this goal? What does it mean to say that everyone will have necessary skills for work and citizenship, and how would we measure our success in attempting to reach the goal? Despite our long history of widespread, expanding literacy, recent adult literacy assessments suggest that we are far from the goal at present.[2] History cannot tell us the answers, but it may provide some understanding of the problems. Literacy is complex; history can illustrate some of the intricacies with which policy must reckon. This chapter highlights some of those complexities. The first is that literacy is not just a skill, or even a set of skills, but has a content. Because literacy has a cultural content, it is not neutral. Acquiring or transmitting literacy has an ideological dimension. In the nation-building process, especially in countries with an ethnically diverse population, literacy training is typically coupled with an effort to unite the public politically, culturally, and linguistically. The state uses literacy to create consensus and cohesion. But how unitary can public print culture be? Whose culture should it represent? On the other hand, what are the consequences of supporting a print culture that is extremely diverse? These issues have taken different forms at different times in American history, and they are salient in the current debates about school curriculum.

Second, even if we agreed on the proper content of literacy, it is nonetheless difficult to measure literacy abilities and to say how much literacy a person needs. We can define it functionally, as in the current goals: literacy will allow individuals to "compete in a global economy and exercise the rights and responsibilities of citizenship." The Literacy Definition Committee of the National Adult Literacy Survey avoided specifying particular functions like economic or political participation and left the purpose more general: literacy, they said, is "using printed and written information to function in society, to achieve one's goals, and to develop one's knowledge and potential."[3] Both of these definitions emphasize the active use of literacy abilities to accomplish social goals, but they don't tell us what abilities will be emphasized, how they will be measured, or what level of competence would be considered necessary to achieve a national goal of successful functioning literacy. The techniques used to measure literacy have changed continually over time, as have the criteria for determining an adequate level of literacy.

The third complexity revealed by history is that literacy is rooted in the social structure and is thus stubbornly unequal. Literacy is associated with power, with advancement, and with status. Power relationships and group competition militate against our ideal of equal opportunity when it comes to literacy. For most of our history, advantaged Americans have kept women, nonwhite people, and poor people from full access to education. Such outright discrimination has reduced over time because of the struggles of oppressed groups and because our political principles challenge our prejudices. But advantaged people have the appetite and the resources to acquire more and more education themselves, and our literacy needs and expectations are continually rising, so the gaps between groups continue at higher levels. Thus, the complicated history of literacy is characterized by converging rates of literacy at lower levels and increasingly visible divergence at higher levels as literacy expectations rise.

The fourth complexity is that literacy training goes on in two quite different arenas—in the preparatory world of elementary and secondary education and, for some, in adult literacy training programs. So when we say we want to improve adult literacy, we may try to improve elementary and secondary education so that future generations of adults will have better literacy abilities or we may try to affect adult literacy rates directly by improving adults' literacy. It is very difficult to alter national average literacy rates through adult training. Despite some well-known and demonstrably successful campaigns for adult literacy training in various periods, the nation's long-run, rising literacy rate has been more a product of the continually increasing level of school attainment in the population. This process has worked because we have had almost all of the population in schools in their youth, whereas we have never had more than a tiny portion of the adult population in basic education programs. There are good reasons to put resources into adult literacy training, but it will not raise the national average literacy rate very much. On the other hand, as we shall see, there are reasons to doubt whether the historical strategy of continually increased schooling will work in the future to improve the quality of general literacy in the population. History doesn't provide policy blueprints; it provides food for thought.

A fifth complexity is that America is a multicultural nation. Literacy in the English language is part of the enculturation of children in literate English-speaking families. For those whose first language is not English, however, English language literacy can be seen as a hurdle, an opportunity, an imposition, or an imperative. The language history of the United States is complex, and Americans' ambivalence about our multilingual society has meant that encouragement for non-English literacy has ebbed and flowed at different periods. Although this chapter is about English language literacy as a national goal, this complexity is hovering in the background with the others.

TRADITIONAL LITERACY IN COLONIAL NEW ENGLAND

A selective overview of the history of literacy in the United States will touch upon these complexities. Let us look first at the stereotype of highly literate seventeenth-century Puritan New England, a favorite spot for historians seeking the origins of Anglo-American culture. Historians of British colonial America have traditionally emphasized the New England colonies, the Puritan religion, and the high education levels of the initial settlers.[4] But in the first book-length study of literacy in American history, Kenneth Lockridge challenged the idea of widespread high literacy among the first English colonists in New England. Only about 60 percent of the men and 30 percent of the women in the first generation could sign their names. Lockridge's figures show New England literacy rising sharply for both men and women in the seventeenth century, a rise that he attributed to the powerful influence of Puritanism. The purposes of literacy in this society, Lockridge argued, were conservative. He portrayed the initial colonists as living in a predominantly oral, premodern environment similar to that of European peasants.[5] Recently, historians have rejected the premodern-modern dichotomy. David Hall has used instead the term *traditional* to summarize the wide circulation of a limited number of steady-selling texts, focused mostly on religion. People read these texts over and over. In this sense, the literacy environment was more sparse than later.[6]

In this regard colonial New England was typical of other provincial situations in the early modern West, not exceptional. Individuals with high levels of education and extensive libraries were unusual, but many families owned a few books, and there were no newspapers or magazines. The purposes of literacy were predominantly conservative; in most situations readers were receivers of authoritative text about religion or law. Reading fare was rounded out by popular forms that were more responsive to daily life and local events, like almanacs, histories, captivity narratives, sermons that reported strange occurrences, and execution confessions.[7] Because there were relatively fewer texts, people tended to read them repeatedly; certainly this was the case with the Bible, by far the most common book.

Some scholars have called this repeated reading of fewer texts "intensive" reading, as contrasted with the quicker reading of competing texts in later centuries. Even in later times, of course, intensive reading survived and was important, not only in Bible reading but in the rereading of favorite books and stories or in the absorbing experience of a novel.[8] But in the seventeenth century, it was the main mode of reading.

Yet the seeds of change were present in the colonial situation. Transatlantic commerce fostered literacy and the development of coastal towns, imperial political relations produced strain and controversy by the late seventeenth century, and centrifugal forces pressing the colonists away from the European metropolis caused this highly literate population to develop a book trade and indigenous newspapers. Printed publications became more secular, more diverse, and more polemical in the eighteenth century. The center of gravity in colonial printing shifted to politics.

THE NINETEENTH CENTURY: POLITICS AND THE INDIVIDUAL

Eventually, in the nineteenth century, the diffusion of information, the expansion of literacy, and the diversity and dispersal of the population led to publications that supported individualism and pluralism.[9] For several decades, however, republican politics dominated the purposes of literacy, as Michael Warner's recent work argues.[10] His work suggests a two-stage evolution away from the cohesive, traditional world view of seventeenth-century reading matter. First came the legitimation of different views on public issues, that is, arguments within the public sphere so central to republican politics. Only later, and somewhat inhibited by the republican focus on public discourse, came the legitimation of printed publications for individualistic, nonpublic uses, like the reading of novels. By the mid–nineteenth century, however, despite the persistence of authoritative, traditional texts and despite the continued importance of politics in American print matter, American literacy was accommodating novels, women's journals, story papers, and farm magazines alongside cheap daily newspapers and high literary journals.[11] As Richard D. Brown has written, by 1850 "America had gone from a society where public information had been scarce, and chiefly under the control of the learned and wealthy few, to a society in which it was abundant and under no control other than the interests and appetites of a vast, popular public of consumers."[12] As mass literacy spread out to find new niches in the advanced capitalist society of the late nineteenth and early twentieth century, it drifted farther from its old moorings in religion and politics toward the potent generative forces of advanced capitalism: commerce and consumption.[13]

Each new stage of expansion, diversification, and fragmentation of reading fare brought anxieties to some elites, yet worries about pluralism seem to have been offset in American history by an environment that fostered the diverse uses of print. Unlike the English, most American writers who commented on literacy thought that the key to social order was more education, not less.[14] From Thomas Jefferson to Horace Mann to John Dewey, American educators have argued that democracy cannot work without an intelligent reading public. Although free common schooling was accompanied by large doses of Anglo-American cultural conformity and although the first amendment guarantee of a free press was at times contravened, both were nonetheless crucial to the development of competing ideas in print.

The early nineteenth century saw a narrowing of the gap in literacy between white men and white women. It is not clear how big the gap had been in the late eighteenth century; Lockridge's signature-counting estimates, showing a two-to-one advantage for white men over white women (90 to 45 percent), have been challenged by recent scholars. Some argue that many women who signed an "X" could nonetheless read,[15] and other historians have discovered rates of female signing as high as 70 to 90 percent in some areas.[16] On the other hand, no one is suggesting that educational opportunities were equal, even at the elementary level. Clearly, men had higher literacy rates in the early national period. By 1850, this gender advantage seems to have almost disappeared among whites, if we take seriously the U.S. Census figures on self-reported literacy, which showed white female and male rates both over 90 percent.[17] But having achieved that low-level parity, white women faced educational discrimination at the secondary and collegiate levels, and measures of higher level literacy abilities reflected these gender biases; some even remain today. Gender differences illustrate the general pattern in the history of literacy; while gaps narrowed at rudimentary literacy levels, they persisted at higher levels, and as the nation raised its literacy expectations these gaps became more apparent and more important.[18]

Discrimination was even greater across racial lines. Whites only gradually and begrudgingly extended some public schooling to minorities; nonwhite groups had to fight to get better public schools and to attain literacy. If there was anything that united African-American leaders from slavery through Reconstruction and through the civil rights struggles of the twentieth century, it was the importance of education and literacy, even in a world where discrimination prevented black Americans from attaining high-literacy jobs. Similar attitudes prevailed among Hispanic and Asian-American leaders.

New and excluded groups faced a culture of printed words, a country where whites emphasized the value of public schooling, a country where the combination of capitalism and protected free speech guaranteed that printed matter would continually expand into new markets, new topics, and new purposes. Recognizing the importance of print, excluded groups in U.S. history have made literacy and education a central goal, a tool by which to assimilate or to assert group rights.[19] Freed blacks after the Civil War, said Booker T. Washington, were "a whole race trying to go to school," and the foreign language press, paradoxically, was more influential in assimilating European immigrants to American institutions and traditions than any Americanization program designed for the purpose.[20]

Beneath the placid surface of the history of literacy rates is a lot of political turbulence, ethnic competition, cultural aspiration, and personal transformation. Thus, the nineteenth century closed with many different groups striving to create for themselves not only literacy skills but distinctive reading materials. The foreign language press thrived, regional centers of publication pulled away from New York and Boston, specialized publications increased in number, the development of national brand advertising fostered a revolution in cheap magazines, and the rotary presses churned out yellow journalism as well as huge runs of big-city papers that reached farther and farther into the hinterland. At the turn of the century, diverse publications bristled with differing ideas while the instruments of standardization were in their infancy: syndicated columns, newspaper chains, wire services, marketing surveys, and widespread secondary education. The dramatic tension between diversity and standardization has remained in play from that time to our own, as new groups developed various ways to express themselves in print and became part of the pluralistic literacy scene. But as time passed, commercial reading matter became more standardized, and high schools gave more and more young people a smattering of common academic culture.

THE TWENTIETH CENTURY: EXPANDING LITERACY IN INDUSTRIAL SOCIETY

By 1900 elementary school attendance was almost universal among whites, even though many went for only a few years. Over 90 percent of native-born whites claimed that they could read, and the percentage of blacks who said they were literate was increasing rapidly.[21] A few groups, like Native Americans, were caught in a much more severe attempt both to suppress their culture and to exclude them from white institutions; thus, they were at a huge disadvantage with regard to English print literacy. Even for the remainder of the population, the length and sophistication of one's literacy training depended upon gender, wealth, and ethnicity. Nonetheless, America had moved successfully toward the goals of widespread rudimentary English language literacy for most people and a higher, more critical literacy for a smaller elite. Daniel and Lauren Resnick charted the evolution of these goals across the history of industrial France and the United States. In the early twentieth century America had two literacy goals: first, competent, passive English literacy for all, a goal inherited from the "civic-national" phase of literacy's evolution and, second, the more active "elite-technical" skills reserved for a minority of the population in an evolving industrial society.[22]

The simple two-tiered depiction, however, leaves out a great deal of activity in the areas between rudimentary mass literacy and highly trained critical literacy. Gaps were narrowed, secondary education expanded, the book reading market widened apace, and literacy expectations expanded. Not only were more blacks able to say they could read at the rudimentary level, but black colleges increased in number and the black intelligentsia debated an agenda for an educated middle class.[23]

The percentage of seventeen-year-olds who had graduated from high school increased from 2 percent in 1870 to 6.4 percent in 1900, then to 17 percent in 1920 and to 51 percent in 1940.[24] Active book readers tend to be high school attenders, so the book market thrived as education expanded. Book reading was probably not limited to high school graduates, however. In 1919, 15 percent of low- and medium-income white urban dwellers in one survey said they purchased books. The same survey showed that 96 percent purchased newspapers. Newspaper reading was ubiquitous at the turn of the century. A survey of industrial workers in 1890 discovered that newspaper purchasing rates varied from 62 percent among coke workers to 92 percent among glass workers. In a 1901 survey 95 percent of low-income, urban, employed workers said they purchased newspapers or books (most, presumably, buying newspapers).[25]

Concerns about illiteracy one hundred years ago were focused either on European immigrants or black Americans. Many European immigrants were illiterate, and many were non-English speaking; some were both, and often commentators just equated the two. Concerns about the assimilation of immigrants led to the establishment of Americanization programs and to immigration restriction, which came in 1921. The Americanization classes, like most adult education ventures, touched only a tiny percentage of all immigrants, most of whom became familiar with the English language and American institutions in other ways.[26] The heavy rates of European immigration from 1880 to 1920 kept the illiteracy rate high among the foreign-born in America; it was 12 percent in 1880 and 13 percent in 1920, without much variation in the interim.[27] When immigration was restricted, of course, the anxieties about the immigrant threat receded. Indeed, the literacy problem alleviated, since the illiteracy rates among immigrants' children were much lower than among the first generation.

Black illiteracy was a different kind of problem. There was no new influx of illiterate black Americans from abroad, so after 1865 their illiteracy rates gradually decreased. Northern white missionary teachers and southern blacks mounted extensive schooling efforts during Reconstruction, and blacks continued these efforts after Reconstruction collapsed. But there was much mixed opinion among whites on the subject of education for black Americans, as there was for Hispanics. Most American elites, unlike their English and continental counterparts, believed that popular education for working-class whites would lead to assimilation and good behavior. For nonwhites, however, some harbored the even more conservative notion that safety and social order was served by keeping the group ignorant.[28] In reaction to northern philanthropists' late nineteenth-century efforts to promote industrial education for southern African Americans, the *Richmond Dispatch* called black schools "hotbeds of arrogance and aggressions," and the *Farmville Herald* of Virginia said that "when they learn to spell dog and cat they throw away the hoe." Hispanic Americans and other nonwhites faced similar antieducation views. In Texas, one school superintendent said that keeping the Mexican "on his knees in an onion patch . . . does not mix well with education."[29] Despite these barriers, nonwhite illiteracy decreased. We have separate national figures only for blacks, whose self-reported illiteracy rate went from 81 percent in 1870 to 45 percent in 1900 to 23 percent in 1920. As in the earlier case of white women, the convergence of these crude literacy rates masked remaining gaps at higher levels, and these gaps were greater for minorities than for women.

THE DISCOVERY OF FUNCTIONAL ILLITERACY

With entry-level literacy becoming so common, attention turned in the 1920s and 1930s to the quality of reading abilities among those counted as literate. Experts invented the idea of "functional literacy." One literacy expert said in 1920 that some who were "not classified as illiterates" nonetheless "lack facility in reading and writing."[30] William Gray, a leading reading researcher, remarked in a speech to the National Education Association in 1930 that one had to look beyond the high nominal literacy rates in the U.S. census. Millions of people, he said, "have learned to engage in the very simplest reading and writing activities but have not attained functioning literacy." Taking up the question, the National Education Association concluded that functional literacy should be defined by the number of grades one had completed in school. They suggested as a threshold for functional literacy that six grades of school should be completed.[31] This standard was not immediately adopted, but other agencies soon proposed more modest standards, and grade level soon became the measuring stick for functional literacy. One might think that this was hardly better than asking people if they could read, since going to school does not guarantee learning. Everyone knows of children who have gone to school and remained far behind grade-level reading ability or even illiterate. On average, however, school attendance does correlate with increased learning, so the grade-level definition was a modest advance. The Civilian Conservation Corps used third grade as an equivalent of functional literacy in the 1930s, and the army used fourth grade during World War II. The Census Bureau escalated the standard to fifth grade in 1947 and to sixth grade in 1952.[32] The old notion, that mass rudimentary literacy was adequate to our national needs, was giving way to a more demanding goal.

Two other changes occurred in literacy as a public issue during the early decades of the twentieth century: first, state and federal governments got concerned and began to urge action and, second, their attention more often turned from the focus on immigrants and minorities that had been common in the nineteenth century to a more general concern with low-literacy adults in the whole population. One famous program that became a model for state intervention elsewhere began in Rowan County, Kentucky, in 1911. Cora Stewart and a group of public school teachers volunteered to open the county's schools to adults at night, and they visited homes throughout the county to recruit students. Nearly one-third of the population enrolled. The teaching materials included a newspaper about local events produced specially for these "moonlight schools" and a recently published math book that discussed rural problems. The moonlight schools reported great success in teaching literacy, and Stewart became a popular advisor and speaker to groups elsewhere.[33] Publicity surrounding programs like the moonlight schools tended to portray literacy as an either-or proposition, despite the experts' turn to higher level definitions of functional literacy. In only seven or eight weeks, said Stewart, wholly illiterate people could learn to read. This notion—that one was either literate or not and that it was relatively easy to teach reading to adults—flew in the face of developing professional knowledge, but echoes of this attitude have persisted in the public mind and in government rhetoric even down to our time.

While adult literacy programs wrestled with the relatively small but troubling percentage of people who were totally illiterate or could barely read, the average American got more and more schooling. By midcentury, the country was well educated by several measures. The Census Bureau reported that only about 3 percent of the population said they couldn't read or write at all. Only 11 percent of the population had fewer than five years of schooling, the general standard of functional illiteracy at the time.[34] Over 98 percent of all children aged seven to thirteen were enrolled in school, as were 71 percent of those aged sixteen to seventeen. Among seventeen-year-olds, 59 percent were high school graduates. Eighteen percent of all twenty-three-year-olds held bachelor's degrees, double the proportion of ten years earlier.[35]

But what of the quality of literacy? Were Americans satisfied with the quality of learning in their schools? Many were, but criticism was mounting and, by the end of the decade of the 1950s, criticism of the public schools was rampant. The story of school reform brings us beyond the history of print literacy, but we cannot understand our current literacy goals without some attention to the history of these more general school reform efforts. Indeed, one can see the succession of contrasting school reforms since 1950 as a process in which the nation edged toward a goal of inclusive, critical literacy.

We have already seen that the common definition of functional literacy by grade level had risen to fifth grade by 1950. This upgading of expectations continued. In 1960 the U.S. Office of Education used a sixth grade standard, and in the 1970s some experts concluded that every adult needed to be able to read at the twelfth grade level.[36] This level of reading ability implies not just more vocabulary and more comprehension, but advanced literacy skills, such as (in the Resnicks' words) "the ability to gain information from reading and use that information in new contexts." Jeanne Chall argues that, to function well in today's society, everyone needs to be able to read to understand new subject matter and to sort out multiple viewpoints on issues. And even the middling level of the new adult literacy levels defined by Kirsch and his associates demands that readers be able "to search fairly dense text" for information and "to integrate information from relatively long text that does not contain organizational aids such as headings." As we get to the fourth and fifth levels, the need to make inferences increases, as does the need to synthesize or compare complex texts.[37] If all adults are to read at this level, then all children must have a curriculum loaded with cognitive work—not academic in the old sense of rote memorizing and following set procedures, but a highly academic curriculum in a new sense. And if we are to increase the percentage of adults in the current population who have such skills, we would have to increase vastly the availability, quality, and relevance of programs for low-literacy adults.[38]

Critical literacy skills for all was clearly not the goal in 1950. In the area of adult literacy training, the large number of draftees rejected from service in World War II because of low literacy caused a ripple of concern, and the Carnegie Foundation put some money into literacy programs for black Americans, but literacy was not an important item on federal and state social agendas. As for the public schools, they were managing to turn out a population most of whom met the fifth grade functional literacy standard. High schools widely adopted a version of progressive education known as life adjustment education, which targeted the middle 60 percent of the school population for a less academic curriculum, emphasizing academic learning for the top 20 percent and trade education for the bottom 20 percent.

SCHOOL REFORM AND RISING LITERACY GOALS

After 1950 a series of school reforms gradually, tacitly, and cumulatively established the new literacy goal and moved the nation unevenly toward it. There were two phases of school reform debate in the 1950s. Both sets of critics advocated a more academic emphasis, but they differed in two other ways. The academic critics of the public schools in the early 1950s were concerned about the whole range of traditional disciplines, including history and literature. Second, they argued that all children should study the same curriculum. Their chief spokesperson, Arthur Bestor, a historian from the University of Illinois, was adamant about the undemocratic nature of the life adjustment curriculum because it envisioned a more academic curriculum for college-bound students than for others. This practice, Bestor fumed, was based on the belief that 60 percent of the students "are incapable of being benefited by intellectual training," a falsehood that "declares invalid most of the assumptions that have underlain American democracy."[39] Whatever the merits of his critique, Bestor was urging an across-the-board rededication to academic learning for the critical tasks of citizenship, an impulse relevant to today's goal of inclusive, critical literacy.

Bestor and other academic critics did not have very much influence on actual school practice in the mid-1950s. After the launching of the Soviet satellite Sputnik in 1957, school reform pushing for tougher academic work had more influence, but it took a different direction. It emphasized math, science, and foreign languages more than history, geography, literature, or the arts, and it emphasized special courses for academically talented students.[40] One feature of this curriculum reform movement relevant to today's goal of critical literacy was its emphasis on critical thinking and on the student as an active learner. Whatever the eventual pitfalls of the new math, the new science, and the new language labs, this reform period nudged many schools toward more emphasis on active intellectual work, at least for some students. And the high SAT scores of the early 1960s made this period seem like the heyday of academic learning in high school to some later critics.

By the mid-1960s, under the influence of the civil rights movement and President Lyndon Johnson's War on Poverty, attention had shifted to another portion of the school population equally relevant to any goal of universal, critical literacy: low-achieving disadvantaged children. Arguing on grounds of both equal opportunity and the creation of a productive work force, Congress passed such programs as Head Start and Chapter 1 of the Elementary and Secondary Education Act of 1965, aimed at raising the basic reading and math abilities of pupils in low-income areas. Twenty-five years and billions of dollars later, the evaluation verdict on these programs is still mixed, suggesting positive but modest pay-off; nonetheless, whether from these programs or the pressures put on elementary schools to reorient their goals and instructional efforts, the achievement scores of minority and white students have partially converged between 1970 (when the National Assessment of Educational Progress began monitoring school achievement) and the present. This suggests indirectly that the shift in the national educational agenda had some effect.[41]

But it also created some backlash. The red tape of federal regulations, plus the reduction in instructional time for other school subjects like social studies and science, created frustration among local educators. And the attention to skills, without much talk about content, lent itself to criticism. It was wrong on two grounds, critics said. First, it was cognitively naive. All skills had to be rooted in some knowledge of subject matter.[42] Second, it represented a failure of nerve about standards. Opponents of the 1960s reforms and the accompanying ethos of pluralism charged that educators had become moral relativists and were afraid to stand for anything—whether content or values—because they might be charged with promoting a biased history, something that was the property of privileged groups.[43] At its worst, this stereotype portrayed schools as places where anything goes, where the goal was simply to make kids feel good about themselves. Such criticism of the public schools gathered force in the late 1970s and the 1980s, depicting the 1960s and 1970s as a time of reinforced ethnic identity in inner-city schools and of laissez faire smorgasbord curriculums in suburban high schools.[44]

Added to this were the recession of the 1970s, the threat of Japanese economic productivity, and the declining scores on college entrance tests. The picture of decline in the eyes of some observers was devastating. Had American literacy and school achievement steadily expanded and improved for a century and a half only to decline just when the United States was faced with serious trouble in the global economy? Had the great pluralistic experiment finally slowed to a standstill through lack of consensus and will? Had the strategy of more and more schooling for more and more people finally failed to pay off with the advanced skills we needed?

Anxieties about decline—in the schools or in the society more generally—were nothing new in American history, of course. They have recurred periodically since the days when the Founding Fathers feared that excessive democracy would degenerate into chaos without the strong rudder of a monarchy. The decline of republics was a commonplace of their historical understanding.[45] In the late nineteenth century critics of the Gilded Age saw corruption and gaudy display everywhere. Some became good government types and pursued reforms like the civil service. In a similar vein urban reformers of the 1890s aimed to clean up the corrupted school system by centralizing school boards and getting them back in the hands of more responsible elites.[46] And in the 1950s, when the American dream had resulted in most white middle-class families having the *Saturday Evening Post* on their coffee tables and a TV in the corner of the living room, critics following the Frankfurt school agonized about the threat of such mass culture.[47] Their heir in our day, Allan Bloom, bemoaned the decline of serious book reading, the rise of rock music, and the spread of cultural relativism in *The Closing of the American Mind*.[48] Meanwhile, E. D. Hirsch wrote about the decline of shared knowledge in our culture due to the retreat of the schools from content. "We cannot assume that young people today know things that were known in the past by almost every literate person in the culture."[49]

DECLINING LITERACY OR RISING EXPECTATIONS?

Have literacy and shared knowledge declined? It is a complicated question that has engendered interpretations of various kinds, from careful, social science reviews of the assessment literature to polemics more visibly shaped by politics and educational philosophy.[50] The test scores tell a mixed picture. Some scores went down, some went up, and some stayed the same from the 1960s to the 1980s. Some of the declines are attributable to artificial causes, like a changing population taking the test. But in the 1970s, on some highly publicized tests, like the Scholastic Aptitude Tests, there were some real declines. However, for most tests, such as reading achievement tests, the score declines were for a given grade level, so they were offset by the rising school attainment rates. (National average school attainment among twenty-five- to twenty-nine-year-olds rose two years between 1960 and 1980.)[51] This phenomenon led the famous Excellence Commission of 1983 to remark, almost as an aside, that "it is important, of course, to recognize that the average citizen today is better educated and more knowledgeable than the average citizen of a generation ago—more literate, and exposed to more mathematics, literature, and science."[52]

In the midst of all the talk about decline, the most telling trend in reading scores was one that showed virtually no change—the report from the National Assessment of Educational Progress that, although minority reading scores had improved relative to whites over the period 1970 to 1988, the national average was almost unchanged. This was not a decline, but it was a stagnation over a period of nearly twenty years, at a time when literacy demands and expectations were rising and concerns about literacy were linked to prominent national problems.[53]

There are many series of comparable test scores on reading ability and on the general knowledge demanded by college entrance tests, especially after 1950. They are hard to interpret, but the data are plentiful. Comparable scores across time for knowledge in specific content areas are much harder to find, so it is difficult to assess E. D. Hirsch's complaint that so few people today know what virtually everyone used to know about Shakespeare, Dickens, and Ulysses S. Grant. The *New York Times* sponsored a history quiz in 1976 and was able to compare the results with identical items posed to a similar population in the 1940s. Young people knew about the same small stock of information at both dates. Recently, a more comprehensive review of the available assessments of history knowledge has been conducted, with the same result: no decline over time.[54] One reason for the illusion of decline is that, if people like Hirsch are comparing high school students in the 1930s with high school students in the 1990s, they are comparing 50 percent of the age group then with 95 percent of the age group now. Many commentators are coming to the view that the main problem is not decline. It is that we are not meeting new, more demanding goals. Daniel and Lauren Resnick underlined "the novelty of our present situation." Commenting on the back-to-basics movement, they said, "There is little to go *back* to in terms of pedagogical method, curriculum, or school organization. The old tried and true approaches, which nostalgia prompts us to believe might solve current problems, were designed neither to achieve the literacy standard sought today nor to assure successful literacy for everyone."[55] Irwin Kirsch and his associates wrote that, "during the last 200 years, our nation's literacy skills have increased dramatically," but that there have been "periods when demands seemed to surpass levels of attainment. Today although we are a better educated and more literate society than at any other time in our history, we find ourselves in one of these periods of imbalance."[56] And in the American Federation of Teachers' magazine, recently the editors commented that the crisis in American education "is not, as has been suggested, the result of 'decline' from some Golden Age, since if a Golden Age ever existed it existed only for the few." The schools, they judged, "are educating more students and more difficult students to levels attained in earlier times by only a small and favored group." The problem, rather, is that the schools are not doing well enough to meet our needs and not doing well enough in relation to other industrialized nations.[57]

Obviously, the impression of decline has been heightened by the anxieties about America's standard of living and role in the world and by our sometimes forgetting that we have raised our goals. We now aim for knowledge-based, critical literacy for all adults. That goal is daunting enough in itself, but it is complicated by two further matters about *what* and *whose* literacy we are talking about. The debate about empty or content-free skills versus content-based knowledge raised the issue of standards: do we believe in some traditions and some knowledge that can properly be attached to literacy in the United States? If so, what are they? If we define literacy this way, to include the traditions and cultural context in which one learns to read, the national adult literacy issue becomes even more complex; for it is then not just a matter of achieving necessary *levels* of ability, but a matter of finding the appropriate knowledge and traditions to create both coherence and inclusiveness, common ground and a sense of ownership, received knowledge and active participation.

LITERACY AND DIVERSITY: WHOSE CONTENT?

The content and context of literacy have in the past been decided implicitly at the state and local level by school curriculums and lesson plans and at the national level by textbooks and other teaching materials. There has often been dialogue and disagreement about the curriculum on grounds of cultural diversity, and the mainstream curriculum of American schools has gradually and partially accommodated more diverse viewpoints and traditions as it evolved. Analogously, adult literacy educators have periodically attempted to adopt materials related more realistically to the lives of their clients.

Recently, the debate about curricular diversity has heated up. Two polar opposites are depicted. Those who believe the schools' curriculums are too narrow say they are based on a glacially evolving male Western tradition, which leaves out a lot of people; those who think the schools have already given too much ground to diversity say that the cacophony of cultures leaves too little common ground to develop tolerance, common political principles, and common social commitment. No one seems to have found the magic formula for adjudicating a compromise between these extremes in the present cultural and political environment, but ultimately this conflict is relevant to how we define effective adult literacy.

With regard to the literacy issue, advocates of diversity argue that a more pluralistic resolution is required not only because it would be fair according to our democratic, pluralistic commitments but also because effective literacy training demands it. Commentators ranging from anthropologist John Ogbu to the Secretary's Commission on Achieving Necessary Skills to adult literacy expert Hannah Fingeret have recently argued that effective literacy training is impossible without attending to the culture, needs, and histories of the groups involved and that the groups must be collaborators in determining the content and context of literacy.[58]

School reform did not cease while this dialogue was going on. In fact, school reform in the 1980s moved to the states and to an emphasis on the average abilities of the whole school population, not on the educational needs of particular groups. While the controversies over diversity brewed in the background, many activist governors and top school chiefs assumed that there was sufficient consensus about common content and that the problem was to get the schools to focus on it. They believed that the

problem was not what to teach but a lack of resolve, discipline, and resources. State reforms in the 1980s attempted to rededicate schools to
academic learning through new state requirements, including periodic
testing and more courses for high school graduation. They provided new
funds, including better teacher salaries and, in many states, new teacher
certification requirements. In some states, future teachers were required to
take more liberal arts courses, maintain higher grade-point averages, and
pass mandatory writing tests. At its best, the widespread, state-level education reform said two things: that every student was expected to learn and
that schools needed more resources. The results of these reforms were not
dramatic; test scores were not turned around, schools were not transformed. It perhaps is a measure of the urgency of the reform impulse that
the lack of quick results from the state reforms did not deflate the reform
movement; rather, it pushed it energetically in two new directions. Thus, in
the late 1980s and early 1990s, many states and individual school districts
took up the piece of the mid-1980s agenda that had been least implemented
because it was the most difficult: school restructuring. In Dade County,
Florida, in Chicago, in New York, and in far-flung small cities like Easton,
Pennsylvania, and Appleton, Wisconsin, educators actually reversed the
historically potent trend to centralized control of schools and experimented with site-based management, involving more decision-making
authority for building principals, teachers, and parents. The expectation
was that control belonged closer to the community and the classroom and
that decentralization would energize schools and focus resources on improved learning. It is too early to tell yet whether restructuring will lead to
better learning. If it does, it will be relevant to the goal of effective, high-
level adult literacy.

NATIONAL GOALS AND STANDARDS

At the same time, and in striking contrast, a movement began in the 1980s
to create not just national goals but national assessments and national
standards concerning those goals. Pursued by new agencies such as the
National Council on Educational Standards and Testing, the National
Board for Professional Teaching Standards, and the National Education
Goals Panel, as well as some existing organizations like the National Assessment of Educational Progress, the movement sought to specify in some
detail what the national goals meant, how they could be measured, and
what levels of competence would be needed to function well in American
society. This movement has continued during the Clinton administration
and is embodied in the legislation called *Goals 2000*, which retains the goals
enunciated at Charlottesville and creates the National Education Standards and Improvement Council to encourage the development of content

standards, performance standards, and new assessment instruments.[59]

The movement for national standards and assessment faces several obstacles. Given our traditions of local and state control of curriculum, Congress has been hesitant to get involved in curriculum issues, so the federal government's role in the standards effort has been ambivalent. Second, the energetic move toward decentralization experiments, as noted above, stands in contrast to the national standards movement. Third, there is widespread dissatisfaction with traditional paper-and-pencil testing; better assessment is on the horizon, but it seems expensive and unproven. At this early stage, the new forms of assessment lack the widely accepted technology of validity and reliability associated with standardized multiple-choice tests. Thus the movement toward a set of national goals, assessments, and standards has been controversial even though it has been pursued in a noncoercive way. Still, the call for national education goals and assessment has much appeal in government and business circles where currently fashionable quality management theories demand carefully established goals and carefully measured progress.

The emphasis on standards and assessment is directly relevant to the goal of effective adult literacy. Neither the teachers of elementary and secondary schools nor the educators who work in adult literacy training can proceed very effectively toward better critical adult literacy skills without more consensus on how to define and measure necessary adult literacy skills. We do not yet have such agreement. Some have argued that the school language curriculum is not structured to foster the kind of reading skills that adults need.[60] Others have argued that the school-to-work link is weak in the United States and that the literacy and thinking skills learned in schools should be aligned with those needed in the work place.[61]

There are several dangers inherent in such attempts to align school learning with general adult literacy tasks or with work-place roles. With regard to school literacy and adult literacy, the authors of *The Subtle Danger* urged educators to "reconsider the literary emphasis in the K–12 reading curriculum" and find a place for "the literacy skills students sorely lack— skills of logic, inference, and synthesis."[62] Assistant Secretary of Education Chester Finn sounded the alarm for the traditional curriculum, calling the report an "insidious" and "misguided" attempt to subvert the teaching of literature in favor of trivial everyday tasks and diluted standards.[63] One challenge, then, is to overcome the resistance from people who want the schools to do a better job with the traditional curriculum, not to change toward a better fit with adult roles The second problem to avoid is the very trivialization they allege. Any attempt to have schools teach children more effectively for adult roles runs the risks of merely presenting children with formulaic solutions to concrete adult tasks. As Kirsch and his associates argue, we do not need programs in which "discrete functional tasks, such as filling out a job application form or using a bus schedule" are "referred to as competencies that are then taught in isolation." We need, instead, to uncover, analyze, and teach the "ordered set of skills and strategies" that seem to be needed to accomplish reading involving narrative, documents, and numerical work.[64]

Those who have recently called for a tighter school-to-work connection will do well to study the history of vocational education. Throughout the twentieth century, vocational education within the schools has run the risk of bad predictions of two different sorts. First, schools have made predictions about individual students' future vocational roles. If one is going to train students in school for adult work, it is very difficult to escape these sorts of predictions, which in turn tend to stratify the curriculum and preempt decisions students should be making for themselves, at later stages. The second area of wrong predictions is that schools have had to select occupational training programs on the hunch that they would be stable enough and profitable enough to provide jobs for students trained in them. These predictions have not typically turned out well.[65] One solution to these problems, now proposed by many reform commissions, is for schools to teach all children the kind of general knowledge and problem-solving abilities needed in high-performance work places, whether in service, professional, or manufacturing sectors, and then seek to link schools to specific jobs with better apprenticeships and other transitional processes beyond the school's instructional program. Both of these goals differ from traditional vocational education. The first goal, teaching general knowledge and problem solving needed for all high-level work, is inseparable from the new adult literacy goal. In report after report during the past five years, commissions and government agencies have concluded that the American work force needs smarter workers and that schools must be substantially redirected and restructured for students to reach that goal job.[66] Expressing the goal in terms of work-place literacy demands should not obscure the fact that precisely the same abilities—higher order thinking and reading abilities—are urgently needed for citizenship, at a time when public issues have become more and more complex and media coverage is typically simplistic.[67] Indeed, the very vision of a high-performance work place, with front-line workers sharing decisions and using critical literacy skills, is itself a vision of a more democratic work place than those of the old industrial production system, and thus the issue of adult functional literacy illuminates one connection between our economic system and our political system. Some are skeptical that high-performance work places will ever become the norm in the American economy, but it is a forced option, made more urgent by the progress of some other nations toward the goals of high literacy and work-place reorganization. Fortunately, as difficult as the literacy goal will be to reach, if we steer clear of the twin shoals of vocational education—stratification and trivialization—the literacy reform movement is consistent with our best political principles. In its insistence on high-quality literacy for all, it will have to address the prospects of disadvantaged students, who currently have a disproportionate risk of low literacy.

THE GOAL OF HIGH-LEVEL ADULT LITERACY

The history of literacy and education in the United States, as well as every commission on literacy, education, the economy, or citizenship in the past ten years, encourages us to interpret the Charlottesville mandate to mean that every adult should attain at least a moderate level of critical reading ability. If that is the case, we will not come very close to full realization of the goal by the year 2000 or even by 2010. Even if adult literacy remains a high priority and even if schools and adult literacy training programs gain substantial new resources, this goal is the hardest of the six goals to attain in one decade because it targets the whole age range of our population for improvement. In contrast, looking at the goal of school readiness, if we had perfect consensus, effective intervention, and ample resources, we could reach the goal in five years because it targets children from birth to five years. Similarly, if we had perfect consensus, effective intervention strategies, and ample funds, we could implement the science and math learning goal in about seventeen years because it refers to what seventeen-year-olds can do. But to bring the whole population of all ages closer to criticial functional literacy will take not only consensus, effective strategies, and very substantial resources, but more time.

Historically, expanding literacy has been attained by increasing the amount of schooling people had. But the schools have never attempted what is now proposed—critical reading abilities for all students—so just having more of the same schooling will not work. It will take not just more schooling, as in the past, but more effective schooling. Even if the schools succeed in moving in that direction, it will take a few generations for those cohorts of improved readers to move up through the age structure of the population.

While we attempt to restructure the schools to provide the kind of reading and thinking skills needed for high performance work and active citizenship, it is therefore imperative that we improve and expand literacy training for adults. Even though the national average reading ability is much more likely to be affected by better schooling of children, there are at least three reasons for investing in better adult literacy training. First, it will take too long to reach our goal through the schooling of children, even if the schools succeed. We have pursued both strategies in the past and will certainly need to do so if we are to approach the new, rigorous goal of universal, high-performance literacy in the meaningful, midterm future. Second, opportunity is one of our ideals. We don't give up on people at a certain age. Indeed, now more than ever, lifelong learning is for most people a necessity of modern life. Now is especially a time of difficult adjustments as the economy moves from a national to a global plane and from an industrial to an information base. Two generations of workers have been undergoing painful dislocation, and we need to provide them with retraining opportunities. Third, history does not imprison us. Even though adult literacy training has not affected a very large proportion of adults in the past and thus has not affected overall literacy rates very much, it could. To do so, literacy programs need not only to expand but to improve in accessibility, relevance, holding power, and integration with other services. Much good research and program innovation is taking place at present, so it is the right time to expand adult literacy services.

This historical essay has highlighted some of the complexities of literacy: that it is not just a skill but has cultural content, that it is difficult to define and to measure, that it is rooted in an unequal social structure, and that solutions to adult literacy involve a dual strategy of schooling and adult training opportunities. History tells us that the goal of critical adult literacy enunciated at Charlottesville is new and ambitious but has been developing for some decades and that the process of expanding literacy, closing gaps between groups, and raising literacy expectations is continuous in the history of literacy. History cannot tell us how to reach the goal of universal, critical literacy or whether we will have the determination and resources to continue the attempt when interest flags and the short-term results are not dramatic.

If we understand the national literacy goal to aim at critical literacy skills for all Americans, it is audacious. It is an ideal to reach for, not an expectation that we can fulfill literally or completely. If we define the literacy standard rigorously, we will certainly not reach the goal by the year 2000. But if we could get halfway there in the next twenty years and do it in ways that escape the biases that have historically encased literacy attainment in our society, then in my opinion—as a citizen, not as a historian—the country would be immensely better off for it and the investment would be repaid, economically and morally.

NOTES

The writing of this essay was supported by the Office of Educational Research and Improvement, U.S. Department of Education. The author's research on the history of literacy, on which the essay is based, has been generously supported by the Spencer Foundation, the Wisconsin Center for Education Research at the University of Wisconsin-Madison, and the Benton Center at the Department of Education, University of Chicago. This chapter does not represent or reflect the official position of these agencies.

1. Carroll Campbell et al., *The National Education Goals Report: Building a Nation of Learners* (Washington, D.C.: National Education Goals Panel, 1992), 40.

2. The best assessments are Irwin S. Kirsch and Ann Jungeblut, *Literacy: Profiles of America's Young Adults* (Princeton, N.J.: Educational Testing Service, 1986); Irwin S. Kirsch, Ann Jungeblut, and Anne Campbell, *Beyond the School Doors: The Literacy Needs of Job Seekers Served by the U.S. Department of Labor* (Princeton, N.J.: Educational Testing Service, 1992); and Irwin Kirsch, Ann Jungeblut, Lynn Jenkins, and Andrew Kolstad, *Adult Literacy in America: A First Look at the Results of the National Adult Literacy Survey* (Washington, D.C.: U.S. Department of Education, 1993).

3. Kirsch and Jungeblut, *Literacy*, 3.

4. Samuel Eliot Morison, *Puritan Pronaos: The Intellectual Life of Colonial New England* (New York: New York University Press, 1936), 82–85.

5. Kenneth A. Lockridge, *Literacy in Colonial New England: An Enquiry into the Social Context of Literacy in the Early Modern West* (New York: Norton, 1974).

6. David D. Hall, "The Uses of Literacy in New England, 1600–1850" in *Printing and Society in Early America*, ed. William L. Joyce, David D. Hall, Richard D. Brown, and John B. Hench (Worcester, Mass.: American Antiquarian Society, 1983), 24 and "Introduction," passim.

7. See David Paul Nord, "Teleology and News: The Religious Roots of American Journalism, 1630–1730," *Journal of American History* 77 (June 1990): 9–38. The contrast between the seventeenth and eighteenth centuries should not be made too starkly. For the pluralist, competitive aspects of seventeenth-century New England print culture, see David D. Hall, *Worlds of Wonder, Days of Judgment: Popular Religious Belief in Early New England* (Cambridge: Harvard University Press, 1989), 43 and chap. 1, passim.

8. William J. Gilmore, *Reading Becomes a Necessity of Life: Material and Cultural Life in Rural New England, 1780–1835* (Knoxville: University of Tennessee Press, 1989), 264–69; Cathy Davidson, *The Revolution and the Word: The Rise of the Novel in America* (New York: Oxford University Press, 1986), 72–73.

9. Richard D. Brown, *Knowledge Is Power: The Diffusion of Information in Early America, 1700–1865* (New York: Oxford University Press, 1989); idem, "From Cohesion to Competition" in *Printing and Society*, 300–309.

10. Michael Warner, *The Letters of the Republic: Publication and the Public Sphere in Eighteenth-Century America* (Cambridge: Harvard University Press, 1990).

11. Davidson, *Revolution and the Word*; Michael Denning, *Mechanic Accents: Dime Novels and Working-Class Culture in America* (London: Verso, 1987).

12. Brown, *Knowledge Is Power*, 286.

13. I owe much thinking about this evolution to conversations with Janice Radway in our roles as co-editors of a forthcoming volume in the ongoing History of the Book in America, supported by the American Antiquarian Society and the National Endowment for the Humanities.

14. Carl F. Kaestle, "'The Scylla of Brutal Ignorance and the Charybdis of a Literary Education': Elite Attitudes toward Mass Education in Early Industrial

England and America" in *Schooling and Society*, ed. Lawrence Stone (Baltimore: Johns Hopkins University Press, 1976), 177–91.

15. Lockridge, *Literacy in Colonial New England*, 38–39; E. Jennifer Monaghan, "Literacy Instruction and Gender in Colonial New England" in *Reading in America: Literature and Social History*, ed. Cathy N. Davidson (Baltimore: Johns Hopkins University Press, 1989), 53–80.

16. Gilmore, *Reading Becomes a Necessity*, 127; Linda Auwers, "Reading the Marks of the Past: Exploring Female Literacy in Colonial Windsor, Connecticut," *Historical Methods* 13 (1980): 204–14.

17. Maris A. Vinovskis and Richard Bernard, "Beyond Catharine Beecher: Female Education in the Antebellum Period," *Signs* 3 (Summer 1978): 856–69. See also Lee Soltow and Edward Stevens, *The Rise of Literacy and the Common School in the United States: A Socioeconomic Analysis to 1870* (Chicago: University of Chicago Press, 1981), 156–58.

18. This theme is pursued in Carl F. Kaestle, "Literacy and Diversity: Themes from a Social History of the American Reading Public," *History of Education Quarterly* 28 (Winter 1988): 545–47. See also Gita Z. Wilder and Kristin Powell, *Sex Differences in Test Performance: A Survey of the Literature* (New York: College Entrance Examination Board, 1989).

19. On the reactions of enslaved blacks to white literacy, see Warner, *Letters of the Republic*, 11, and the references there; also, Janet Duitsman Cornelius, *When I Can Read My Title Clear: Literacy, Slavery, and Religion in the Antebellum South* (Columbia: University of South Carolina Press, 1991).

20. See Mordecai Soltes, *The Yiddish Press in America: An Americanizing Agency* (Philadelphia: Jewish Publication Society, 1925), and Carl Wittke, *The German-Language Press in America* (Lexington: University of Kentucky Press, 1957), chap. 11.

21. John K. Folger and Charles B. Nam, *Education of the American Population* (Washington, D.C.: Bureau of the Census, 1967), chap. 4.

22. See Daniel P. Resnick and Lauren B. Resnick, "The Nature of Literacy: An Historical Exploration," *Harvard Educational Review* 47 (August 1977): 370–85.

23. James Anderson, *The Education of Black Americans in the South, 1860–1920* (New York: Oxford University Press, 1988); August Meier, *Negro Thought in America, 1880–1920* (Ann Arbor: University of Michigan Press, 1963); Michael G. Fultz, "Education in the Black Monthly Periodical Press, 1900–1910" in *Education of the Afro-American Adult*, ed. Harvey G. Neufeldt and Leo McGee (Westport, Conn.: Greenwood Press, 1990), 75–112.

24. Abbott L. Ferriss, *Indicators of Trends in American Education* (New York: Russell Sage Foundation, 1969), 378–79.

25. Carl F. Kaestle, Helen Damon-Moore, Lawrence C. Stedman, Katherine Tinsley, and William Vance Trollinger, Jr., *Literacy in the United States: Readers and Reading since 1880* (New Haven: Yale University Press, 1991), 164. See also David Paul Nord, "Working-Class Readers: Family, Community, and Reading in Late 19th-Century America," *Communication Research* 13 (April 1986): 156–81.

26. Frank Thompson, *Schooling of the Immigrant* (New York: Harper & Brothers, 1920), 32–34.

27. Sanford Winston, *Illiteracy in the United States, from 1870 to 1920* (Chapel Hill: University of North Carolina Press, 1930), 58.

28. Kaestle, "Elite Attitudes," 185–86.

29. Anderson, *Education of Black Americans*, 97; Herschel T. Manuel, *The Education of Mexican and Spanish-speaking Children in Texas* (Austin: University of Texas Press, 1930), 77.

30. Winston, *Illiteracy from 1870 to 1920*, 15.

31. William S. Gray, "Catching Up with Literacy" (Paper presented at the 71st Annual Meeting of the National Education Association, Washington, D.C., 1933), 280; Wanda Dauksza Cook, *Adult Literacy Education in the United States* (Newark, Del.: International Reading Association, 1977), 43.

32. Kaestle et al., *Literacy in the United States*, 92

33. P. P. Claxton, *Illiteracy in the United States and an Experiment for Its Elimination*, bulletin 20 (Washington, D.C.: Bureau of Education, 1913); Cora Wilson Stewart, *Moonlight Schools for the Emancipation of Adult Illiterates* (New York: E. P. Dutton, 1922).

34. Cook, *Adult Literacy Education*, 64.

35. Ferriss, *Indicators of Trends*, 378, 380, 389.

36. Kaestle et al., *Literacy in the United States*, 92; Carmen St. John Hunter and David Harman, *Adult Literacy in the United States* (New York: McGraw-Hill, 1979), 27; John B. Carroll and Jeanne C. Chall, *Toward a Literate Society* (New York: McGraw-Hill, 1975), 8; see also Jeanne S. Chall, "Policy Implications of Literacy Definitions" in *Toward Defining Literacy*, ed. Richard L. Venezky, Daniel A Wagner, and Barrie S. Ciliberti (Newark, Del.: International Reading Association, 1990).

37. Resnick and Resnick, "Nature of Literacy," 382; Chall, "Policy Implications of Literacy Definitions," 58–59; Kirsch, Jungeblut, and Campbell, *Beyond the School Doors*, 26.

38. See Hannah A. Fingeret, "Changing Literacy Instruction: Moving beyond the Status Quo" in *Leadership for Literacy: The Agenda for the 1990s*, ed. Forrest P. Chisman and Associates (San Francisco: Jossey-Bass Publishers, 1990), 25–50, and Gordon Berlin and Andrew Sum, *Toward a More Perfect Union: Basic Skills, Poor Families, and Our Economic Future* (New York: Ford Foundation, 1989), 24–38.

39. Arthur Bestor, *Educational Wastelands: The Retreat from Learning in Our Public Schools*, 2d ed. (Urbana: University of Illinois Press, [1953] 1985), 82.

40. Barbara Barksdale Clowse, *Brainpower for the Cold War: The Sputnik Crisis and National Defense Education Act of 1958* (Westport, Conn.: Greenwood Press, 1981).

41. Ina V. S. Mullis and Lynn B. Jenkins, *The Reading Report Card, 1971–88: Trends from the Nation's Report Card* (Princeton, N.J.: Educational Testing Service, 1990), 13–15. On the evaluation of Head Start, see Marshall Smith and J. S. Bissell, "Report Analysis: The Impact of Head Start," *Harvard Educational Review* 40 (1970): 51–104, and R. Haskins, "Beyond Metaphor: The Efficacy of Early Childhood Education," *American Psychologist* 44 (1989): 274–82. On Title I and the Elementary and Secondary Education Act, see Julie Roy Jeffrey, *Education for Children of the Poor: A Study of the Origins and Implementation of the Elementary and Secondary Education Act of 1965* (Columbus: Ohio State University Press, 1978); Gary Natriello, Edward McDell, and Aaron Pallas, *Schooling Disadvantaged Children: Racing against Catastrophe* (New

York: Teachers College Press, 1990); and Commission on Chapter 1, *Making Schools Work for Children in Poverty* (Washington, D.C.: Council of Chief State School Officers, 1992).

42. See Thomas G. Sticht and B. A. McDonald, *Making the Nation Smarter: The Intergenerational Transfer of Cognitive Ability* (San Diego: Applied Behavioral and Cognitive Sciences, 1989), and Robert Glaser, "Education and Thinking: The Role of Knowledge," *American Psychologist* 39 (January 1984), 93–104.

43. Diane Ravitch and Chester E. Finn, Jr., *What Do Our 17-Year-Olds Know? A Report on the First National Assessment of History and Literature* (New York: Harper & Row, 1987), 8.

44. Frank E. Armbruster, *Our Children's Crippled Future: How American Education Has Failed* (New York: Quadrangle, 1977); Paul Copperman, *The Literacy Hoax: The Decline of Reading, Writing, and Learning in the Public Schools and What We Can Do about It* (New York: William Morrow & Co., 1978); Arthur G. Powell, Eleanor Farrar, and David K. Cohen, *The Shopping Mall High School: Winners and Losers in the Educational Marketplace* (Boston: Houghton Mifflin, 1985).

45. See Gordon S. Wood, *The Creation of the American Republic, 1776–1787* (Chapel Hill: University of North Carolina Press, 1969), 92, 123–24.

46. David B. Tyack, *The One Best System: A History of American Urban Education* (Cambridge: Harvard University Press, 1974).

47. Bernard Rosenberg and David M. White, eds., *Mass Culture: The Popular Arts in America* (Glencoe, Ill.: Free Press, 1957); see also Patrick Brantlinger, *Bread and Circuses: Theories of Mass Culture as Social Decay* (Ithaca: Cornell University Press, 1983).

48. Allan Bloom, *The Closing of the American Mind: How Higher Education Has Failed Democracy and Impoverished the Souls of Today's Students* (New York: Simon & Schuster, 1987).

49. E. D. Hirsch, Jr., *Cultural Literacy: What Every American Needs To Know* (Boston: Houghton Mifflin, 1987), 8. On complaints about decline that recurred as schools became more and more inclusive, see Lawrence A. Cremin, *Popular Education and Its Discontents* (New York: Harper & Row, 1990), 1–12.

50. See Kaestle et al., *Literacy in the United States*, chaps. 3 and 4 and the works cited therein, for examples.

51. Thomas D. Snyder, *Digest of Education Statistics, 1993* (Washington, D.C.: Department of Education, 1993), 17.

52. National Commission on Excellence in Education, *A Nation at Risk: The Imperative for Educational Reform* (Washington, D.C.: U.S. Department of Education, 1983), 11.

53. Mullis and Jenkins, *Reading Report Card*, 20.

54. *New York Times*, 2–4 May 1976; Dale Whittington, "What Have Our 17-Year-Olds Known in the Past?" *American Education Research Journal* (Winter 1992): 776–78.

55. Resnick and Resnick, "Nature of Literacy," 384, 385.

56. Kirsch, Jungeblut, and Campbell, *Beyond the School Doors*, 2.

57. *American Educator* (Winter 1992): 19–20.

58. John U. Ogbu, "Understanding Cultural Diversity and Learning," *Education-*

al Researcher 21 (November 1992): 5–14; Secretary's Commission on Achieving Necessary Skills, Learning a Living: A Blueprint for High Performance (Washington, D.C.: U.S. Department of Labor, 1992); Fingeret, "Changing Literacy Instruction."

59. House of Representatives, Goals 2000: Educate America Act: Conference Report, 103d Cong., 1st sess., Rept. 103–446.

60. Richard L. Venezky, "The Origins of the Present-Day Chasm between Adult Functional Literacy Needs and School Literacy Instruction," Visible Language 16 (1982): 113–26; Richard Venezky, Carl F. Kaestle, and Andrew Sum, The Subtle Danger: Reflections on the Literacy Abilities of American Youth (Princeton, N.J.: Educational Testing Service, 1986).

61. For example, Commission on the Skills of the American Workforce, America's Choice: High Skills or Low Wages! (Rochester, N.Y.: National Center on Education and the Economy, 1990), chap. 7; Secretary's Commission on Achieving Necessary Skills, Learning a Living, 51.

62. Venezky, Kaestle, and Sum, Subtle Danger, 43.

63. Chester Finn, "'None Too Subtle Danger' Lurking within New Report," Education Week, 11 March 1987.

64. Kirsch, Jungeblut, and Campbell, Beyond the School Doors, 115.

65. Larry Cuban, "Enduring Resiliency: Enacting and Implementing Federal Vocational Education Legislation" in Work, Youth, and Schooling: Historical Perspectives on Vocationalism in American Education, ed. Harvey Kantor and David B. Tyack (Stanford: Stanford University Press, 1982), 44–78; Harvey Kantor, Learning to Earn: School, Work, and Vocational Reform in California, 1880–1930 (Madison: University of Wisconsin Press, 1988), 142–48.

66. See, for example, Commission on the Skills of the American Workforce, America's Choice; Secretary's Commission on Achieving Necessary Skills, Learning a Living; William B. Johnston and Arnold E. Packer, Workforce 2000: Work and Workers for the Twenty-first Century (Indianapolis: Hudson Institute, 1987). On the complicated issue of whether jobs are becoming "smarter" or "dumber" in general, see K. I. Spenner, "The Upgrading and Downgrading of Occupations: Issues, Evidence, and Implications for Education," Review of Educational Research 55 (Summer 1985): 125–54.

67. Francis Schrag, Thinking in School and Society (New York: Routledge, 1988), 127–34; W. Russell Newman, The Paradox of Mass Politics: Knowledge and Opinion in the American Electorate (Cambridge: Harvard University Press, 1986).

14 *REEFER MADNESS* AND

A CLOCKWORK ORANGE

WILLIAM J. REESE

Since the 1960s, ordinary citizens who differ on many issues have agreed that drug abuse and violent behavior have increased among young people. For sixteen of the first twenty years of the Gallup poll on education, first taken in 1969, the public ranked discipline as the number one problem facing the schools. In recent years drug abuse has replaced discipline as the leading indicator of youth's decline. Given these concerns, the authors of *The National Education Goals Report* hope that within a decade "every school in America will be free of drugs and violence and will offer a disciplined environment conducive to learning."[1]

Youth's shocking capacity for self-destruction and social disorder flashes across television screens and fills magazines and newspapers. A cover of the *New Yorker* shows children walking to school shouldering knapsacks and assault rifles. The media highlights urban high schools with armed security guards and metal detectors. Approximately 100,000 students reportedly tote a gun (plus other weapons) to school daily; some teachers are knifed, poisoned, or shot. When a poor school district considers free insurance to help cover burial costs for youth killed in drug wars, *A Clockwork Orange* (1971) isn't just a movie anymore.[2]

Are young people in a steady state of moral decline? America's youth clearly have many problems, especially those mired in poverty. Collectively, however, they hardly seem depraved. Violence has clearly accelerated among youth, as among adults, yet a small percentage of schools have the most serious problems. Similarly, although most youths (and adults) experiment with various drugs, only a small minority become addicts or a social menace. The popular press still reports that teenage alcohol consumption increased dramatically after marijuana use declined in the late 1970s, despite evidence to the contrary.[3]

Compared with previous decades, does violence, drug abuse, and a lack of discipline now characterize American youth? If so, what caused these changes and who has defined our understanding of these problems? Will our schools become safe and drug-free?

In this chapter we first examine the concept of a safe, disciplined environment, noting how its definition has changed historically. Social scientists have charted the rise and fall of licit and illicit drug use among high school seniors since the 1970s. Discipline is a more complicated, multifaceted issue, harder to trace precisely over time. Until quite recently, no one kept statistics about sexual harassment or bullies. More empirical evidence exists on smoking patterns than on rudeness, on cocaine abuse than on shake-downs for lunch money.

BEFORE THE 1960S

Are safety, discipline, and drug use as closely intertwined as policy makers assume? Antimarijuana films made in the 1930s, such as *Reefer Madness* (1936), promoted this image. Otherwise decent high school students from respectable families literally went to pot. Puffers soon got lower grades and became implicated in murders and sleazy sex affairs. Today's teenage gang warfare and the related high death toll of minority males only reinforce this image linking drugs and violence.[4]

Discipline, however, has been a perennial educational concern, often unrelated to drugs. The teachers' right to whip, suspend, or expel the unruly was well established by the nineteenth century. Many Ichabod Cranes with a switch in hand taught in the schools (as did more gentle folks). The most popular fictionalized account of rural schools, Edward Eggleston's *The Hoosier-Schoolmaster* (1871), portrays a young teacher fearful of student violence. He needs bulldog determination to face his charges.[5]

Before the 1940s, discipline was central to public education. Schools emphasized moral training and character development, and corporal punishment was common. Violence was hardly unknown on playgrounds or elsewhere. Hollywood heroes glamorized gangsters, FBI agents, and the cavalry. Students who fought mostly used fists, and angry teachers spanked young bottoms with open palms or wooden paddles.

Then, as now, violence assumed many forms. Schoolgirls suffered ridicule as sex objects, bullies extorted money from the weak, and the reckless initialed desks and defaced textbooks. Ethnic neighborhood gangs (which included dropouts) terrorized some urban residents. Students rarely carried weapons to school, but administrators enjoyed the legal right and public sanction to dismiss and expel troublemakers. Today's conservatives naturally bemoan the passing of this golden age.

Since most teenagers still did not attend high school or plan to graduate, educators did not face the challenges presented when secondary school attendance became universal by the 1950s and 1960s. As the labor market for working-class teenagers collapsed during the Depression, high school enrollments grew dramatically. Full attendance forever changed the mission of the high school. Before the 1950s, young men (who commit most teenage crimes) not in school were disciplined by the work place, armed services, or other institutions. When adolescent (and adult) crime rose dramatically in the 1960s, society increasingly indicted public schools for not preventing a problem not of their making.[6]

The 1940s and 1950s witnessed a growing nervousness about school crime and misbehavior. During the 1940s, as more women worked outside the home and many fathers fought overseas, Congressmen, social scientists, educators, and other citizens complained about the failures of youth and their families. As one prescient observer noted in 1984, the "problems of discipline and violence in schools did not begin with television, rock and roll, school desegregation, or Vietnam."[7]

Discussions of school violence and classroom safety centered on teenagers and the high school. In sensational articles in the 1940s, J. Edgar Hoover said even girls were part of a teen "crime wave" sweeping the nation. Congressional hearings on juvenile delinquency also made the headlines. Many citizens believed that juvenile crime was growing.[8]

Movies such as *The Wild One* (1953), *Blackboard Jungle* (1955), and *Rebel without a Cause* (1955) framed popular images of violent, troubled, insecure, hostile youth that were imitated in dozens of other films. Marlon Brando and his motorcycle gang behaved shockingly. Students in the *Blackboard Jungle*, set in a New York City vocational high school, were beer-swizzling, knife-wielding gang members who assaulted teachers, desecrated property, and defied authority. James Dean's character, in turn, taught America that even middle-class boys removed their coats and ties after school and donned their blue jeans and T-shirts, engaging in knife fights and deadly drag races to prove their manhood. Even privileged teenagers could not find social approval, love, or guidance at home or at school.[9]

Did the real world resemble the movies? The evidence was ambiguous. In congressional hearings on juvenile delinquency, testimony emerged that understandably made teachers, principals, and parents anxious. Some students were bringing weapons—mostly knives, brass knuckles, and some guns—into a few urban high schools, especially where ethnic and racial tensions simmered.[10]

Violence in some schools had probably increased, as high schools struggled to incorporate new working-class populations into urban systems. Still, fear for public safety came from many sources. This was the era of the bomb shelter, when schoolchildren everywhere practiced the art of duck and cover, hiding beneath their seats on command to survive an atomic blast from the Russians. Schoolchildren wore dog tags. If new forms of fear and violence pervaded America's schools, they grew from many seeds.[11]

Dress codes remained common in the 1950s and early 1960s, though some institutions seemed more lenient. Very little social scientific research was conducted on school crime and violence, but teachers did not ordinarily work in blackboard jungles. Critics did blame progressive educators for low academic standards and slack discipline in the schools. Still, youthful misbehavior or actual delinquency failed to match the most shrill rhetoric.[12]

Many students identified with Holden Caulfield in J. D. Salinger's enormously popular novel, *The Catcher in the Rye* (1951). But neither Holden nor the popularity of comic books, Elvis, Little Richard, or Jerry Lee Lewis made most youth violent creatures. It was also the age of tent revivals, church on Sunday, and Pat Boone.

Professional education journals expressed real concern for delinquency and the prospect of unsafe schools, yet they seemed complacent compared with some congressional hearings or Hollywood movies. A National Education Association survey in 1956 revealed that teachers had a growing fear of student misbehavior yet thought only 1 in 100 students were troublemakers, mostly found in slum schools. Fist fights at lunch time, running in the corridors, speaking out of turn, chewing gum, throwing spit wads, and traditional student misbehavior and pranks remained familiar complaints. An article on "the maladjusted child" in 1952 said that "stealing and rowdyism" were among the most serious "acts of student indiscretion." In 1957 two preeminent social scientists listed among "student misbehavior . . . inattention, carelessness, underhandedness, and smoking."[13]

Historian William Graebner's study of Buffalo in the 1950s demonstrated that local police called every street corner gathering a "gang." To combat ethnic gangs and after-school rumbles, city leaders sponsored chaperoned dances. Here, as elsewhere, middle-class parents feared that working-class youth, a growing presence in high school, would contaminate the "better" students. Some youth were certainly violent. In 1960 Buffalo police confiscated sawed-off baseball bats, lug wrenches, and a pickax before one rumble. While gun fights were routine on television and on the big screen, teenage fights, however brutal, still relied on fists.[14]

Through the 1950s the prominent *California Journal of Secondary Education* emphasized that teachers, like society, wanted schools to discipline and control as well as to educate students. "Despite its cry for more of the 3 R's, society also wants its youth taught obedience, self control, and respect for adults, law and order." In 1955, the journal's editor dedicated a whole issue to juvenile delinquency. But he claimed that teachers mostly worried about the "Troublesome 1 Percent."[15]

Peers grew in importance in the lives of youth. One writer in 1956 said that teenagers now seemed different, since they increasingly felt free "to express resentment more fearlessly in the classroom, at home, and in public places." The editor added: "Wherever high school teachers gather, a perennial topic of complaint is discipline. Adolescents, teachers will tell you, shift erratically from apathy to rebellion." But school rebellion still largely meant tossing paper wads and talking out of turn.[16]

SCHOOL SAFETY AFTER 1960

As crime in general increased in the 1960s and 1970s, school safety problems also accelerated, especially in major cities. One study claimed that juvenile crime nationally increased by 246 percent between 1965 and 1977. That "violence is as American as cherry pie" seemed apropos, as many forms of crime increased in the 1960s and then further accelerated. School crime apparently leveled off by the mid-1970s, although urban gangs and the proliferation of cheap hand guns (and worse) still undermine public order. Incivility, claim many observers, characterizes America's schools. But schools generally reflect (and sometimes are safer than) society.[17]

Although many citizens debate the causes and magnitude of social disorder, conservatives have often used rising crime rates for political advantage. After Richard Nixon's law and order campaign in 1968, even neoconservative Democrats later blamed contemporary woes on the sixties. As the nation veered rightward after 1968, polls ranked discipline as the leading school problem. *Discipline* lacks precise definition. But a broad consensus emerged that the young should respect authority and behave.[18]

What caused the escalation of school vandalism and violence? Since the late 1960s, various people have blamed the youth culture, liberalism, radical professors, poverty, declining family values, racism, peer groups, Communists, arbitrary teachers or school administrators, an irrelevant curriculum, spoiled baby boomers, large class or school size, and so forth. A distinguished panel of social scientists in 1974 pointed out more simply that the numerical increase in the fourteen to twenty-four age group in the 1960s was unprecedented in this century. For the first time, many of the males in this group (perpetrators of most crimes), especially teenagers, were increasingly not in the work force but in school.[19]

Although increased levels of incivility and violence were undoubtedly rooted in multiple sources, some vocal critics blamed relativism in the schools. Educators by the late 1960s often stopped teaching traditional

values, sharing society's belief that morals were private matters. Even
conservatives in power, while espousing law and order, also weakened
respect for authority. Government officials lied about the war in Vietnam,
broke laws to undermine critics and antiwar protestors, and later coined
new words like *coverup* as Nixon fell from power. The young had a multi-
tude of negative role models.[20]

Antiwar campus revolts also spawned new ideas about students'
rights, even in high schools, but more fundamental to social disorder was
the erosion of the inner-city economy. In 1964 a teacher wrote in the *Journal
of Secondary Education* that "the blackboard jungle" was now a living reality
in many cities. One writer, already an anachronism but anticipating Principal Joe Clark and his baseball bat, said schools should expel the "hoody"
element. Traditional order was eroding in urban education, and declining
neighborhoods meant declining schools. By 1968, the *Journal of Secondary
Education* ominously announced: "NEEDED: A Policy for Riot Control in
Schools and School Districts."[21]

A small percentage of secondary students actively participated in the
civil rights movement or in antiwar protests. But sit-ins, student boycotts,
peace rallies, and participation in Moratorium Day became more common
in some high schools. Adult authority weakened. Students demanded alternative newspapers and casual dress and even sued schools for their civil
rights. These actions were unprecedented. One professor opined in 1970
that youth were rightly disgusted, since teachers lacked "rapport" with
students and taught irrelevant courses. Three out of five principals polled
by the National Association of Secondary School Principals had encountered some "student protest" the previous year.[22]

Criticisms of insensitive, racist, thoughtless teachers were hardly new.
But several best-selling books in the 1960s focused on the horrors of racism
and urban school decay. These writers challenged the status quo but hardly told students to engage in violence or vandalism. Few teenagers read
these books, but school violence increased, which occurred in a context of
urban riots, political assassinations, and the Vietnam War.[23]

A 1964 NEA report on school violence revealed that teachers increasingly worried about personal safety, and the first systematic national study
of school vandalism, by the Office of Education in 1969, estimated that the
annual destruction of school property (not including medical bills for students and teachers) exceeded $100 million. The NEA soon doubled the
estimate. In one crime-infested school in Los Angeles, grateful students
named a security cop "teacher of the year."[24]

Historian Jeffrey Mirel documented the rise of uncivil behavior in Detroit. Given the widespread urban riots, what happened seemed natural.
By 1969, Mirel wrote, assaults on person and property multiplied, terrify-

ing many teachers. "It is impossible to catalog the number of violent incidents in the Detroit schools . . . Literally hundreds of incidents, including shootings, stabbings, rapes, student rampages, gang fights, assaults, arson, bombings and bomb threats, extortion, and vandalism occurred in the schools or on school property."[25]

With school and society simultaneously shaped by greater social conflict, educators feared more than the troublesome 1 percent. Now high schools were educating those previously excluded from secondary schools and whose families faced a deteriorating economy. The conservative demand for law and order intensified. In its first poll on education in 1969, Gallup asked: "How do you feel about the discipline in the local schools— is it too strict, not strict enough, or just about right?" Only 2 percent thought the schools too strict, 49 percent said not strict enough, 44 percent said it was about right, and 5 percent did not know or failed to answer. Besides favoring stricter dress codes, the majority said discipline was the "biggest problem" facing the schools.[26]

In 1974, big-city superintendents helped Gallup frame its first direct questions on school vandalism and crime, indicating which educators knew most about the subject. When Gallup asked in 1975 whether schools should teach "morals and moral behavior" (admittedly vague), 79 percent of those polled said yes and only 15 percent said no. The figures in the next decade were almost identical.[27]

SCHOOL SAFETY IN THE 1970S

Government reports claimed that school violence and vandalism peaked sometime by the mid-1970s. However, many citizens, lay and professional, emphasized the prevalence of adolescent violence. In 1976, even National Public Radio opened a program on school violence by saying, "Violence and vandalism in schools are problems that won't go away . . . they seem to have reached crisis proportions." Guests on the program came from across the educational spectrum and worried about escalating violence. A contributor to *Adolescence* in 1978 agreed that teenage crime had reached "near crisis proportions."[28]

Were youth feeding on an orgy of violence? Some schools, like some neighborhoods, were clearly less safe than in the 1950s. By the late 1960s, many urban high schools hired security guards, adding to a prisonlike atmosphere. Not every city's schools had so deteriorated, but more crimes occurred even in the mostly safer suburban and rural schools. Orwellian responses proliferated. Closed circuit televisions appeared in one Dallas junior high school; Parma, Ohio, installed a "radar alarm system" to deter vandals; and intercom systems that detected "unusual noises (e.g., shattering glass)" guarded the Jefferson County, Kentucky, schools. High technology attempted to outsmart thieves and troublemakers. And two government reports on school violence and vandalism, in 1975 and 1977, produced more evidence about errant youth.[29]

Senator Birch Bayh of Indiana, a liberal Democrat, chaired the Senate Subcommittee to Investigate Juvenile Delinquency in the early 1970s. His report was frequently cited in the media: *Our Nation's Schools—A Report Card: 'A' in School Violence and Vandalism.* Noting that in a 1964 survey teachers had said that 3 percent of their students were "discipline problems," Bayh attacked the "rising level of student violence and vandalism." Tossing paper wads and talking back to teachers remained familiar annoyances but now were hardly even reported. Felonies were now common, "including brutal assaults on teachers and students, as well as rapes, extortions, burglaries, thefts, and an unprecedented wave of wanton destruction and vandalism."[30]

The examples were sobering. Violence and vandalism were concentrated in but hardly limited to major cities. In 1964, 15 percent of the teachers sampled by the NEA had been assaulted by a student; a survey in 1973 put the figure at 37 percent. Most crimes involved students against students. Few systems had personnel equipped to deal with violence, which drained school resources, disrupted classrooms, and weakened morale. Albert Shanker of the American Federation of Teachers testified that most school crimes went unreported, since teachers traditionally expected schools to be orderly; to admit otherwise was to admit abject failure.[31]

Other studies indicated that school vandalism and violence rose dramatically in the 1960s and continued its ascent. Of the nation's school districts, 90 percent reported broken glass and windows; arson, burglaries, and attacks on persons and property increased dramatically; and gangs terrorized some places. New York City reported ten thousand school crimes in 1973, a fraction of the real total. Sixteen shootings marred the school year in Kansas City, Missouri, and thirty classmates beat and stabbed an innocent girl in Detroit. Some southern urban schools were "armed camps."[32]

After Bayh's report, the National Institute of Education (NIE) issued *Violent Schools—Safe Schools* (1977). It provided more data on student misbehavior, which the media cited with different degrees of accuracy. "Are crime and violence more prevalent in schools today than in the past?" asked the authors. Many studies showed that "acts of violence and property destruction in schools increased throughout the 1960s to the early 1970s and levelled off after that." School principals surveyed between 1971 and 1976 did not record any dramatic increase in crime, though the rate was much higher than before. The NIE study claimed that only 8 percent of all schools, mostly though not all in large cities, had serious crime problems, a point often downplayed by the press.[33]

Petty theft was common everywhere. The typical high school student had "about 1 chance in 9 in having something stolen in a month; 1 chance in 80 of being attacked; and 1 chance in 200 of being robbed." Most crime was directed by white pupils against other whites or by blacks against blacks, though interracial crime was not uncommon. The study concluded that the racial or ethnic composition of the student body was not a very good predictor of whether violence occurred in a particular school, "once other factors, such as the amount of crime in the neighborhood, are taken into account." About 12 percent of all secondary teachers each month were robbed of something worth over $1 and 0.5 percent were physically attacked, though a huge 19 percent of the attacks required medical treatment. Teachers and students often felt unsafe in some classrooms, halls, bathrooms, stairwells, or parking lots. Rural schools were the safest; large cities were the least safe.[34]

Schools had long suffered the aggravations and costs of crimes against property, and the NIE study showed its extensiveness. Trespassing, breaking and entering, and window smashing was common; a school typically had a 1 in 4 chance of being vandalized each month. Nationally, vandalism cost somewhere between $100 million and $200 million. A violent society had created some violent youth.[35]

Estimates of actual versus reported crime varied enormously. Of all districts included in the study, 1 percent had police stationed in the schools, though 15 percent of the large cities did. Security alarms, paddling (especially in the junior high schools), and other efforts to deter or punish crime became more common as school crime and vandalism increased. As the costs escalated, states increasingly made parents legally responsible for their children's crimes.[36]

INCIVILITY IN THE SCHOOLS

Some pundits quipped in the 1980s that schools had been designed when teachers thought chewing gum was a social problem. As violence and vandalism increased, schools invested more in prevention programs and in security. Like earlier conservatives, the Republican party of Ronald Reagan and George Bush attributed low school achievement to laziness and lax discipline. The famous report, *A Nation at Risk* (1983), argued that schools needed to emphasize personal responsibility and higher academic standards.[37]

Law-and-order Republicans thus popularized familiar themes of social stability and respect for authority. Conservatives routinely criticized violence yet blocked efforts to control the spread of cheap hand guns and assault weapons. Reagan did create, however, a National School Safety Center in 1983 to disseminate information on how to make schools safer. It was located in that cauldron of urban violence, Malibu.[38]

Throughout the 1980s and early 1990s, teachers and administrators worked diligently to create safe schools in some of the nation's most violent neighborhoods. Studies of high schools revealed that the levels of personal violence and vandalism remained relatively high, considering declining school enrollments, though some reduction in crime apparently occurred after the levels stabilized in the 1970s. Even when school violence did decline, children might still face gang-infested streets. The overall effect was chilling. Too many students feared walking to school or using the school bathroom or playing at recess.[39]

In 1986 historian Michael Sedlak and his colleagues described some of the determinants of high school achievement, noting that multiple factors—from peers to home environment to poor instruction—contributed to the high rates of vandalism. Whatever the causes, incivility was common. While violent behavior at school seemed to decline, wrote Sedlak and his colleagues, "this does not mean that tardiness, classroom disruptions, and failure to do homework exact no serious toll on the level of content learning in schools." Student "rudeness" was "widespread" and sapped the morale of teachers. Violence and uncivil behavior remained popular on the silver screen and in too many schools.[40]

Since the late 1970s, some citizens have rediscovered that violence is widespread in American life and lucrative for Hollywood. (Those in authority pursued armed conflict in the Gulf War instead of first pursuing an embargo.) According to a 1988 study, children on average saw an estimated eighteen thousand murders on television before graduation, and the media and children's toys often glorified violence. Access to assault rifles made violence ever deadly, though local schools were often safer than children's homes and neighborhoods. This was little consolation to victims, but it placed things in context. Very few children were killed or violently hurt at school compared with the city streets.[41]

School security measures accelerated in the 1980s and early 1990s, as experts helped administrators learn more about educational "target hardening," or how to make schools and children less vulnerable. New programs taught children about the evils of violent behavior and tried to help victims cope with personal tragedies. The National School Safety Center distributed pamphlets and assorted materials to schools, highlighting effective or experimental curricular programs. Hardening the target especially appealed to those who felt under siege.[42]

The center's *School Discipline Notebook* (1987) quoted Ronald Reagan on the need to learn discipline, especially self-discipline, at school. "Who better to teach the student respect for rules—his principal or someday, the police?" Believing that school crime, like other crimes, seemed to be increasing, the *Notebook* called for well-ordered schools with clear, well-enforced rules on student behavior. Besides explaining how students should walk in the halls, care for their textbooks, and so forth, it enumerated some of the worst forms of student violence, however atypical. "No student knowingly shall possess, handle, or transmit any knife, razor, ice pick, explosive, loaded cane, sword cane, machete, pistol, rifle, shotgun, pellet gun, metal knuckles, or other object that reasonably can be considered a weapon or dangerous instrument in any school building, on any school premises."[43]

The *School Safety Check Book* (already reprinted by 1990) emphasized that academic achievement depended upon safer learning environments. Schools facing or anticipating violence and vandalism had to follow some simple rules: keep gravel off the school yard, remove external door handles except for the front entrance, consider investing in more security devices or police, plant trees ten feet from a building to deter break-ins, "place prickly plantings" near sidewalks to reduce "pedestrian traffic," "add barbed wire to the top of chain link fencing that could serve as a ladder to upper floors or roofs," close campuses, add heavy padlocks to gates, and replace glass windows with Plexiglas. This was the Orwellian and Kafka-like response variously followed at most beleaguered schools to combat disorder.[44]

School disorder had multiple causes: racial and class conflict in areas facing unpopular court-ordered busing, gang problems in major cities, the collapse of economic opportunities for minority males, weakened opportunities for the lower classes generally in a service economy, and long-familiar classroom ills. The lives of youth in some neighborhoods grew more precarious through the 1980s and early 1990s, as the urban teenage murder rate soared. To own a gun was for some males a rite of passage.

Urban schools responded by purchasing more sophisticated security hardware and hiring more policemen ("security agents") and by banning gang colors, hats, and other insignia. Some systems also increasingly sent offenders to the "Student Adjustment Center" for counseling. Briefly, Principal Joe Clark of Paterson, New Jersey, became a national hero and Republican favorite by swinging a baseball bat and expelling troublemakers. The movie based on his life resembled *Rambo* more than *Goodbye, Mr. Chips*.[45]

Given the extensiveness of school violence and crime in the 1980s, administrators advocating more law and order naturally gained some support and publicity. Having a safe school where children and youth have an opportunity to learn is supported by most Americans, and getting tough reflected the national mood. The incidence of vandalism and violence was and remains highest in cities, lower in suburbia, and still lower in the most homogeneous parts of rural America. But violence is widely perceived as rampant, and some believe that no school system is completely safe.

Certainly, the battle zone–like environment in which many poor, minority youth live in major cities is shocking. As Republicans frequently pointed out, minority youth would especially benefit from less school crime; black youth were three times as likely to be victimized and Hispanic youth twice as likely as whites. City school systems have repeatedly formed commissions and study groups to seek ways to curb violence and vandalism. With perhaps 100,000 youth per day bringing weapons to school, this is understandable. Metal detectors, now common in many inner-city high schools, reflect fears for personal safety by students and teachers.[46]

A behavior / discipline task force study in Indianapolis in 1988 revealed social distress all too common in the deteriorating urban core. Children were often noisy and disobedient riding buses, too often swearing, fighting, and causing problems for themselves and others. A survey of junior and senior high school students revealed that 71 percent had seen students carrying knives to school, 25 percent guns, 25 percent nun chucks, and 33 percent Chinese throwing stars. Most teachers and administrators favored identification badges with "photos and names" for all staff, teachers, and pupils. Over half of the students surveyed said teachers lacked control over their classrooms, especially in high school.[47]

The increased violence associated with guns made schools take extraordinary measures to contain violence. Besides confiscating many knives, guns, and even bombs, urban educators invested millions of dollars in school security. School security directors and agents frequently gave interviews to newspapers eager to document the worst scenarios. By 1981 the Los Angeles Unified School District already had a security force of 325. In 1988 the San Diego schools had a security staff of 46 and a budget of $1.8 million, which teachers and administrators would have preferred to spend differently. Despite various attempts to harden targets, hundreds of millions of dollars nationally are expended to prevent school violence or deal with its consequences. A cartoon in the *Phi Delta Kappan* in 1989 said that the first task for a new high school class president was to name a secretary of defense.[48]

The most dramatic examples of school disorder are in metropolitan areas. However, small towns and suburbs have either reported school crime and violence more consistently than in the past or, as many spokespersons claim, are increasingly less safe. An estimated three million school crimes occurred in 1988, and the vast majority of children do not attend school in major cities. Duck-and-cover drills have reappeared; they are called "bullet drills" in Oakland, California, but "earthquake drills" in

Mentor, Ohio. In suburban Winnetka, Illinois, mothers helped guard one school after one frightening incident, and parent patrols and neighborhood watches occasionally appear even in leafy suburbs. Most dramatic are the extremes: when Prince Georges County, Maryland, installs infrared heat and motion detection devices or when New York City's mayor seeks $32 million for school police and metal detectors. But violence is an American, not simply urban dilemma.[49]

Even if school violence is less than that in adjoining neighborhoods, it nevertheless denies everyone the right to enjoy school and reap its full benefits. Although school crime levels increased in the 1960s and early 1970s and then leveled off, the amount of incivility remains higher than citizens, especially youth compelled to attend school, desire or deserve. It is only slightly comforting that, of the five hundred shootings of those under the age of sixteen in New York City in 1991, only one occurred in a local high school. But hand-held metal detectors are now sometimes utilized outside inner cities. One Massachusetts legislator has even proposed mandatory "violence prevention education."[50]

A poll of over a thousand school administrators published in 1993 revealed that urban systems had tightened local security: 20 percent had restricted access by outsiders to their campuses, 38 percent had banned gang clothing and insignia, 21 percent had restricted school use after hours, 17 percent had issued ID cards to students, 5 percent had installed surveillance cameras, and 6 percent had required common school uniforms. The percentages were generally lower but not always significantly so for suburban schools; rural schools were the least likely to restrict student movement and freedom.[51]

Definition of the legitimate requirements for social order will be severely tested in the 1990s as new interest groups redefine what constitutes acceptable behavior. As particular school systems ban beepers, designer clothes, athletic jackets, expensive shoes, and other apparel and promote greater safety, they will also be pressured to respond to two other groups: bullies and those who engage in sexual harassment.

The school bully received increased scrutiny in the 1980s. The National School Safety Center helped publicize this rediscovery of a old problem in *Set Straight on Bullies* in 1989. According to the center, "Bullying is perhaps the most underrated problem in our schools today. Synonymous with fear and anxiety, bullying distracts minds and inhibits the learning process. If the problem goes unchecked, it can destroy lives and put society at risk." An estimated 10 percent of the school population were bullies or were victimized by them. Bullies were hardly a modern invention but, in an age more sensitive to victims' rights, had gained additional interest. Some writers believed that many bullies became juvenile delinquents and denied others their right to an effective learning environment.[52]

Reform-minded scholars, recognizing that violent crimes were relatively rare in the public schools, still believed that many once-overlooked offenses needed more attention. Though the media fed the public an image of schools filled with gun-wielding adolescents, "minor victimizations and indignities" were in fact far more common though depressingly routine. "A student who is coerced into surrendering the Twinkies in his/her lunchbox to a school bully is, by strict definition, a victim of robbery," concluded three researchers in 1987. Apprentice thieves and thugs defaced buildings, stole their classmates' property, engaged in verbal abuse, and expressed their creativity with "rocks, baseball bats, metal bars, spray-paint cans, scissors, screw-drivers, and (presumably large) lollipops."[53]

Under the auspices of the National School Safety Center, the first Schoolyard Bullying Practicum was held in 1987. The center's communications director stated without evidence that bullying was an "escalating" problem, explaining that victims in extreme cases were driven to suicide. Whether confronting bullies was a "normal" part of growing up became a matter of debate. "Adults who would not tolerate physical abuse or verbal attacks on the streets should not treat such behavior lightly when it occurs in the schoolyard among younger people. If ignored, it will perpetuate itself," said the director. The solution: more monitoring and correction for bullies, more sympathy and help for victims. Bullying took many forms: "name-calling, petty theft, extortion of lunch money, harsh pranks, ethnic slurs, assault, sexual molestation, rage, or just minor jostling."[54]

By the early 1990s, after the confirmation hearings of Clarence Thomas, the issue of sexual harassment received more public scrutiny. New reports argued that sexual harassment effectively denied female students equal opportunities in the public schools. By 1993 two states—California and Minnesota—required mandatory sexual harassment training in the schools. California voters in the 1980s had already approved a referendum on a citizens' bill of rights that included children's right to a safe school, and state law permits expelling those in fourth grade and higher if found guilty. Critics question whether errant young children deserve such punitive treatment, but this captures well the power of victims' rights lobbies, whether led by conservative Republicans or liberal feminists. One student in California, cruelly taunted by classmates since eighth grade, sued a local district for failing to protect her from harassment and later settled out of court for $20,000.[55]

The control of bullies and of boys and girls who harass each other has been added to the ever-widening mission of the schools. Hundreds of millions of dollars are now spent to protect property and life and limb; how to promote more civility between students and between students and teachers is apparently the next frontier. To call playground violence typical "rough-housing" and "nothing unusual," as one administrator did, may soon sound anachronistic.[56]

Newspapers, magazines, and television shows frequently feature the pathological and usually atypical examples of school vandalism and violence that can plague particular schools. When middle school pupils in Lorain, Ohio, plot to stab their teacher and classmates wager bets on the outcome, when little children in a Georgia suburb conspire to kill their teacher, when Los Angeles establishes an antigun curriculum, or when New York creates a "grieving room" for students to mourn dead classmates, one can easily forget that the typical mischievous student is guilty only of rudeness and garden variety incivilities. Most do not carry weapons to school or assault anyone. Those who regularly terrorize their schools or classmates seem oblivious to sensitivity training or expensive target hardening.[57]

TRENDS IN DRUG USE

School violence and vandalism obviously have assumed many different forms historically and have complex roots. Inner-city educators note that, while the media cover drug and gang stories, many male teenagers also fight over sneakers, clothes, presumed insults, and girlfriends. Drug turf wars can be deadly, but creating a safe and disciplined learning environment would remain difficult even if drugs and gangs disappeared.

Exactly how serious is America's juvenile drug problem? What explains the increase in drug use by youth in the 1960s and 1970s and the relative decline in use afterward? If our society does not resemble *Reefer Madness*, drug use among America's adolescents remains the highest among industrialized nations. Though rates of adolescent use of marijuana, alcohol, and cigarettes have declined since the late 1970s, these levels, like that of school violence and vandalism, are still much higher than in the 1950s.

Among teenagers, alcohol and cigarette smoking are the most common forms of drug use. Still, the media have often focused on marijuana since white middle-class youth increasingly used it in the late 1960s and early 1970s and it thus became more popular among all teenagers. Like violence, drug use has an old history, has taken different forms, and has been redefined by those holding power. Lower-class drug use is usually stigmatized as deviance; when the middle classes abuse drugs it more likely becomes a medical problem. About 1 of every 400 turn-of-the-century Americans was addicted to opium or its derivatives because of popular and unregulated patent medicines (often containing alcohol) and elixirs for "women's complaints." The addicts—often bourgeois white women— were not regarded as criminals or deviants.[58]

During the same period, marijuana was smoked largely by rural agricultural workers in the Southwest and South, especially Mexican immigrants or Mexican Americans. Its popularity spread among the rural poor in the 1920s and to northern cities as farm workers were displaced from the land. Federal narcotics laws in 1914 began to regulate patent medicines, and the Federal Bureau of Narcotics, formed in 1930, helped lead the campaign against marijuana, used primarily by the poor and some artists and musicians. By 1937 those possessing small amounts of marijuana faced steep fines.[59]

Marijuana use continued among the lower classes through the 1950s and, as described in *The Autobiography of Malcolm X*, among some jazz artists. Beat writers such as Allen Ginsburg and Ken Kesey also publicized their drug experiments, and alarmed high school officials feared a "narcotics problem" in some towns and cities. Some authors in the *California Journal of Secondary Education* believed that the media sensationalized juvenile delinquency, crime, and narcotics, but other educators in the 1950s worried about dope peddlers and the prospect of teenage addicts.[60]

Since marijuana was cheap, easily purchased, and lucrative, claimed one writer in 1952, reefer madness might become a reality. Wherever urban students congregated, drug pushers appeared. "Nearby malt shops and hamburger stands, frequented by a small group of trouble-makers within a school, provide a convenient meeting place," he warned. And too many people naively assumed that only poorer Mexican Americans smoked marijuana.[61]

These fears, like those of mass-scale juvenile delinquency, seemed largely unfounded until the 1960s. Marijuana use among adolescents then accelerated; it steadily increased until about 1978 and 1979, when its use peaked, and then it declined afterward. As one scholar wrote, "A major change in drug use patterns occurred in the mid-1960s, when young people, particularly white middle-class students, began smoking marijuana and taking nonnarcotic drugs such as barbiturates, tranquilizers, amphetamines, and hallucinogens." Teachers had long accused some students of flying on airplane glue, but marijuana had now become pupils' third most widely used drug, after alcohol and tobacco.[62]

During a decade shaped by a peace movement and a youth culture opposed to the establishment, marijuana lost its exclusive association with the poor and artistic communities and became a symbol of revolt. Experts attending a 1962 White House conference on narcotics abuse could hardly anticipate the enormous changes about to occur. In 1968, the *Journal of Secondary Education* published an entire symposium on drugs; 1969 witnessed the first national conference on drug abuse in high schools.[63]

The increase in marijuana use was dramatic, although estimates varied. A 1967 Gallup Poll said that 6 percent of youth had tried marijuana; by 1974 the figure had skyrocketed to 60 percent. Noting that 10 percent of Michigan high school students sampled in one study had tried marijuana, the *Journal of Alcohol and Drug Education* claimed in 1969 that educating youth "about substances that modify mood and behavior" was obviously necessary. Whether drug prevention programs have ever been very effective would remain subject to debate.[64]

In a 1978 article entitled "The Drug Abuse Decade" in the *Journal of Drug Issues*, a physician noted that marijuana use had now spread from a "relatively isolated ethnic minority and bohemian populations to all American youth." The majority now tried or used marijuana. Numerous studies on adolescents and drugs confirmed rising marijuana use. One researcher estimated that "lifetime marihuana use [was] at least 20 percent higher among those 14–34 in 1977 than their counterparts in 1971," with the highest usages among those under twenty-one. Undoubtedly, the usage rate in 1971 far exceeded levels in 1961 or 1951.[65]

Teenagers who hated cutting the grass increasingly enjoyed smoking it, fueling the popularity of Cheech and Chong's *Up in Smoke* (1978). Authors of scholarly essays said youth had "gone to pot." "Teachers and administrators at many high schools and junior high schools in urban and suburban neighborhoods frequently find one or more small groups of students, especially at lunch hour, smoking marijuana outside the school building. Inside the school, marihuana fumes are frequently encountered in bathrooms, staircases, and in other isolated areas." Although the rate of teenage marijuana use remained high in the United States compared to other industrialized nations, its use, which had spread dramatically, actually peaked around 1978–79.[66]

Those sampled by the Gallup Poll fairly consistently regarded discipline as the major problem facing schools. By the late 1970s, however, drug abuse followed right behind discipline in the rankings, assuming second place (except for one year) until 1986, when it was first ranked the "leading" school problem. It remained at or near the top of the list in the coming years, even though adolescent use of illicit drugs, including marijuana and other substances, as well as drinking and cigarette smoking, had actually declined after the late 1970s.[67]

Because drug use among American adolescents is relatively high compared with the 1950s and early 1960s, writers still described a national drug "epidemic" after the problem reached its zenith. Of course, as inner cities lost jobs, the drug trade became more important and essential to underground urban economies, leading to much-publicized violence. Conservative politicians called for a war on drugs. Officials did not launch a war on poverty or fight capital flight from the cities or condemn or arrest many suburbanites who used illegal substances.

The hyperbole about an epidemic enabled politicians to avoid dealing directly with the lost economic opportunities associated with de-industrialization. So complaints about youth seemed to increase despite a decline in drug use. The federally funded Institute for Social Research at the University of Michigan has studied high school seniors and drug use since 1975. Its findings show that in the class of 1990 lifetime marijuana use (and the daily use rate) was the lowest since the class of 1975.[68]

In 1990, marijuana remained "the most widely used illicit drug with 41 percent" of seniors "reporting some use in their lifetime, 27 percent reporting some use in the past year, and 14 percent reporting some use in the past month." Of the class of 1979, 60 percent had reported using marijuana in their lifetime. Other less frequently used illicit drugs also show declining rates of lifetime usage. Between 1975 and 1990, lifetime rates for seniors dropped for hallucinogens (16.3 percent to 9.4 percent), tranquilizers (17 percent to 7.2 percent), heroin (2.2 percent to 1.3 percent), and sedatives (18.2 percent to 7.5 percent). Lifetime use of cocaine was 9 percent in 1975, rose to 17.3 percent in 1984, and fell to 9.4 percent in 1990. Widespread publicity on crack cocaine and the federal war on drugs encouraged citizens to believe drug abuse was the major problem in schools in the late 1980s.[69]

As Michigan's social scientists explain, most illicit drug use is higher for males than females. Also, white youths generally use drugs more than do minority youth (except for a few drugs used more by blacks and Hispanics). Overall, illicit drug use is not tied to any particular economic class but is pervasive compared with the 1950s and early 1960s. The variety of drugs available to youth has grown over time. Although high school seniors lowered their intake of many drugs between 1975 and 1990, by their late twenties over 80 percent of Americans in 1990 had experimented with an illicit drug, 40 percent by age twenty-seven had used cocaine, and 3.5 percent of high school seniors had tried crack. The decline in rates of adolescent drug usage is real, though so are the tragic deaths associated with gang warfare and overdoses. That it is easier to buy drugs or guns than a book in many urban neighborhoods is a national embarrassment.[70]

In recent years, programs such as Drug Awareness Resistance Education (DARE), initiated in 1983 by Police Chief Darryl Gates in cooperation with the Los Angeles schools, have become some of the most publicized efforts to teach young children about the evils of drug abuse. DARE programs now exist in two thousand communities in forty-nine states, as educators and police officers join hands in common cause. In 1993 Marko Grdesic won a poetry contest at the University Elementary School in Bloomington, Indiana: "Don't take coke, / It's not a joke. / Drugs are bad, / They'll drive you mad. / Drug Resistance Education, / has been taught / all over the nation." Whether such programs are effective remains subject to debate.[71]

Alcohol abuse often takes its toll more privately than with gun battles over drug turf, so it rarely makes the news. Since the 1950s, however, alcohol has been the most frequently used licit drug. A contributor to the *Scientific Temperance Journal* in 1945 said the media glamorized drinking. Teenagers, especially boys, learned to drink by watching their parents, neighbors, and peers imbibe, but the media were decisive. "Deliberately devised to teach people to drink, such propaganda permeates the press, the movies, the magazines, the books, and the platform," he warned. Writers frequently claimed that drinking led to juvenile delinquency.[72]

High school teachers and administrators frequently worried about student drinking. One writer warned in 1954 that drinking had increased; perhaps 25 percent of fifteen- to nineteen-year-olds drank. "School authorities are aware that some adolescent students are excessive drinkers . . . Undoubtedly many of these boys and girls are in danger of becoming problem drinkers or alcoholics." The percentage who drank or did so excessively is unknown, but anyone who saw *Blackboard Jungle* watched some of the white working-class students hit the bottle before committing mayhem. White teenagers still drink and binge drink more frequently than do blacks.[73]

Throughout the 1950s and 1960s, more curriculum guides were produced on alcohol abuse, reflecting a growing belief that more teenagers drank. Most educators in the late 1960s, however, feared the rising use of illicit drugs, especially marijuana, because it was alien to white bourgeois life and, unlike alcohol, was associated with the counterculture. Underage drinking was bad but more acceptable: it was legal for adults and even young adults in states with low legal limits. Middle- and upper-class parents who condemned pot did not stop drinking their evening martini.[74]

From the 1940s to the present, alcohol remained the most popular licit drug for most adolescents. Like marijuana and many illicit drugs, alcohol use among seniors peaked in the late 1970s and since then has continued to decline. Studies in the 1970s discovered that about half of all twelve- to seventeen-year-olds had tried alcohol; men were more likely than women to drink or to drink heavily, and the non–college bound drank at higher levels than the college bound. More difficult to conceal than pot, drinking occurred more often outside of classes. But it was the number one teenage drug of choice despite the media attention given to marijuana, LSD, cocaine, amphetamines, and barbiturates.[75]

The University of Michigan researchers emphasize that, contrary to popular belief, teen alcohol use did not increase as marijuana use began to decline in the late 1970s. Both marijuana and alcohol use have decreased. From 1975 to 1990, consistently about 90 percent of seniors have tried alcohol. However, "since 1980, the monthly prevalence of alcohol use among seniors has gradually declined, from 72 percent in 1980 to 54 percent in 1991. *Daily use* declined from a peak of 6.9 percent in 1979 to 3.6 percent in 1991; and the prevalence of drinking *five or more drinks in a row* during the prior two-week interval fell from 41 percent in 1983 to 30 percent in 1991."[76]

Although excessive drinking ruins health, disrupts families and schools, and causes many accidents, steady progress has been made. Federal pressure by the Reagan administration to raise state drinking ages to twenty-one apparently has helped promote less drinking among teenagers. Still, adolescents in the 1990s annually consume about 1.1 billion cans of beer and one-third of all wine coolers. Advertising, adult example, and youth's tendency to experiment will continue to make drinking popular.[77]

Reports on adolescents and cigarette smoking are often discouraging. As chewing tobacco use declined after World War I, adult smoking increased dramatically, surging still higher after World War II. It seemed scandalous when women lit up in the 1920s, but by the 1950s smoking became after alcohol the next favored form of drug use for adolescents. As was true of alcohol, advertisers and movie stars glamorized cigarettes, which teens increasingly used in the 1950s and 1960s. Many schools had traditionally suspended students caught smoking or drinking. By the late 1950s, however, a writer in the *California Journal of Secondary Education* complained that some students smoked despite the penalties. Moreover, said one angry writer, "Some teachers are in favor of a 'bull-pen' or 'bull-pit' where students can smoke openly."[78]

Student activists, demanding to be treated as adults, sometimes gained the right to designated smoking areas at high schools in the 1960s and 1970s. This revolt against authority must have pleased Joe Camel and tobacco lobbyists and shareholders immensely. Traditionally, more males than females smoked, which was borne out by the first national surveys conducted in 1968–69. In 1969, 15 percent of the boys and 8 percent of the girls smoked; a decade later, girls had the dubious honor of taking the lead, since apparently 13 percent of the girls and 11 percent of the boys smoked. Would the flappers have been proud?[79]

Although lifetime, thirty-day, and daily cigarette smoking has declined since the late 1970s, the drop has not been substantial. The lifetime rate peaked with the class of 1977 (75.7 percent) and then declined very slowly to the 1990 rate (64.4 percent). Thirty-day use peaked with the class of 1976 (38.8 percent) but has fluctuated somewhat, about 29.4 percent for the class of 1990. The rate of daily smoking or of smoking a half pack per day has also declined since the late 1970s, but the rates remain alarmingly high; in 1990 the daily use was 19.1 percent and use of a half-pack or more was 11.3 percent. Very little headway was made in reducing the rates after the mid-1980s. A higher percentage of whites smoke than blacks; men and women smoke on a daily basis at about the same rate, but men more frequently smoke a half pack or more daily.[80]

Illicit drug use, alcohol use, and, to a lesser degree, cigarette use among adolescents since the late 1970s have declined. Still, youth drug use is incredibly high by the standards of the 1940s and 1950s or compared with other major industrialized nations. Billions of dollars are spent on educational programs to prevent licit and illicit drug use among adolescents, although these programs are rarely evaluated for their effectiveness. The failure of drug prevention leads to an increase in health problems, spotty school attendance, and other maladies.[81]

The overall levels of school violence and vandalism reached an apogee in the 1970s, and so did various forms of licit and illicit drug use among teenagers. Longing for the days when schools worried about the "troublesome 1 percent" or when levels of drinking, smoking, or marijuana use were very low is hardly constructive for those who seek safe, drug-free schools today.

History provides perspectives, not definitive answers. That youth misbehave, drink, smoke, and take so many risks cannot be stopped by some simple appeal to law and order, the establishment of a particular educational program, or nostalgia for the past. The sources of these dilemmas are multiple, defying simple solutions. By the early 1990s, 11 percent of all AIDS transmission to seventeen- to nineteen-year-olds was through drug use, which thus contributed further to a tragic situation. Education—the typical American solution—remains for many reformers the panacea for every social ill.[82]

The problems of schools heavily reflect the problems of the larger society. If government and corporations continue to fail to create jobs in the inner cities, the destruction of lives associated with the drug trade will continue. A wealthy nation that can marshal the human and material resources to fight wars in distant places can surely attend to crucial domestic needs. As long as the sale of licit and illicit drugs is so profitable, few politicians will assault the tobacco industry or beer and liquor monopolies, and drug cartels will flourish as long as demand for drugs exists. Youth cannot be expected to behave perfectly when adults enjoy so much violence in the movies and on television and solve so many problems at home and abroad with weapons.

In the early 1990s, the Gallup Poll tried to gauge public opinion on the various National Goals for Education. One hope was that, "by the year 2000, every school in America will be free of drugs and violence and will offer a disciplined environment conducive to learning." When asked to rank all of the goals in importance, 55 percent of those polled in 1990 and 63 percent in 1991 ranked this particular one "very high"—indeed, higher than the other ones. When asked in both years about reaching the goal by the year 2000, those responding "very likely" (5 percent and 4 percent) or "likely" (14 percent and 14 percent) were the lowest percentages for all the National Goals. Those polled clearly wanted safe, drug-free schools but recognized the magnitude and complexity of the problem.[83]

NOTES

I thank the members of the History of Education Colloquium at Indiana for their comments on an earlier version of this chapter.

1. *The National Education Goals Report: Building a Nation of Learners* (Washington, D.C.: Government Printing Office, 1992), 136; Stanley Elam, *The Gallup/Phi Delta Kappa Polls of Attitudes toward Schools: A 20-Year Compilation and Educational History* (Bloomington, Ind.: Phi Delta Kappa, 1989), 3.

2. Cover, *New Yorker*, 13 September 1993; *Jet* 7 (4 July 1988): 14; Richard Hackett, Richard Sandza, Frank Gidney, Jr., and Robin Hareiss, "Kids: Deadly Force," *Newsweek* 111 (11 January 1988): 18–19. On the decline of urban schools, also see Diane Ravitch, *The Troubled Crusade: American Education 1945–1980* (New York: Basic Books, 1983), 325–26. The *Hearing before the Subcommittee on Crime of the Committee of the Judiciary, House of Representatives, One Hundred First Congress, Second Session on H.R. 3757 Gun-free School Zones Act of 1990* (Washington, D.C.: Government Printing Office, 1991), 87, shows the differing statistics available on guns and weapons taken to school. The Justice Department estimate is 100,000 guns per day, according to Laurel Shaper Walters, "School Violence Enters the Suburbs," *Christian Science Monitor*, 19 April 1993, 6.

3. U.S. Department of Health and Human Services, National Institute on Drug Abuse, *Smoking, Drinking, and Illicit Drug Use among American Secondary Students, College Students, and Young Adults, 1975–1991*, Vol. 1, *Secondary School Students*, by Lloyd D. Johnson, Patrick M. O'Malley, and Jerald G. Bachman (Washington, D.C.: Government Printing Office, 1992), 13 (hereafter cited as *Smoking, Drinking, Illicit Drug Use*).

4. Leonard Maltin, *Movie and Video Guide* (New York: Signet Books, 1991), 999.

5. See B. Edward McClellan, *Schools and the Shaping of Character: Moral Education in America, 1607–Present* (Bloomington: ERIC Clearinghouse for Social Studies / Social Science Education and Social Studies Development Center, Indiana University, 1992), chap. 2.

6. On high schools, see Robert Hampel, *The Last Little Citadel: American High Schools since 1940* (Boston: Houghton Mifflin, 1986), and Arthur G. Powell, Eleanor Farrar, and David K. Cohen, *The Shopping Mall High School: Winners and Losers in the Academic Marketplace* (Boston: Houghton Mifflin, 1985).

7. U.S. Congress, House, Subcommittee on Human Resources of the Committee on Education and Labor, *Oversight Hearing on the Office of Juvenile Justice and Delinquency Prevention*, 98th Cong. (Washington, D.C.: Government Printing Office, 1984), 657.

8. James Gilbert, *A Cycle of Outrage: America's Reaction to the Juvenile Delinquent in*

the 1950s (New York: Oxford University Press, 1986), 28–29, describes the difficulty of knowing who to believe about the actual incidence of juvenile crime.

9. Gilbert, *Cycle of Outrage*, chaps. 9–11.

10. See *School Safety Checkbook* (Malibu: Pepperdine University Press, National School Safety Center, 1990), 114, and Gilbert, *Cycle of Outrage*, 193–94.

11. John Patrick Diggins, *The Proud Decades: America in War and Peace, 1941–1960* (New York: W. W. Norton & Co., 1988), 198–201.

12. On the attacks on progressivism, see Ravitch, *The Troubled Crusade*, chap. 2.

13. Charles B. Stalford, "Historical Perspectives on Disruption and Violence in the Schools" (paper presented to the annual meeting of the American Educational Research Association, 1977), 3–4; Michael D. Casserly, Scott A. Bass, and John R. Garrett, eds., *School Vandalism: Strategies for Prevention* (Lexington, Mass.: Lexington Books, 1980), 1–2.

14. William Graebner, *Coming of Age in Buffalo: Youth and Authority in the Postwar Era* (Philadelphia: Temple University Press, 1990), 52–53, 87–89, 99.

15. Ralph W. Smith, "Providing for Seriously Unadjusted Junior High School Pupils," *California Journal of Secondary Education* 30 (April 1955): 204, 208; "Symposium: Secondary Schools and Juvenile Delinquency," *California Journal of Secondary Education* 30 (December 1955): 473–93.

16. Donald McNassor, "The Changing Character of Adolescents," *California Journal of Secondary Education* 31 (March 1956): 128–29.

17. Alex Molnar, "Selling Our Souls," *Educational Leadership* 45 (December 1987/January 1988): 78; Francis A. J. Ianni and Elizabeth Reuss-Ianni, "School Crime and Social Order of the School," *IRCD Journal* 114 (Winter 1979): 2.

18. Elam, *Gallup/Phi Delta Kappa Polls*, 3.

19. Panel on Youth of the President's Science Advisory Committee, *Youth: Transition to Adulthood* (Chicago: University of Chicago Press, 1974), 46–64. For a sampling of views, see David A. Sabatino, James E. Heald, Sharon G. Rothman, and Ted L. Miller, "Destructive Norm-violating School Behavior among Adolescents: A Review of Protective and Preventive Efforts," *Adolescence* 13 (Winter 1978): 675–86; John Martin Rich, "School Violence: Four Theories Explain Why It Happens," *NAASP Bulletin* 65 (November 1981): 64–71; and Michael Hass, "Violent Schools— Unsafe Schools," *Journal of Conflict Resolution* 32 (December 1988): 727–58. An excellent analysis of the baby boomers is found in John Modell, *Into One's Own: From Youth to Adulthood in the United States 1920–1975* (Berkeley and Los Angeles: University of California Press, 1989).

20. McClellan, *Schools and Shaping of Character*, 83–87; David Tyack, Robert Lowe, and Elisabeth Hansot, *Public Schools in Hard Times: The Great Depression and Recent Years* (Cambridge: Harvard University Press, 1984), 211.

21. Allen C. Ornstein, "Teacher Training for 'Difficult' Schools," *Journal of Secondary Education* 39 (April 1964): 172–73; R. A. DuFresne, "Perspective on the Dropout Problem," *Journal of Secondary Education* 40 (January 1965): 22–24; Daniel U. Levine, "Stereotypes Regarding Disadvantaged Students," *Journal of Secondary Education* 40 (March 1965): 102–4; John F. McGrew, "NEEDED: A Policy for Riot Control in Schools and School Districts," *Journal of Secondary Education* 43 (November 1968): 291–93.

22. Allan C. Ornstein, "On High School Violence: The Teacher-Student Role," *Journal of Secondary Education* 45 (March 1970): 99; idem, "On High School Violence," *Journal of Secondary Education* 46 (January 1971): 9–15.

23. Cf. Toby Jackson, "Crime in American Schools," *Public Interest* 58 (1990): 31.

24. Stalford, "Historical Perspectives," 4; Casserly, Bass, and Garrett, *School Vandalism*, 11; Karl B. Harris, "Reducing School Violence and Drug Abuse," *Security World* 11 (1970): 18–19, 44–45.

25. Jeffrey Mirel, *The Rise and Fall of an Urban School System: Detroit, 1907–1981* (Ann Arbor: University of Michigan Press, 1993), 333.

26. Elam, *Gallup/Phi Delta Kappa Polls*, 14.

27. Elam, *Gallup/Phi Delta Kappa Polls*, 49, 63, 116–17.

28. *Violence and Vandalism in the Schools* (Broadcast, National Public Radio, week of 22 March 1976), 1; Sabatino et al., "Destructive Norm-violating School Behavior," 675; Phillip Lesser, "Social Science and Educational Policy: The Case of School Violence," *Urban Education* 12 (January 1978): 391.

29. Sabatino et al., "Destructive Norm-violating School Behavior," 679–80.

30. *Our Nation's Schools—A Report Card: 'A' in School Violence and Vandalism*, Preliminary Report of the Subcommittee to Investigate Juvenile Delinquency Based on Investigations, 1971–1975, Senator Birch Bayh, Chairman, to the Committee on the Judiciary, United States Senate (Washington, D.C.: Government Printing Office, 1975), 1, 3. Also see James M. McPartland and Edward L. McDill, *Violence in the Schools* (Lexington, Mass.: Lexington Books, 1977), 79, and "Disruptive Behavior: Prevention and Control" in *The Practitioner*, a newsletter for the on-line administrator, National Association of Secondary School Principals, 2 (April 1976): 1–12.

31. *Our Nation's Schools*, 4–6.

32. Ibid., 6, 10, 17, 23–24, 28.

33. *Violent Schools—Safe Schools*, the Safe School Study Report to the Congress, Executive Summary (Washington, D.C.: National Institute of Education, 1977), 1–2. On the impetus for the report and a sampling of responses to it, see Robert J. Rubel, "What the Safe School Study Means to You," *American Educator* 2 (Summer 1978): 13–16; William H. Evans and Susan S. Evans, "The Assessment of School Violence," *Pointer* 29 (Winter 1985): 18–21; and Julius Menacker, Ward Weldon, and Emanuel Hurwitz, "Community Influences on School Crime and Violence," *Urban Education* 25 (April 1990): 68–80.

34. *Violent Schools—Safe Schools*, 2–4.

35. Ibid., 3.

36. Ibid., 6.

37. For a critique of the conservative reaction to the 1960s, see Ira Shor, *Culture Wars: School and Society in the Conservative Restoration, 1969–1984* (Boston: Routledge & Kegan Paul, 1986).

38. For one view of the politics behind the establishment of the center, see Anne C. Lewis, "Misinterpretations of Educational Issues Abound as Election Year Gets under Way," *Phi Delta Kappan* 65 (March 1984): 443–45.

39. Media coverage highlighted extreme cases: see, for example, "Classroom Disarmament," *Time* 131 (1 February 1988): 56; "Childhood's End," *Time* 139 (9 March 1992): 22–23; and "Kids: Deadly Force," *Newsweek* 111 (11 January 1988): 18–

19. On the chilling effect of even infrequent violence, see Powell, Farrar, and Cohen, *Shopping Mall High School*, 108; on those afraid to go to school, besides the previous reports by Senator Bayh and the Safe School Study, see John R. Hranitz and E. Anne Eddowes, "Violence: A Crisis in Homes and Schools," *Childhood Education* 67 (Fall 1990): 4–7, and Frank S. Pearson and Toby Jackson, "Fear of School-related Predatory Crime," *Sociology and Social Research* 75 (April 1991): 117–25.

40. Michael Sedlak, Christopher Wheeler, Diana C. Pullin, and Philip A. Cusick, *Selling Students Short: Classroom Bargains and Academic Reform in the American High School* (New York: Teachers College Press, 1986), 95.

41. Molnar, "Selling Our Souls," 78.

42. For a flavor of this vast literature, read Alex Rancom, Jr., "Police on Campus: The Order of the Day," *Thrust* 18 (October 1988): 50–51; "Student Safety Top Priority," *USA Today* 117 (December 1988): 6–7; John A. Calhoun, "Violence, Youth, and a Way Out," *Children Today* 17 (September-October 1988): 9–11; "Robberies Push Detroit's School Board to Propose District-wide Dress Code," *Jet* 77 (25 December 1989): 29; and Donald C. Becker, "Impact of Crime and Violence on Schooling: Is There a Solution?" *Contemporary Education* 55 (Fall 1983): 45–47.

43. *School Discipline Notebook* (Malibu: Pepperdine University Press, National School Safety Center, 1987), quotation by Reagan on cover and end quote from p. 44.

44. *School Safety Check Book* (Malibu: Pepperdine University Press, National School Safety Center, c. 1990), chap. 4; Stuart Greenbaum, Blanca Gonzalez, and Nancy Ackley, *Educated Public Relations: School Safety 101* (Malibu: Pepperdine University Press, National School Safety Center, 1987).

45. Lallani Sarmiento, "Schools Ban Hats over Gang Activity," *Social Policy* 20 (Fall 1989): 13–14; "School Bans Beepers to Stop Gangs," Bloomington, Ind., *Herald-Times* (4 March 1993): C3; "Will Changing Dress Codes of Students Help Curb Crimes?" *Jet* 82 (11 May 1992): 16–18, 54; "Getting Tough," *Time* 131 (1 February 1988): 52–56.

46. David Peter, "The Tide Turns against the School Crook and Bully," *Times Educational Supplement* 3524 (13 January 1984): 14.

47. Indianapolis Public Schools, *Behavior/Discipline Task Force Study* (Indianapolis: IPS, 1988), 10, 19, 49–54.

48. Sidney Thompson, "Vandalism-cutting Techniques That Worked for Us," *Thrust* 11 (October 1981): 12–14; Rancom, "Police on Campus," 50–51; Julius Menacker, Ward Weldon, and Emanuel Hurwitz, "School Order and Safety as Community Issues," *Phi Delta Kappan* 71 (September 1989): 56.

49. Eleanor Guetloe, "School Prevention of Suicide, Violence, and Abuse," *Education Digest* 54 (February 1989): 49; Diane M. Rotundo, "Walking Education's Mean Streets to Curb School Crime," *Education Digest* 58 (February 1993): 40, 42; Ted Guest, "These Perilous Halls of Learning," *U.S. News and World Report* 106 (13 March 1988): 68–69; Hillary Mackenzie, "A Blackboard Jungle," *Maclean's* 105 (16 March 1992): 30.

50. "Guns and Condoms in Schools: Protection Racket," *Economist* 321 (30 November 1991): 29. The magazine reported that this was the first in-school murder in New York in a decade. Also see Walters, "School Violence Enters the Suburbs," 6.

51. Walters, "School Violence Enters the Suburbs," 6.

52. Stuart Greenbaum, Brenda Turner, and Ronald D. Stephens, *Set Straight on Bullies* (Malibu: Pepperdine University Press, National School Safety Center, 1989), 3; David and Barbara Bjorkland, "Battling the School Yard Bully," *Parents* 64 (April 1989): 195; Stuart Greenbaum, "What Can We Do about Schoolyard Bullying?" *Principal* 67 (November 1987): 21–24.

53. James Garofalo, Leslie Siegel, and John Laub, "School-related Victimizations among Adolescents: An Analysis of National Crime Survey (NCS) Narratives," *Journal of Quantitative Criminology* 3 (1987): 331.

54. Greenbaum, "Schoolyard Bullying," 22–24.

55. Editorial, "Harassment in the Schools," *Christian Science Monitor*, 26 March 1993: 20; Elizabeth Levitan Spaid, "Schools Grapple with Peer Harassment," *Christian Science Monitor*, 21 January 1993: 3.

56. *New York Times*, 17 June 1993.

57. David Holstrom, "L.A. Aims to Rebuild Sense of Community," *Christian Science Monitor*, 19 March 1993, 7; "Childhood's End," 22; "The Knife in the Book Bag," *Time* 141 (8 February 1993): 37.

58. Joseph H. Brenner, Robert Coles, and Dermot Meagher, *Drugs and Youth: Medical, Psychiatric, and Legal Facts* (New York: Liveright, 1970), 4–9.

59. Brenner, Coles, and Meagher, *Drugs and Youth*, 6–9.

60. Frank R. Scarpitti and Susan K. Datesman, eds., *Drugs and Youth Culture* (Beverly Hills: Sage Publications, 1980), 9–18; Mabel-Ella Sweet, "Narcotics: The Responsibility of the School," *California Journal of Secondary Education* 27 (May 1952): 293–94; Oscar E. Shabat, "A Critique of Articles on Narcotics," *California Journal of Secondary Education* 27 (December 1952): 493–96.

61. Sanford Rothman, "Narcotics among High School Boys," *California Journal of Secondary Education* 27 (May 1952): 291.

62. Scarpitti and Datesman, *Drugs and Youth Culture*, 14.

63. Robert L. DuPont, "The Drug Abuse Decade," *Journal of Drug Issues* 8 (Spring 1978): 173; "Marijuana: A Study of the Issues," *Journal of Secondary Education* 43 (May 1968): 196–235.

64. Scarpitti and Datesman, *Drugs and Youth Culture*, 22; Editorial, "Two Important Studies of Adolescent 'Drug Use,'" *Journal of Alcohol and Drug Education* 14 (Winter 1969): 40; David J. Hanson, "The Effectiveness of Alcohol and Drug Education," *Journal of Alcohol and Drug Education* 27 (Winter 1982): 1–13.

65. DuPont, "Drug Abuse Decade," 175; Bruce D. Johnson and Gopal S. Uppal, "Marihuana and Youth: A Generation Gone to Pot" in Scarpitti and Datesman, *Drugs and Youth Culture*, 82.

66. Johnson and Uppal, "Marihuana and Youth," 93.

67. Elam, *Gallup/Phi Delta Kappa Polls*, 183.

68. Mark Fraser, "Family, School, and Peer Correlates of Adolescent Drug Abuse," *Social Service Review* 58 (September 1984): 434–47; *Drug Use among High School Seniors, College Students and Young Adults, 1975–1990*, Vol. 1, *High School Seniors* by Lloyd D. Johnston, Patrick M. O'Malley, and Jerald G. Bachman, University of Michigan Institute for Social Research, National Institute on Drug Abuse (Washington, D.C.: U.S. Department of Health and Human Services, 1991), 51 (hereafter cited as *Drug Use among High School Seniors*).

69. *Drug Use among High School Seniors*, 27, 52.

70. Ibid., 14.

71. Marko Grdesic, Untitled award-winning poem, University Elementary School, Bloomington, Ind., 1993; Kirsten A. Conover, "How DARE Began and Spread," *Christian Science Monitor*, 22 January 1990, 14. On local responses (and their frequently ineffective nature), see Wilhelmina E. Holliday, "Operation SPECDA: School Program to Educate and Control Drug Abuse," *FBI Law Enforcement Bulletin* 55 (February 1986): 1–4; Barry M. Wolf, "The Struggling Adolescent: A Socio-Phenomenological Study of Adolescent Substance Abuse," *Journal of Alcohol and Drug Education* 26 (Spring 1981): 51–61; and Constance Lignell and Ruth Davidhizar, "Effect of Drug and Alcohol Education on Attitudes of High School Students," *Journal of Alcohol and Drug Education* 37 (Fall 1991): 31–37.

72. John L. C. Goffin, "Alcohol and the Adolescent," *Scientific Temperance Journal* 53 (Autumn 1945): 89; Fred Slager, "The Role of the Public School in Relation to Alcohol," *Scientific Temperance Journal* 53 (Spring 1945): 45–48; Francis W. McPeek, "Youth, Alcohol, and Delinquency," *Scientific Temperance Journal* 52 (Summer 1944): 35–38.

73. Arthur Lerner, "How Fare the Alcoholics in School?" *California Journal of Secondary Education* 29 (April 1954): 186.

74. Gail Gleason Milgram, "Analysis of Alcohol Education Curriculum Guides," *Journal of Alcohol and Drug Education* 20 (Spring 1975): 13–16.

75. G. Nicholas Braucht, "Psychosocial Research on Teenage Drinking" in Scarpitti and Datesman, *Drugs and Youth Culture*, 109–15.

76. *Drug Use among High School Seniors*, 52; *Smoking, Drinking, Illicit Drug Use*, 13.

77. Fred M. Hechinger, *Fateful Choices: Healthy Youth for the 21st Century* (New York: Hill & Wang, 1993), 114–17.

78. Dorothy E. Green, "Teenage Smoking Behavior" in Scarpitti and Datesman, *Drugs and Youth Culture*, 147–50; Norman Schacter, "Smoking—'An Administrative Headache,'" *California Journal of Secondary Education* 33 (October 1958): 340.

79. Green, "Teenage Smoking Behavior," 150.

80. *Drug Use among High School Seniors*, 13, 33, 52, 71.

81. *Smoking, Drinking, Illicit Drug Use*, 19; Michael D. Newcomb and Peter M. Bentler, *Consequences of Adolescent Drug Abuse* (Newbury Park, Calif.: Sage Publications, 1988), chap. 1.

82. Deborah Holtzman, John E. Anderson, Laura Kann, Susan L. Arday, Benedict Truman, and Lloyd J. Kolbe, "HIV Instruction, HIV Knowledge, and Drug Injection among High School Students in the United States," *American Journal of Public Health* 81 (December 1991): 1596–1601.

83. "The 23rd Annual Gallup Poll of the Public's Attitudes toward the Public Schools" in *Annual Editions/Education*, ed. Fred Schultz (Guilford, Conn.: Dushkin Publishing Co., 1992), 20.

CONTRIBUTORS

David Angus, Professor of Education at the University of Michigan

Patricia Albjerg Graham, Charles Warren Professor of the History of Education at the Graduate School of Education, Harvard University, and President of The Spencer Foundation

Carl F. Kaestle, William Vilas Professor of Educational Policy Studies and History at the University of Wisconsin

Joseph F. Kett, Professor in the Corcoran Department of History at the University of Virginia

David L. Kirp, Professor of Public Policy at the University of California, Berkeley

Michael W. Kirst, Professor of Education at Stanford University

Jeffrey Mirel, Associate Professor of Education at Northern Illinois University

Gary B. Nash, Professor of History at the University of California, Los Angeles

Paul E. Peterson, Henry Lee Shattuck Professor of Government and Director of the Center for American Political Studies at Harvard University

Diane Ravitch, research fellow at the Brookings Institution and senior research scholar in the School of Education at New York University

William J. Reese, editor of the *History of Education Quarterly* and Professor of Education, History, and American Studies at Indiana University at Bloomington

Michael W. Sedlak, Professor of Education at Michigan State University

David Tyack, Professor of Education at Stanford University

Reed Ueda, Professor of History at Tufts University

Maris A. Vinovskis, Professor of History at the University of Michigan

LIBRARY OF CONGRESS CATALOGING-IN-PUBLICATION DATA

Learning from the past : what history teaches us about school reform /
edited by Diane Ravitch and Maris A. Vinovskis.
    p.   cm.
ISBN 0-8018-4920-9 (acid-free paper). — ISBN 0-8018-4921-7 (pbk.:
acid-free paper)
1. Educational change—United States. 2. Education—United
States—History. 3. Education—United States—Aims and objectives.
I. Ravitch, Diane. II. Vinovskis, Maris.
LA217.2.L43   1995
370'.973—dc20   94-27015